GROWING ROOTS
The New Generation of Sustainable Farmers, Cooks, and Food Activists

STORIES AND RECIPES

KATHERINE LEINER

Photographs by Andrew Lipton

SUNRISE LANE PRODUCTIONS
DURANGO, COLORADO

Printed in the USA on recycled paper
ISBN # 978-1-60358-288-9
Library of Congress Control Number: 2010928293

Book cover and interior design and production: Peter Holm, Sterling Hill Productions
Production: Abrah Griggs, Sterling Hill Productions
Illustrations by Leslie Lee

Published by
Sunrise Lane Productions
1689 Sunrise Lane West
Durango, Colorado 81301

Growing Roots: The New Generation of Sustainable Farmers, Cooks, and Food Activists is distributed by Chelsea Green Publishing Company

U.S. Trade Bookstores and wholesalers:
Please contact Chelsea Green Publishing, 85 North Main Street,
Suite 120, White River Jct., Vermont 05001
Orders: 800.639.4099, offices 802.295.6300
Quantity Sales: special discounts are available on quantity purchases for groups or individuals. For details please visit
www.growingroots.info

The recipes in this book were chosen by the subjects of the profiles and are tried and true.

Recipes on pages 40–43 are reprinted with permission from *The Farmer and the Grill*, by Shannon Hayes, published by Left to Write Press, Richmondville, NY, © 2007.

Recipes on pages 78–79 appear courtesy of Elspeth Pierson and her blog, www.diaryofalocavore.com.

Recipes on page 118 are from *Jiibaakweda Gimiijiminaan* (pages 3, 12, 22, 38.)

Recipes on pages 164–166 are Copyright Jessica Prentice, 2006.

Facts on page 192 were taken from the Algalita Marine Research Foundation "Plastics are Forever" online brochure

Recipes on pages 242–243 are compliments of market shopper.

Page 74 excerpt from *Grub: Idea For An Urban Kitchen* by Anna Lappé and Bryant Terry, copyright © 2006 by Anna Lappé & Bryant Terry. Used by permission of Jeremy P. Tarcher, an imprint of Penguin Group (USA) Inc.

Make the world a better piece of ground

WENDELL BERRY

Contents

Foreword
Deborah Madison

We talk a lot, and with enthusiasm, about farmers markets and CSAs, urban gardens and hand-crafted foods —all the delicious and encouraging things happening with food. Something that doesn't get talked about all that much is the age of American farmers. We have numbers for those farming on a large scale rather than those running the small farms and food businesses that mesh so well with the new foods and their makers. The average age is somewhere around fifty-five to fifty-seven. That's not old. It's a good number if age equates with experience and wisdom. But it's also an age when many are thinking about cutting back, retiring from whatever it is they've been doing, maybe especially if that's been farming, which is more physically demanding than an office career. Where will our food come from when these typical American farmers finally throw in the towel, which they have every right to do?

Some of us also wonder who's going to start independent restaurants in a world of chains? Who's going to sign up for making cheese, composting, raising beef and saving saving seeds, for being food and health activists? Who among the younger generation is drawn to a life that promotes sustainability through farming, cooking, organic food production, and gardening?

It turns out some pretty wonderful young people are taking up these reins with skill and intelligence. In this book you will meet a smart bunch of young people who are deeply engaged in these pursuits. Their enthusiasm is infectious. They seem surprisingly wise. Most aren't super-young — some in their twenties — but more in their thirties, a few pushing forty, with more than a few years of experience under their belts bringing their visions and ideals to life.

When Katherine's book was in its early stages, her working title was *Young and Hungry* suggesting a cadre of young people consumed by a hunger for knowledge and an opportunity to live in the world in a particular way. Even though the title of the book changed, the subject remains the appetite of young people with vision to do good work in food and farming. If you need encouragement about the future, this book is a gift.

It's a pleasure reading what these people have to say about what they're doing with their lives, how they spend their days and what they make of their futures. They all have great stories. Taken together they comprise a national sampling of on-the-ground, in-the-trenches food visionaries. You meet people who are busy growing herbs and greens on the roofs of their restaurants, young women cooking organically in the middle of Nowhere, Utah, farmers who both juggle and hunt, a young couple who makes biodiesel, another one who grows and dispenses herbs for health, and more. Did I say cook? They all cook, though most of them aren't chefs — recipes are happily scattered throughout the book. These are people who see the value and pleasure of providing their own delicious nourishment. One of the most compelling aspects of these stories is discovering how these young people became aligned with the lives they've chosen.

When I was researching my book *What We Eat When We Eat Alone*, I found that all those who were figuring out how to cook for themselves had a parent, usually a mother, who cooked. That was their reference point, what gave them the desire and the confidence to get started. Among the young folks in *Growing Roots*, there's also frequently a parent or other family member who points the way. "I learned to cook and sew from my Uncle Mark," says one. "I come from a family that cares about the environment and thinks about energy consumption and food," says another. "I've been mushrooming since I was five. I used to go with my father."

Parents, it turns out, do affect their children, and many have passed on their enthusiasm and passion by including their children on walks in the woods, trips to the barn or hours spent in the kitchen. Some of these members of the next generation have parents who preceded them in some aspect of the business they're in today, parents who were ranchers, winemakers, food activists, and so on. Some enter their world because they once tasted something so delicious, better than they ever got at home, that it inspired them to learn to cook and taste more.

In my generation we were the hippies, the Zen students, the renegades who broke with our families, ignoring the directions of our college educa-tions. We became farmers, or decided to make cheese, wine, or bread; we became activists and the parents of these young people. Seeing how this has all worked out is a wonderful thing. We are connected. The stories in *Growing Roots* leave no doubt in my mind that this generation is poised to take their dreams even further than we did. Which is exactly how it should be.

Deborah Madison
Galisteo, New Mexico

Deborah Madison is the author of *Local Flavors, Cooking and Eating from America's Farmers Markets*, and *Vegetarian Cooking for Everyone.*

Preface

I began this project after my youngest child graduated from college and left me an empty nester. I had no one to cook for, no one to share meals with. I felt the quiet most often in the kitchen. It was clear that I needed to get out of the kitchen for a while, so I hit the road. In the spring of 2007, I began traveling back and forth across the nation interviewing what I now know is a new breed of young people who find passion in good food. Their sustainable lifestyles revolve around food that has been grown locally, without pesticides, herbicides, hormones, or chemical fertilizers. They understand that the privilege of healthy eating does not come easily. It comes from hard work on the land, in the schoolroom and by using the political process.

I grew up with a mother whose ideas about food were simple. She wanted to know where our food came from. If it was meat, poultry or fish, what it had eaten and how it had lived and died. She believed strongly that vegetables and fruits should be organic, grown locally and not sprayed with poisonous chemicals. When my children were growing up I fed them the same kind of good, clean food. Like my mother's kitchen, mine was the center of our home.

Sometimes we take for granted the wholesome food we are lucky enough to have. Despite my grandmother's mantra, "The whiter the bread the sooner you're dead," my sister and I traded our whole wheat, homegrown tomato and raw cheese sandwiches as quickly as we could for anybody's baloney or ham on squishy white bread.

In the last several decades our food supply has come under the control of a few multinational corporations. Genetically modified crops are becoming pervasive. More and more of us realize that this inexpensive, mass-produced, processed food comes at a high cost (most of it hidden) to our health, our communities and our environment.

Mostly, what I learned interviewing these people is how they have found passion in their lives, in their work, and in the food they eat. This is the kind of passion we all crave and I was seeking to renew in myself when I began this journey.

Healthy food is a right for everyone. The young people profiled here, living and working across this wide nation of ours, are examples of the possibility of democratizing our food system to produce healthy, nutritious food for all. Sitting at their tables, I became reinvigorated, enthusiastic again about my food choices. I hope you find their stories as enlightening and inspirational as I do.

Katherine Leiner

DEDICATION

To Andrew who was by my side every step of this journey.
And in memory of my mother.

Acknowledgments

This book would not have been possible without the enormous generosity, passion and eager willingness of each of the people featured as profiles. As Alice Waters said, years ago there would not have been enough folks to fill a book like this. Now there are so many around the nation who get up each morning to live thoughtful, joyous lives that revolve around food, that I couldn't fit them all in this book.

It takes courage to create and coordinate a healthy environment for our food; the ability to work hard and persevere even when luck and weather work against you. Thank you to everyone who fed me along the way, literally and metaphorically. I am forever grateful to my friends across the country, my writers' group in New York City (LOLs), and my art sharing group in Durango. Thanks to my assistant Mariah Richstone. To Debra Greenblatt who introduced me to Mary Cleaver, who introduced me to Gabrielle Langholtz who said quite simply over a glass of wine and a plate of local cheese, "this is a good idea for a book." To my editor JoAnne McFarland who has both a sharp eye and a gentle ear, so I believed her when she said "CUT!" Many thanks to Margo Baldwin and everyone at Chelsea Green Publishing who took this book under their generous wings. To Peter Holm and Abrah Griggs at Sterling Hill Productions for their patience and pulling this all together. To Marcy Murphy for her careful transcriptions. To Beth Stevens for her support and continued enthusiasm, and Joseph Browning for his humor, generosity, and web talents. To Jacqui Daniels (Sally Anne McCartin and Associates) for her imaginative promotional support. And to Dana Lee for permission to use her mother Leslie Lee's HARVEST graphics which are scattered through the book, as Leslie's memory is through my own life. To Lynn Eames for her continued design support and friendship. To Patricia Janoff at the Carnegie Hill CSA in New York City, who makes it possible for New Yorkers in my area to get fresh, farm food. To Grant Pound and the Colorado Art Ranch (www.coloradoartranch.com) for giving artists and writers a platform for discussion. My deep appreciation also to Deborah Madison for her continued splendid work and kind words; to Michael Pollan for putting this renewed food movement on all of our radar; and to Alice Waters, for her good food and continuing resolve to see that children are exposed to healthy food and have an opportunity to grow their own. To Robert Kenner for his groundbreaking documentary, Food, Inc. and to A.E. Hotchner and his work with Newman's Own. To Rosemerry Wahtola Trommer, whose orchard in Delta County next to the Gunnison River filled my heart. Many thanks to my sister, Marie Gewirtz, for all her advice and our shared history; my nephew, Julien Gervreau, who is always there for me, rain or shine, and his fiancé Serena Johnson. And most of all to my blessed children, Dylan and Makenna and my daughter-in-law Andrea, all of whom appreciate our family's bounty and offer me their continued friendship and their own examples of joyful lives and good food. Last of all, I will be forever grateful to Luna, my puppy.

I am happy to have had the opportunity to work on this book. It has opened my mind and my heart. And I have crossed paths with extraordinary people and food.

Introduction

SPRING ■ *It is May. My sturdy little cattle dog, Luna, no longer fits under the seat in the airplane cabin, so I decide to drive from New York City to Durango, Colorado, where I own a log house fifteen miles outside of town. Already I miss my daughter who usually travels with me. She graduated from college and almost straightaway got a great job with a major publishing house in NYC. After so many years of close-up mothering, I feel fragile about the alone time that stretches before me. But I am looking forward to the drive. I'll listen to books on tape and music. I'll stop when I want to and walk with the dog. I've Googled natural food stores, farmers markets and restaurants that serve local produce and local meats all along my way.*

I find all kinds of seasonal fruit, local cheeses and bread. I even manage to get Luna several big beef bones that come from local farms. My third day on the road, after driving all morning and afternoon, it looks like I'm about to run out of gas. I pull off the highway and drive a few miles along a back road. Finally I spy a small farm with a sign out front that reads: EGGS FOR SALE. *I leave Luna in the car with the windows cracked, and following the sounds of a tractor, come upon a young man plowing his back field. I wave him over, telling him how sorry I am to interrupt his work, but I need some gas. He shuts off his tractor and jumps down. Before long he's telling me he's just graduated from college and has come home to help his parents for the summer while he tries to decide what he wants to do for the rest of his life. He speaks to me as if we are old friends.*

He admits that while he was in college he missed home and his family's goats. He walks me back to the car. "You can let the dog out. This is a dog-friendly place." He and I take turns throwing a stick for Luna as we continue to talk about the pros and cons of farming. He gives me several gallons of gas and tells me about another farm eight miles down the road that's also a B & B. "Looks like we're due for our first tornado of the season." At the B & B I hunker down for a night of wind and pounding rain, Luna shivering beside me.

That young man is one of many young people I meet along the way who has returned to a family farm, started their own farm or interned at someone else's farm. Some sell their produce at farmers markets or become chefs using local foods. When I actually begin to do research, they seem to be everywhere: in the newspapers and magazines, on the radio, and on TV, in cities like New York, growing vegetables and raising bees on apartment building rooftops.

After I arrive in Durango I stroll through my own garden, the grasses green and high, dandelions everywhere. Bulbs are already coming up, a brilliant field full of daffodils and tulips against the white trunks and spring green of aspen leaves. The back garden is wild with lupine and apple blossoms, the daisies just starting. I glance over at my empty vegetable beds and remember how delicious the summer's yield was, but also how hard it had been to grow food at eight thousand feet in arid southwestern soil.

Once I settle in, I begin searching in earnest for young farmers as well as anybody involved with sustainable food. At the Durango Farmers Market alone there are more than thirty food vendors, two-thirds of them under forty years old. I meet folks in Telluride, Montrose, Mancos, and Ridgeway, and begin informal interviews. By summer's end, I've gathered lots of information.

Dan and Becca James

The James Ranch ■ Durango, Colorado ■ www.jamesranch.net/cheese

FIRST FALL ■ *By the time I am ready for my first formal interview, the chamisa in Durango is about two feet high, broad blooms of yellow against the wild silver sagebrush. Gamble oak and mountain mahogany turn the hillsides red, while yellowing aspens and cottonwoods tower above them. All of this color against the backdrop of huge blue spruce. Due to recent rains and early frost in the mountains, the fall colors come on stronger and faster. Across the county, people pull up last-minute tomatoes and basil. Apples weigh heavy on their branches. All the seasons in Durango are beautiful, but particularly fall. I feel a bittersweet tenderness as gardens across La Plata County are being put to bed; wood gathered up, chopped and piled high; the first fires built. Snow is in the air.*

Among the many organic farms, ten miles northeast of Durango is a magnificent multi-generational family-run business featuring a diverse group of products: organic vegetables, grass-fed pigs, cows and chickens, eggs, organic flowers, organic artisan cheese, and raw milk. I grab my tape recorder and start out.

The James Ranch sits on 450 acres of high altitude irrigated land, beyond which are the wide vistas of red mountaintops known as Missionary Ridge. Jersey milk cows peacefully graze the high mountain grasses in the lush Animas Valley and drink from the spring-fed mountain ponds. Becca, Dan and their three children are the picture of rosy good health, and take the stewardship of their land very seriously. Throughout the interview they comment again and again about how grateful they are to live on such a generous land.

Dan: Becca and I are one of four families that currently have come home to my family's 450-acre ranch. The corporate life did not appeal to my dad. My mom and dad knew they wanted to raise a large family in a rural area, so soon after my father and mother were married, they decided they didn't want to live in California. They had a dream of owning land in the west, and as soon as they could, they went looking for it. They looked at a lot of ranches, and finally got the green light from my grandfather when they discovered the prime real estate north of Durango.

Before long, my parents were deep into the cattle business and as our family of five children grew up, they encouraged us to leave, go to college, learn something that would later be useful on the ranch. "Come home with an enterprise," they said. I couldn't wait to get out of here after high school.

My parents had the wisdom to know that you don't fully appreciate what you have until you no longer have it. As my sisters and brothers and I came home, other ranch families asked my parents and us how to get their own kids to come home.

Becca: I met Dan in Seattle at the University of Washington. We were both on the rowing team. Right after we graduated we got married, in Spokane where I'd grown up. We lived in Seattle for five years — Dan worked in a big seafood company and I worked for an advertising agency before going back to school for interior design. When we started thinking about a family, we decided we wanted to be here in Durango, our kids growing up with their cousins in this environment.

I basically grew up in the suburbs, but we had a big lot and my parents were really wannabe farmers. They had a big garden, so we always ate homegrown fresh vegetables. My dad hunted, so we ate venison and grouse — you know, we were the weird family on the block. My family was on a budget so we'd also get the cheap cuts of meat, you know, at Safeway. We baked our own bread, made our own granola — no sugar cereals!

Dan laughs and says:

It's really interesting to look back at my parents' food choices. Some of them may have been a function of having five kids and not having a lot of time. We had a huge garden, lots of great meat, and my Mom is a great cook. We had a little trout-catching business that was one of our jobs as kids. People would come catch trout out of our ponds and pay by the inch — Meadow Brook Trout Farm we called it. That was our first entrepreneurial experience, and although our parents stocked the ponds, the kids ran the business.

The James boys, Grady and Mason, take me down into the field to show me the ponds. Grady says that one of his and Mason's jobs is to bring the goats up every day when the ranch market is open. He does a lot of art, and he shows me a poem he wrote called "Theme in Red" about the red cliffs

and the big fire that occurred in Durango in 2002. *Forest fires are a part of the cycle of nature, Grady tells me. He assures me that when he grows up, he'll continue to live and work on the farm. I know for sure, he says.*

Dan: By the time I got around to making a decision to come home, my siblings were already deeply involved, one with a large vegetable garden.

The vegetables and flowers at the James Ranch are produced by one of Dan's sisters, her husband and their daughters. They garden with organic methods, and the scrumptious array includes seasonal black and red currants, asparagus, greens, cucumbers, tomatoes, five kinds of potatoes, onions, peas, beans, summer and winter squashes and a variety of pumpkins. This year they have my very favorite — small succulent artichokes! Their girls are in charge of the magnificent flower production.

Another of my sisters and her husband have a flock of laying hens, and a landscape tree farm.

It is a native tree farm specializing in mature

Colorado blue spruce (towering ten to twenty-five feet high). The trees have matured in the pastures of the James Ranch since 1978. Their three boys help with gathering eggs from the flock of hens.

And my parents were raising grass-finished beef. Amazing grasses have always been our number-one resource. The James Ranch has "cool season" grasses, lots of clover, high elevation, beautiful dry air and great soils, allowing the cows to do well all season.

The girls, as we like to call them, have a very good life. We're breaking all the dairy rules, really. They are one-hundred-percent grass fed. We milk once a day. And we leave the calves on for ten weeks. They actually meet us at the gate for morning milking and then wander up through the oaks to the milking barn.

Our animals have a much longer life span than those in a conventional dairying system. We only milk while the cows are on grass (May to November). The seasonality of our operation gives the

RECIPES ■ Dan and Becca James

Kefir is a fermented milk drink prepared by injecting cow, goat or sheep's milk with kefir grains. Using kefir grains to make kefir is easy. Once you have obtained kefir grains either from an online source or from a friend or neighbor (the "grains" – not really grains at all – grow and multiply, and therefore need to be divided and shared) you plop them into some milk (the actual quantity is not important) and let it sit on the counter for between 24 to 36 hours. The length of time you let the milk culture sit depends upon your personal taste (how thick you like it) and how warm the room is. The warmer the room, the faster your milk will culture. The finished consistency will be like runny yogurt, but may "gel" a bit more and separate (just blend back together). Strain out the kefir grains either with a strainer (never letting the grains touch metal) or with very clean fingers and put them into a clean jar. Cover them with milk, and in another 24 to 36 hours you will have more kefir. You can let the grains go dormant in the back of your fridge in a little milk if you get tired of making it or are going on vacation. Even after a few months they can be resurrected, but it may take a batch or two for them to get back to full strength.

Dan's Kefir Smoothie with Blueberries and Ginger

  2 cups raw kefir
  2 bananas
  1 cup frozen blueberries
  ½ cup grape juice
  1-inch piece of ginger, peeled and very thinly sliced (to taste)

Blend up and enjoy! Makes about 1 quart of smoothie, and can easily be cut in half.

Dutch Apple Pancake

  4 tablespoons unsalted butter
  3–4 large apples (whatever you like for pie works well here) peeled and thinly sliced
  4–8 tablespoons (depending on sweetness of your apples) sugar (granulated or dehydrated cane juice like rapadura – available at most natural food stores)
  1 teaspoon cinnamon
  4 eggs
  ½ cup all-purpose flour
  ½ cup milk
  1 tablespoon sour cream
  ¼ teaspoon salt
  Grated zest of one lemon

Preheat oven to 400 degrees. Melt butter over medium heat in an oven-proof sauté pan. Add apples, sugar and cinnamon. Sauté for about 5 minutes while preparing the batter. In a mixing bowl, beat eggs. Add flour, milk, sour cream, salt and zest. Beat until a smooth batter forms. Pour over apple mixture and bake until puffed and golden – about 25 minutes. Cut into wedges and serve directly from the pan.

  This recipe can easily be doubled and done in a larger pan. I have made this recipe with whole wheat flour, whole spelt flour and with a mixture of oat and brown rice flours with good results. The oat and rice combo is heavier, but a good gluten-free alternative.

Becca's Macaroni and Cheese

Personally, I don't think you can ever have too many good recipes for mac and cheese!

cows a good break from producing milk and insures that only the highest quality, grass-fed milk goes into our artisan cheeses. Our cheeses seem to have a richer, more complex flavor that reflects the grass the cows have been eating. The grass also boosts levels of CLA, omega-3, fatty acids, vitamin A & E and beta-carotene.

We make cheese in batches of fifty to one-hundred and fifty gallons in a round vat imported from Holland; the wheels are pressed and brined for three to seven days and aged anywhere from two to twenty-four months. The whey is mixed with grain and fed to the pigs, which are also rotated on our lush pastures in the same manner as our cows. We produce our pork without the use of chemical fertilizers, pesticides or antibiotics.

We make aged raw milk cheeses. At the moment they include the following:

1 pound pasta such as fusilli or penne

1 to 1.5 pounds of cheese (see note on cheese below), grated

½ cup (¼ pound) unsalted butter

½ cup flour

4 cups milk

½ to 1 teaspoon salt (see cheese note again)

½ teaspoon freshly grated nutmeg

Dash cayenne

Pepper to taste

Cook pasta in boiling salted water until al dente. You want it slightly undercooked to avoid mushiness in the final product.

Melt butter in a large sauce pan. Add flour and cook, stirring frequently for about 3 minutes. Slowly add milk. Cook over low heat, stirring occasionally at first and then constantly as it starts to thicken. This sauce will still be rather thin but will thicken more when baked. After the sauce has thickened a bit, add nutmeg, salt, cayenne and pepper. Remove from heat and add ⅔ of the cheese, reserving ⅓ for the top. Stir until the cheese is melted. Combine the pasta and cheese sauce and pour into a 9×13-inch pan. Top with remaining cheese. Bake at 350 degrees for 30 minutes. It should be bubbly. Turn on the broiler for the last minute or two if the cheese on top did not get as brown and crispy as you like. Let it sit for 5 to 10 minutes, if you can wait, and then serve. Serves 5.

Note on cheese: This recipe can be created with many different cheeses. Choose cheeses available in your area, or your favorite types. You can use one kind of cheese for the sauce and one for the top. Don't use more than two types, however, because the flavors will become muddy. Make sure the cheese you select melts well. In the recipe, I give a range for the quantity of cheese. Depending on your preferences and the flavor of the particular cheeses, you can adjust the quantity in the cheese sauce with good results.

I also give a range for the amount of salt to add. This depends upon the saltiness of the cheese you are using.

Rice Gratin with Spinach and Sausage

2 cups brown rice, cooked

1 pound spinach, steamed and chopped (or 1 pkg. frozen chopped spinach)

1 pound sweet Italian sausage, browned

Good Italian-style cheese such as fontina, Parmesan, Andalo (that's ours), or pecorino

Béchamel Sauce:

¼ cup minced onion

2 cloves garlic, minced or pressed

4 tablespoons butter or olive oil

4 tablespoons flour

3 cups milk

Salt and pepper to taste

¾ teaspoon grated nutmeg

1½ teaspoon fresh thyme or 1 teaspoon dried thyme

Preheat oven to 375 degrees. Cook onion in the butter for 1 to 2 minutes, then add garlic and sauté 1 more minute. Add flour, cook 2 to 3 minutes. Whisk in milk, then cook, stirring frequently until it begins to thicken. Add salt, pepper, nutmeg and thyme. Combine rice, sausage, spinach and Béchamel sauce in a baking dish (9×13 inch or similar). Bake for 25 minutes at 375 degrees. Serves 5.

Belford is our signature cheese. It's similar to an aged gouda but has some cheddar qualities.

Andalo is an Italian-style cheese made from whole cow's milk. It has a piquant flavor and is good with dried fruit or fresh figs in the fall. We grate it over pasta or a soufflé.

Leyden is a traditional Dutch-style cheese with a lemony flavor made with whole cumin seeds.

Becca: What we're working on as a whole ranch is building a new facility. We have quarterly family meetings where we discuss expanding the building where the cheese is made. We'll have a bigger, better retail facility, and more room for dairy processing so that we can continue to do cheese but expand our volume and expand into other products like yogurt, kefir, ice cream. We want to try to make this truly sustainable for our family. The addition might include a restaurant, a certified kitchen, a place for

workshops and possibly some housing for interns. We also want to provide opportunities for future generations who might want to move back here.

Dan: We're trying to think two generations down the road. Little enterprises — for those future generations. My parents have always been stewards of the land. Our family spent two years discussing the issue of holistic management, revisiting the deep questions in agriculture rather than cashing in big by growing condos. We talked about quality of life. What makes us happy? Where do we want to raise our children and grandchildren? Do we have a responsibility to the land? Fifty years ago family farms lined the Animas Valley in Durango. People knew who grew their potatoes and asparagus and who raised their beef. There was a relationship between the family sitting down to eat a meal and the family who grew the meal. All of us at James Ranch want that back, not only for the health of our family, but also for the health of our community.

Dan heaved a sigh. He ruffled the hair of each of his boys and smiled over at his daughter, Stella. Then he looked out at the colorful autumn mountaintops of Missionary Ridge and the San Juan Mountains.

We're in the final stretch of our season. It's a beautiful transition in the fall.

Becca: You know, the end of the farmers markets in November coordinates with the end of our season. Our lives are very much in rhythm with nature in that we are super busy in summer, when it's high production. We're making our products and selling our products — the tourists are here, the markets are open and everything's going, going, going. And then it just sort of does this gentle sigh into winter. And the grass rests and the plants rest and the animals rest. And then, we rest.

Samantha (Sam) Johnson
Raw Food Cook ■ Durango, Colorado

My second interview is with a young woman who grew up in Southern California within reach of many farmers markets and lots of small family farms. Used to being able to get good produce year round, and eating primarily raw foods, Samantha has worked extensively with raw food chef, Juliano. Now she lives in a yurt in rural Southwest, Colorado. Hers is a simple life in a beautiful mountain valley where she integrates seasonal cooking and sustainable living with the study of pre-med/naturopathy. Samantha has also been mentored by Katrina Blair, a kind of folk hero in Durango who is profiled in this book.

Sam: I grew up on forty acres in Topanga, California. I've always had plenty of space to get lost on.

I come from a family that cares about the environment, thinks about energy consumption and food. Through the years I've been part of almost every food fad you can imagine: vegetarianism, macrobiotic and now raw. I also grew up in the fashion world. My grandmother was Olga, the "First Lady of Lingerie," and my mom is a designer of athletic wear.

As a kid I didn't realize what a privileged life I was leading — all that sky and fresh fruits and vegetables. I went to private schools in Los Angeles and spent a year in Switzerland. After high school and a semester or two at Pierce Junior College in L.A., I traveled with my boyfriend through Mexico and then Central America. I came back with a broken heart and a stomach parasite. I spent a year getting

RECIPES ■ Samantha Johnson

Coconut Jerky and Macadamia Nut Cheese Wrapped in Butter Lettuce

This is one of my favorite raw treats. It's probably more of a summer dish – but I do eat it in winter. Whenever I can, I use my hands to chop and mix, so I wash them constantly.

Coconut Jerky

5 baby coconuts (you can find them in health food stores or specialty stores like Whole Foods)

Place the coconut on its side and crack it open with a large knife or cleaver. Spoon out the coconut meat leaving behind all of the shell and the brown skin. Clean with water. Set aside and then add to marinade.

Marinade

1 cup olive oil
1 cup balsamic vinegar
1 cup Nama Shou or any kind of high quality soy sauce
1 tablespoon hot pepper sesame oil
1 cup apple juice

Add a pinch of each:

Red pepper
Chili pepper
Cajun spice
Celtic sea salt

Add the cleaned coconut into the marinade and let it sit overnight (the longer the better), stirring a few times. Place marinated coconut onto a dehydrator sheet (I use Teflex) and dehydrate overnight. Turn the coconut onto other side and dehydrate until chewy. Sprinkle on wrap.

Macadamia Cheese

1 cup macadamia nuts
1 cup cashews
3 cloves garlic
1 inch piece of ginger, peeled
1 teaspoon red pepper flakes
1 teaspoon Celtic sea salt
¼ cup soy sauce
¼ cup lemon juice
¼ cup water or coconut water

Put all the ingredients into a blender and blend until they are smooth and creamy. If you add too much liquid in the beginning it won't be creamy - careful!

Butter Lettuce Wraps

1 head of butter lettuce
2 tomatoes chopped
1 cucumber, cubed
pepperincinis, minced
macadamia cheese (see above)
coconut Jerky cut into small pieces
salt
olive oil

Mix all the ingredients together with your hands. Take a lettuce leaf and fill it with a scoop (as much or as little as you desire), adding a pinch of salt and a sprinkling of oil. Eat up! Serves 5.

Oatmeal With Whipped Coconut Cream
Great for breakfast!

Oatmeal ingredients for one serving:

⅛ cup each of: oats, barley, rye and wheat berries (All grains should be soaked overnight to soften and activate)

Toppings:

Apples, cubed
Walnuts and/or pecans
Maple syrup or agave nectar
Cinnamon

Coconut Whip Cream:
- 2 Thai baby coconuts (scrape meat and drain water into cup)
- ¼ cup honey
- 1 teaspoon vanilla extract

Add all the ingredients to the blender except for the coconut water, which should be added slowly until the coconut becomes smooth and creamy.

Place mixture of sprouted grains in a bowl with coconut cream and optional toppings. Serves 5.

Winter Herb Salad with Citrus Vinaigrette

Sometimes I just need a little salad in the winter…
Cooking time: Including the marinating ½ hour

- 6 rainbow chard leaves (cut in small slivers, leaving as much of the stalk as possible)
- 3 kale leaves
- Cilantro, about one handful (remove leaves from stalks)
- ¼ cup dill
- ¼ cup basil (remove from stalk and sliver)
- ½ cup sun-dried olives, chopped
- ½ cup sun-dried tomatoes, slivered

Makes 4 servings.

Citrus Vinaigrette

- ½ cup olive oil
- ¼ cup apple cider vinegar
- ¼ cup orange juice
- 2 Tablespoons agave nectar
- 1 teaspoon salt

After you have made the dressing let the chopped kale and chard marinate in it for ¼ hour before adding the rest of the ingredients and serving.

Juliano always says about eating raw: "I am enjoying the most exquisite, unique, decadent food on the planet and my mentor is not some fancy cooking school, but the earth itself."

my health back. During that time I started working with the raw food cook, Juliano (www.planetraw .com), and began learning how to "uncook," or to cook raw. More like assembling, really. I changed my eating habits and lifestyle, and my energy soared.

It feels like my life keeps getting smaller and smaller, simpler and simpler. I live in a yurt, and from CFL lightbulbs to the green power energy blocks I buy from La Plata Electric, I'm always trying to save. I have a composting toilet, and I think solar is in my future, and maybe a windmill, since there is plenty of wind year round. In the winter

These are the superfoods I try to eat on a regular basis: beans, blueberries, broccoli, pumpkins, salmon, spinach, tomatoes, turkey, walnuts and yogurt.

months I heat with a wood stove. The insulation is pretty good. In the walls it's recycled jeans, and that's what covers the water pipes. There's a crank in the dome to let the heat out, but it was pretty cold this last winter. The floors are reclaimed wood, and the loft wood comes from my mom's old desk.

During the summer, I cook part-time at the Turtle Lake Refuge Café (a nonprofit restaurant). I have become an expert at assembling gourmet meals from wild weeds and our local southwest permaculture plants. As we learn more about what we have in our own backywards we'll be able to conserve more energy and become healthier, physically and emotionally. As we learn more about the benefits of

wild foods we'll be more adamant about protecting the remaining wild lands.

It's a little more difficult eating raw in the winter, especially when temperatures drop below zero. Our immune systems can be more compromised. Winter is when I miss California, being able to eat raw foods from my garden year round. I'm not naturally attracted to squash, potatoes or pumpkins, and I know I should be canning and stewing; I need to learn how and I will. Over the long haul there are times for cleansing, times for raw food, macrobiotic and certainly times for eating meat. Eating meat seems to keep me more in balance in the winter months. I find I don't crave a lot of salads. I sear my meat and fish — which has to be organic, grass-fed, no pesticides or hormones.

Often I feel like a contrarian. I'm always watching what I eat; it's hard to exist on a day-to-day basis eating this way unless you make it the most important thing in your life. Every day I learn some new way of saving or giving. I really want to make a difference in my own small way, be part of creating a sustainable world.

It's time to make the early fall trek back to New York City. Not because I have to, not because a child needs me to help get organized for school, but because it's what I have always done. So I close up the house and pack up the car. It's time for Luna's and my last walk around the ranch roads, a walk I've taken with my daughter at the end of summer for many years. Most of the oak trees have turned their burnt red, and the cottonwood leaves are a bright marigold. Down by the pond, the cattails are beginning to open, letting their cotton fly. All of this against the brilliance of the dark pine green of the firs and the high-altitude blue of the sky that surrounds my twenty acres. It's been another summer without a vegetable garden, but the flowerbeds sprouted all kinds of things, including the lush Russian sage and hollyhocks now in full bloom. The strong pull toward New York City and away from Durango is always hard for me. The Welsh call this longing to be in all places we call home, hireth.

Once I'm on the road, I accomplish the drive back in record time for me: four days. I listen to books on tape about gardening and cooking. I'm excited about the two Durango interviews and the ones I have lined up for the fall in the northeast. I'm excited to see the new apartment my daughter has moved into, which she's sharing with two other young women. She's raved about her kitchen, and asked me to bring honey from Durango and some of the plates she's been collecting for years.

Even before going to my own apartment, I stop by my daughter's new place. I hang around admiring everything for so long that I almost lose my loneliness.

That Monday morning I stop at the Union Square Greenmarket, where I've shopped for many years. I walk around the cheerful market, with the incongruent background noise of car horns and taxis screeching, scoping out a couple of young farmers. I have short conversations with each of them, getting information about where their farms are located and if they use any pesticides or additives. Second stop: Carnegie Hill CSA (Community Supported Agriculture), with pickups on Tuesdays at the Heavenly Rest Church on 90th Street and Fifth Avenue. There, Patricia Janof gives me a long list of young Hudson Valley farmers. Third stop is to set up a meeting with Mary Cleaver.

Mary owns The Green Table, tucked in the far corner of the Chelsea Market, and she is, according to many, a real guru in the food world. Mary offered to get me a meeting with the feverishly busy Gabrielle Langholtz, then publicity director of the Greenmarket. There are forty-six farmers markets throughout the five boroughs of New York City, and if anyone knows the young farmer and food set in the area, between Mary and Gabrielle, they know them all. All of us have dinner obligations, but we meet in the late afternoon at The Green Table.

Gabrielle: But we must order something from Mary's menu, particularly if you haven't eaten here before. How can we possibly sit here talking about food with so many divine possibilities on that menu? And wine, we must have a plate and a glass of wine.

That's Gabrielle for you. Her smile and overall presence light up a room when she walks into it; her enthusiasm about food is contagious. And Mary is also a wonder. Not only do they know folks up and down New York State, but also across the country. For over an hour they throw out names and descriptions of people from New York to California. As they play off of each other, the excitement grows so that everyone in the small cozy restaurant seems to share it.

By late September, almost everyone has returned to the city from vacationing. In late fall and the upcoming winter months, New York comes alive. There's an air of pulling in, letting go. There's more time to be spent indoors. Museums fill with new exhibitions, there are new plays on and off Broadway. Even before Thanksgiving, the sparkle of lights and the gorgeous holiday windows at Tiffany's, Saks, Lord and Taylor's and Bloomingdale's mark the real beginning of the holiday season. Then the huge tree in Rockefeller Plaza goes up, and skating begins in the plaza and at Wollman Rink in Central Park. New York is magical. And so is the Union Square Greenmarket, which continues through the fall and winter months.

I begin to write emails, setting up meetings and interviews for spring. I continue my reading as I am assembling those transcripts I've already collected. I cook a lot for friends and, when alone, I try to love it — the peace, the quiet. I do my yoga and take walks in the park with Luna.

That autumn, during one of Luna's and my walks in Central Park, the last leaves showing off the almost-bare boughs of the gracious trees, I think of my mother, how she used to talk about her childhood in Salt Lake City. She always longed to live on a farm, to grow her own food. She grew up as a Mormon, and her own mother always had a full larder. My mother was always ahead of her time, searching out the latest nutritional and health tips. She'd had breast cancer when quite young, and felt strongly about preventative health care.

When my family moved from Washington, D.C., to California, my mother searched out Adele Davis (author of Let's Eat Right to Keep Fit*) for health advice. She sought out organic produce. She read Rachel Carson. She never sprayed her garden, not even the citrus trees. Even way back when, my mother knew what was going on.*

By the end of February the weather is warmer and I am ready to start really digging into my project. When I tell my sister's son, born and raised in Sonoma County in California, immersed in the sustainable food movement since he was a kid, that I am working on a book about sustainable eating he gets really excited. "Come out, Auntie Kate. I'll set you up with folks here." So after I find someone to look after Luna, I fly out and follow the road map my nephew has made for me. First stop, Julien's office in the small business center of Healdsburg. The view from his desk: a sunny blue sky and a beautiful urban vegetable garden.

Julien Gervreau
Original Matters ■ Healdsburg, California ■ www.original-matters.com

FIRST WINTER ■ *Julien's office is not far from the farmers market, where he introduces me to the farmers and vendors, many of whom he went to high school with or worked with after graduating from Connecticut College in 2003. It was a very conscious decision for him to move back to his home turf and work in wine country. Julien says he has watched the attitudes of the people in his community shift from "conventional to eco." He believes that with its abundance of natural resources, northern California is on the leading edge of sustainable mindfulness. In recent months he and his mother, Marie, have partnered in a new business called Original Matters, which specializes in the branding of organic and biodynamic wine, and will soon expand to include the sustainable business practices for water resources and wellness.*

Julien: This book seems to me to be a call to action. Preserving agriculture as a way of life is no longer a fringe thing, it's no longer just about conscience. By emulating the ways and methods of each of the individuals profiled in this book, I believe we can change ideas about food. Knowing where it comes from, putting a face on the farmer, that's a small but significant step. If we cook dinner with friends just one time a week, that is another step. We can go to the farmers market and then have the basics on hand in order to whip up quick meals with real food: butter, olive oil, tomatoes, spices, pasta, lettuce. We can pick up our pastured meats and seasonal vegetables on the way home from work. Let's face it, eating is not just about food. It's also about community.

Julien and his fiancé, Serena, who holds a master's degree in public health from Columbia University, went to Nicaragua for six months to help raise awareness and money for natural resource and

public health related causes in the small town of San Juan del Sur.

During our time in Nicaragua, we collaborated with various nonprofits and the local government to launch a municipal recycling program, with a focus on separating plastic from solid waste and diverting it from landfills, streets and beaches. In conjunction, we made an educational presentation about the positive human and environmental health impacts of reducing, reusing and recycling to over 1,300 students in San Juan del Sur. We delivered biosand filters to 500 families outside San Juan del Sur. These filters eliminate up to 98 percent of intestinal parasites and bacteria from

RECIPES ■ Julien Gervreau

Breakfast: **Gallo Pinto with Sautéed Vegetables and Eggs**

Gallo Pinto, which roughly translates to "spotted rooster," is considered a staple in the Nicaraguan diet.

   2 cups cooked rice
   1 cup cooked red beans
   ½ cup white onions, diced
   3 teaspoons olive oil
   1 cup of chopped red and green peppers
   4 eggs
   Salt
   Hot Sauce

Pour vegetable oil in frying pan over medium heat. Sauté onions and peppers until cooked. Add entire pot of cooked beans. Over low-medium heat, stir in cooked rice and simmer for 5 minutes. Add salt to taste. Serve eggs, prepared any style, over the Gallo Pinto mix and add hot sauce to taste. Serves 4.

Lunch: **Nicaraguan Nacatamales**

Tamales are found throughout Latin America, and are most often enjoyed as a weekend treat. In Nicaragua, nacatamales are made with pork, chicken or fish and wrapped in a plantain leaf.

   ½ pound of Masa (corn flour)
   ¾ pounds of butter
   6 diced garlic cloves
   2 cubes of chicken or vegetable bouillon
   2 pounds chicken (either breasts or legs)
   1 cup white rice (soaked in warm water for 30 minutes)
   4 potatoes, thinly sliced
   2 green bell peppers, thinly sliced
   1 yellow onion, thinly sliced
   2 tomatoes, thinly sliced
   10 whole plantain (or banana) leaves
   Approximately 10 feet of twine or string

Dissolve corn flour in enough water to produce a thick dough. Melt the butter into a large pot, sauté garlic and add in the bouillon. Slowly mix in the corn flour dough.

   Crisscross two plantain leaf halves on a counter or flat surface and place 1 cup of corn flour dough in the middle.

Fold the following ingredients into the dough: 2 medium sized chicken pieces (or 1 chicken wing), 1 scoop of rice, 2 slices of potato, 3 slices of green bell pepper, 2 slices of onion and 2 slices of tomato.

   Wrap tightly all four sides of the plantain leaf and secure with twine or string.

   Steam all 10 nacatamales for 3 hours so that the raw ingredients cook thoroughly. Serves 10.

Snack: **Tostones (Fried Plantains)**

Tostones, twice-fried green plantains, are a favorite snack and side dish throughout Central America and the Caribbean.

   2 Green plantains, peeled and sliced diagonally into
      1-inch pieces
   2 tablespoons Olive or vegetable oil
   Your favorite cheese
   Salsa, ketchup or hot sauce for dipping
   pinch of Salt

Heat oil in skillet over medium-high heat. Add the plantains to the hot oil and fry until brown on all sides. Place on counter and flatten each slice with a cup until each piece is between 1 and 2 inches in diameter. Put flattened pieces back into the frying pan, until each side is crispy. Remove excess oil with paper towel as desired and add salt to taste. Serve with a slice of your favorite cheese (fried or cold), and salsa, ketchup or hot sauce. Serves 4.

Dinner: **Fish Filet with Garlic Sauce**

   1½ sticks of butter
   2 tablespoons olive oil
   4 garlic cloves, diced
   4 fish filets (red snapper or dorado)
   2 limes

Melt the butter into a pan and sauté garlic. Preheat broiler and lightly brush both sides of clean fish filets with olive oil. Broil fish, skin side up, for 3 to 4 minutes, then flip the filets over and spoon on garlic butter sauce. Broil fish for additional 3 to 4 minutes. Garnish with limes and parsley if desired. Serve with rice and steamed vegetables of your choice. Serves 4.

ground water, providing these families with clean water for generations to come. We've kept a record of our experiences on our blog: www.wanderlust-chronicles.wordpress.com.

Our time in Nicaragua has taught us that before people can have a sustainable food movement, they must have a healthy natural environment and know how to conserve natural resources.

Here in the United States, we've begun to incorporate what we learned in Nicaragua into our own daily lives and our future plans: natural resource management and public health, respectively. We'll see what happens. Meanwhile, we go to the farmers market twice a week and cook with friends at least once a week.

Alex Hill
Mushrooms ■ Healdsburg, CA ■ www.DiscoverwineCountry.tv

FEBRUARY ■ *Julien says that even in high school Alex knew what he wanted to do. Sure enough, upon first meeting I can feel Alex's self-confidence. Maybe it's because of his family's deep roots in Healdsburg. Maybe it's because he has always had a plan. Alex works with his father making wine. But he's a mycologist at heart.*

Alex: I've been mushrooming since I was five. I used to go with my father, run around the forest in Mill Creek — miles and miles, it was so overgrown, dark, perfect, two to three weeks after the first hard rain in late October, when the weather turned cold. My dad had his secret places, then they became mine. I always go out expecting to find nothing. If I'm looking for chanterelles (golden and black), I go out three weeks after the first hard rain. I've got a spot near the Tanoak and around the huckleberry bushes. I've got a sweet place in the Dry Creek Valley that's full of porcinis. Under the pine needles that have built up on the soft forest floor I find the matsutakes (so white and delicate, spicy

and clean). I sift through the needles. You can smell them. My dad used to say they smelled like old socks. They're tough, with a chewy texture that the Japanese prize above all others. A few shavings can really change the taste of a pasta or soup. Morels are at a higher elevation, say about five thousand feet. I found a patch last year in the Sierras, in the El Dorado National Forest. They're my favorite of all mushrooms, I think, so beautiful to look at, with this great meaty odor.

But I love all mushrooms — oyster, shitake, portobello, button, cremini — cultivated in dark, damp areas indoors on beds of compost. But there's nothing like wild mushrooms. When I go out hunting, all my senses come alive. For me, finding a mushroom in the woods is a miracle. Ecologists actually say that wild mushrooms are on the decline because of pollution, deforestation and global warming, but they're still out there. I've always got my head down sniffing around like some wild animal, hunting for a little mound. I've gotten lost at Salt Point — so focused on the ground, almost like a meditation, that I didn't notice it was getting dark. Suddenly the trees were creaking and I looked up and had no idea where in the world I was.

I don't hunt mushrooms for money — too much competition — but I love "getting my eyes on," as they say, and of course cooking with them. Put them in a pot with onions and butter and the smell will fill the whole house.

I love Healdsburg. I love all of Sonoma County. Some here worry that our quiet little farming town will become another Napa Valley, buttoned up and high-priced. I guess that's bound to happen in any area where you can pick out of your garden year round. Not too many places left in America where you can do that.

I grew up playing baseball and swimming in the river. I did well academically. I went to Sonoma

State University majoring in wine business strategies, and now I'm working on an MBA. I spent six months in New Zealand during the wine harvest, then went to Italy during the picking season to study Amarone wine. I spent a bunch of summers working in restaurants. I worked at Chateau Souverain with my friend Jamie Peterson, who owns and runs Peterson Vineyards. That's where I learned about simple cooking and how to season foods.

I interned for my father at Blackstone Vineyards a couple of years ago when he was head winemaker there; now he's gone off on his own. At that time,

Andrew Weil says, "One learns mushrooms in one way: through people who know them, not in books or by looking at pictures."

RECIPES ■ Alex Hill

In the summer, I jumpstart my day with either banana & berry muesli or:

Oyster Mushroom Scramble:
Time: 5 minutes

> 5 eggs, free range
> A couple of drops of truffle oil
> A large handful of Oyster mushrooms
> A handful of parsley

Beat the eggs with a fork in a medium-size bowl. Pre-heat medium-size skillet. Sauté the mushrooms for one minute. Pour eggs into the skillet and begin to scramble over the mushrooms. Add truffle oil. Just before the eggs are at your desired consistency, add parsley. Place on warmed plate with your choice of toast. Serves 2.

Lunch: White Matsutakes with Cabbage
Time: 40 Minutes

> 2 Matsutake mushrooms, baseball size
> 1 tablespoon butter
> 1 head of white cabbage

Sauté the sliced mushrooms in a medium skillet over low heat for 30 minutes. In a separate skillet cut the cabbage into 4 parts and cook covered with ½ cup of water and lid until soft. Put the cabbage on a plate and drape the mushrooms over each portion. I usually have a little rice on the side. Serves 4.

Dinner (or Thanksgiving): Wild Mushroom Stuffing
(I got this from Alice Waters. We used to make it at Santi Restaurant, although I changed it a bit for my taste.)
Time: 30 minutes
Will stuff a 12 to 14 pound turkey

> 1 pound chanterelles
> 4 tablespoons unsalted butter

2 shallots, peeled and finely diced
4 cloves garlic, minced
Salt and freshly ground black pepper to taste
1 cup onion, finely chopped
¼ pound smoked bacon
1 turkey or chicken liver, diced
1 day-old baguette, crust removed, to make 4 cups cubed
3 cups milk, or as needed
1 teaspoon Italian parsley, finely chopped
1 lightly beaten egg, if desired

Clean mushrooms and cut in half crosswise. In a large skillet over medium heat, melt 2 tablespoons butter, and add shallots and ¼ teaspoon of the garlic. Sauté until soft, about 2 minutes. Add mushrooms and season with salt and pepper to taste. Sauté until mushrooms are softened, about 8 minutes. Chop coarsely, then place in large mixing bowl.

In the same skillet, melt remaining butter. Add the onions and the remaining garlic. Sauté until softened, about 3 minutes. Season with salt and pepper to taste, and add to the bowl of mushrooms.

Return skillet to medium heat and add bacon. Cook until crisp, then remove bacon, either saving the fat for another purpose or discarding it. Add diced liver to pan and sauté over medium heat until browned, about 2 minutes. Drain well, season with salt and pepper to taste and add to mushrooms.

In a large mixing bowl, combine bread cubes with enough milk to saturate them. Drain bread, squeezing gently. Add to the mushrooms and mix gently. Add herbs and mix again. If you desire, add egg to bind stuffing.

Mushroom and Fennel Bread Pudding
(Adapted from Aida Mollenkamp)
Time: 1 hour

> 3 tablespoons unsalted butter
> ¾ cup white onion, coarsely chopped

another intern was flying in from Brazil to work for the summer. My dad asked me to pick her up from the airport. I waited in baggage claim for Paula, and it was love at first sight. Six months later, June 2006, I asked her to marry me. Paula is from a small town about five hours outside of Rio de Janeiro. She has her masters in food and dairy science, and works at the Petaluma Creamery. Her specialty is

12 ounces Cremini mushrooms (about 4 cups), coarsely
  chopped
2 cups fennel (1 medium bulb), coarsely chopped
⅔ cup celery (2 medium stalks), finely chopped
2 cups heavy cream
1 cup low-sodium chicken broth
4 large eggs
12 ounces ciabatta or other country-style bread (about 8
  cups), coarsely diced
1 cup aged pecorino such as Gran Pecorino (about 3
  ounces), coarsely grated
1 tablespoon fresh Italian parsley, finely chopped
1 teaspoon fresh sage, finely chopped

Melt butter in a large frying pan over medium heat until
foaming. To prevent overcrowding, cook vegetables in
batches: add onion and cook until soft, about 3 minutes.
Season well with salt and freshly ground black pepper, then
mix in mushrooms, fennel and celery. Cook until soft and
mushroom juices have reduced, about 10 minutes. Remove
from heat and let cool slightly, at least 10 minutes.

Heat the oven to 375 degrees and arrange the rack in
the middle. Butter a 9×13-inch baking dish and set aside.
Whisk together cream, chicken broth and eggs in a medium
bowl until well combined.

Add bread, cooled vegetables, cheese and herbs to
cream mixture, and stir until bread is well coated. Season
well with salt and freshly ground black pepper, then
turn into the prepared baking dish. Allow bread to soak
until well saturated, at least 15 minutes. Meanwhile,
bring about 10 cups water to simmer in a large pot over
medium-high heat.

Once bread has soaked and water is simmering, set the
baking dish in a large roasting pan and add enough hot
water to reach ⅔ of the way of the sides of the baking dish.
Bake until custard is set and top is lightly browned, about 50
minutes. Serve warm or at room temperature. Serves 6.

raw milk and its byproducts, like raw cheeses. She's
a good cook and makes great goat cheese, though I
do most of the cooking at home.

My father and I just bottled our first vintage of
wine in the style of Amarone, made by harvesting
ripe red grapes and allowing them to partially dry,
traditionally, on racks in the loft of a barn. This
process, called *appassimento* in Italian, means to
dry and shrivel. This concentrates the remaining
sugars and flavors and is similar to the production of *Vin Santo*. The length of drying time varies
according to producer and the quality of the grapes.
It's full bodied and complex — good with meats. It
will be our first wine released from the Langhart-
Hill Wines.

I play on the Peterson Winery baseball team from
the early spring through the summer with a bunch
of old friends, Jamie Peterson included, of course.
I've got a small garden, access to good food all
year, I love wine and I love to cook. Food relates to
the way we think and feel. I try to eat organically,
but local is more important to me at this point.
Tomatoes are just starting to appear at our farmers market. And figs, mmmm . . . figs! Paula and I
are just enjoying the early spring and the bounty of
fresh produce around here. We have a Fuyu persim-
mon tree that is so prolific in the fall that we use
persimmons with everything.

I also host a video podcast called "Profiles in
Wine" at www.DiscoverwineCountry.tv.

Jamie Peterson

Peterson Winery and Vineyards ■ **Dry Creek Valley, Healdsburg, California**
■ **www.petersonwinery.com**

FEBRUARY IS SPRING IN CALIFORNIA ■
Jamie Peterson, like Julien and Alex, is a native of Sonoma County living in Healdsburg. He's one of four children in what he says is "a real twentieth-century family" (his mother remarried and had another child). Jamie went to the Woolman School in Nevada City, a Quaker boarding school located in the Sierra Nevada foothills and focused on environmental study. Now he is a winemaker.

Jamie shares an 800-square-foot house with his girlfriend, Jessica. In the backyard, a jungle of vines runs up poles and fences and creeps along the ground. The 1800-square-foot garden has raised beds. Jamie orders most of his seeds from Jeremiath Gettle's Baker Creek Heirloom Seed Catalogue in Mansfield, Missouri. Jamie and Jessica mostly cook in. Once a week they eat out at either Scopa or Santi (where Jamie once worked), both local restaurants that use as much local food as they can.

First I checked out Jamie's garden, then we drove the five miles to Bradford Mountain, where most of the Peterson vines grow. We ended up back at the winemaking facility located at Timber Crest Farms on Dry Creek Road.

Jamie: I finally got my tomatoes yesterday. I've got thirty-five tomato vines, and I think I'm up to eight different kinds of heirloom tomatoes. Did you know that Baker Creek Seeds opened a store in Petaluma, just down the road? Now I can actually go in and get my seeds rather than ordering them through their catalog. Most of these melons are from Baker Creek Seeds. Melon craziness over here! I planted them a little too close together. I ran the drip tubing and then put the plastic mulch over it, so it really cut down on the water use. Even though I've doubled the amount of garden space, I use way less water. I'll harvest the sunflower seeds. These aren't edible,

they're too small, but my stepmom has been using them for wild bird rescue. She's got tons of birds to feed. I did plant six of the edible ones that I'm drying right now. I roast the big ones and take them to our baseball games. The guys like them.

My mom and stepdad bought property up in Canada — Salt Spring Island — where they're starting to farm, and they've got a gray-water system for some of their plants. I will collect rainwater here when the rainy season hits.

Peterson winery is just north of Healdsburg in the Dry Creek Valley. My father's background is not just in winemaking, but also in viticulture. He came to Dry Creek Valley in 1983.

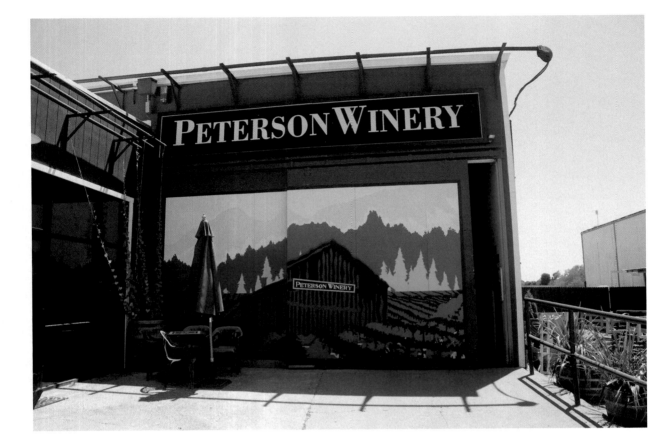

For over twenty years, the winery was located in an old red barn that was beginning to sag and sway. In 2005 we moved to Dry Creek Road at Timber Farms. After we moved, in 2006, I was given overall responsibilities as winemaker. The Peterson approach to winemaking is to capture the essence of vintage and vineyard, a philosophy we call Zero Manipulation — low-tech, high-touch! The evolution of Peterson wines to wines with soul accelerated when I became assistant winemaker in the summer of 2002.

At the edge of Dry Creek Valley, there are thirty-two acres that my dad cleared and planted in the 1980s. The elevation is one thousand feet, red-clay soil. It is so distinctive that people label it Bradford Mountain. It's a lot different up at the very top than down closer to the water. Grapes are picked at higher sugar content to get the perfect balance; they're really great grapes because the land is nearer to the ocean. We originally planted it in the 80s,

but unfortunately something was wrong with the rootstock: it wasn't resistant to a certain disease, so basically it all died out. He had to replant.

On the left of the grove are our newly planted grapes and on the right are the Syrah. My dad and I planted the Syrah in 2000. These little guys, this first row, is basically sacrificial because of the nearby trees. Down on the terraces we have Viognier planted. We have a little drip line to get this established. The well is across the road. It's pretty good, but we had to put in a second one for the other vines down below.

This vineyard that stretches down there *[he points down the hill]* gives us about six tons of grapes in a good year which is enough for 350 cases, 4,000-odd bottles. Down below *[he points beyond]*, past where the Cab and the Zin are planted, I think, we get another two- or three-and-a-half tons an acre. We are definitely a boutique operation. We do about five thousand cases total — some of the big

wines. We don't tweak or homogenize the wine to obtain consistency of flavors.

Our grapes for Peterson wines are grown in traditionally farmed vineyards. Of course each vintage varies from year to year due to the weather. All Peterson wines originate from small plantings, so there's a consistency of location in our wines.

I really like all parts of the wine business: the smells, the taste, and the not really being sure of what we're going to have until we have it. I love tasting the grapes out in the field, which is really the beginning of the birth of the wine.

During harvest time I'm up early and out sampling a few of our vineyard grapes to see where things are. If we're picking, I help oversee that, too. In between, I'll come back to the facility and get the grapes cleaned up and sorted, picking out leaves for crushing and de-stemming. The grapes fall through an auger near the bottom of the tank, and there's a cage with holes in it. Inside the cage are the paddles, and the paddles gently knock the grapes off the stems, and the stems go out one end and the whole grape drops down below. We don't actually crush the grapes, we leave most of them whole — it preserves more of the fruit without extracting too much of the tannin. We have a bunch of open-top tanks, four bigger four-ton, and three smaller ones that hold three tons of grapes. The juice drops to the bottom and the skins rise up above. When the skins and the juice separate, you have to mix it to get the juice mixed in. Then the grapes are left to ferment. We'll have to get in here to mix up the fermentation a few times, so I'm always in two places at once. The press is called a basket press, very gentle on the grapes. It helps so that we don't have to filter the wine because it's so gentle you get pretty good juice yields, but you don't break the skins and seeds and then have to filter.

wineries, that's their smallest tank. We do a lot of little lots. The machines we use are called twelve vineyard workers! It's all picked by hand. Because of the steepness of the grade, we don't even run tractors up here.

We have other vineyards that grow grapes for our wines. One of them is the West Vineyard, the source for our Tradizionate Zinfidel. Bernier Vineyard is also a traditional dry-farmed vineyard that supplies us with grapes. We didn't get their grapes last year because they had a lot of frost damage. But we're getting them again this year.

Once we get into the grape season, my dad and I look at the grapes from each vineyard and evaluate weather, soil and site. Zero manipulation is a discipline we follow to capture the character and balance in the grapes; it means using the most gentle traditional winemaking practices possible to maximize the flavors, aromatics and texture of the

In my life, I try hard not to be a consumer. I reuse everything, eat no fast foods, go to the farmers market and often invite friends over for dinners. My stepmom owns the organic Downtown Bakery where I get my bread. I go mushroom hunting with

Alex Hill, ride mountain bikes, play third base for our baseball team, and read fiction and gardening books. My cooking mentors are Deborah Madison and Mollie Katzen. My favorite foods are Italian and Thai.

For breakfast I'll eat poached eggs, tomatoes, truffle salt and toast. For lunch, a burrito or a BLT (bread from the bakery, tomatoes from the garden), bacon from Big Johns, our local supermarket. In the summer, the main thing we cook for dinner is pasta. We love mac and cheese and tomatoes or pasta primavera.

Five years from now I hope to be right here making wine, maybe able to buy a house in the area, or else build a house up by the vineyard. Jessica will have her vet license and my dad will hopefully be able to retire and just run his vineyard. It's all about the wines, and the heart and soul of what goes into them.

As I was leaving, Jamie gently picked a small melon. It fit perfectly in the palm of his hand.

From Jere Gettle's heirloom melon seeds. I'd let it ripen for two days.

I let the melon ripen for two days and then cut it open at breakfast out in the beautiful California sun. Its juice runs all over my hand and down the back of my arm; its delicate, sweet taste, sweeter than a

cantaloupe, and juicier, makes me smile. I want to meet Jere Gettle and visit Baker Creek Heirloom Seed Company. For now, Julien Gervreau, Jamie Peterson and Alex Hill make this world of sustainable food that I was getting into seem smaller and smaller and smaller.

In the northeast it's still early spring. Each one of these early interviews is a day trip from New York City, and usually includes some spectacular walk with Luna and a delicious meal.

Gabrielle Langholtz

Editor of *Edible Manhattan* (www.ediblemanhattan.com) and *Edible Brooklyn* (www.edible brooklyn.com) ■ Brooklyn, New York

---

SECOND SPRING MARCH ■ *Six months after our first meeting at The Green Table, I meet Gabrielle for the second time at the Fort Greene Farmers Market in Brooklyn. She joins me there at 8:30 A.M., already having been to two other markets. She's waiting in front of a vegetable stand snacking on the first spring rhubarb.*

Gabrielle: I'm so excited this morning about this rhubarb.

She breaks a stalk into pieces and chews on it without so much as a puckered lip.

I don't much like dessert, but my boyfriend, Craig Haney *[livestock manager at Stone Barns Farm in Tarrytown]*, really loves it. Over the last couple of summers I've really gotten into baking desserts as a way to show how much I love him. And today it begins again. In the winter I get sick of just apples, and now, all summer long I can make apricot tart, gooseberry fool. Things I've never made before.

In the spring and summer time I get up early because the dawn comes much sooner and there's lots to do. I like to be at one of the markets by 8:00 A.M. Many of the forty-six markets are open multiple days of the week. I might get to the Bronx first thing, eat a tamale for breakfast, or I might go to Watertown Heights, or to Jackson Heights, Queens. There's an amazing selection of food everywhere. Each one of our markets is so different.

We've moved on to a fishmonger, and now snack on fresh raw scallops from Long Island Sound, thumbnail size and so sweet.

Our biggest and most famous market is Union Square, open four days a week, year round. Most days, I spend a lot of time running around talking to the media, or folks on the city council at City Hall. Last week I had a meeting in east Harlem to talk about letting food stamp clients know they can spend their food stamps at the farmers markets.

Even as a kid I was always interested in food. I loved to cook. I can still remember my first two cookbooks. One was a cartoon cookbook with a recipe for peanut butter on celery. What a good idea, right? Many of the other recipes indicated that you needed a grown-up to help because there was a knife involved. I loved that cookbook. My favorite recipe — which required a grown-up's help — was Cabbage Soup for a Crowd.

I have one brother and one sister. We moved around a lot. I was born in Indiana but mostly grew up in suburbia around America. California, Alaska for six years, Oklahoma for six years. I went to high school on the Upper East Side of New York City, college in Virginia, and like a lot of young people in those years, although I wasn't a science-centered student, I was interested in the environment. I majored in English and Art History.

I spent all my personal time paying attention to food. I bought a little farm share and started making pesto. I had Indian food parties. I had no money for cookbooks, but I'd check them out of the library. I was a vegan, and was interested in the ecological impacts of my eating choices. I would visit farms during my college weekends and people would ask why I wasn't at a culinary school. I told them, I wanted "real" work, a "real" job, I didn't want to work in a kitchen. I still don't. Of course, now I'd love to go to culinary school if I had the money.

During the summers in college I interned at the Metropolitan Museum of Art. The summer after my junior year I interned at *Fortune* magazine. Then *Fortune* hired me right out of college to do their event planning. It was during the dot-com boom, and they had a big budget. I was on this great career path. I loved my colleagues, but

it wasn't work that I found really gratifying. We'd have these brainstorming meetings and I was there all right, I just wasn't offering up my best. Instead I was at the farmers market bringing home tomatoes, photographing them, inviting friends over for dinner. It never occurred to me that I could make a living from it.

Then, *Fortune* magazine sent me to Paris for an event that was to be held at Versailles, hosted by Chirac for about a thousand CEOs and heads of state. I stayed for a month at the Georges V Hotel, one of the most beautiful hotels in the world. I was inside working around the clock, but I was missing the first strawberries at the farmers market and all the flowers, and my friends at the stands. On the last day of the conference, I walked through the Parisian farmers market, just a couple of blocks away. I took a whole roll of film. I had this moment of conversion, a moment of decisiveness, and I went back to the hotel and called up the Greenmarket office in New York City. I started there in January of 2001.

Finally, a job I loved. Every day was alive for me. I was working with people who were as excited as I was about the work, hard work but varied and rich. I was brainstorming, and it was a totally different feeling than when I was with *Fortune*. I was using my imagination, all of it.

On Tuesday, September 11, 2001, when the first plane hit, I was at the Union Square Market, not at the World Trade Center where we'd had a market set up at the foot of the towers on Tuesdays and Thursdays for twenty years. We could see the flames, see the fire trucks racing down Broadway after the first tower fell. That was the worst moment of the day.

Later we learned that everyone had been evacuated, they just left their stands, just walked away. Our market manager took everybody's keys to go back and get the trucks — and we didn't hear from him for hours and were beside ourselves. He couldn't get to a phone so he walked all the way home to Brooklyn.

For the rest of the month, it was really confusing because mid to late September is a really key harvest time for our farmers. They couldn't bring trucks into the city. A lot of our markets shut down. All the farmers who had been there that morning lost their trucks.

I continued working full-time with the Greenmarket but was also employed there doing cooking demonstrations. Two days a week I worked on a farm, weeding and harvesting. I did a dinner with Alice Waters at the Whitney Museum. Then I volunteered at Chez Panisse [*Alice Waters's restaurant in Berkeley*]. I wrote the guide for one of Michael Pollan's books. I became the editor, first for *Edible Brooklyn*, then for *Edible Manhattan*, which was amazing because it was an opportunity for me to pull back the curtain on our city's eats, revealing every spellbinding, unctuous tale. The wheels were turning for me. My life kept building on food, and I was aware of how it was feeding me and nurturing me, and it made me realize that if your heart's not in what you're doing, how can you love it and innovate and connect?

The third time I interview Gabrielle, I drive up to Tarrytown, where Gabrielle lives (having moved from her beloved Brooklyn) with her now-husband, Craig Haney, and their 9-week-old baby, Bessie Hudson Haney. It's a dark, cold April day, pouring rain. I ring her bell twice and finally call out, "Gabrielle." After several moments I hear, "Come in." Gabrielle is sitting on the couch, nursing Bessie. At her feet are stacks and stacks of neatly piled books.

Gabrielle: I can't believe I forgot you were coming today. The place is a mess and I'm in the middle of editing for deadline. I'm so sorry. I feel like I have no sense of time anymore. That started during labor . . . maybe before, maybe just after I got pregnant when I said to myself, Something's got to give here. Editing the two *Edibles* and having a baby, it's more than enough work for me right now — six issues a year with *Edible Manhattan* and four issues with *Edible Brooklyn*, and I get to work at home.

I thought long and hard about how I could keep all my jobs. I could put Bess in daycare eight A.M. to eight P.M., but then, why have a child? Despite the financial stress, I want to hold my child, nurse her and be a mom. If I miss anything, it's the community of Brooklyn. Suburbia is different, there's no center to it, really. I've never had a master plan. I've never been able to see the future. I know I want to change people's perception of food. Like a lot of people in this movement, I know I have to make a living, but I am motivated by something other than money, a belief in something bigger. I feel there's something really brave about this work. When I was younger I had this kind of activist notion about overthrowing things, dropping out. But now I want to be part of the change. I want to impact people who don't agree with my ideas, yet, or understand them. People have said that my greatest strength is that I believe so fervently and am so passionate about healthy food and will fight for it.

Gabrielle looks up from her nursing and says she hears her husband's truck pulling in. He's home to make himself a sandwich, see Bess and check in on Gabrielle.

Hi! [*Craig comes into the living room and leans over Gabrielle and kisses her.*] I completely forgot Katherine was coming this morning. After you make your sandwich can she speak to you for a minute?

Craig: Sure!

Gabrielle: We first saw each other across a field at Stone Barns Center for Food and Agriculture [*where Dan Barber has his Blue Hill restaurant*]. The second time was in a crowd at a Lucinda

Williams concert in Central Park. We officially met at the Union Square Greenmarket, where we drank sauerkraut juice and talked to Jen Small and Mike Yezzi (of Flying Pigs Farm). Later that night we went square dancing. Craig missed the last train back to Tarrytown. *[Gabrielle laughs.]*

We went back and forth between Tarrytown and Brooklyn after that. Soon we knew we wanted to get married, knew we wanted a child. Neither of us worried about the order of things. If anything, it was kind of timed so the delivery would happen during Craig's slow season.

Before becoming the livestock manager at Stone Barns, Craig worked at an 1840s farm, part of a living history museum in Cooperstown, N.Y. About six years ago his first marriage ended, and he moved down to Tarrytown drawn by the concept of Stone Barns as an educational setting and the offer of a great position as livestock manager.

Craig: Dan Barber was buying meat from my farm upstate for his New York City Blue Hill Restaurant. After they settled on the restaurant for Stone Barns, they talked about setting up a livestock farm and a vegetable farm.

While he finishes making his sandwich, Gabrielle tells me about the Stone Barns operation.

Gabrielle: Craig's pigs live in the woods, so he brings them food and water every day. He brings in a boar when it's time for breeding, and helps with the births. Last Friday, a sow went into labor and hid in a shelter where Craig was pretty sure another sow would follow. They're so social and they're used to sleeping together. The sow would most likely crush the new bunch of piglets, so Craig set up a spot for her, brought in hay and kept the other curious sows away. He does the same during lambing season. He's more hands off, but when they're born he has to castrate the males, dip their umbilical cords so they don't get infected, dock their tails with a rubber band. That's late April, early May.

The sheep move to fresh grass every day, and the grass is just beginning now. At the moment the sheep are still in the barn. So much of what Craig

does is about moving the animals to fresh pasture. He moves the meat chickens, the egg chickens, moves the sheep, every day. The pigs move once a month since they're in the woods and not eating grass. He has lots of poultry: turkeys, geese and the chickens.

Craig returns with his sandwich.

Gabrielle: Craig made a ham on Monday night and yesterday I took some of it and made it into a frittata with Craig's eggs — it was delicious. This is making me hungry!

Craig: Do you want me to make some sandwiches?

Gabrielle: No, it's okay.

Craig: When I was a high school senior I thought I was going to be a lawyer. I used to go to the courthouse to listen in on court cases. I grew up around older people which helps explain why I spend a lot of time thinking about the heritage of the animals around me, mostly their genetic heritage — where they come from, what they used to do and why, and

what they would like to do now. I like moving the animals, especially the sheep and the turkeys. They get pretty excited, they know the routine.

From the moment I saw Stone Barns, I knew I could work there. I loved the land. Stone Barns is eighty acres, but Mr. Rockefeller owns five hundred acres of a larger cattle farm surrounding us. The state owns another seventeen hundred, so that's twenty-three hundred acres.

I ask both of them what they feel is the single most important thing that has happened in the food world in the last ten years.

Craig: Maybe Stone Barns. Stone Barns is a farm, a kitchen, a classroom, an exhibit, a laboratory and a campus. It's all about community-based foods. To have this kind of facility available to the public —

everyone, but especially kids, gets to see where our food comes from, learn how it affects our health, the health of the land, the community and the environment *[see www.stonebarnscenter.org]*.

Gabrielle: Michael Pollan's book, *The Omnivore's Dilemma.* It has informed so many different kinds of people, bringing ideas to the forefront that many had never heard of. It is so persuasive, has had such public appeal, has been so amazing for shifting public opinion.

She pauses for a moment. Looks over at Craig. Caresses Bess who finally, after nursing, has fallen asleep in her lap.

Craig, I'm starved. Can I have a bite of that sandwich? It looks so good.

They both laugh.

Jen Small and Mike Yezzi
Flying Pigs Farm ■ Sushan, New York ■ www.flyingpigsfarm.com

After my interview with Gabrielle, I feel I am on my way. Several days later I head back upstate. I have frequently shopped at the Flying Pigs Farm stand at the Greenmarket in New York's Union Square. There Jen Small and Mike Yezzi showed me a generous selection of pork cuts: chops, tenderloins, smoked ham steaks, bacons, sausages, hocks, fresh belly, butt shoulder and leaf lard (pure hog fat). I sautéed them, barbecued them and braised many of them, and knew their delicious, tender flavor. On a fine, crisp March morning, not a cloud in the sky, I drive up to Shushan, New York, to visit their farm and meet their pigs. I remember reading in one of Shannon Hayes's cookbooks that every

farmer needs four best friends: a border collie to move the livestock, a guard dog to protect them, a good barn cat for catching mice and rats and a pig to handle the rest. Mary Cleaver (The Green Table in Chelsea Market) raved about these pigs and the farm, but when I pull up in front of the small yellow farmhouse, and see the pigs running wild in the field with the view of Battenkill River Valley beyond, it takes my breath away. Mike Yezzi and his beautiful, spirited little daughter, long blond hair trailing behind her like a comet's tail, run up from the field to meet me. Mike tells me he's on duty that day while Jane's baby brother, Charlie, naps, and Jen works part-time with the American

Farmland Trust. Jen has a master's degree in public health; Mike has a law degree as well as a master's degree in public health. They both have full-time jobs besides the farm to take care of. Jen raises money for Williams College, in addition to working for AFT, while Mike works for a company that manages homes for the elderly.

Mike Yezzi: If you'd told either of us ten years ago that we'd be best known for pig farming, we'd have said you were crazy!

All the pigs run toward us. Jane screams with glee as they gather around her and she pats their heads. I stroke a pink one with smoky gray spots. It looks up at me like a dog might, completely friendly. I instantly fall in love.

That's a Gloucestershire Old Spot cross. *[Mike reaches over and pets its floppy ears.]* Those two with red-haired bristles are Tamworths, and the black ones are Large Blacks or Large Black crosses. All of them are rare heritage breeds as determined

by the American Livestock Breeds Conservancy, and are at risk of extinction.

In an earlier interview, Jen had told me that these breeds had gone out of favor when lard went out of style. Since lard is no longer popular as a commercial fat, there is little use for a pig that produces a lot of it. And they don't do well in confinement. They're not efficient. They eat more and take longer to grow, moving around and eating a varied diet of grass, weeds and wildflowers. That's what gives their meat such a fine texture and makes them so tasty.

Jen and I met at Union College as undergraduates. Then we went to graduate school together. She was actually in the public health program before me. She was working at the University of Massachusetts while I was going to law school. Then I got my master's in public health, and began working for a nonprofit nursing home group doing compliance and regulatory work.

Jen's father grew up in the house next door to what is now ours, which dates to the 1830s. Jen

RECIPES ■ Jen Small and Mike Yezzi

We like this recipe because it can be made with almost any kind of smoked pork on hand. And because smoked pork is already cooked, one only needs to heat it through, which results in a hot meal in just a few minutes.

Smoked Pork Chops, Ham or Sausage with Wine and Sauerkraut

  1 slice of bacon*
1 onion, peeled and coarsely chopped
½ can or ½ bag of sauerkraut**
2 whole cloves
2 bay leaves
¼ teaspoon caraway seeds (optional)
4 crushed juniper berries (optional)
1 pound sliced smoked ham, a smoked ham steak, smoked pork chops, or even a smoked pork sausage such as kielbasa
About 1 cup white wine

In a deep skillet fry the bacon.* Remove the bacon from the pan and eat it. Sauté the onion in the bacon drippings that remain in the pan for about 2 minutes. Add the sauerkraut, cloves, bay leaves, caraway seeds and juniper berries to the pan and combine. Nestle the ham, ham steak, pork chops or pork sausage into the sauerkraut mixture, and pour about 1 cup white wine over the top, just enough to almost cover. Bring to a boil, and then turn the heat down and simmer for a few minutes, until the pork is hot and much of the liquid has evaporated. Serve the pork and sauerkraut with boiled potatoes and your favorite mustard. Serves 2 to 4.

  *It's faster and more economical to save your bacon drippings in a can in the fridge. Then when you need to add flavor to beans, soups, chicken, eggs or almost any other dish, you scoop out a small amount.

  **If you like sauerkraut that is very sour, just pour into a strainer and press out the liquid. If you do not like it that strong, pour into a strainer, rinse with water and then press out the liquid.

spent her summers up here. Her mother and father would come up on the weekends. In the mid-90s, a developer wanted to buy this farm and the one next door and cover the land up with houses. You can imagine how it would have changed the character of the road and the rural community. So the family got together, and we all worked it out and we wound up buying the farm. We were still in grad school and had no money but we also felt we had no choice. It was either buy it or lose it forever. For more than two years we redid the house on weekends and during our vacations while living near Jen's job. We did all the gutting and rough framing. We moved into the house in 1999. Of course then we needed to figure out something to help the land pay for itself, and what to farm. We looked at dairy animals, but the expense of the equipment and milking twice a day made that impossible; we both have office jobs. The cost of llamas or alpacas or fencing cattle was huge, so we decided on pigs. We thought, We'll get them in the spring, get rid

of them in the fall; if we don't like it, we haven't invested too much.

So in 2000 we got three pink pigs from neighbors down the road. It takes six or seven months from birth to slaughter for those pink guys — and it worked out so well that we did another fifteen. Jen did some research, we got some good advice, and so looked into rare heritage pigs, and found somebody in Connecticut working with Large Blacks. There's not a lot of them around, so we got seven of them. We also learned that Durocs, a breed started in this country in 1860, were scarce in the area, so we got seven of those. Of the ninety-two million pigs processed in the U.S. each year, Durocs are actually one of the main breeds, so they really didn't need help. Of the rare heritage breed pigs, there's fewer than two hundred registered of the Large Blacks and the Old Spots in North America, and fewer then five hundred of the Tamworths. Worldwide population of Blacks is two thousand and Tamworth, five thousand. About this time we

went down to the greenmarket in New York to meet people, see if there was room for us and see if people would be willing to pay the additional costs of rare, pasture-raised pork. Mary Cleaver, who at the time was doing catering for the 9/11 recovery workers, had gotten a grant from the National Pork Board and basically bought out our inventory to feed the workers. Then we met Peter Hoffman, who owns Savoy Restaurant. They both continue to be our big supporters.

The next year we had fifty-seven pigs and sold them at Cadman Plaza. The following year we started at Grand Army Plaza in Brooklyn.

Once the house was finished, we let the pigs help us clear the outside, all 150 overgrown acres. The pigs helped manage the land by using their strong snouts to root up the shrubs and plants, converting overgrown patches into these grassy pastures. Because the pigs have so much space, the land stays clean and they stay healthy.

I saw an HBO documentary not long ago called Death on a Factory Farm, a close look through undercover footage at animal cruelty at an Ohio factory hog farm. As I look at these beautiful creatures and see the way Jane is playing with them, it makes me shudder to think that anyone can possibly treat any animal inhumanely.

As Jane walks through the crowd of the pigs, they bump into her right and left. She laughs, petting them and cooing. Suddenly she looks up at me. "Do you like my boots? You know, I don't have any dogs. I have five cats. They sleep on my mom and dad's bed. I was a ballerina last Halloween."

I wonder if, in the months that these beautiful, friendly pigs are around, Jane and her brother Charlie get attached to them? Mike nods.

But she knows they will go. She understands as much as she's able to.

On Thursday evenings, after dinner, we leave the kids with a sitter and drive two hundred miles to New York City, getting in around one A.M. On Fridays, we do restaurant deliveries and work the

Union Square Greenmarket. We stay at a friend's apartment on Friday evening and then work both Union Square and the Grand Army Plaza Greenmarkets on Saturdays. We leave for home and arrive at about ten P.M. to relieve the babysitter. We see the kids on Sunday mornings. The markets are year round. We've done thirty-nine to forty markets so far this year. It's a perfect balance for us. Sometimes we will trade with others at market for fresh fish and great cheeses, or cider. We actually have our own chickens and eggs. Sometimes we'll raise some beef and lamb.

We also do mail order one or two days a week. We ship across the country but mostly in the Northeast.

Five years from now I hope we will still be farming, doing more things ourselves, more value-added products, cured meats, continuing to work with other small farmers.

We breed some of our pigs, but we primarily buy piglets from breeders throughout the Northeast who raise pigs to our standards. We'll still sell at farmers markets and still work with restaurants. We're now working with Savoy, Back Forty, Il Bucco, Mas, Telepan, Gramercy Tavern, Diner and of course Mary Cleaver's The Green Table. We've thought about adding a slaughterhouse. The slaughterhouse we use is about an hour away, and scalds and scrapes the skin, which is what restaurants want. We do twelve pigs a week.

The butcher that does our retail cuts, like bacon, is a really good smoker. We produce no-nitrate bacon for people who don't want the nitrates.

Pork from heritage breeds is moister, and has a better flavor than conventional hybrids or some of the more common breeds. It may seem odd to use rare breeds for pork, but they will not survive unless a market can be created for them.

Our pigs eat grains, vegetables and fruits, grass and plants that grow right here on the land. No antibiotics or animal parts in the feed.

We're right on the Battenkill River, with beautiful views of Vermont. Up on the hill its one of the higher points around, you can see the Equinox

TIP ■ We recommend turning down the heat on our bacon, and cooking it a little longer at more moderate temperature. It reduces the formation of nitrosamines.

clearly — its just a great view. It's hard work, but worth it.

So far, we have just the right balance of urban and rural. People at both markets have made this possible; they have been so good to us. We started with three pigs in 2000, and we finished a little over five hundred in 2008. One of the things we're talking about is if we want to grow, and how much? Maybe we'll just stay at five hundred and from there we'll just get more efficient. This week we ran out of roasting chickens and soup chickens and eggs — people were very upset about that. Peter, who works at the Union Square stand, said there was actually a fight over the last soup chicken, and he had no idea who was first in line. "I'm going to come back in a minute and you'll tell me who's going to buy that chicken," he told them.

When we started all of this, we thought it was just about preservation, keeping out development, keeping it agricultural land.

Mike shook his head.

We wanted to save a farm and ended up becoming farmers, raising heritage breeds — preservation again, just like the farm. Agricultural heritage is disappearing, and many of these breeds are on the brink of extinction. And just like Mary Cleaver and Peter Hoffman advised us, these breeds taste better. Our work is all about relationships. And we've made some good friends. We've created a good life for ourselves.

Having had the pork from Flying Pigs Farm, one thing is for sure. The taste of that meat incorporates all that the animal has eaten: fresh grass, bright sun, clean water. Incredible taste. Always a reminder for me of how important it is to know where your food comes from, to be able to put a face on your farmer.

Shannon Hayes
Sap Bush Hollow Farm ■ Schoharie County, New York ■ www.shannonhayes.info

---

MARCH ■ *Not far up the road from Flying Pigs Farm, Shannon Hayes may not call herself a full-time farmer but she does farm, eating the food she raises with her husband, Bob Hooper, and her parents at Sap Bush Hollow Farm in Warnerville, New York. She travels the world studying great food, agriculture and rural living. She makes her own soap, composts her garbage and plans to homeschool her unvaccinated daughters.*

Shannon would admit to having a number of degrees in sustainable agriculture, and to being a prolific writer, with articles, essays and columns appearing all over the place including www.farm totable.org and The New York Times. *She is a wonderful cook as proven by many of the recipes from her two books* The Grassfed Gourmet *and* The Farmer and the Grill. *Her third book,* Radical Homemaker: Reclaiming Domesticity From a Consumer Culture, *is an examination of what Shannon sees as a return to family first, and the high cost of working outside the home.*

Shannon would certainly say she is always a loud voice for local causes in her community, be they weighing the possible effects of the construction of wind turbines or the high cost to small farmers of putting electronic tags on farm animals under the National Animal Identification System.

But not long ago, Shannon Hayes wrote an essay for her blog, Shannonhayes.info, acknowledging that she was coming apart at the seams. She said she had become a new stereotype that echoed an old lifestyle: The Supermom.

We are overeducated overachievers, side-stepping the conventional rat race for an alternative maelstrom. When you approach us at the weekly market we offer to sell you our eggs, or grass-fed steak or freshly processed chicken. But really, we are selling you more than that. We are selling you our lifestyle. "Buy from me because we represent your values." What I really feel like saying is "Buy from me, because I want to pick up a bottle of gin on the way home." Somehow, on our paths toward this noble life, one more group of girls has fallen prey to another impossible feminine ideal. And I, for one, am crumbling under the pressure of Über-Momming. Our gardens are a mess, my kids are throwing up on the way to the market, my fingers ache from milking the cow, we're running out of homemade soap, and attachment parenting is causing my back to ache . . . and despite our best efforts, our four-year-old still longs to be a Disney Princess.

On a chilly spring morning I pull up in front of the Hayes-Hooper home. I imagine I will be walking into a hippie house of chaos. Instead I find a tidy, spacious, elegant, recently renovated 1200-square-foot solar-heated addition with a wide loft upstairs that has open bedrooms and a bath. Things seem pretty peaceful in the household. The children are not screaming: one plays quietly while the other naps. Bob, an environmental educator, is at work in his office. Shannon's halfway through the breakfast dishes after having risen earlier to write. She makes us a pot of tea.

Shannon: This summer was great. I did nothing but relax! *[She laughs sarcastically.]*

Shannon gives me a tour of the house, including the cold cellar, a long kitchen counter of poured concrete, the masonry fireplace that heats the whole house and a full larder.

There's a giant crock of sauerkraut down in the basement. In the cold room on the north side of the

house I've got a couple of bushels of squash. I've got more sauerkraut going here in the kitchen, and I have a half-gallon of lacto-fermented beets. Lacto-fermentation is a way of preserving food by building bacteria. I also make kimchee. And then I did a gallon of pickles. We've got lots of fruit, winter storage apples, cherries, peaches, pears, apple butter, green beans and corn. And all the meat from the farm, that's a given.

However, I do not kill, not even a fly. I can do the evisceration and I can do the boning. My mom was desperate for help with the chicken processing, but I was just so squeamish she finally said, "Shannon, you do not have to kill anything." And it turns out there are some people who are good at it, and others who aren't.

My mother and I have a very close relationship. She had my brother when she was twenty-one and I was born when she was twenty-three. When I decided to come back to the farm, my parents put the challenge to me: "You want to come back to the farm, great, come back with a job that will give you a livelihood without taking money from our income." So I had to find ways to earn money without drawing on their resources. I don't take direction very well and I have an entrepreneurial kind of mind. I like being my own boss and being in control of my own thing. So we have a partnership. I'm responsible for certain enterprises, like our weekly farmers market. My husband and I run it on our own twenty weeks out of the year. Also I've developed a line of eleven different sausages. My parents

Mushroom and Olive Burgers

¼ cup fresh chives, finely chopped

¼ cup fresh mushrooms, diced

¼ cup oil-cured black olives, pitted and finely chopped

3 tablespoons fresh oregano, finely chopped, or 1 tablespoon dried

1 ½ teaspoons coarse salt

2 teaspoons coarsely ground black pepper

1 clove garlic, minced

1 ½ pounds of ground beef, ideally 80 percent lean

Combine the chives, mushrooms, olives, oregano, salt, pepper and garlic in a medium-size bowl. Mix well. Add the ground beef. Using your hands, mix until all the ingredients are thoroughly incorporated into the meat. Loosely shape the beef into 4 meatballs, then gently flatten each ball until it is just shy of 1-inch thick. With your fingertips, make a small well in the top of each patty to prevent the meat from getting fluffy over the flames. Set the patties aside while you light the grill and brush off the cooking grate.

When the grill is medium-hot and you can hold your hand 5 inches above it for no more than 3 or 4 seconds, brush it down lightly with vegetable oil, then set the patties directly over the flame, with the well facing up. Grill, covered, for about 4 to 5 minutes per side for medium burgers, remembering that for safety, ground beef should be cooked to a minimum internal temperature of 160 degrees. Serves 4.

Short-Ribs Marinated in Cayenne and Garlic

4 cloves garlic

1 tablespoon cayenne pepper

1 small onion, peeled and cut in half

1 tablespoon coarse salt

1 tablespoon white peppercorns, coarsely ground

1 tablespoon black peppercorns, coarsely ground

4 tablespoons cognac

4 tablespoons olive oil

4 tablespoons red wine vinegar

4 bay leaves

4 sprigs fresh rosemary

3 to 5 pounds short ribs

Add the garlic, cayenne, onion, salt, peppercorns, cognac, olive oil and vinegar to the large bowl of a food processor.

Puree to make a paste. Rub the paste into the meat, then set the ribs in a plastic bag. Set the bay leaves and rosemary on top, then seal the bag tightly and refrigerate several hours or overnight.

When you are ready to grill, remove the ribs from the bag, but do not blot off the paste. Allow the meat to come to room temperature, then grill as directed in the *asado (grilled short ribs)* recipe below.

If using a charcoal grill, light the coals and allow them to burn until they are covered with a layer of gray ash. Pour a line of coals down the left and right side of the grill, and place a drip pan or cast iron skillet in the center. If cooking with gas, light the front and back burners only. Put your rotisserie attachment in place, spear the meat on the spit (if the ribs are flanken style, thread the spit between every second or third rib, zigzag). Allow the meat to turn on the spit and slowly roast for 2 to 3 hours, until the tissue along the exterior of the bones begins to pull away and the meat, when sliced, appears nearly well done throughout (although there should still be ample juices). As you cook the meat, be sure to leave the lid of the grill open. You want to make sure that the temperature *at the spit,* where the meat is, remains around 300 degrees. To gauge this, you should be able to hold your hand right next to the rotating meat for 8 seconds.

Ten minutes before you serve the ribs, splash them liberally with the *salmuera*. Allow them to continue to turn on the rotisserie so that a salty crust forms. When you serve the meat, pass the *salmuera* bottle separately so your guests can add additional sauce as desired. Serves 3 to 5.

Salmuera (Argentina and Brazil's salt-saturated garlic water)

5 to 6 cloves garlic, finely sliced

1 tablespoon black peppercorns, coarsely crushed using mortar and pestle

1 tablespoon white peppercorns, coarsely crushed using mortar and pestle

7 tablespoons coarse salt, plus extra

1 clean, empty 750 ml wine bottle and cork or stopper

Combine the garlic, black and white peppercorns and 2 tablespoons salt in a medium-size saucepan. Pour in 3 cups water, then bring the mixture to a rolling boil for 30 seconds. Turn the heat off and allow it to cool for 5 minutes.

Using a funnel, add 3 tablespoons salt to the bottom of the wine bottle. Then pour in the garlic water, including the sliced garlic and ground peppercorns. Cork the bottle. Using your thumb to hold the cork in place, shake vigorously until all the salt is incorporated into the water. Add 2 more tablespoons salt and shake again. If all this salt is absorbed and none has collected on the bottom of the bottle, add additional salt.

In a good salmuera, the water must be *completely* saturated with salt. This means you must continue to add salt and shake until the water will absorb no more and a small pile of salt has gathered on the bottom of the bottle.

Shave off a corner of the cork to allow the mixture to be easily drizzled (we use a pour-spout stopper), then store at room temperature for up to 3 months, adding more salt, pepper, garlic and hot water to taste to enrich the flavor after each use.

Before applying to the meat, place your bottle of salmuera on the grate of your grill to heat up. For maximum flavor and efficient cooking, always be sure your salmuera is hot before you use it. Once you've splashed it on the meat on your grill, be sure to set the salmuera on the table so that your guests can add more to their meat to taste.

Carolina Pulled Pork

1 batch Paprika-Pepper Spice Rub
1 batch Vinegar Mop
1 batch Southern-Style Butter Barbeque Sauce
Optional: 1 can beer or 2 cups apple cider
1 pork shoulder roast, 4 to 10 pounds (either Boston butt or picnic roast will work)

Several handfuls of hickory chips or chunks, soaked in water for a minimum of 30 minutes. (If you are using a gas grill, only use wood chips, and you will need only about 2 cups.) Note: As an option, our good friend and barbeque aficionado Frank Davis suggests soaking the smoking wood in apple cider or beer for extra flavor.

Thoroughly coat the pork shoulder in the spice rub, reserving any extras for the vinegar mop. Wrap the meat in plastic

and refrigerate for 1 to 2 days.

On barbeque day, remove the meat, unwrap it and allow it to come to room temperature.

If using charcoal, start the grill and warm it until the temperature inside the cooking chamber is about 220 degrees. If using a gas grill, light the grill, turn all burners to high, then put the 2 cups soaked wood chips in a foil tray and set it down directly over one burner. Close the lid and preheat the cooking chamber (all burners still on high) until smoke billows out. Turn all off but the one burner beneath the wood chips and allow the cooking chamber to come down to 200 to 230 degrees (if the chamber won't cool down that low, get it as cool as you can, then plan for a shorter cook time).

Set a drip pan in place on the cool side of the grill. If you like, pour a can of beer or 2 cups apple cider into the pan to add additional moisture and flavor to the smoke process (this is optional, as the meat will smoke just fine without it). Lay the pork shoulder on top. If possible, arrange the meat so that the fat cap is facing up. If the roast is too tall, or if it won't balance with the fat cap on top, lay the meat on its side and arrange it so the fat cap faces the heat. This will help protect the meat from drying out or overcooking. If using a charcoal grill, toss some soaked wood chips or chunks directly on the coals. Put the lid in place. Open the vents of the lid partially and arrange them so they are directly over the meat. If using gas, simply close the lid.

Smoke the meat for roughly 1 hour 15 minutes to 1 hour 30 minutes per pound, adding coals as necessary (or adjusting the dial on your gas grill) to make sure the temperature of the cooking chamber stays between 200 and 230 degrees. Each time you add coals, brush the meat down with the vinegar mop and add a few more wood chips or chunks to the fire. If using gas, baste with the mop once per hour. When the meat is fork-tender with an internal temperature around 185 to 200 degrees, it is ready. Remove the meat from the grill and allow it to rest 10 to 15 minutes before pulling it apart. Pass the meat with the barbeque sauce, allowing guests to pour it on themselves. Serves 4 to 10.

Paprika-Pepper Spice Rub

⅓ cup ground black pepper

¼ cup coarse salt

⅓ cup sucanat, turbinado or an unrefined or partially
    refined sugar

2 tablespoons dry mustard

⅓ cup mild paprika

1 tablespoon granulated garlic

1 tablespoon onion powder

1 teaspoon celery powder

Combine all the ingredients in a small bowl. Mix well.

Vinegar Mop

Remaining paprika-pepper rub left over after seasoning
    the meat

3 cups cider vinegar

1 small onion, minced

2 tablespoons honey

2 teaspoons coarse salt

1 teaspoon ground black pepper

2 cloves garlic, minced

1 to 2 teaspoons cayenne pepper (optional)

¼ cup ketchup

Combine all ingredients in a medium-size bowl and whisk
well.

Sweet Tomato Barbecue Sauce

This sauce is excellent over eggs when making scrambled,
over-easy, or when you scramble and stuff into a tortilla with
the sauce on top.

1 tablespoon butter

1 medium onion, finely chopped

1 cup strong, black coffee

3 cloves garlic, minced

½ cup honey

½ cup cider vinegar

4 tablespoons honey mustard

4 tablespoons tomato sauce

1 teaspoon salt

1 teaspoon freshly ground black pepper

Melt the butter in a saucepan over medium flame. Add the
onions and sauté until translucent. Stir in the remaining
ingredients and allow the sauce to simmer, uncovered, until
lightly thickened, about 20 minutes. If desired, season to
taste with additional honey, vinegar, salt, and pepper. Serve
warm. If refrigerated in an airtight container, the sauce will
keep several weeks.

manage the farm on a daily basis. As my daughters Saoirse and Ula get older, we begin working together during the growing season.

When it comes to adding value, that's where I come in. I do a lot of food preservation, which helps to bring down our costs, and I do a little ancillary business: taking animal fats and rendering them into soaps. I do a lot of speaking engagements in the winter. Not long ago I spoke to the American Dietetic Association, letting the dieticians know that the organic food movement hasn't gone away — I broke down why food costs what it does, what happens in subsidies and where the money goes. For example, I'm at a farmers market and two ladies come up and poke at my meat. And one says,

"This must be really expensive." And I say, "It's $15 a pound." And they say, "That must be a $50 leg," and I say, "Actually it's $64, which allows me and my family to live at 200 percent of the poverty level, to qualify for assistance if we so desire, and to not have health insurance."

We live on $40,000 in income from our farm proceeds, our investments and my essays and cookbook sales.

I did my undergraduate work at SUNY Binghamton, and although I took a job after graduation for a year as a schoolteacher in Japan — I never really wanted to leave here. But I had this language skill and I had to prove that I wasn't here just because I was scared to leave. My Japanese is fading fast, but my French and Spanish are pretty good. When I first came home I got a job in rural development. This county was hit by some devastating floods in 1996, and I was hired to run a housing rehabilitation program for low-income homeowners. I did that for a year, completely burned out, and then went to grad school at Cornell.

I feel very attached to this land. When I met Bob, he was working at L.L. Bean in Maine. I knew if I was going to have a partner in life, he had to be willing to come here. As much as I love other places, this is the place where my heart beats strongest. Bob, who is sixteen years older than I am, understood that.

Initially we rented the upstairs and lived with my family, like in the olden days. My parents didn't require that we get married first.

Now that we have children, I hate the idea that I'm supposed to send them to somebody else for however many hours a day. It's such a short period of time, eighteen years, and I'm going to keep them with me. If it's not working, then school's always an option. If I'm not doing well at it, I'm not going to make them suffer through my bad teaching.

We feel we have such a good life, and we have the opportunity to expose our kids to this work. Eventually, if they want, they can become part of what we do.

I'm second-generation American. My grandmother farmed in Germany. She was twelve years old when her family fled Europe, just as Hitler was coming to power. Her family ended up in Hoboken, New Jersey.

My grandfather is Irish. My grandmother would never have married a German man. She didn't want one lick of German showing through in her family. She made sure everyone was raised Catholic and that we were Irish to the core.

There are sixteen cousins in my generation, all raised on farms, but I'm the only one farming now. Aside from Japan and a few other travels, farming is all I've ever really known.

Nobody I know talks about the hardships of

farming. There's the constant pressure to make it look good because that's what the consumer wants. During one busy summer I started feeling like I was fighting a losing battle. All the farmers at the farmers market, everyone looked so perfect, and I just broke down and lost it. I felt really overwhelmed, like personally I was a disaster, a disgrace; and that's when I wrote that essay. I sent it to two friends who I trusted to be sympathetic. Then the essay took on a life of its own and I began receiving letters from women all over saying, "I'm falling apart, too." I've pretty much gotten over that.

In five years time from now I want to be right where I am, but my children will be older, I'll be in more structural school mode and won't be dealing with diapers.

Until 1950, agriculture was an entrepreneurial venture, multiple generations figuring out different ways to make a living on the land. It was not so

much making an income as it was making a living. They were providing for themselves and selling their surplus. The wife might crochet booties for babies in the community to bring in extra money, she might make pies, she might sell her preserves. They had crops and livestock and all kinds of things. After WWII, when we industrialized, the farmer stopped being an entrepreneur and started being a blue-collar worker. And it became about moving a single product, a single commodity, and it wasn't anywhere near the diversified entrepreneurial creative process that it was prior to that.

In the 1950s, this little town was considered nonviable, the farmlands were too hilly, the farmsteads too small, so industrialization didn't happen here. People didn't have power, we didn't get the technology. We still don't have high-speed Internet. We've

stayed entrepreneurial as a culture and as a town. In places with big, wide, open, rolling fields that were perfect for cultivation, perfect for technology — when industrialization happened those farmers were usurped. In fifty years' time that farmstead culture disappeared. But now it's coming back and all over there's this rebuilding, learning to live within one's means again, not live on credit.

Bob and I do everything together. When it's meat cutting day, I'm usually down there. When its chicken processing day, he's on the farm. Today we're here together, which is a nice thing. When we're canning we're doing it together, when we're doing firewood, we're doing it together. Raising the kids . . . There are couples that do well when they're apart and couples that just want to be together all the time; that tends to be how we are.

Whether or not I alone will inherit the farm is always a touchy subject. I don't think my brother wants to be involved. It's important to me that the land stays in the family because I feel it's all we have. With our limited income, we can't really go anywhere or do anything else. One of the reasons we built this addition was that it was the cheapest way for me to get a little privacy for my family. When the time comes, our girls will be able to decide how they want to live, suburban or on a rural farm.

The Shaw Family
Garden of Spices ■ Greenwich, New York

STILL SPRING ■ *It is raining so hard I can barely see out the windshield. The roads are slick and I'm driving slowly.* "Don't rush," *Ben Shaw said. Three and a half-hours up the New York thruway in Greenwich, New York, I pull off on River Road, cross the railroad tracks and proceed down the road onto the muddy drive of the Shaw's seventy-acre poultry farm. I heard from Mary Cleaver that at Thanksgiving the Shaws' turkeys are the best, and that the rest of the year they can be counted on for scrumptious chickens, ducks, Guinea fowl and rabbits. Well worth the drive, Mary promised.*

I have no idea what to expect when I knock on the beautiful oak-carved door. Ben Shaw opens it, stretching out one hand to greet me while the other supports four-month old Andrew on his left hip.

Ben has a neatly trimmed beard, twinkling eyes and a wide, warm, welcoming smile. Standing behind him is his wife, Jeannette, and behind her, their eight other children. "Welcome, welcome!" *Jeannette cries.* "Come into our home."

I follow them in through a small mudroom into a large open kitchen. In the middle of the room there's a wooden chopping block with a delightful array of food — homemade bread, a bowl of mashed potatoes, corn. There's a chicken in the oven of the beautiful old stove that Ben found for Jeannette when they first moved in. "We're hoping you're up for a big supper in the middle of the day. We couldn't let you drive all the way up here and not feed you."

The children all bustle around the kitchen gathering napkins, cutlery and plates, scurrying to set the

dining room table in the next room. Jeannette says, "Since we homeschool the children, everything can be used as a lesson and today, we are cooking and preparing to be interviewed by a writer. After you ask us questions, we have prepared questions for you, too!"

Ben: My grandfather was a farmer, so my dad grew up on a farm until he left to start his own excavating business. I grew up helping him in that business. When Jeannette and I first married I was a public school teacher, but because of the budget cuts in the county I ended up getting a pink slip. From there I became a human resource and safety director for a construction company that did heavy highway road and bridge work. I did that for six years. During that time we started homeschooling the children. Because of my job, I found myself spending more and more time away from home. I

was on my way to becoming vice president, but I felt a real conflict. We were having more and more children. Our oldest, Ruth, spent most of her time with Mom, but our oldest boy, Caleb, seemed to be getting bored.

Jeannette: He was hungry for Dad.

Ben: It was a real breaking point for me. One morning sitting on the couch I said, you know, I'd really like to sell the house and move out to the country.

Jeannette: We both had always wanted to be farmers and felt kind of displaced in the village we were living in. We put out a FOR SALE BY OWNER sign and within four days we were lucky enough to have a buyer.

Ben: We found this place at the right time and for the right price. I quit my high-paying corporate job and we began trying to decide how to make a living off of the farm. We ended up choosing pastured poultry because it didn't take a huge upfront investment like milking cows would have. We also opened up a state-certified processing facility so we could sell our poultry to local restaurants and down in the city through "Farm-to-Chef." Thanksgiving is our big time — lots and lots of people come up here to get turkeys.

We've been doing it for over three years now — our bills are paid and we're making a living.

Jeannette: We make our living on the poultry, but I grow the herbs too. We have a bulk food store where I sell all kinds of culinary and medicinal herbs.

The kids all listen intently, waiting for their turn. Finally one of the little ones asks me to explain how a story gets made into a book. He says shyly that he wants to be a writer and an artist. I share with him that I sometimes write books for children and give him a little information about how a manuscript becomes a picture book. I suggest that perhaps all the kids introduce themselves and tell me a little about what they like to do, what they want to be when they grow up. Very excited, they start clapping their hands, motioning for me to follow them into a large room with a piano, several guitars, a mandolin on the wall and several overstuffed chairs.

Ruth: I'm Ruth Eden Shaw and I'm eleven. I play the piano some and I like cooking with Mom. I help butcher the chickens. I like it. I want to be a missionary, and go to China, maybe, when I'm older.

Caleb: I'm Caleb Bernard Shaw. I'm named after my grandfather. He's eighty-eight. I'm ten and I like farming and playing the mandolin. I like oxen and I used to have one but we had to get rid of him. I like building things. We're going to build a shed soon. I want to be a dad.

Benjamin: I'm Benjamin Luke Shaw and I'm eight. I'm a blacksmith like Papa. I like making things with metal. I made the curtain rods in the kitchen. Caleb helped me. I want to be a fireman.

Sarah: Hi. I'm Sarah Faith Shaw — I'm seven. I play the guitar. I'm learning chords.

Elijah Franklin Shaw: I'm six. I have a puppy. A white puppy. Dogs are my job. And I collect the eggs. I think there are fifty chickens. Sometimes I collect the eggs three times a day. The compost bucket is my job, too. I like to write and draw.

Levy Arrow Shaw: *[He holds up 5 fingers.]* I want to be a fireman. I was playing the ukulele, but it broke. It was behind the heater and it cracked. I found a recorder at a garage sale. It cost a quarter.

James Malachi Shaw: Four. I want to be a fireman. I play the guitar, too.

Luke: I'm Luke Stephen Shaw.

Jeannette: And this is Andrew Benjamin Shaw — four months old. I think he's a go-getter. He already wants to pull himself up and get going.

Jeannette passes little Andrew to Ben, grabs up her guitar, and gets comfortable. She puts her fingers in place, then looks up at the group. Each of them has an instrument, and when she nods they all begin to sing and play together.

Jeannette: We'll have more children, the Lord willing. Children are a blessing, so we want to be rich!

Ben: A normal day begins for us at five. We wake the children at quarter to six or so.

Jeannette: We all read our Bibles in the morning.

Ben: Morning devotions. After that the boys and I go outside to do chores, which change seasonally. We're starting to get a lot more chores right now because we have loads of chicks coming in. Eight o'clock we come back inside for breakfast.

Jeannette: Ruth's the director of breakfast affairs and Sarah's her right-hand lady. I oversee, and while that's going on I get the laundry started. Laundry is constant throughout the day.

Ben: We do breakfast and then breakfast cleanup, and once that's done we shift over to school. Even the younger ones, we sit down and do simple stuff — like James, even though he's not school-age we sit down and he does his math every day, and Luke usually does some drawing. Everyone sits down for a couple of hours. Then I take the young ones and we do things out in the yard. Mom continues lessons with the older children, English and spelling. I'm the math and science guy. And then when school's finished up, usually the older boys come out and give me a hand with whatever I'm doing.

Jeannette: I make lunch, then there's quiet time.

Ben: There are different homeschooling curricula — we do a lot of cutting and pasting of various programs. The reading curriculum that we used teaching Ruth and Caleb wasn't what Benjamin needed. We have a friend from Honduras who teaches Spanish to the children. We have art on Fridays.

Most of what we do is centered on building the children's lives. Anything I choose to take on as a business endeavor, of course I want to be profitable, but I also want to assess how it's going to affect the children. When I was away working in the corporate world, the boys especially became very, very tense. When I began to stay home, a lot of that tension dissipated. When children have their parents around they feel more peaceful.

As the children get older, we find we can do more and more; canning, for instance. But we learned early on not to take on too much — canning is a lot of work. A can of beans is not worth causing fights and arguments. We don't believe that we've got to be entirely self-sufficient. It's unrealistic and not necessary.

All of our meat comes from either this farm or local farms, but I do a lot of bartering.

Certain things don't work with a family our size;

Caleb's Veggie Dip

1 cup mayo
½ cup sour cream
1 tablespoon dill
1 teaspoon onion powder
1 teaspoon garlic powder
¼ cup vinegar

Mix and enjoy! Serve with cut up raw vegetables. Serves 10.

Garden of Spices Goulash

2 onions
3 carrots
1 parsnip
1 rutabaga
1 turnip
¼ cup vegetable oil
4 tablespoons paprika
12 small new potatoes
2 cups chicken broth
2 to 4 teaspoons cornstarch
1½ cups water
2 tablespoons chopped parsley
4 pounds cooked chicken or turkey
2 to 4 tablespoons flour
1 16-ounce can stewed tomatoes

Fry onions, carrots, parsnip, rutabaga, turnip and potatoes in the oil. Add paprika, tomatoes and chicken broth. Mix cornstarch and water and add to the pot. Cook 15 minutes. Add sour cream, meat and parsley. Serves 10.

Garden of Spices Chicken Hearts

4 pounds hearts
Oil, ¼ inch deep
3 tablespoons onion powder
2 onions
2 pinches cayenne pepper
1 teaspoons thyme
2 teaspoons cumin
¼ cup red cooking wine
¼ cup vinegar
2 teaspoons oregano
2 3-ouce cans tomato paste
1 cup water
Salt and pepper to taste

Sauté oil, hearts and onions in a pan. Then add onion powder, cayenne, thyme, cumin and oregano. Add tomato paste and water. Simmer for ½ hour. Add wine and vinegar. Simmer for another 15 minutes. Add salt and pepper. Serves 10.

Garden of Spices Chocolate Cake

2 cups sugar
2 eggs
¾ cup baking cocoa
1 cup milk
½ cup oil
1 cup strong coffee
2 cups whole wheat flour
1 teaspoon baking powder
2 teaspoon baking soda
1 teaspoon salt

Preheat oven to 350 degree. Cream together eggs, sugar and cocoa. In a separate bowl, mix together dry ingredients. Combine wet and dry. Mix milk in, then oil, then coffee. The batter will be thin! Bake 40 minutes.

organized sports — we couldn't get to nine different games on a weekend. Farmers markets are time-consuming and economically draining for us with small children.

Benjamin has the most interesting combination of what he likes doing: baking and auto mechanics. He does all of the maintenance on all the vehicles on the farm!

As far as the garden goes, each of the children has different ideas about what they'd like to grow. Last year Caleb wanted to grow giant pumpkins. He actually earned $350, but with expenses he probably netted $200. So he's doing it again this year.

As you can see, we pasture the chickens — the grass has just started to grow. In the barn near the orange fence, we have birds ready for slaughter. And then we have some ready to come out from under the brooder and go out into the pasture. In fact I was setting up a shelter for them just this morning.

We go back inside and the kids show me their big recipe book. They all have their favorites — some they've invented and some old-timers. Everybody seems to have a job in the kitchen in order to get the

food on the table in a timely manner. Caleb shows me his recipe for veggie dip (see sidebar).

We gather around the table. After the food is passed around, Ben motions, and everyone grabs hands and bows their heads. Ben says the prayer, and we dig in. It is a meal fit for a king, as my mother used to say. We all talk about the delicious chicken, the centerpiece of the meal, and how grateful we are for its life.

Jeannette: If you're going to kill and eat the animals, it's not a good idea to get too attached to them. When an animal comes on the farm, we very quickly announce to the children whether this is an animal that's going to be around for a while, giving us service such as milk or something, or if it has a short lifespan here.

Ben: As for vegetables, we grow tomatoes and most of the vegetables for our household. Herbs, as Jeannette mentioned, are for sale. Potatoes come from a farm out on the other side of Saratoga; it's not worth my time to grow them because they're so cheap and they take up a lot of space and labor.

Jeannette: We'll grow more chickens.

Jeannette and Ben ask who else I've interviewed for the book, and if one profile has led to the next. They want to know if lots of other families live on their farms, and whether I have an interest in farming. They are excited to learn that there are others around the U.S. living in some of the same ways they've chosen, and that not all of them come from farming backgrounds. They ask if there is a common thread in the book. Yes, I say, the common thread is the absolute passion that each feels for the way they've chosen to eat and to live.

Ben: It matters to us that our children be exposed to a lot of different cultures. Now that some of them are a bit older, Jeannette and I are able to spend some time away from home; we can bring a bit of the world back for them.

Jeannette: I'm getting my certification as a childbirth educator. I also volunteer at a crisis pregnancy center. Now that Ben works at home, I'm free to go out for a few hours one day a week.

Ben: And I go once a week into the local jail and do a Bible study. I come back with stories from the jail about what the men are dealing with whatever's suitable for young ears. Living on the farm, we get a lot of visitors from all over the world who share themselves with us.

Jeannette: When I was growing up here, I only knew one black man!

Ben: And only the French teacher spoke another language, and not even that well. So you see, we want something different for our children.

After lunch we walk around the farm. It's raining, but the kids all still have their afternoon chores to do, and they want to show me the chickens.

Ben: As Elijah said, we typically get three dozen eggs a day. The chickens' lives are nine weeks from chick to freezer. All the chickens are pastured out there. *[Ben points to a wide expanse of field.]* That's Pepé, our guard donkey. The turkeys are around for 20-25 weeks. We can raise a twenty-to-twenty-five-pound turkey in twenty weeks. At Christmastime we also sell lots of ducks.

Jeannette: This is our garden. We have raspberries over there; garlic's coming up along with the beans. Pretty much by Memorial Day everything's in. Over there we have the herbs.

Ben: What's the tea you say cures even before you taste it?

Jeannette: *[laughs]* Composition Powder. It has cayenne, cloves, bayberry, a couple of other things.

Ben: That's the tea if one of the children complains about not feeling well, Jeannette says, "Oh I'll get you some Composition Tea," and we say, "Wait, I feel better!"

We end up back at the house. In our absence, one of the children has taken the pies out of the oven. We all huddle around breathing in the sweet aroma.

Jeannette: Sometimes when we have pie leftover, we eat it for breakfast.

Ben: We hope that the close relationships we have now with each of the children will last as we all get older.

The pies are raspberry, apple and pumpkin.

Jeannette: Give Katherine a slice of each!

We sit down and spend the next few minutes eating.

And like everything else at the Shaw House, the pie is divine.

Josh Viertel and Juliana Sabinson
New Haven, Connecticut ■ www.slowfoodsusa.com

ANOTHER PERFECT SPRING MORNING ■ *I'd already heard about Josh by the time he started working at the Yale Sustainable Food Project in 2002. Over the next several years our paths crossed many times.*

I visit Josh and his girlfriend, Juliana, for this interview at their sunny, fourth-floor apartment while they are still living in New Haven. There is a fire going in the brick fireplace when I arrive, with three comfortable chairs pulled up in front of it. They show me around their home, its walls covered with Juliana's artwork. The well-appointed kitchen is a work of art in its own right. After we settle ourselves by the fire, Juliana brings in a tray filled with goodies: homemade bread (which Josh proceeds to toast over a rack in the fireplace), organic butter, rhubarb jam and hot tea and coffee with steamed milk. Sublime.

Josh: I grew up in a family that really loved food. Over meals we discussed the times, and got into arguments about political candidates and whatever issues were going on.

In 1995, during my junior year at Fieldston High School in New York City, I spent a semester at the Mountain School in Vermont. Like all the students there, I saw chickens slaughtered, ate grass-fed lamb and beef, worked in the gardens, picked vegetables, and helped out in the kitchen. I liked being in the woods and I liked haying. I don't remember consciously thinking it was a life-changing experience. Now I can see how my time there was probably the foundation for seeing how the environment, public health and social justice all come together around food, agriculture and how we use them.

In 1999, my second year in college, I took a year off. I hiked the Long Trail from Canada down to the Massachusetts border with Vermont, following changes in the foliage that start in the north where the weather's coldest and work their way south as the days get shorter. It was an incredible experience.

Then I did hurricane relief work in Honduras. But what was most transformative during that year away from college was going to Sicily with the WWoof program *[www.wwoof.org]* where I worked on a farm hauling grapes and where I met a wonderful guy named Agro who was an Albanian refugee. I told him how I wanted to work with sheep, so Argo introduced me to a shepherd he worked with and got me set up.

That's how I learned about cheese making, hauling a lot of wood and following sheep around. It changed me socially, culturally and physically. I picked a lot of asparagus and mushrooms that year,

and we ate a lot of fantastic simple peasant food, most of it wild-crafted. For breakfast it was usually day old-bread, and since we were making ricotta cheese, we'd just take a scoop off the top while it was hot and put it on the bread, let it soak through and then just eat it. As the season progressed, I tasted wild brassicas *[broccoli relatives]* that had this peppery, broccoli taste. And then when the wild mint bloomed, and the oregano, I'd mix that with the cheese. I could really follow in a meaningful way a connection between a specific place on earth and the food produced by that land.

Connections within the community in Sicily are built around shared work and the land. Certain things for the people are just physical. For me, an intellectual Jew from Westchester County whose family was completely nonphysical, this was a revelatory moment — well, not a moment exactly, but rather a revelatory experience.

When I went back to school, I thought, I can't just write and read. I've got to make this part of my daily life. And I wanted to share the experience with others. So I talked the biology department out of a greenhouse and started growing food there.

My friends would show up at parties with a six-pack of beer, I'd show up with a bunch of French breakfast radishes and a head of good lettuce. I wrote my thesis on physical work as a response to the modern experience, which can be very alienating — looking at how physical work can reaffirm and bring back reality for human animals. So I was writing and growing in the greenhouse and noticing how it brought people together — huge numbers of people gathered at my apartment and also at the greenhouse, where they wanted to work.

This simple peasant work I was doing was becoming popular, and seemed to make people want to be around it; it seemed like people were craving it. It made me realize that there was a real lack and it ran deep. I wanted to create ways in which I could work on giving this service to people.

I knew that it was a total privilege to get to "decide" to go to Sicily and pretend to be a shep-

herd. It would have been a really different experience if I didn't have a return ticket, and wasn't returning to Harvard. I was able to choose my own adventure and create access to something like the greenhouse, for people who already had plenty of food choices. I don't believe that food that's good for us, that connects us to land through shared work, should be a privilege for the elite. It really should be a universal right. Finding a way of incorporating that idea into the sustainable food movement became something I was really interested in.

After I graduated I got a job at the Mountain School for a year as an environmental science intern. Because it was just a one-year position, I knew I would have to figure out what to do afterwards. When you're in this field, it seems like eventually all roads lead to Alice Waters. So I just threw myself in front of her and said, "Here's my background, here's what I've done, and I want to move to California and help you do this work!" She said, "Well, really

you should move to New Haven, because they're starting this program at Yale and it seems like you'd be a perfect fit for the Yale Sustainable Project." As I left her office I thought, you know what, this is too cool an opportunity to pass up — sure it was a long shot, because initially there would be no money, and nothing like this had been done before, but if Alice Waters was behind it, I thought it might just work. So I began to write up a proposal, and later on sent a letter to President Levin of Yale. It all took a while, and after I left the Mountain School, things weren't yet in place at Yale.

In the interim, Juliana and I moved to Connecticut to start a small vegetable farm. We called it Mamabrook Farm, after a brook we love in Vermont. We lived above a maintenance garage on the grounds of a mansion. We were given access to a pool, and to a piece of land the size of a soccer field. Juliana and I began turning the soccer field into a garden. Late that summer the produce started coming up, and we sold it at the Mt. Kisco farm market.

Late fall 2002 everything came together and I started working full-time at Yale.

Juliana: We met during the summer of the year Josh spent at TMS. I was up in Vermont for the summer. At the time I was very cynical and very young — I didn't want a boyfriend. After meeting Josh I went back to high school in New York and wrote my senior thesis on Virginia Woolf. At the last moment I scrapped the entire thesis and rewrote it, adding some of the letters between Josh and me. At that point I didn't know what I wanted to do with my art or if I wanted to go to college — but I knew I wanted to work on a farm. I didn't have a life yet in the same way Josh did. I had to work very hard to get one. Now I work with kids and much of my artwork is about domestic space — how a woman's role has always evolved and revolved around housework and children. I also work in the Yale garden.

Josh: Five years later, what started out as organic food for only one college at Yale — Berkeley Hall — has turned into a sustainable dining program for all the colleges: 40 percent of all food on the menu

could afford, and since he had no marketing costs, they are relatively easy to grow, and we guaranteed the volume, it worked out. Then we went to a local processor and asked if he could turn the tomatoes from George into salsa. He told us how much garlic, green peppers and onions he would need, and we asked George to grow them. We went back and forth and brokered this deal. Then we found a local printer to do labels. Every step of the way we impacted the local economy in a positive way, reducing the carbon imprint and making a wonderful-tasting salsa with a story behind it that's connected to our place!

George is one of a dozen farmers in the Harvest Program. Incoming freshmen are broken into groups of eight and taken by upperclassmen on trips to work on local organic farms before actually coming to Yale and moving in. So their first experience here is that they go and work together on a small farm. It might be the same farm that's growing the tomatoes for the salsa or growing potatoes — and that's where they might meet some of their best friends. We create a real connection between food and place by saying, "Hey look, welcome to this part of the world which isn't just a set of university buildings and a prestigious name. This part of the world has land around it, and the land makes it possible for you to work here and eat here."

Juliana: Although this place has been incredible for us, neither Josh nor I feel that it's a place we want to live forever. When you are involved in this kind of work, it's hard not to feel a pull toward California.

Josh: I agree. My connection to this place comes from farming and fishing. I know what's happened with this land because I work it. The sad part is now I put on a tie and spend most of my time in an office. I'm a bureaucrat. I administer this program. But I know what's on the land because I pick it — today it's asparagus and rhubarb. And I fish. I have a little boat that folds up on the top of my car. I know the water cycles and I'm connected to them in a very physical way. You hook a fish; you're actually connected to that ecosystem. You put a shovel

is local, seasonal and organic. We eat all the locally grown greens by Christmas, then turn to California for organic salad greens. The only source of poultry that meets our demand is not certified organic, but certified humane, free range and not raised in cages. Our milk is all local and organic. Beef is grass-fed from New York State; coffee, tea, chocolate and bananas are fair-trade and organic.

There's a couple that makes kettle corn in a cart outside the medical school. They'd been doing it for years. We asked if we found them an organic source for ingredients and offered them a good volume, would they be interested? They now make organic kettle corn in huge volumes. Pretty cool!

It's amazing the impact we have now. Take salsa, for instance. We make twenty-five, twenty-six thousand pounds of salsa a year, and that's only one of six-thousand products that we use. Not all of them in that volume. We went to a local grower, George Pertle, and asked him if he could grow enough salsa tomatoes — roughly twenty-four thousand pounds — and he said he'd do it. We told him what we

Breakfast: Spit in Your Eye

Both of our parents made this for breakfast for us when we were little kids, and we both loved it. Especially the name.

2 ½-inch slices of good bread, ideally a sourdough with some whole grain or rye in it (but not super-dense rye bread, which won't work)

2 good eggs (by good, I mean from a farm where hens are out on pasture. The yolks should be orange, not pale yellow, and they should "stand up" in the pan, not spill out all over the place)

Butter or olive oil

Salt to taste.

Garnish/Side: Chopped fresh herbs (whatever is on hand, chives, basil, tarragon, parsley, etc.), or some stewed tomatoes, or fresh tomatoes, chopped with fresh herbs, and a little garlic, etc.

Cut a square out of each piece of bread. Put some fat in the pan (oil or butter) and get it hot but not smoking (olive oil will start to ripple, butter will melt, but don't let it brown and foam). Lay the bread in a big cast-iron skillet with a lid that fits. Flip it once to coat on both sides. Brown it on one side, then flip it, browned side up. Crack one egg into each hole. Clamp the top on, and turn the heat down.

Check after a minute or two, and take out as soon as the egg whites have set and become opaque on top. If it isn't happening, you can either toss in a splash of water and clamp the lid back on (the steam helps to cook the tops), or you can flip the eggs to have them over easy).

Salt them and serve with whatever garnish is around: chopped fresh herbs (chives, basil, tarragon, parsley, etc.), or some stewed tomatoes, or fresh tomatoes, chopped with fresh herbs, and a little garlic, etc.

Lunch: Salad

We eat salad all the time, nearly year round. It almost always includes some greens, but in the hottest part of the summer, we stick to fruit and tomatoes in particular, because lettuce and other leafy greens are not happy in the heat. We love the greens that come in the fall especially. The bitter ones have a sweetness to them. If there are good eggs, we like to soft-boil one and split it on top of the salad. (Tip: Plunge an egg into boiling water, reduce to a simmer, and cook for between

6 and 7 minutes, then remove immediately, plunge into iced water, crack the shell lightly, and after 10 minutes, carefully peel it, then split it the long way, on top of the salad.)

With a soft-boiled egg, a little toasted bread on the side, slivers of anchovies or even some boiled and quartered potatoes, cooled and tossed on top, a salad is lunch.

Salad Dressing

This is our old standby. Sometimes we will use strong mustard instead of anchovies; sometimes we will use neither. Sometimes we just use salt, vinegar and oil. Always, we discuss it.

This version is strong, and goes well with strong greens like escarole, radicchio, etc.

1 clove of garlic

2 anchovies (if salt-packed, run under cool water, separate fillets from skeleton, and rub away any scales)

Salt (we tend to use kosher salt for its consistency)

Red wine vinegar (try to use real, living vinegar. It is hard to find but it is worth it)

Olive oil (this is the place to use the good stuff)

Chop the garlic very fine. Put a little pile of salt on top (maybe 2 teaspoons, or a tablespoon). Using the flat of the knife, rub the garlic and salt together back and forth against the cutting board till they become a paste, with no chunks of garlic left. Chop up the anchovies and add them to this paste, rubbing them into it till it is uniform. Transfer into a wooden salad bowl, and whisk in red wine vinegar. Keep whisking, and add in olive oil, a little at a time, till it emulsifies (becomes all one, and a little thicker). In general I think I use about twice as much oil as I use vinegar, but I never measure, so I'm not sure. Taste it on a piece of the salad. Adjust by adding more salt, more vinegar, more oil, etc. Toss the salad in it. If you made too much, pour it out of the bowl first so that you don't overdress it. When the greens are good, go easy on the dressing.

Dinner: Roast Chicken with Root Vegetables

This is a nice dish for fall. Substitute whatever root vegetables look best. We like to make this as a Sunday supper. If there are just two of us, we tend to eat the dark meat, which we like the best, and to make chicken salad for leftovers out of the white meat. If we are feeling virtuous, we then make stock out of the carcass. Also, Josh likes to fry up the liver in butter, and then crisp some sage leaves in the browned butter. Put the liver on toast, and pour the butter and fried sage leaves on it, and a little salt. Juliana thinks it's gross.

Note: It is crispiest on the outside and tenderest on the inside with the dry salt cure, but if you don't have twenty-four hours to wait, don't worry about it. It will still be great.

1 small chicken (1.5 to 3 pounds) raised on pasture

Potatoes: 4 midsized or equivalent (yellow fleshed like yukon gold or carolas are best, but what you've got will work)

Carrots: 6 midsized carrots (not itsy-bitsy skinny ones, ideally not the big honkers either, but better too big than too small)

2 midsized onions or 4 smallish ones (not little pearls, though)

A hefty bunch of sage

A head of garlic

Kosher salt (a handful or two)

Fresh cracked pepper

Olive oil (quarter cup)

One really large cast-iron skillet (you can use a roasting pan if you don't have one, but you should have one)

Prepare the chicken 12 to 24 hours ahead of time:

Rub the chicken dry inside and out. Slide individual sage leaves under the skin all around (you may need to make a little cut with a small knife at the edge to get it started). Rub a bunch of sage leaves inside the carcass and leave them there. Generously coat with salt, and some fresh-cracked pepper. (I like to roast peppercorns in a dry cast-iron skillet till just before they burn, and then crack them up with a mortar and pestle or a grinder. It makes them really fragrant, and it makes the kitchen smell great.) Place on a rack over a plate, so the skin is exposed all around, and put in the refrigerator for 24 hours, uncovered (I use some chopsticks across a plate because we don't have a rack). Flip it once partway through.

Cooking it (roughly an hour and a half before serving):

Set the oven at 400 degrees.

Cut the carrots into sections about 2 inches long (and

in half, if too big to imagine on your plate as is). Cut the potatoes into chunks you could imagine sitting on your fork. Cut the onions in half through the root nub, leaving them intact, so they hold together. If really big, cut in quarters. Peel the garlic cloves, but leave whole. Toss all the vegetables together in a bowl with the olive oil, and with salt and pepper to taste. Make sure that your skillet, with the chicken in the middle, can accommodate the vegetables all around the edges, without them being piled more than one layer deep (otherwise they will steam, not roast). If it is too small, switch to a roasting pan, or put some of the vegetables in another skillet or sheet pan.

Heat up the skillet on the stovetop. If you splash a bit of water into it, it should hiss and dissipate quickly, but not be so hot that it is smokes. Lay the chicken in, breasts up, thighs down, and let it sizzle there for a minute. Toss the vegetables all around it. Slide it into the oven. Use a spatula to turn it after 25 minutes.

Check it after 45 minutes. It should be browned on the outside. When done, the leg should wiggle easily, it should be browned on the outside, it should smell like really good roast chicken, and when you stick a knife into the joint between leg and thigh, the juices should run clear. If it isn't done, leave it in and check it after 10 minutes. If it is browning too fast, turn the oven down and lay some tinfoil over the browning parts. Remove from the oven when done, and let it rest for 10 minutes before carving. I like to serve it in the pan.

Dessert: Crostata with Fruit/Jam/Whatever Is Looking Good

This dessert is versatile, and cooks while dinner is being eaten. It works with any fruit in season, with fruit you have frozen, or with jam as well.

I make the dough the day before I'm having friends over, or earlier in the afternoon, and I try to make a few extra servings so I can keep it in the freezer (I wrap it in plastic wrap, then in tinfoil to keep for a month or two). I roll it out and shape it with fruit on it, on a sheet pan before friends come over, and leave it in the fridge, then I put it in the oven when we sit down to dinner, and hop up once or twice to check on it and take it out. Then it is ready right when it is dessert time.

Dough

½ pound (2 sticks) cold unsalted butter

2 cups flour

¼ cup superfine sugar

½ teaspoon kosher salt

¼ cup ice water

Keep butter cold, cut into cubes (put in fridge). Put flour, sugar and salt into food processor, pulse to combine. Add butter, toss to coat. Pulse 15 times (till butter forms peas). Run motor and add ice water a little at a time, process 10 seconds, stop before it turns into a big mass. Add just enough water to make it hold together. Turn it out onto foil, press into 7-inch disk. Let it rest an hour in the fridge. It will last two days in the fridge, two weeks in the freezer.

Topping

¼ cup flour

¼ cup superfine sugar

½ stick butter (4 tablespoons)

Combine flour and sugar. Cut in butter till crumbly.

Crostata instructions:

Preheat oven to 425 degrees. Roll into 12- to 16-inch circle (defrost first if frozen). Dust with flour to keep from sticking. (I also use a small sheet of marble that I put in the freezer first.) Lay on parchment paper on baking sheet (if you need to you can flip one side over the other, so it is gently folded into a half circle to transfer more easily, then unfold once on the sheet). Spread fruit on top (less is more, especially with wet fruit). Leave a 2-inch ring free of fruit around the outside, and don't put more than one layer of fruit down. Pleat over the edge, top exposed fruit with crumble. Bake 20 minutes or more (longer bake makes for jammier fruit, which I like, but don't burn, if need be, put foil over top to keep from over browning). Let cool 10 minutes.

in the ground; you're connected to the ground. So I do feel a connection to this place.

I'm working on structural change in institutions around sustainability and food. I'm on the board for SlowFoodUSA and also Slow Food Nation. I think it's hard to be involved in big nonprofits that are trying to change the world when you're in a rural area. What you're talking about is major structural change in a system — in a food system — and dealing with turning structural racism in the food system to structural equality, and turning structural classism in the food system to structural equality. That involves dealing with the press and the government. So I can't see myself in a totally rural area doing that.

We held a summit here at Yale last fall because we realize that on every college campus there is a small group — four people, a dozen people, maybe even more, but a relatively small group — pushing for change in the dining halls, and perhaps pushing against an administration that doesn't really care. We decided to try and bring them together and

let them look each other in the eye and go, "Holy shit, we're part of a national movement now." So we did this in the northeast in partnership with an incredible organization called The Food Project and Brown University. We thought maybe we'd get sixty people at the most, but we got 175. And those 175 people were leaders on their campuses for sustainable food. And you figure this is just in the northeast. So we have to describe this as a movement!

If you want to do this on your campus, you need a group. You have to find those students and connect with them; strength will grow from that. Some colleges are really focused on what their undergraduates want. Some just don't care. And so if they don't care, you've got to find the thing that they do care about. That's true of making change anywhere, figure out what the people who have the capacity to make the change care about, and frame the thing you want in terms of their desire, or in terms of their fear. That's how you make change happen.

Start by asking a lot of questions. You've got

to create cultural change if you're going to create policy change. Generally I think lawyers and politicians follow culture; they don't create it. But I think the movement happens from within, everyone collectively deciding on values or coming to a place where they care about something different from the norm. At Yale, we work with students to create a culture where you can't walk across campus without something about food and agriculture being in your face. Whether it's a talk being given by Michael Pollan or Eric Schlosser, or a group of students coming together to talk about the role of food in their social justice work. This is what Yale is about now.

The politics of food today is a complicated and scary issue. To do the right thing with food means doing something that a lot of people perceive as elitist. That's a perception we can overcome only by talking about food, real food, in a way that doesn't hurt the land, doesn't hurt the people who grow it. The fact that we live in a world that doesn't give equal access to good food is a justice issue. We need to talk about that in a straightforward way. Historically, the way we've talked about it is to say, "Food that's good for you costs more, and that pits the do-good liberals against poor people." That's an impossible place for a politician because it just doesn't sound populist, it doesn't sound egalitarian, it isolates people.

We walk over to the Yale garden, passing old buildings, the sky wide open, not a skyscraper in sight. At the garden there are fruit trees and greenhouses. Juliana points out how all the wood they used to build the raised beds came from a local boardwalk, and the stone came from Yale's buildings and old factory buildings from the mill economy.

Josh: Welcome to the farm!

Juliana: I can't wait until the summer when we can start having pizza parties up here.

She points to the new brick pizza oven.

Juliana: There's an article I just read about setting up a garden on the lawn of the White House.

Josh: Alice Waters has been pushing for that.

Teresa Heinz said she'd do it if Kerry was elected. Times are changing.

Juliana: It would be beautiful, wouldn't it? Roosevelt had sheep that mowed the lawn during his presidency.

Josh: And we're in a war. We need Victory Gardens. Something like 40 percent of produce eaten during WWII was grown by Americans on their own plots.

Juliana: Maybe we can convince Obama to have a garden.

In September of 2008, four months after our visit, Josh Viertel is named the first president of Slow-Food USA. The new position of President bolsters strategic and capacity-building leadership within SlowFood USA (www.slowfoodusa.com).

Josh: I imagine Slow Food over time having a membership and a reach that enables the organization to put real pressure on federal policymakers in the next food and farm bill discussion, in the same way that the Natural Resources Defense Council or the Sierra Club can affect policy for the environmental movement. I'm concentrating on that.

I'm also going to focus on the young people. When I look at what young people are doing in the sustainable-food movement, I think that their creativity and sense of humor — but also their complete unwillingness to compromise — are just the kind of jet fuel we need right now.

Take Sam Levin. He's fifteen years old. We worked really hard to get him into the opening session of Slow Food's Terra Madre in Italy this last October. He's from western Massachusetts, and started a small farm on campus at his high school and had the food from that farm going to the cafeteria. Sam got up and spoke in front of nine thousand people, got a standing ovation. I think he showed up Carlo Petrini *[founder of Slow Food International]*, who's the most charismatic speaker in the world. That energy for me is really important.

Josh and Juliana moved to Brooklyn and live in a light-filled loft that was once a chair factory. It's home, at least for now, they agree.

Andrew Coté: Beekeeper

Silvermine Apiary ■ Norwalk, Connecticut ■ www.beeswithoutborders.org/

LATE MARCH ■ *According to Einstein, "Without the honeybee, in four years, there would be no mankind."*

In the middle of a Connecticut suburb, a few blocks from an elementary school and a small park, there are houses from the 1950s clad in aluminum siding. They sit alongside other houses that are up to four hundred years old. A former artists' colony spread over Norwalk, New Canaan and Wilton, Connecticut, Silvermine (named after the nearby river) seems like a comfortable, mostly middle-class neighborhood. Three hand-carved wooden bears and seven wooden beehives sit out on one of the neatly mowed front lawns. These belong to Silvermine Apiary and Andrew Coté, the fourth generation in his family to tend bees.

Andrew: A bee's job is to pollinate flowers, to gather nectar to bring back to the hive so the colony can live and thrive. Did you know that bees have pollinated one out of every three bites of food we take? Watermelon, apples, peaches, onions — we wouldn't have them without the industry of the honeybee.

While Andrew talks, he has started up a metal smoker; inside there's a piece of burlap that causes a smoldering fire. He waves the smoker in front of the hives.

Burlap burns cool and quiets the bees so I can inspect the hives.

He smiles, enjoying the quiet that he and the smoker create.

I was a solitary kid. I read a lot, I didn't do drugs, not even once. That was never for me. Maybe because of the reading I knew the world expanded beyond Norwalk, not that Norwalk isn't a great place. The first time I traveled abroad I went to London with a school group. There were more girls on the trip than boys, just like in a beehive. There

are more girls, you know, because after the males have serviced the queen, they die.

I quit high school when I was fifteen went to Greece and backpacked through Europe a little bit. Then when I was seventeen, I went to Hong Kong and then back to England, down to North Africa and after that, Central America. I worked all kinds of jobs to support my wanderlust: hotel kitchens, a kebab shop in Wales, spent a summer taking care of sheep in Ireland, drove a taxi in New York, was a cinema projectionist. I wanted experience.

When I was twenty-one I moved to Ecuador and got a job teaching at a high school for a year. It was before the Internet, so they couldn't check up on my diploma. Then, after a series of bad or at least mediocre school experiences, I ended up at Friends

World College, part of Long Island University, in Kyoto, Japan.

As far as food goes, as a kid I ate a pretty typical 1970s diet of a lot of garbage: feedlot hamburgers, hot dogs, loads of processed food. Meals were home-cooked but supplemented with pizza. My father was a phenomenal cook when he was at the firehouse, he cooked for ten-plus guys — great sauces, and we're not even Italian. My mother made a lot of lasagna. Now, for eight months of the year I get most of my food at the farmers market, or Whole Foods in a pinch. I still have a soft spot for pizza, which sustains me when I have to be at the farmers markets for eighteen hours in a day.

Andrew continues waving the smoker in front of the hive.

Back to the bees. The smoker makes them more docile. Some say that it makes them think there's a fire and they've got to fill up on honey — and if they fill up with honey, it's harder for them to sting. It also inhibits their ability to send out danger pheromones to other bees, to let them know that someone is invading their hive — the beekeeper.

I've got seven honeybee hives here and thirteen more in the backyard — each is its own independent colony, about sixty-thousand in each with one queen. The design of my hives is about a hundred and fifty years old — they were designed in the 1850s by Reverend Langstroth, and are moveable frame hives, standard ten-frame equipment that can weigh up to three hundred pounds. I also use some Top Bar Hives, where one bar is placed on top of the hive where the bees naturally build their comb. This idea is really thousands of years old.

Each frame can be removed to check on the bees and the honeycomb. This hive design is used a lot by organic beekeepers — I use only organic methods on my hives and most of the 200-plus hives I tend. No pesticides or herbicides.

I believe Colony Collapse Disorder (CCD) — which we don't have in Connecticut, but which has affected many states and countries *[see www.tree hugger.com]* is at least in part due to the fact that bees have been saturated with pesticides — from the plants they eat, poor nutrition, to the treatments they're getting for the disease.

CCD is a mysterious disappearance of worker bees due to an ailment that has yet to be pinpointed, but which may be caused by drought, pesticides or herbicides.

When I check on the hives, I look first for the queen. If I don't find the queen, I want to find eggs; if not eggs, larvae; if not larvae, pupa. In that order, so I can make sure the hive is healthy. I'm looking at the pattern in which the queen lays her eggs — if

it's a healthy pattern or a non-healthy pattern, and what I see here is — oh! Something's not good . . . they're making a new queen. The workers probably didn't like her, they may have killed her, or she may have died on her own — a blue jay may have eaten her. It happens. Not so unusual.

When I'm working with bees I feel meditative, it feels calming. I'm really in the moment. I don't see how you can look at one of these honey frames and see what the bees do and not be at peace. Can the world be random? Perhaps. But I have a hard time looking at a beehive and thinking that there's not some order or some plan. Just my opinion.

Bees first came to this country with the Pilgrims, around 1609, to pollinate. The first pilgrims died in a sea of food — there were more nuts and fruit and berries here than they knew what to do with. Wild turkey; more food in New England than anywhere else, and they almost died because all they wanted was salted pork. They didn't bring a cow but they brought encyclopedia sets — I mean, really inap-

RECIPES ■ Andrew Coté

My friend Sherri Brooks Vinton, a food advocate, helped me with these recipes (to the point where they are in fact hers, but the ones that I like the best).

Roasted Chicken with Ginger-Honey Glaze

- 1 tablespoon olive oil
- 1 pasture-raised chicken, cut into 8 pieces
- ¼ cup Andrew's Local Honey
- 1- to 2-inch knob of ginger
- 2 cloves garlic
- ¼ cup soy sauce
- Pinch red pepper flakes

Preheat oven to 375 degrees. Lightly oil a roasting pan and arrange chicken pieces in it. In a blender or food processor, puree remaining ingredients. Pour mixture over chicken. Roast chicken, basting occasionally, until thighs reach 165 degrees and juices run clear, about 35 to 45 minutes. Remove from oven and rest for 5 to 10 minutes before serving. Serves 4.

Honeyed Carrots

- 2 tablespoons butter
- 1 pound carrots, peeled
- ¼ cup water
- ¼ cup honey
- 1 tablespoon lemon juice, optional

Sauté whole carrots in butter in a large skillet until beginning to brown, about 5 minutes. Add water and honey and bring to a boil. Reduce heat and cover. Simmer carrots until cooked through, about 5 minutes. Remove lid and reduce cooking liquid to a syrup just thick enough to glaze carrots, about 2 to 3 minutes. Stir in lemon juice, if using, and serve. Serves 4.

Couscous Salad with Honey and Pistachios

- 2 cups water
- 2 cups couscous
- 2 tablespoons butter
- 1 teaspoon salt
- ¼ cup yogurt
- ¼ cup honey
- 1 cup small or diced vegetables (such as whole peas or edamame, diced carrots, diced zucchini)
- 1 small red onion, diced
- ½ cup pistachios
- ¼ cup parsley, finely chopped

Bring water to a boil. Add couscous, butter and salt, cover and remove from heat. After 5 minutes, fluff with a fork. Meanwhile, in a large bowl, whisk together yogurt and honey. Add fluffed couscous and remaining ingredients and stir to combine. Serve immediately or cool and refrigerate for up to two days. Serves 4.

Honey Yogurt

- 2 cups whole milk yogurt
- ¼ cup honey

Line a colander with a coffee filter. Pour yogurt into lined colander and set over a large bowl. Place colander and bowl in the refrigerator and drain for at least an hour and up to four. Save resulting liquid whey for another use. Stir honey into yogurt. Use to top desserts or serve with breakfast granola. Makes about 1½ cups.

propriate things. Most of them died within the first year.

I wake up a little bit before the sun gets up. I don't use an alarm clock. In March, April, early May, I might have to wait until nine or ten to go out, until it's warm enough to open up the hives and inspect them, safely. Sixty degrees, because I believe lower temps freeze the eggs. Some beekeepers say a lower temperature is acceptable — I don't agree with that. But if you ask ten beekeepers, you'll get eleven opinions.

The kitchen in Andrew's house seems to be the central hub of activity. There are large machines, sinks, bookcases and a special shelf filled with dozens and dozens of jars of honey with names like Pengwen, Kandakaw and Skarbazer — honey made by Iraqi bees. The jars are among dozens that Coté has personally collected during his travels to Iraq,

The queen bee mates once in her life in a mating flight where she mates fifteen to twenty times.
She stores the eggs for up to four years, though she is only a prolific layer for two.
The drones all die immediately after mating as their barbed penises tear off and remain in the queen.

India, Nigeria, Zimbabwe, Moldova and Guatemala. For Andrew this honey is proof that beekeeping can lift people out of desperate circumstances.

Prior to the 1990 war there were half a million hives in Iraq. Now there are twenty-thousand. I traveled there in 2005. That's because when the Iraqi troops withdrew from Kuwait, they set the oil wells ablaze, spreading noxious smoke as far north as Baghdad. Some fires burned for years, killing off many of the honeybees. Beekeepers have not been able to move about freely to tend their hives due to the ongoing war.

I traveled to Iraq under the auspices of the U.S. State Department to help the Iraqis, the Kurdish minority in particular, reestablish their beekeeping traditions. Just recently I've incorporated Bees Without Borders as a nonprofit so I can continue to do work I've been doing for years on my own dime. Our mission is to empower people living in destitute conditions in isolated areas of the globe, teach them about underused resources, how to create a cash crop from maintaining hives, harvesting honey and honey products.

I have trips planned this year and next to Cuba and the Ukraine. I'd like to go back to Iraq and also to Afghanistan. Really, I'll go anywhere I'm needed. I think bees are a great tool for connecting people. I have had great conversations with beekeepers without having a common language. If there's a woman whose husband has been killed and she has eight children and through beekeeping she can send one of her children to school, then the program is

a great success. If she can make another twenty dollars a month, then it's a huge difference to her and her family. Twenty dollars to people in these circumstances is life changing. I don't presume that we know more about bees than they do, but I do know that we may have more information available to us. I stand on the shoulders of all the men and the women at the beekeeping club and all of the authors of the books I've read.

There are any number of health properties bees give us, and getting stung by bees is supposed to be good for arthritis. I know MS patients who want to be stung, who claim that it helps them. I will give people bees for free but I won't sell them because I don't ever want to be caught up in the whole medical thing. Apitherapy (the medical use of honeybee products) is big. I believe the oldest working man is a 105-year-old beekeeper, a fellow in Kansas.

Bee pollen provides vitamins and minerals along with proteins, free amino acids, hormones and trace elements. No other food on earth offers such a broad spectrum of natural nutrition. All over the world honeybee pollen is recognized not only as an ideal food source, but also as a food source with wide-acting medicinal properties, including the ability to:

1. Restore lost sexual desire and energy
2. Alleviate menstrual cramps
3. Speed the healing of wounds
4. Alleviate depression and fatigue
5. Normalize digestive problems
6. Alleviate migraine headaches
7. Relieve various prostrate problems
8. Improve fertility
9. Greatly improve energy levels

Common misconceptions about bees: They won't attack you unless you do something foolish and startle or disrupt them. Another is the misuse of the word *swarm*. People always say, "He's swarming me!" One bee is not a swarm, and usually that one bee is a she. No one has died from honeybee stings in the last half century in the States, and yet every third person in New York City who passes by my hive display loudly proclaims, "Oh, I'm deathly allergic to bees." I ask if they carry an EpiPen, and the answer is usually no.

In five years I see myself still on this porch, but with a nice fence around the property. Maybe I'll have a small apartment in New York City, be one of those people with a country and a city home. I hope Bees Without Borders will have at least two more headquarters: one in South Africa to serve Africa, and one in India to serve parts of Africa and Asia. And maybe one in Hungary to serve Eastern Europe. There are more beekeepers in Hungary than in any other European country, per capita.

I have no interest in expanding my own beekeeping. I have just enough work, and it's hard enough to do it right just the way it is. Lately, I've been scaling back.

Ian Cheney and Curt Ellis
Producers of *King Corn* feature documentary ■ New York ■ www.kingcorn.net

APRIL ■ *The cherry blossoms are in bloom. It seems like every time I turn around the Mountain School program comes up. Ian Cheney and Curt Ellis met there in their junior year of high school. Ian and Curt both say that their time at the Mountain School profoundly shaped their thinking and who they are in the world today. They've worked together since college, and when I first met them they had just released the film,* King Corn. *In it Ian and Curt move to the heartland to learn where their food comes from. With the help of friendly neighbors, genetically modified seeds, nitrogen fertilizers and powerful herbicides, they plant and grow on one acre of Iowa soil a bumper crop of America's most productive, most subsidized grain. When they try to follow their pile of corn into the food system, what they find out raises troubling questions about how we eat and how we farm. Recently they created a sequel to* King Corn *called* Big River *which explores what happens when fertilizers, pesticides and herbicides used to grow corn hit the river. They are also working on two documentaries;* Truck Farm, *about an urban farm grown in the back of a 1986 Dodge truck, and* The City Dark, *about the disappearing night sky.*

Curt Ellis: I grew up on the outskirts of Portland, Oregon, the youngest of six kids. My parents had ten acres and a big vegetable garden. My mother loved to cook. She really believed that the best food you could feed your children was fresh food, made at home, straight from the garden. I was allergic to cow's milk, so I drank goat's milk straight from a local farm — it came in glass bottles. We got eggs from the farm down the hill, and Mom bought lamb straight from farmers so we always had these strange cuts of meat in butcher paper in the freezer. Growing up in the Oregon area, there was a broad interest in food. Local and sustainable was just more accepted there. By the time I got to college, dirt was something I missed. Somewhere in my head I think I always wanted to be a farmer, so I missed the connection to the real things, like dirt and green plants, the magic that happens when you plant a seed and watch it grow.

Ian: I grew up on a boarding school campus near Boston. My parents were teachers, and my mom cooked every night. She loved cooking. There was never any mention of organic food. I ate like everybody else around me, hot dogs and potato chips, and spent my spare change on Twinkies and grape soda. I grew up in the land of Dunkin' Donuts. I remember going to McDonalds on a family road trip and being angry that I was only allowed to order one cheeseburger. I thought, "When I grow up I'm going to have a red pickup truck of my own and I'm going to order as many cheeseburgers as I want!"

It was during summers in Maine that my food became more local, because that's the way everyone ate there. The food from the farm stand down the road was much better and cheaper.

Curt and I did go the Mountain School together but I didn't see a lot of him there. He was always wandering around the farm looking at tractors. I spent most of my time writing bad poetry.

Curt: In college we wound up living in the same dorm our freshman year, so we started spending more and more time together and bonded over trips to Dunkin' Donuts. Unbeknownst to us at the time, more than a dozen ingredients in those glazed donuts contained corn, everything from the propylene glycol on down to the cornstarch.

In college we got interested in food and agriculture issues. We were both environmentalists, but to some extent we were becoming disenchanted with the *50 Simple Things You Can Do to Save the Earth* approach to environmentalism. For us the most

logical connection to the planet came through the food we were eating. Ian spent a summer in Senegal looking at the changing farmers markets and food culture. I majored in history but did most of my papers on topics like the country life movement in America, and the changes in small farms and Amish agriculture.

Ian: In our sophomore year, I started a group with a couple other people at Yale to begin looking into where our dining hall's food was coming from. The group was called "Food from the Earth" because that was all we knew about it. It was really our way of saying we'd love to have a more intimate connection with the sources of our food, try to buy more local organic foods in Connecticut and bring them to the school.

Curt: Ian was really more involved in the creation of the Yale Sustainable Food Project than I was, but we worked together senior year doing a series of events called Farm Week. We released sheep across

campus and kicked all the Frisbee players off the green. We hauled a kiddie pool filled with manure into the middle of Old Campus so people could put on tall rubber boots and romp around in it. We were trying to reconnect people to agriculture.

Ian: Curt was mostly excited about bringing farmers to campus! [*Laughs*]

Curt: Which we did. We wanted to connect those of us in that sort of transitory college town to farmers just ten miles from the school. The culmination was the final meal at the end of the conference, when we got to work with Alice Waters on a big dinner.

Ian: Later that summer I got a call from the head of Berkeley College, one of the residential colleges at Yale, and he said, "Hey, it looks like something's going to happen!" Josh Viertel was hired that year.

Curt: Josh made the program much bigger and better than we ever did or even imagined.

After graduation Ian went to forestry school, and

I drove across the country with my mom, then spent a couple of months building kitchen cabinets for a beach house, and then I moved to Elizabethtown, in the Adirondack Mountains in upstate New York, near a cousin who worked as a documentary filmmaker with PBS. My cousin and I worked on this colossal project building a house using trees that were cut down and milled in town. We had these great evenings up there, drinking the local moonshine and talking about food, which was what I was interested in, and talking about films, which my cousin, Aaron, was interested in. Ian came up a number of times.

Ian: On one of the weekends I went up to help pound nails, we got to talking about a film. I don't even remember at this point whose idea making the film was. We were going to call the film *What's Eating America,* and it was going to be in three parts, three films — *Breakfast, Lunch* and *Dinner,* tracing everything back to their sources, including strawberry pickers in California and their plight; chemicals like the methyl bromide used in that process and things like that.

Curt: Migrant labor problems. *Lunch* would be about fast-food hamburgers and where they come from.

Ian: Cattle farms, dairy farms in Indiana, and tomato pickers in Florida — the sky was the limit.

Curt: We realized it was like making a movie about the entire world, probably take us thirty or forty years and $30 or $40 million, and thirty or forty guys like us to do it. *[Laughs]*

Ian: As we started researching the film, Aaron was finishing another film in Australia. That summer after I graduated from the forestry school, Curt and I set out across to meet with people much smarter than we are, like Michael Pollan *[Omnivore's Dilemma],* Wes Jackson [The Land Institute and MacArthur Fellow], David Kline [Amish farmer and author] and Alice Waters [Chez Panisse].

Research showed us that corn was everywhere. We found that so much of the landscape was covered in corn that if we wanted to make a film

about where our food came from, corn was just going to be king of the story.

Curt: Driving through Iowa, we met this incredible farmer named Chuck Piat who belonged to the American Corn Growers Association. He had a real belly laugh and a deep understanding of the way that our food system is being driven into the industrialized production of corn. Ian and I discovered that both our great-grandfathers came from the same corner of rural northern Iowa.

Ian: It was actually Aaron who became obsessed with the idea of using that for the film, using our grandfathers as a story piece.

Curt: So the film began because of a series of coincidences. We were amazed by this northern Iowa connection that we had through our roots, and we were both blown away by the fact that we were full of corn and had no idea! We figured our grandfathers must have passed each other on the street at some point, but who knows if they knew each other.

Ian: Our process became about putting ourselves in our grandfathers' shoes in order to understand why we have the food landscape that we have. It doesn't help to just point fingers and vilify. We need to put ourselves into the shoes of our predecessors and understand why they might have created this system. That process was very novel to me, to think about my great-grandfather's decisions. It's also given me insight as to why I grew up eating the way I did.

The process of making *King Corn* radically changed the way I thought about food. We saw very early on where the food was coming from, we lived in the landscape that provides most of our calories — two-thirds of Iowa is corn and soybeans. Seeing cattle raised in close confinement, hogs raised in sheltered, extremely close confinement — the same with chickens, dairy cows, layer hens. And smelling those places really changed me in a way that just reading about them never could. I really believe it's hard to change your food habits. And yet the process of living in those places and smelling those places and shooting footage of those places really turned my stomach. It's hard to eat those meats now.

Curt: Making a film's a terrible experience as far as food goes. You spend six months on the road eating in airports, shopping malls and movie theaters where there really isn't anything that good to eat. I find it really hard to eat meat that comes out of that industrial food system. I'm just not comfortable with the way the animals are raised. And after you see it enough times, you taste it. I'm not a vegetarian, I just eat grass-fed. It's more expensive to get good meat these days, but I think it is the most important thing we can do.

Ian: When I eat at a friend's house, I don't ask where the meat comes from. Maybe I should, but my overriding ethic is one of being polite. If I go to the grocery store and don't find any grass-fed beef and don't ask for it, I have to kick myself because why would they ever supply it if I don't ask for it? So that's been a shift for me. I don't eat as much meat as I used to but I still believe in eating some.

Having learned more about how humans evolved to eat as farmers, as hunter gatherers, eating wild lean meats, fish, berries, nuts and greens has given me a deeper understanding of what my body needs. And I've tried to remain committed to that.

Curt and I went hunting when we were living in Iowa. It took us about three to four hunting seasons to finally track down a deer. Then it was pretty harrowing to have to field dress it. It was hard. It was a big deer. It wasn't quite dead when we shot it so we had to cut its throat, and I had a really dull knife from Wal-Mart, and suddenly there I was, having grown up eating chicken nuggets and hamburgers, never once having to kill anything that I ate — there I was, killing an animal that was blinking at me. After the deer died, it was remarkable how quickly we were able to think about it as food, as dinner, how careful we became about cutting it up in a certain way.

But that gave me pause. When we were hanging the deer in the barn to let it drain out, I thought, if I had to do that every time I wanted a chicken sand-

PHOTO COURTESY TAYLOR GENTRY

wich, if I rolled up to a McDonalds and ordered a chicken sandwich and they said okay, here's the chicken, you kill it and then pull out the feathers and hand it back to us and we'll make you that sandwich, I really wouldn't eat that many chicken sandwiches. Or maybe I would become very accustomed to it, I don't know. Either way, it made me want to take more responsibility for what I was eating.

That said, I also believe in convenience. I also deeply believe in affordability. Some days I enjoy traveling around, tracking down a local farm and trying to meet the farmer and find a chicken, learn its story. Other days, I want to be working on my films or working on my writing and I want to walk to the corner store and buy food that comes from a good place — but have it be convenient and have it be affordable and right there for me.

Of course we know that affordable doesn't mean cheap. Cheap food isn't cheap. The ecological costs are enormous, and the health care costs are enormous. We're seeing epidemic rates of Type 2 diabetes

RECIPES ■ Ian Cheney and Curt Ellis

Breakfast: Tofu Breakfast Sammiches

With which Ian convinced Curt to eat (and love) tofu
Preparation time: 5 minutes

- 2 English muffins
- 2 tablespoons mayonnaise
- 1 teaspoon hot sauce
- 2 ½-inch slices tofu slices, ½-inch thick, firm, dried with paper towels
- 2 handfuls spinach, washed
- 2 slices cheddar cheese (from contented cows!)
- 1 tablespoon Olive oil
- Salt and pepper to taste

Heat a skillet over medium heat. Add a tablespoon of the olive oil. While that heats up, mix the mayonnaise and hot sauce in a small bowl. Now, with the oil hot but not smoking, return to the skillet, add the tofu, and brown the bottom side. Flip tofu and top each piece with a slice of cheddar. Start your English muffins toasting, and add the spinach to the skillet, being careful not to crowd the tofu. When the muffins are done, slather each with a dollop of spicy mayonnaise, add a tofu slab (the cheese should be melted and the bottom brown), and top with spinach. Season with salt and pepper to taste, and enjoy with a twelve-pack of grape soda.

Lunch: Dingleberry Picnic

Our favorite shoot-day meal
Preparation time: 5 minutes

- 1 handful green peppercorns, in brine
- 1 wedge semi-soft cheese
- 1 Piece smoked chicken (from liberated fowl!)
- Loaf baguette

Slice the bread! Slather the cheese! Chop the chicken! Top with dingleberries! Enjoy on the tailgate of a pickup or the fender of a tractor.

Dinner: Truck Farm Arugula Salad

From our second small-scale farming experience
Preparation time: 4 to 6 weeks

- 1 1986 Dodge pickup truck or similar
- 1 12V cordless drill with ¼-inch bit
- 40 square feet root barrier
- 40 square feet drainage mat
- 40 square feet jute mat
- 25 cubic feet lightweight gaia soil or similar
- 10 cubic feet organic compost and potting soil
- Water or rain
- 1 packet heirloom arugula seeds
- 2 tablespoons organic lemon
- 3 tablespoons extra virgin olive oil
- Handful feta cheese
- Salt and pepper to taste

Park pickup truck in pleasant location. Drill 30 to 40 holes in the bed of the truck, spaced regularly throughout with special attention to corners, and being careful not to puncture gas tank. Cut root barrier to fit bed of truck and lay flat. Cut drainage mat and lay on top of root barrier. Empty gaia soil over drainage mat and spread to an even thickness of approximately 8 inches. Spread jute mat over gaia soil, and then compost/potting soil mix to an even thickness of approximately 2 inches. Make a shallow row in the soil with your finger or a stick – an ice/snow scraper also works well – and sow the arugula seeds into the soil every inch or so. Cover lightly with ¼-inch of soil, pat gently, and water regularly. When the arugula is 4 to 5 inches tall, cut at the base, wash, and toss with the remaining ingredients. Eat! Discard truck and repeat.

and obesity and heart failure, and we can start to put a price tag on those things. And it's costing all of us. Our tax dollars pay for corn subsidies, so we're subsidizing the raw material for junk food. Through Medicare our tax dollars pay to treat diseases created in part by those foods. I don't begrudge anybody the right to treatment for being sick, but, well, I think you see my point.

Good, clean, organic foods are still expensive for people. The response to that is, well, let's just try to grow more of it and make it less expensive. Why can't we imagine more ways of growing better

Dessert: Homebrewed High Fructose Corn Syrup
A sweet substance that may or may not be safe to eat
Preparation time: 2 to 3 days.
Active time: 90 minutes

Ingredients
 A few gallons water
 One little droplet sulfuric acid
 3 or 4 cups corn
 A few teaspoons alpha-amylase
 A few teaspoons gluco-amylase

Equipment
 Stovetop
 12 quart stockpot
 Wooden spoons for stirring
 Cuisinart or blender (or mortar & pestle)
 French press coffee maker
 Drip-coffee filter with filter
 2 cups diatomaceous earth
 Jar (for the final product!)
 Goggles
 Gloves
 Teaspoons and measuring cups

Add one droplet of sulfuric acid to a gallon of water. Heat on stove to 140 degrees. Reduce heat to low. Add 4 cups of corn and soak overnight at 140 degrees. Physically damage the corn (grind up in Cuisinart). Add back into stockpot, heat to 140 degrees, and add alpha-amylase. Soak overnight at 140 degrees. Spoon mixture into French press coffee filter and press down! Pour liquid back into stockpot. Heat to 140 degrees. Add gluco-amylase and bring to a boil. Bring to a boil for 1 minute, then simmer for 15 minutes. Filter through diatomaceous earth and enjoy!

foods and apply the same entrepreneurial spirit that we applied to growing corn and soybeans and other processed foods? Why can't we apply that same spirit and ingenuity on a larger scale to foods that we know are good for us, and growing practices that we know are good for the land? Who can

untangle all of the ways in which our crappy diets are actually costing us money?

Curt: The gains we got in the 2008 farm bill were so minimal it was like rearranging the deckchairs on the *Titanic*. And the real problem is the commodity payments. Until we fundamentally reconsider the farm bill as a food bill, its not going to matter if we get twice as much funding as last time for farmers market programs or organic research. Prices are naturally high in the market place; farmers are not going to be left in the lurch if the commodity payments go away right now. The reality of the food price crisis is an opportunity to reconsider how we want to feed six billion people. We don't want to feed them with high fructose corn syrup and factory farmed meat. We want to feed them foods that promote health.

I hope to be farming in five years. I hope to be farming within one year, but I don't know whether I can pull that off. I'm moving to Texas (Austin) because I'm marrying a wonderful woman. Ian is jealous that I'm not marrying him, but . . . *[Laughs]* It's a common law marriage with Ian! I have several fellowships that should provide half-time financial support to create communication pieces that relate to food and food policy. I'm writing an article on ethanol right now, and working on some op-eds about the food crisis and doing some video work related to that. Ideally I could farm half the day and do this fellowship work the other half. Then I'll either have to get a job or become a real farmer. I look forward to having children, and I hope when that happens I can raise them on the farm.

Ian: I don't think I'm going to live on a farm in the near term. I like the idea of growing my own food, but I also like the idea of trying to change South Boston into a place where it's easier to eat well. When it comes to the way I want to eat, I don't simply want to avoid the big grocery stores, the conveniences stores, the fast-food restaurants and just put all my energy, money and attention into the CSA (Community Supported Agriculture) concept. Even though I do believe it is important to

spend my money on foods that sustain good food networks, I also believe in wading into the main-stream food landscape, trying to shift that big beast in a better direction. That's what our film *King Corn* was trying to do.

I think I fell in love with filmmaking a little more than Curt did. Recently we did this film about a green building in Boston, *The Greening of Southie.* It's the first green residential building in Boston. It's a story about how a building is made, like *King Corn* is about where our food comes from, how we've become disconnected from that. I see them as intertwined stories.

We're now doing a film about light pollution, about disappearing views of the night sky. That one's a little bit removed from the food story, but at its core is this question: What do young people lose when they grow up without being able to see the night sky?

As far as having kids? I don't even know where my next meal is coming from! I would have to become a really successful filmmaker to be able to support a child. I love the idea of raising a little buddy or two, but . . . maybe having kids would be another way of sustaining my interest in these issues.

Anna Lappé

Author/Activist ■ Brooklyn, New York ■ www.takeabite.cc/

MAY ■ *I'm on the F train heading to Brooklyn to meet Anna Lappé, daughter of author/activist Frances Moore Lappé who wrote* Diet For a Small Planet, *and the late toxicologist Marc Lappé. In her own right, Anna is a nationally recognized author with dozens of articles, two books under her belt and a third one brewing. Her first book, co-written with her mother,* Hope's Edge: The Next Diet for a Small Planet, *chronicles social movements on five continents that address the root causes of world hunger and poverty. Her second book,* Grub: Ideas for an Organic Kitchen *co-written with chef Bryant Terry, combines Anna's treatise on the contemporary environment of organic foods and sustainable agriculture with Bryant's delicious menus.*

It's a warm, breezy day. At the end of a beautiful block of brownstones, I climb ten steps and ring

Anna's buzzer. She opens the door and as she leads me up the stairway to her apartment, I'm struck by her sweet, open face and the sense of energy that she exudes.

Anna: My parents divorced when I was very young, and of course I spent time with both of them. Their professional lives really mattered; they felt passionate about their work. Both my parents tried to figure out how they could be part of global efforts to make the world a better place, to try to address injustices suffered by the world's most vulnerable people. That influenced me in a fundamental way, to ask what are we on the planet to do, how to make sense of our time in this world.

Although the food was different in each household it was a normal part of our family life to have

all our meals together. When I was writing *Grub*, I remember coming across studies about how few families have meals together anymore. I cannot

remember a single night when we did not have a meal together. Even in the mornings, my mom would make my brother and me breakfast, every

---

In *Grub* Anna describes what happened one evening at a dinner party.

I got to talking . . . about my work. "It's a rip-off," one of the guests said when I mentioned organic foods. "It's a big propaganda campaign to get us to pay more for our food, and what difference does it make anyway?" Maybe you've had a conversation like this one and wished you could instantly conjure up the most compelling reasons for eating organic food, what I call "Grub." Consider the following "Grub Cliff Notes." It might help next time you're in the hot seat. . . . But no need to jump from the hot seat to a pedestal. It's safe to assume that most of us share common values: that we like clean air and clean water, that we'd like to see people in the world fed and healthy and treated fairly, that we like for ourselves and our loved ones to live long lives, free from cancer, debilitating obesity, and other serious illness. So start from there. After all, that's what Grub is all about.

10. No More Mouthfuls of Additives
Processed foods contain all kinds of additives – from sweeteners and colorings to preservatives – many of which have been linked to illnesses, including allergies, headaches, asthma, growth retardation, and heart disease.

9. Worry Less About Consuming Food that May Make You Sick
While scientists study which pesticides on the market are carcinogenic or are endocrine-disrupters and while regulators battle it out with the food industry, we can ensure peace of mind by choosing food grown without chemicals and organic meat and dairy.

8. Opt Out of Being a Guinea Pig for Genetically Modified Foods
While we are doing the research to understand how GMOs affect our environment (and our bodies), you don't have to be the guinea pig. Since labeling GMOs in food is not required in the United States (as of this writing), choosing organic or Non-GMO or GMO-free is the only way to ensure you are not eating GMOs.

7. Miss Out on Hydraulic Fluid in Your Burger
With strict guidelines for acceptable feed, organic, sustainably raised meat lessens your risk of exposure to foodborne pathogens and other contaminants (even hydraulic fluid, calculator parts, metal shards – you get the idea). Eating organic meat and dairy also means you're not consuming products raised with hormones and antibiotics.

6. Get a Nutritional Bang for your Hard-Earned Buck
Whole foods have been shown to have higher nutritional content and more fiber than their processed foods counterparts. Evidence for the nutritional benefits of organic food is also mounting.

5. Claim Your Power
You decide exactly what's in your food; you control the salt, sugar and fat. The more you prepare meals for yourself the more you know how much of that stuff is in there.

4. Celebrate the Spirit of Your 'Hood
When you eat local foods, you're supporting local businesses and farmers. The local economy will thank you.

3. Earn Karma Points
When you raise your fork, or slurp from your spoon, you know there's a better chance that no farm workers, farmers or processing workers were exploited in the process of getting the food to you.

2. Protect Food and Cultural Diversity and Food Traditions
Farmers throughout history have saved and shared seeds and raised a diverse variety of plants and animals. When we choose Grub, we help keep these traditions alive.

1. "Yum" – Enough Said
This could well be the number-one reason for many of us; let's face it, this food also tastes better – way better.

day. Whenever my mom made dinner she had NPR on, listening to *All Things Considered,* and to this day just hearing the jingle to that show, it's Pavlovian, my mouth begins to water. My mom's was definitely a "diet for a small planet" kitchen. The worst junk food I could find in her house was peanut butter and rice cakes!

I grew up in the San Francisco Bay area, so I wasn't the only one having cream cheese and jelly sandwiches on whole wheat bread for lunch. I don't have memories of getting made fun of, but probably that has a lot to do with where I grew up.

I never had serious teenage rebellion like some kids have with their parents. We shared very similar political beliefs, yet I also felt very independent. I feel like I was given so much opportunity by both my parents to really be who I wanted to be.

During graduate school at Columbia University, I was really frustrated. Classroom learning felt so limiting. At the time, my mother was still living in Vermont, trying to decide what her next project would be. My brother and I encouraged her to write a thirtieth-anniversary sequel to *Diet for a Small Planet.* Finally my mother agreed to write something on the condition that I help her. My grad program let me use our work as my graduate thesis.

So we started work on *Hope's Edge,* and it's funny, we laugh about how much we were able to do in nine months, it all just came together. We both wanted it to be a journey book with a strong connection to *Diet for a Small Planet,* the original book. We also wanted it to be personal. After the book came out I organized an extended educational speaking tour. Then I moved to Brooklyn and began working on a couple of different projects that came out of the lessons I learned working on *Hope's Edge,* particularly the powerful ripple effects of our food consumption and the choices made by U.S.-based multinational companies around the world.

In the book, there is a scene where we're driving up into the foothills of the Himalayas and we see a row of eucalyptus trees with Pepsi logos on them. The day before we had been to an incredible

celebration for Indian drinks, all indigenous, from plants grown locally, and all very good for you, with medicinal benefits or cooling effects or hydration benefits, things which Coke or Pepsi do not have. I was reminded of an internal Coca-Cola Inc. memo that Ben Barber (author of *Jihad vs. McWorld*) quoted in a speech that said we have to kill the tea culture in India. If they're drinking tea or water or any of their other traditional drinks, then they're not drinking our products. Seeing those Pepsi logos, and knowing that the communities we were visiting had an easier time finding sodas than finding potable drinking water, was a powerful moment for me. It encapsulated the ripple effects of U.S.-based multinational food companies and the Americanized diet we're pushing on the rest of the world. I wanted my next project to focus on that.

I had just met Bryant Terry and I thought it would be a perfect time to work together on a book about how we might have a positive rather than a negative effect. I take no credit for the deliciousness of his recipes; he just came up with them all on his own. He'd call me and describe his latest concoction; they always sounded amazing. Meanwhile, I was working on the exposé part, and I'd send him drafts and he would say, "Great, great, keep going."

Now I'm working on a new book about food and climate change. I'm on my own, which is exciting and terrifying at the same time!

FLASH FORWARD SIX MONTHS ■ *I am a guest at the annual fundraiser for Anna and her mother's foundation, the Small Planet Fund, founded in 2002 to raise support and recognition for social movements around the world addressing the root causes of hunger and poverty.*

The event takes place in New York City's elegant downtown restaurant Colors — an employee-owned restaurant started by the survivors of the World Trade Center's Windows on the World restaurant. The evening celebrates the sixtieth anniversary of the United Nations Declaration of Human Rights, and honors Lucas Benitez, one of the most visible advocates for farm workers' rights.

Afterward, I have a brief catch-up with Anna who tells me her new book is out: Diet for a Hot Planet: The Climate Crises at the End of Your Fork and What You Can Do About It.

JULY NEWS ■ *Anna is now married and has a daughter, Ida Marshall-Lappé, born July 11, 2009.*

My daughter has mostly cleared out her closet, her desk and her bulletin board. One day when she comes to pick up some clothes, she leaves me a note saying that I should use her room for an office. I stand in the middle of it with the note in my hand remembering all the late hours she sat at her desk writing stories, poems, her thesis for college. The room still feels like hers. I wonder if I can do it.

Next stop, Truro, Massachusetts. The glorious Cape. I'm going to spend several days walking on the beach with Luna.

Elspeth Hay
Wellfleet, Massachusetts ■ www.diaryofalocavore.com

MAY ■ *I am looking for an oysterman. Tourist season's not yet in full swing, and at the sea's edge locals picnic, enjoying the cool water grit of the sand before the summer crowds descend. Provincetown's restaurants and art galleries are half empty, and the inhabitants of second homes in Truro have not yet arrived. I've picked up a copy of Mark Kurlansky's book,* The Big Oyster. *There seems to be a lot of history behind the oyster. Since early times, shell middens have been found along the Atlantic coast of the U.S. The early Native Americans covered their dead (including their dogs) with oyster shells. Oysters originally came from New York (one of the oyster capitals of the world) but by the 1820s most of New York's natural beds had been overharvested. Soon after, the saltwater flavor of the oysters in Wellfleet, Massachusetts, became heralded as the best in the world and were even imported by the Queen of England.*

Luna and I take a walk along the harbor in Wellfleet. I've been directed to a small clapboard house at the end of the dock, where John Mankevetch, the assistant shellfish warden, works in the early mornings. He knows a lot about oysters (he's been shell fishing since he was a boy), knows the people involved and the laws. He cautions me, "It's not like farming cattle. We're not going to feed the masses with oysters. We're growing treats for the wealthy." In Kurlansky's book, I'd read that even in early times, when the poor had gathered oysters and often ate them on a daily basis, they were still considered a delicacy. As a traditional food of the northeast though, I want to include an oysterman in my lineup. So, after my chat with John, I hike back up the road to the local fish shop, "Mac's Shack," open year round. The owner directs me to **Elspeth Hay,** *a vibrant locavore and contributing editor to the quarterly magazine* Edible Cape

Cod. *She has a blog (www.diaryofalocavore.com), a weekly four-minute shout-out on NPR Radio about local, sustainable food on the Cape, and is not only willing to direct me to an oysterman, but knows just about everything sustainable happening on the Cape. We meet at a popular local restaurant, the Native Oyster.*

Elspeth: I grew up in Brunswick, Maine, just north of Portland. My father is a professional bird watcher — he takes people on bird-watching outings to places like Antarctica and Brazil. My mom's an editor. They wrote a book together about bird watching when my sister and I were little and

RECIPES ■ Elspeth Hay

Warm Brussels Sprout Salad

4 pieces bacon
2 stalks Brussels sprouts
1 medium-size apple

Fry the bacon in a large, heavy-bottomed frying pan. While it cooks, wash and halve the sprouts from the Brussels sprout stalks. Set aside, then core and dice the apple. When bacon is done, remove from pan and set aside. Sauté sprouts over medium heat until they begin to soften, about 8 to 10 minutes. Add apple and bacon, cut into small pieces, and continue cooking for several more minutes, adding olive oil if needed. When sprouts and apples are tender, serve warm, over greens. Serves 4.

Calico Slaw

Turnip and carrot chilled salad is an excellent lunch accompaniment to a grilled cheese or leftover roast chicken sandwich.

4 cups grated Eastham turnip (about ½ medium turnip)
2 cups grated carrot (about 5 medium carrots)
1 cup grated white onion (about 1 medium onion)
1 cup grated apple (about 1 and ½ pieces fruit)
¼ cup cilantro, chopped fine
½ cup olive oil
½ cup cider vinegar
Sugar, salt and pepper to taste

Mix together the turnip, carrot, onion and apple. Toss with cilantro, and a dressing of the olive oil, cider vinegar, and sugar, salt and pepper to taste. Serve chilled. Serves 4. NOTE: If you make this slaw in midwinter, do not, I repeat, DO NOT grate the vegetables. Being a bit less firm than they might have been in the fall, they will simply turn to mush. Instead, julienne them into long, thin strips. This will yield a much better texture come February.

Applesauce Fig Cake

(adapted from *The Silver Palate Cookbook*, by Julee Rosso and Sheila Lukins)

2 sticks butter
2 cups sugar

2 cups applesauce
1 teaspoon vanilla
1½ cups white flour
1½ cups whole wheat flour
1 tablespoon cinnamon
1 tablespoon nutmeg
2 teaspoons baking soda
1 cup chopped figs*

Preheat oven to 325 degrees. Butter a 10-inch bundt pan. In a mixing bowl, cream the butter with the sugar. Add the applesauce and vanilla; mix well. Sift in dry ingredients: white flour, whole wheat flour, cinnamon, nutmeg, and baking soda. Add the figs; stir well. Pour batter into bundt pan and cook approximately 1 hour, or until firm but moist. Let cool in pan 15 minutes; turn onto serving plate and let cool completely. Serves 10 to 12.

*Fig trees can survive in the northeast as long as they are well protected over the winter. They go dormant during periods when temperatures stay between 20 and 40 degrees. Their roots and trunk base can be well insulated with wood chips or other thermal protection, and they will do quite well outside. The fruit makes one of the best treats both fresh and dried.

Mixed Bag Applesauce

Take as many **sweet apples** as you'd like and wash them in cold water. Put on a large pot with 1 to 2 inches water to boil, and drop in apples, whole or sliced. When tender, crank the apples through a food mill or press them through a fine mesh sieve, catching pulp in a large mixing bowl. Add **cinnamon**, **nutmeg**, **lemon juice** and **sugar to taste** (all are optional), and serve chilled or hot.

Tomato sauce

This is one of my go-to dishes . . . it's easy and can be eaten on pasta, with veggie sticks, grilled cheese, pureed into soup, even . . . everything!

5 tablespoons fat drippings
1 cup of chopped white onion
½ to ¾ cup red wine

⅓ cup fresh herbs
salt and pepper to taste

Drop 5 tablespoons fat drippings into a hot pan. Add 1 cup of chopped white onions, and sauté until translucent. Add 6 cups chopped tomatoes. Add ½ to ¾ cup red wine and bring to a boil. Turn to low and simmer until reduced by a third. Season with ⅓ cup fresh herbs (rosemary, thyme, oregano or basil) and salt and pepper to taste. Serve generously over fresh pasta. Serves 6 to 8.

Blackberry Jam with Apple Pectin

Blackberry jam puts a little bit of July into any breakfast
   3 quarts of fresh-picked blackberries
   3 finely chopped tart, early apples
   9 cups sugar

In a large, heavy bottomed, nonreactive pot, heat the blackberries and apples over medium heat until the fruit begins to weep. Add sugar and stir until dissolved. Bring to a slow boil, stirring frequently, and continue to simmer about 25 minutes, until the liquid begins to sheet off a wooden spoon.

Keep in mind that jam thickens quite a bit as it cools; you can always turn off the heat, let the mixture cool, and keep cooking if it's not thick enough – this is better than making 7 jars of rock-hard jam. Test as you cook by pouring a small amount of the liquid onto a plate and waiting to see its consistency as it cools over the next few minutes.

When jam consistency is right, pour into 7 sterile pint jars, leaving a half-inch of head room. Take care to clean rims of jars with a cloth dipped in boiling water and to seal with sterile lids. Screw caps on tightly as tightening later may break the seal. Leave upside down on a cloth to cool overnight; check seals, label and store in a cool dark place.

Makes 7 pints plus a little extra for eating fresh.

we got dragged all over the state. Now I wish I knew more, but we just revolted against the whole bird thing then. There's a lot of being quiet and walking slowly, and we were just not into that.

Before we were born, my parents made all their own yogurt and bread. They kept chickens, and did all sorts of cool things. Then when we were born it all kind of went out the window. At least we always had dinner at home. Every night.

I've always been interested in food. When I was at Middlebury College I ate mostly from the salad bar. The food wasn't labeled organic, but I think Middlebury's right up there with the forerunners of local and organic in colleges. I got interested in writing about food back then — I wrote a column for the local paper called "Good Seasoning," talking about a different local ingredient each week. So that was good, but it was hard for me to find fresh local produce. Here on the Cape it's hard, too. I moved here after college and live with Alex, one of the owners of Mac's Shack. He kind of revolts against my local eating and wants things like orange juice and bananas. There aren't very many local farms (Cape Cod Organics, Matt's Organic Gardens, Watts Family Farms and a few others) but there's tons of seafood. I joined a milk co-op that gets its milk from a farm in Dartmouth, MA; that's the closest place. Every week I pay $3.50 for a half-gallon of organic raw milk and then once every four months I do the pickup. We rotate, filling the car with coolers.

For vegetables and fruits, I go to the farm market in Orleans or Hyannis. We buy grass-fed beef from the farm where I get my milk. We get lamb from Barnstable, and next week we're getting two hundred pounds of pig; hopefully I'm going to split it with somebody because I really don't know what to do with two hundred pounds of it. The hardest thing to find is butter. There are a few things, like flour, butter, anything that requires more land, that are really hard to find here because there's no land for farming. I found flour in Maine — that's the closest source.

If you're looking for an oysterman you should try Chad Williams. Not only does he have his own grant *[basically a chunk of mud out in the ocean which the oystermen call their farm]* but he owns a restaurant called The Juice, which serves his oysters along with other local fish and produce. His wife, Rumiana, manages the front of the house. His father's the landlord and his mother's the prep cook. He's been oystering since he was a kid and he's an amazing cook. He's always got live music and seems like everyone in town is there at some point during the weekend. Always a crowd!

Charter (Chad) Williams
Wellfleet, Massachusetts ■ Oysterman ■ www.thejuicerestaurant.com

The next day, Charter Williams, dressed in shorts and a faded T-shirt, looking and acting much more like his nickname, Chad, agrees to take me out to his grant for early-morning oystering. "Great morning for oystering!" he announces, shaking my hand. We are at his restaurant, The Juice, on the corner of Bank and Commercial Streets. He has coffee ready for me. I had a delicious dinner there the night before: a half-dozen oysters, blackened scallops over local greens from Barnstable, day haddock in soft tacos with a spicy coleslaw, and rhubarb-strawberry pie for dessert. The sun's just coming up. After we down the coffee, Chad throws a couple of steel baskets into the back of his pickup. He's wearing knee-high rubber boots, and hands me a pair of heavy rubber-and-canvas gloves and a short, sharp knife as we jump into his pickup. Chad pops a CD into the player, telling me he loves reggae. We cruise down King Phillip Road, a tree-shadowed dirt lane, swaying to the beat of Bob Marley.

Chad: I grew up in an apartment above a restaurant. My dad and mom had several restaurants through the years, a flower shop, and an ice-cream shop. During the time my dad was fishing, he rented the restaurant out to different people. When I was maybe five or six it was a pizza place called Upper Crust Pizza. I'd come down and watch this guy, Eric, make pizzas and stuff, and he let me hang out in the kitchen. I used to lean up against the wall and watch him make pizza. My mom was a good cook, too. Now she does all the prep, all the desserts, all the soups for me. I do the main courses.

My roots are deep in Wellfleet. I love it. Even as I pursue other things, go to school, this will always be a good place for my wife and me. We're invested.

It's low tide, and in the pickup we head right out onto the hard-packed sand, where we pass two or three other parked trucks. Chad parks his pickup way above the water line at the head of his grant.

My dad's had this grant for twenty-five years. He used to work it a lot. He was my age, around twenty-eight, when he got into the fishing industry here in town. There are two ways to get a grant — somebody passes it on to you, like my dad did to me, or you get on the list and you wait your turn until a piece of land comes up. When my parents were looking at grants, they wanted one close to town that would be suitable for a shellfish farm, a good tidal inlet where you could actually reach it by car — as we're doing this morning. So my dad got this grant. It's three acres, and now it's mine. My farm.

RECIPES ■ Chad Williams

Chilled Salmon Sandwich with Lemon Dill Aioli

1 pound salmon filet
4 ciabatta rolls
2 carrots, julienned
1 cucumber, thinly sliced
¼ pound mixed salad greens
1 lemon
½ bunch dill
½ cup heavy mayonnaise

For salmon: Season salmon with salt, pepper and squeeze of lemon, and bake at 350 degrees for 10 to 12 minutes. After cooled, place salmon in refrigerator for 30 minutes.

For aioli: Combine juice of 1 lemon, dill and mayonnaise in small mixing bowl and whisk. Add black pepper to taste.

For sandwich: Slice ciabatta rolls and toast. Spread aioli on both sides of rolls. Layer greens, cucumber and carrots on bottom half of rolls. Gently flake apart salmon, leaving bite-size pieces intact, and divide among rolls, placing fish on top of vegetables. Serve open-faced with lemon wedges. Serves 4.

Seared Scallop Salad with Honey Vinaigrette

½ pound baby arugula, locally grown if available
½ pound sea scallops, tendon removed
Edible flowers such as nasturtiums
1 lemon, sliced into wheels or wedges
1 shallot, minced
1 tablespoon Dijon mustard
3 tablespoon honey, preferably from a local source
¼ cup Apple cider vinegar
¼ cup olive oil
12 slices of cucumber, cut on the bias
Fine sea salt and black pepper to taste
1 tablespoon canola oil

For the dressing:
Place shallot, mustard, honey and vinegar into a mixing bowl. Whisk until all elements are incorporated. Once mixed thoroughly, continue to whisk while adding olive oil in a slow but steady stream. Set dressing aside.

For scallops:
Place nonstick sauté pan over medium-high heat and add just enough canola oil to lightly coat the pan. While pan comes up to temperature, season both sides of scallops with sea salt and pepper. Once oil is hot but not smoking, gently add scallops to pan, being sure to deliberately place flat side of scallops onto the hot pan to ensure a good sear.

My dad also got involved with some fishing boats and started processing sea clams in the basement of our building. He would go down to the harbor, buy big surf clams that were coming off the boats, and bring them back, process them, chop them up for chowder, or into strips for fried clams, things like that. He started *Cape Cod Clam Company*, wholesaling in Boston, selling stuff to Legal Seafood Restaurant. He had a fifty-five-foot boat called the *Nordstrom* that we actually lost in the "perfect storm." The boat sank off of Block Island, Rhode Island. I was pretty young then. That's when my dad started phasing out of the business. That's just about when I started getting interested in it.

There are two ways to grow oysters. You can either catch the wild seed that occurs naturally in the harbor, or buy seed. If you choose to catch wild seed you use a Chinese hat, a plastic, cone-shaped, rigid mesh. The hats, are coated with a concrete mixture high in lime and cement and then put out into the

Allow scallops to sear for approximately 1 minute, moving with a small spatula if necessary. After a nice sear has developed, flip scallops over, let cook on the other side for 1 minute and remove from heat.

In a large stainless bowl, toss arugula with dressing and divide among four large plates or salad bowls. Place 3 slices of cucumber (fanned out) on the very top of each mound of arugula (this will act as a platform to keep the scallops as the center of attention).

Divide the cooked scallops among the 4 plates, placing the scallops atop the cucumber slices in the center of the plate. Add a few edible flowers and garnish with lemon wheel. Offer fresh cracked pepper to guests. Serves 4.

Haddock Provencal over Herbed Israeli Couscous

2 pounds haddock filets cut into 4 8-ounce portions
3 cups chicken or vegetable stock
2½ cups Israeli Couscous (Moroccan couscous may be substituted, however cooking method will differ)
1 bunch chives, finely diced
1 red onion, finely diced
4 tablespoons olive oil
1 cup fresh tomatoes, diced
½ cup crushed tomatoes
1 large white onion, medium dice
¼ cup kalamata olives, sliced
¾ cup dry white wine
2 tablespoons chopped garlic
1 bunch parsley, chopped
10 fresh basil leaves, finely chopped

For Sauce:
Heat ½ of olive oil in large saucepan. Add white onion to saucepan and cook until onions are translucent. Add fresh tomato and half of herbs. Let cook down for 5 minutes. Add wine, crushed tomatoes, garlic and olives and cover, leaving a cracked lid so steam can escape.

Simmer sauce for approximately 15 to 20 minutes on low heat. The longer the sauce cooks, the better it will become; however be sure to not let it cook down too much, as we want it to retain a sauciness. Once sauce is done, remove from heat and let sit while the rest of the meal is prepared. At this point add salt and pepper to taste.

For couscous:
Heat remaining olive oil in medium saucepot. Sauté red onion, chive and remaining herbs until aromatic. Add stock and bring to gentle boil (covered). Add couscous to boiling stock, stir, cover and reduce temperature to a light simmer. Cook couscous until all stock has been absorbed, remove from heat and let stand.

For fish:
Arrange filets in large roasting pan preferably three to four inches deep. Season with sea salt and fresh ground black pepper. Cover fish with sauce and bake in a 350 degree oven for 10 to 12 minutes or until fish flakes easily.

Serve fish over couscous with a generous ladle of extra sauce over the top. Finish with parsley, fresh lemon and salt and pepper to taste. Serves 4.

water in July, where oyster seeds (called "sets") are floating, just looking for somewhere to attach in order to begin their life. *Cultch* are shells that have been thrown back into the water. They provide good material for seedlings to attach and cling to until they have grown bigger in the fall. When you break the cultch apart — it's called *culling* — you have all these little oysters that you can put into various-size mesh bags, where they continue to grow. By September they should be the size of a quarter.

The other way to go is to get the seeds from a hatchery — we've done that over the past couple of years. These are places with indoor tanks, where in the winter they kind of trick the seeds into spawning by changing the temperature of the water. Then the seed is collected and grows up from there. You're kind of getting a head start. I'm going to get some next week. They'll be about two millimeters, basically like coarsely cracked pepper. You put these seeds into different-size bags, starting them out in three-quarter-millimeter green mesh. As they grow you put them into the next-size mesh bag. If you start with, say, one thousand you can eventually turn them into two bags of five hundred, staying on top of breaking them down as they grow. It's anywhere from a two- to three-year process.

When the end of December rolls around, it gets cold, ice starts to develop in the harbor. You don't want to leave your oysters out here because there's a chance that the ice will become so powerful it can take all your bags as the tide goes out. They can travel miles away. You can lose your entire investment in one tide, doing that. In years past, we've brought them inside and put them in a pit in the basement. As long as the temperature is around forty degrees or so, they just go into hibernation mode. You can keep them for up to two months. When the ice clears out, we bring them back out. The oysters have a little drink, and they're back to life.

Now we've got this disease to deal with called Dermo, or *Perkinsus marinus*, a parasite that is affecting the oysters in this area. It is persistent if winter temps don't get cold enough to kill it. It affects the juvenile oysters — when they are about 2.2 inches, just about the time they are ready to be sold, in late August, early September — all of a sudden the oysters start dying. There's nobody home when we come to empty the bags. Harvest time you can usually count on, say, ten to twenty thousand oysters — but now, with Dermo, by the end of August most have died. What we did last year was, instead of bringing the oysters in, we left them, cut the bags open and sprinkled them out, looked to see how many survived on their own.

Some fishermen think that it's climate change that has brought Dermo. I'm not sure — it still gets pretty cold up here in the winter and generally the cold keeps the oysters clear of most disease. It's still too early to tell why it's sticking around.

When I am culling *[breaking the small oysters off the larger ones]*, which is done continually, my knife is an important tool. Nowadays they make knives with big black handles — for shucking —

but I prefer this smaller one, it feels better in my hand. When you're sorting through the oysters, breaking off stuff that you don't want, in order to make a nicer oyster that you might put on a plate, you can sometimes use a plastic knife, but I couldn't find my plastic one today.

To the left of Chad's grant is a friend named Jim, operating his mother's thirty-year-old grant that he uses mostly for clams. To the right is another friend, Clinton Austin, who's working on his mother's farm.

On the way back to the restaurant, Chad shows me the lay of the land, the big houses owned by the tourists, or "lizards," as he calls them, who come up for the summer to sit out on the hot rocks. Obviously they depend on the tourists, but there is also some animosity between them.

Some of them don't like having our grants in their front yard, blocking their views; we've had some disagreements about that. But they love to come to the restaurant for the shellfish!

He points out a huge pile of fishy smelling shells.

It's legal to come here and dump your empty shells. It's the town cultch — so clam shells, oyster shells, scallop shells are dumped here. A big barge filled with these will be taken to different parts of town; the shells will be put out in the ocean wherever the warden thinks they'll best catch wild seed.

Everything else in the world has gone up in price except shellfish. Wholesale they fetch fifty cents a piece. Here on the Cape, in a restaurant you'll pay anywhere from $1.50 to 2.50 per oyster. In Boston or New York, double that. Used to be that fishermen would say, Eat oysters in months that have an R in them — cooler months, except for September. The other months the oysters are spawning. A good fisherman or cook knows when an oyster is bad. If it's open when he picks it up, it's bad; if there's mud in it when he shucks it, it means the shell wasn't properly closed. In July, when the oysters are spawning, they get translucent, with not as much body to them. Doesn't mean they're bad though; just not as tasty. Some restaurants open up one

hundred oysters at the beginning of the day, then put them in the fridge — there's a million different things that can happen between the time they are opened up and when they're placed before you. I like to open them and then eat them immediately.

Other things can happen to make an oyster go bad, like if the knife is dirty during shucking, or if the cook prepped a chicken just before they shucking the oysters. Clams will sometimes have an open gap, but if you tap them, they should close up. Means they're still alive. Same with mussels. If you're served a fish soup and some of the shellfish haven't opened, don't eat them; it means their muscles aren't working and they've already died. A fresh shellfish releases when it dies.

It's a tricky business. Right now I have a perfect life — fishing in the morning and then cooking in the evening. What could be better?

Since I grew up in California, where there's always so much fresh food year round, I ask both Elspeth and Chad to tell me what kind of local produce they have access to in the winter. There is quite an array of food available through the cold winter months. Just for the heck of it, here they are, in alphabetical order:

Apples, Beets, Brussels Sprouts, Cabbage, Carrots, Cauliflower, Celeriac, Cranberries, Daikon, Garlic, Horseradish, Jerusalem Artichoke, Kale, Kohlrabi, Leeks, Mushrooms, Onions, Parsnips, Pears, Potatoes, Pumpkins, Rutabaga, Shallots, Sprouts, Sweet Potatoes, Swiss Chard, Turnips, Winter Squash.

Fish: Cod, Crab, Haddock, Hake, Littleneck Clams, Lobster, Monkfish, Mussels, Nantucket Bay Scallops, Oysters, Pollock, Quahogs, Sea Clams, Sea Scallops, Soft Shell Clams.

Although many of the restaurants close up for the winter, there are natural food stores and lots of the restaurants, markets and businesses that have committed to buying locally grown fruits, vegetables, sea food, preserves and wine.

For information about which fish are safe to eat and not endangered, go to www.edf.org or www. montereybayaquarium.org/seafoodwatch.

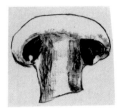

I like being able to go into my new office, close the door behind me, turn on the CD player and work. It feels like a den, and although it still smells like my daughter, I am beginning to feel like it's becoming mine. Her books still fill the bookcases, and I like that. I don't have to clean up when I stop work. I can just leave my papers everywhere.

It's time to head west for the summer. Over the winter months I lined up dozens of interviews. I pack up my files, my notes, my maps. It will probably take about two weeks to get back to Durango, then later in the summer I'll head farther west.

MID-MAY ■ *My first stop is the Reading Terminal Market in Philadelphia. After wandering around for some time, I find the only stall — Fair Food Farm-stand — that has local organic produce along with meat and cheese. I ask the vendor if she knows any local young farmers. "Mostly they're middle-aged, but I think I remember that the Jamisons have a daughter who's into cooking local foods." The Jamison Farm is a lamb farm. I call and set up a meeting for mid-morning the next day. Before leaving the market I stock up on cherries, shelled peas and a good hunk of local cheddar.*

Latrobe, Pennsylvania, in Westmorland County, has an almost suburban feel until I make a right turn and head up a narrow rural road, following the handmade wooden sign to the Jamison Lamb Farm. There's Sukey Jamison waiting for me at the end of a long drive, flanked by fields full of honeysuckle and currants. We have a good look around the lamb fields, get a glimpse of the processing plant and the freezers, and I learn how Sukey and John met in college, bought the farm and started raising lamb for their kids.

Of their three children, they feel Eliza is most likely to return to the farm one day. She attended the Culinary Institute, worked in many of the finest restaurants in New York City, and is now up in Rockland, Maine, working at Primo, a world-class restaurant. I look forward to the possibility of an interview with Eliza later in the summer. I ask Sukey where to have lunch and get a taste of Jamison lamb. She directs me to Six Penn Kitchen in Pittsburgh.

Chris Jackson
Six Penn Kitchen ■ **www.tedandhoney.com**

I arrive just in time for lunch and order the lamb special. They serve it with local greens and tomatoes from the kitchen's own rooftop garden. I ask if I can meet the chef, and soon a handsome man approaches my table. He beams when I reveal that I've just come from the Jamison Farm. Chris takes me up to his rooftop garden that overlooks the entire city. He has all kinds of herbs, including spicy bush basil, citrus lemon basil, lavender, rosemary and cayenne peppers from Thomas Jefferson's garden. The tomatoes that are just starting to grow will form the heirloom tomato plate later in the summer. Chris also has a variety of heirloom melons.

Six months later, Chris's sister calls him to say that the best spot in the world has opened up in Brooklyn. A few days later Chris serves notice at Six Penn, ties things up in Pittsburgh and moves himself and his family to Brooklyn. Three months later Ted and Honey opens in Cobble Hill, Brooklyn. (Ted was Chris's boyhood nickname and Honey was his sister's.) The menu is quite different from Six Penn, though still local, mostly organic and scrumptious. The atmosphere is friendly with lots of books, crayons and larger kid-friendly tables. Chris says that he sometimes longs for the busy nights of fine dining at Six Penn, but he's happy to be in Brooklyn with new regular customers.

I do have a small but successful garden at Ted and Honey, where this year I grew herbs, peppers, curry, edible flowers and lots of other things. We used

RECIPES ■ Chris Jackson

Tomato Aioli

This recipe for Tomato Aioli goes well with all kinds of meats!

  2 tablespoons tomato paste
  2 tablespoons honey
  2 each Roma tomato, halved and roasted***
  1 tablespoon whole grain mustard or Dijon
  4 tablespoons sundried tomatoes
  2 tablespoons lemon juice
  3 tablespoons parsley, chopped
  2 tablespoons roasted garlic cloves (or 1 tablespoon fresh
      garlic, chopped)
  1 tablespoon dry mustard
  1 cup light or blended olive oil
  3 each egg yolks
  Salt and fresh cracked pepper to taste

Cut Roma tomato or fresh garden tomato in half and put on baking sheet cut side up. Drizzle with olive oil, salt and pepper and roast in a 350 degree oven for ½ hour to expel and intensify all flavors.

Place all the ingredients except the oil into a food processor or blender and start the motor on high. With motor running, slowly but steadily add the oil through the feeding shoot nd watch for the ingredients to start to emulsify – to form a thick yet silky aioli/mayonnaise consistency. Stop motor and check for seasoning. Add more if you like.

Serve with anything from a great BLT with summer tomatoes, lettuces and crisp bacon to grilled/smoked pork chops off the grill, or even make a wonderful corn on the cob rolled in tomato aioli then rolled in finely grated parmesan cheese, chili powder and lime juice! Makes about 2 cups.

everything in it. We also teamed up with a farmer in Pennsylvania who started an heirloom organic farm specifically for growing tomatoes, jalapeño peppers and garlic for us. Sadly the tomatoes got the blight and we only had a few shipments. I did can, jar and pickle the remainder of his jalapeños, and worked on a salsa recipe for him to bring to a canning facility. We will regroup this next year and see what happens.

I don't think I could ever be without my relationship with the Jamison Farm. I am proud to be using their world-famous lamb in several of my summer/fall and winter menu items. This lamb will be the highlight of our slow-cooked lamb barbeque sandwich, which is doused in North Carolina–style sauce and served with house-made coleslaw and house-made pickles. The lamb will also be featured in the Merquez sausage panini special, with roasted eggplant, baby arugula from Satur Farms in Long Island, and our house-made harissa aioli. Also, very soon we will start to feature Ted's Almost Famous

— a concoction of Jamison Farm lamb bolognese sauce with fresh pasta and feta cheese!

One of the many things I begin to notice as I make my way west is how many more restaurants serve local foods. There are more farmers markets, and all in all, more and more folks under forty involved in the new sustainable movement. Every small town seems to have an Edible *magazine or some way of broadcasting the local organic fare.*

Dan Neufeld

Daisy Flour, Annville Flouring Mill ■ Annville, Pennsylvania ■ www.daisyflour.com/ annville-mill/historic

STILL MAY ■ *Next morning I head to Annville, Pennsylvania, a township in Lebanon County. I drive through a thunderstorm, the car literally hydroplaning, blown across the road by the wind. I pass mile after mile of young cornfields. It's a quiet town, not a lot of traffic. The sun's trying to come out as I round a corner and start down a swooping hill that ends directly at 545 West Queen Street and the 270-year-old limestone mill called Annville Flouring Mill.*

The mill, originally built in 1740, is powered by the Quittapahilla Creek that sits directly behind it. Looking in the direction of the creek, the mill and the three or four surrounding buildings, it's as if no time has passed at all. It is the oldest mill in the United States to be continually operating as a commercial flourmill. In its early days it was also used to saw lumber and process wool.

McGeary Organics of Lancaster now owns the Annville Mill, which is run by Dan Neufeld.

Dan Neufeld: My grandfather was a miller. I'm not sure if that had anything to do with me becoming a miller, but it sure might have. I went to Kansas State and they had a milling school there. During the summers I did internships and after graduating, I got placed in a mill. At that time, there was pretty much one-hundred-percent job placement for millers.

I came out here to Camp Hill, Pennsylvania, and spent two years over at Harrisburg, working for ADM [*Archer Daniels Midland*], then five years out in the Minnesota-North Dakota area at a small private mill, and now I'm working for McGeary. This is my first opportunity to work with organic wheat and oats.

The process for milling is pretty much the same as for conventional grains except we work with 100 percent organic wheat. No chemicals are allowed on this property. Our fields cannot be sprayed with herbicides or pesticides or the like for three years prior to crop planting. After that, we're not allowed to add any chemicals or enrichment to our process, in the way that nonorganic flour is produced in many conventional milling plants.

I grew up on a farm — just a few acres, mainly cattle. My dad once worked at a nuclear power plant. We have a family reunion every July. We go when we can make it. It's mainly Dad, his two sisters and a brother, a bunch of their aunts and uncles. I've got cousins scattered all over.

RECIPES ■ Dan Neufeld

Banana Nut Bread

½ cup butter

1 cup sugar

2 eggs

¾ cup mashed banana (about 3 medium)

1¼ cup spelt flour

¼ cup ground flax seed

¾ teaspoon baking soda

½ teaspoon salt

Dash of cinnamon

Handful of chopped pecans

Blend until mixed. Grease and flour a loaf pan. Bake at 350 degrees for 35 to 40 minutes, or until no crumbs stick to a toothpick.

Recipe submitted by Lisa Howard Tobin of Lancaster, PA.

(Daisy Flour friend) John Donohue's Quick Pizza Recipe

If you're in a hurry you can make this pizza in about an hour, although an hour and a half is a more realistic timeframe.

Pizza dough:

1 packet active dry yeast (about 2 teaspoons)

1 teaspoon salt

1 teaspoon sugar

¼ cup olive oil

1 cup warm water

1 cup Daisy whole wheat pastry flour

2½ cups Daisy spelt flour (more or less)

Mix together the yeast, salt and sugar then add the oil and water. Combine and then add the whole wheat flour and mix with a wooden spoon. Start to add the spelt flour, half a cup at a time, beating with the wooden spoon, until the dough starts to come together. Turn the dough out onto a floured surface and knead the remaining flour into the dough until the desired consistency is achieved. The dough shouldn't be too sticky and should have some strength when tugged on. Coat a large mixing bowl with a layer of oil and form the dough into a ball. Put the dough into the bowl, turning it over so all sides are coated with oil, and then cover the bowl with an overturned plate. Allow the dough to rise for about an hour.

This hour gives you the perfect amount of time to make a batch of pizza sauce! You can also prepare the toppings.

About 20 minutes before the dough is finished rising, preheat the oven. For a crispy pizza crust, a short bake at high temperature is the best. A starting point might be 450 to 500 degrees. When your dough is ready, prepare a baking sheet by spraying with a cooking spray or oil and then sprinkle with cornmeal. Punch down the dough, removing any CO_2 bubbles, and start to stretch or roll the dough out into a pizza shape. Top with toppings and place in the oven. Depending on how hot the oven is, 10 minutes should do it, but keep an eye on the pizza to make sure that it isn't burning. Experiment to find the best temperature/time for your combination of oven, baking sheet and pizza stone if you are using one.

My favorite toppings are vegan, but feel free to add cheese – preferably fresh mozzarella, not the shredded kind.

John's homemade pizza sauce

Sundried tomatoes, kalamata olives, green olives, fresh basil, crushed red pepper and mushrooms brushed with oil so they don't dry out. Mix with a favorite pizza seasoning.

Make sure that the ingredients are fresh.

Bonus Recipe for Pizza Sauce! (adapted from *Vegan with a Vengeance*)

2 teaspoons olive oil

2 cloves garlic, minced

½ teaspoon thyme

1 teaspoon oregano

1 teaspoon salt

afresh ground black pepper

4 plum tomatoes, chopped

2 tablespoons tomato paste

In a saucepan over medium-high heat, add the oil and garlic. Stir for a few minutes, allowing the garlic to turn golden; be careful not to burn it. Add the spices and stir. Add the tomatoes and paste, turn up heat until tomatoes release some liquid, simmer for about 10 minutes. Turn the heat down to low and allow the sauce to thicken until it looks done, maybe another 10 minutes or so. Turn off the heat and allow the sauce to cool a bit. When cooled, put in blender and blend

until smooth. Feel free to leave some of the sauce chunky if you prefer.

That's my pizza.

Whole Wheat Ricotta Gnocchi with Swiss Chard

Betsey Sterenfeld owns a cooking school called Essen. She made this batch of gnocchi (using Daisy Flour) for her family in Lancaster after returning from a food exploration trip to Italy.

Gnocchi:

2 cups whole milk ricotta
2 large eggs, lightly beaten
1½ cups grated Parmesan, divided
¼ teaspoon grated nutmeg
1⅜ cups Daisy whole wheat pastry flour

Stir together the ricotta, eggs, 1 cup Parmesan, nutmeg and ¼ teaspoon each salt and pepper. Add the flour, stirring to form a soft, wet dough. Divide dough in half. With lightly floured hands, roll each half on a well-floured work surface into about a 1-inch-diameter rope. Cut the dough into 1-inch pieces. Make small indentation in center of each piece.

Set the formed gnocchi in a single layer on a floured, parchment-lined baking sheet while you form the rest of the dough.

Meanwhile, bring a large pot of salted water to boil. Working in two batches, cook the gnocchi in the boiling water until they have all risen to the surface, about 3 to 4 minutes. Scoop the gnocchi into a colander with a slotted spoon while you cook the second batch.

Sauce:

Olive oil
4 cloves garlic
3 pounds swiss chard
½ pound speck, roughly chopped
Red pepper flakes
Parmigiano-Reggiano

Add olive oil and garlic to pot. Heat to medium. Sauté garlic until cloves are aromatic and a light brown color. Remove garlic from pan. Add speck and cook until crisp. Add chard stems. Lightly season with salt and red pepper flakes. When stems begin to tender, add leaves. Cook until leaves wilt, but are not mushy.

Transfer the cooked gnocchi to the skillet with the chard. Sprinkle with remaining cheese and toss. Serves 6 to 8.

Grandma Whitcraft's Chocolate Cake

Charyl Dommel's family recipes come from Lititz, PA, a Moravian community. They date as far back as the beginning of Daisy Flour in the late nineteenth century.

2 cups sugar
2¼ cups Daisy whole wheat flour or white pastry flour
¾ cup cocoa
2 eggs
2 teaspoons baking soda
1 teaspoon baking powder
1 teaspoon vanilla
½ cup oil
1 cup coffee (liquid)

Stir in at end:
1 cup cold milk

Bake at 350 degrees for 35 to 40 minutes in a 9×13-inch pan.

Recipe submitted by third-generation baker Charyl Dommel, who says "Grandma always topped this cake with caramel icing."

When I was young we mostly ate farmgrown products and we did a lot of hunting for rabbits, quail, doves, that kind of game. Growing up I knew how to shoot. Our closest neighbor was a good quarter mile away, and there probably wasn't another neighbor for a good 2 to 3 miles after that. Closest town was fifteen miles. That's where my school was. We took the bus 'til one of us learned how to drive. There were seventeen kids in my graduating class, three of them foreign exchange students. I'd say about half the class went to ju-cos *[junior colleges]*. I think I'm the only one that got a four-year degree.

I have two daughters, ages two and three, and my wife is a medical transcriptionist. We met in college. She knows all the fancy words.

Since I've been here working, everything has changed for me. Before I was always just one of the shift millers, not really in charge of much, just keeping the mill running. Now I'm pretty much in charge of everything that happens. New things happen every day. Broken machinery. Drivers getting upset. I have to know when a load of wheat or oats is due in, see to it that it gets milled, from start to finish.

At first I didn't think I would be able to taste the difference between conventional flour and organic. My wife says organic flour is easier to roll out, holds it form, and it bakes different. Bakers learn to adapt their recipes. Old-timers say it acts like flour before it was mass-produced.

Dave Poorbaugh, president of McGeary Organics, bought the mill in 2002 and resurrected the venerable Daisy Flour. He says that in the 1800s any "self-respecting housewife in Lancaster, PA, baked with Daisy Flour. She'd walk — or take a trolley — to the corner grocery store, and carry home a small two-pound bag. She would use it quickly, knowing from experience that it would spoil if kept too long in the cupboard." Daisy Flour, a regional product, is still made via a very slow, very old process. The

starch is not destroyed, as can happen when flour is processed fast and hot.

Daisy dough does not crack or form lumps that have to be reworked. In the old days, if you kept flour in a bin, you would be sure to sift it well, to get the weevils and weed seed out. Because the grain is 100% organic, if you keep it too long it has a chance of getting bugs in it, so the bags are stamped with an expiration date.

As we walk through the building, Dan points out all the nooks and crannies, explaining what the machinery actually does.

This is a beautiful old building, isn't it? Sometimes when I'm here alone, I get a cold feeling and the hair on the back of my neck stands up. I feel like I'm being watched. I think every guy here has experienced that at one time or another. Our night shift guy carries a baseball bat around with him.

In five years' time I hope to be right here doing what I'm doing now, overseeing the mill, producing Daisy Flour. We'll probably have all-purpose whole wheat by then, and we'll be milling bread flour in addition to our pastry flours. Nate Pirogowicz grows a lot of our wheat in Lisbon, Ohio, not too far away.

Several years ago McGeary Organics acquired a pinch of twenty different varieties of heritage wheat seeds (from the 1700 and 1800s) from the USDA. The following year they had a handful. This year they will plant that handful, and by 2010 enough heritage wheat will have grown up that they'll be able to start milling it.

Freshly ground wheat really does taste different from the flour you buy in the grocery store.

Nate and Shelley Pirogowicz
Wheat Farmers ■ Columbiana County, Ohio

Next stop is New Lisbon Village, on the north bank of Middle Beaver Creek. Originally known for its iron and whiskey production, New Lisbon is now a hodge podge of mills, tanneries, cement works, salt works, carpenters, gunsmiths and hotels. As I enter the town, I pass a small cemetery on my left, not more than several dozen old headstones and a carnival on my right, with a gorgeous Ferris wheel: Columbiana County Fair. There's no movie theater and I don't see a bookstore, but I know there's a college nearby. I pull up to a small ranch house with no front yard, park the car, leaving Luna with all the windows wide open, and ring the bell. Nate and Shelley Pirogowicz invite me in.

Nate: I grew up on forty acres, about an hour northwest of here, still in Ohio. We had a decent-size beef herd. It was conventional. When I was twelve, I started working on the dairy farm next door to us, a five hundred-cow, 2500-acre dairy. I never even heard of organic until I went to college, Ohio State ATI. *[Agricultural Technical Institute].* That's where Shelley and I met.

My second year there I get work on this farm. Turns out it's organic. Shelley comes to visit me one day when we're cultivating the soybeans and I tell her, "This is the stupidest thing I've heard of. If you ever see me cultivating organic again, shoot me!" Well, here I am. Now I've got my own organic farm.

I started doing a lot of trucking for this guy, taking all his beans up to Ann Arbor, Michigan, to get turned into soymilk. I find out what he's getting for the crops, I do the simple math and I realize there's a lot more money to be made here than in conventional crops. At the time conventional prices were way down, we were just breaking even at home. I mean, this guy's farming three hundred acres and the farm itself is paying my wages and buying new machinery. I'm thinking, How's he doing this?

So that was the first big reason I even got involved in organics, the money. At the time, that farmer was making four hundred percent more on soybeans. Corn was about two hundred percent more than conventional. And he raised spelt.

So, yeah, a considerable amount more money. Then you get to thinking the whole process through, and yeah, it just makes more sense. You have less cash input, but it's more labor intensive because you have to go in and work the ground. You can't just no-till. And then you plant, but you have to keep cultivating it, so that takes a lot more time. And to do a good job you have to go slower, so that burns up time. I guess farming's labor intensive all the way around, whether it's conventional or organic.

After a while what happens with a lot of the big conventional guys who go with fertilizer and pesticides for their corn and soybean rotation is you suck all the nutrients out of the soil. Most guys just put enough fertilizer back into the soil for what the crops needs for the year. But the different sprays and whatnot kill the microbes in the soil, along with the earthworms that are a huge, huge help to any kind of dirt as far as conditioning the soil. Some guys use hydrous nitrogen, which turns the ground rock hard. You've got to work harder and harder, put more nutrients in, you have to put more fertilizer in, and then of course, it's all going to end up in the water, the streams. If you overspray and try to plant soybeans the next year, your beans won't grow.

Certain weeds have actually grown immune, so now they've got to keep developing different sprays because the weeds and whatnot have mutated.

I use no GMO seeds. I only use seed raised organically or raised naturally without any seed treatment of any sort. I'm a dealer for Blue Rover Hybrids out of Ames, Iowa.

Our fields vary from year to year. We raise corn,

too — our rotation goes corn, oats, wheat . . . we interplant — or interseed clover or alfalfa with the wheat. And then it'll go back to corn or soybeans from there. We farm about three hundred acres and we try to keep about seventy-five acres of each crop.

Nate's other full-time job is with Kurt Klingel-hofer, whose thirty-year millwright business, K&S Millwrights, builds, installs and repairs machinery in feed mills, grain systems, grain setup, anything to do with feed and grain handling. They work all over Ohio, Pennsylvania, Indiana, North Carolina and Illinois. Klingelhofer always wanted a farm but never had the time or money to actually do it. Now money's not an issue and Nate has time, so they've become partners in the farm. Nate says they are both workaholics.

If it wasn't for Kurt, we couldn't get done near what we do. He's saved my life a few times! Especially getting started. It takes so much more work to get ground that hasn't been farmed for a couple

of years and to get it to where it's in decent condition. Kurt's really helped.

Most of our wheat and oats go to McGeary's Organics, a mill in Pennsylvania. The corn goes east for either organic chicken feed or feed for organic dairies.

Honestly, I started out for the money and I'm still in it for the money. If it's not worth your while, then why do it? Especially in these times. The more I do organic farming and the more I learn about it, the more benefits I see. This is my seventh year of organics. When I started, I thought since I'd farmed my whole life I could do this. But I was never more wrong. You have to forget everything you know about farming, everything. In the beginning I was on the phone, calling guys for help, visiting people. The Internet. There are a few books out there, but not many. There are some good websites; one's from Rodale Institute in Pennsylvania. I learned a lot from Matt Peart, who had an organic farm

where I used to work. I drove him crazy for a while. Dean Mackelvane, who's the largest organic farmer in Ohio, farms over twelve hundred acres. I called him a lot.

There were years I sat in my combine seat and said to myself, "I'm not doing this next year." But you got to keep going.

Shelley: My full-time job is as a Future Farmer of America teacher. I teach five days a week at Southern Local, which is the school I graduated from. It's really nice because I feel like by being there and helping, I'm kind of making a difference in my own school, my own community. I teach grades nine to twelve, all elective courses in agriculture. We cover all kinds of things: simple agriculture science, plant science and animal science related to livestock. We study pigs, sheep and cattle. We debate organic farming vs. conventional farming. This week we're at the fair. Many of my students are running the food stand in four-hour shifts. I have eighty to ninety students a year with an average class size of fifteen to twenty. We have a small

school. Most of the kids are looking for information they can take back and apply to their own family farms.

Shelley is one of four kids. One of her brothers lives an hour away and is a herdsman on an Angus beef farm. Her sister is a teacher in town, and her other brother works in town.

Nate: In the past there have been incentives for being organic. As organic farmers, it costs us a minimum of $600 to be certified, just to do the paperwork. The government will reimburses all but $100 of that.

People I know who dabble in selling fruits and vegetables organically say sales have shot way up, because the average smart consumer that knows organic foods are going to be safer to eat.

For the guys at McGeary Organics, since they're processing our wheat themselves, it goes straight from me to them and into their mill and then ground into their flour — Daisy Flour. The only thing you have to worry about is that the truck that hauls it from here to there is clean. We document

RECIPES ■ Nate and Shelley Pirogowicz

Vegetable Casserole

2 pounds of mixed vegetables (carrots, broccoli and
    cauliflower)
1 can of condensed chicken soup (or chicken broth)
¼ cup of milk
¼ cup of sour cream
2 cups of prepared stuffing (can be a mix)
1 cup of cheddar cheese, divided

In a saucepan, combine chicken soup, milk and sour cream
and heat until warm. Place mixed vegetables in a greased
9×13-inch baking dish. Spread prepared stuffing over top
the vegetables and sprinkle with cheddar cheese. Pour
chicken soup mixture over the top and sprinkle with remaining cheddar cheese. Cover and bake at 350 degrees for
about 45 minutes to 1 hour, or until vegetables are tender.
Serves 4.

that we've cleaned the trucks before we load them and everything is on the up and up.

I had a truck come in one time that had actually hauled conventional grain before me. We had to sweep it clean. Another time we had a truck that had hauled nickel to a stainless steel plant. I wouldn't put my wheat on it because even after we swept it, the nickel was still embedded in the aluminum of the trailer. You've got to make sure about everything, that's the hardest part about organic, you have to write down every little thing you ever do. I mean they want the date you plowed your field, the date you harvested a field, exact yields.

I follow Nate and Shelley's truck up to their farm. Along the way we make a brief stop on the narrow farm road and Nate motions for me to get out of my car. He points to an area where the ground seems to have been cut short in concentric circles.

Nate: Crop circles. Farm graffiti, yeah. You'll see these big crop circles in the wheat and stuff out west. That's somebody trying to do a bad job of an initiation, here.

We get back in our vehicles and I follow them farther up the road to their farmland.

Nate: The wheat's real short this year. It's probably because our spring has been real wet, cold, and we planted late. Just had a bad start. Normally they'd be waist high, four feet. Rye and spelt can be a lot taller.

Nothing's irrigated. When it's dry, I wish I could irrigate. Our ground is sandy shale. It doesn't hold water. The saying around here is, "You're always two weeks away from a drought." Now since we're organic our ground is getting better at holding water, the organic matter tends to hold moisture a little longer. But we still have the sand and shale which lets the water run right through it. In wet years it's a blessing because I can be planting before a lot of guys, and harvesting before them. They're out there getting stuck while I can get right through. But you get a dry year, it gets ugly real quick.

We don't actually own the land. We rent. The woman I rent from doesn't even want money, she just wants the ground taken care of. Her family homesteaded this place. It's been in her family for generations. We came in and started farming differently from everybody else, and she got real excited. She loves what we're doing.

There are two hundred and some acres here. A lot of it is in the woods though, timber, a lot of white oak. The Amish do logging and come in with a team of horses and drag the lumber out.

Shelley: We'd both like to live out of town. I grew up on a beef farm. That's definitely something we're interested in.

Nate: I think about farming every day. I love my job with K & S Millwrights. I've worked into a foreman position, which means I don't have to work quite as hard and the money's really good. I hate talking politics, but the more I farm organic, the more I learn that the better you take care of the dirt and the earth, the more they take care of you.

Lora Krogman
Angelic Organics ■ Caledonia, Illinois

Next morning, promptly at nine A.M. I am back at Angelic Organics. Lora Krogman has just returned from town with ice — lots of ice — the coolers are broken and the broccoli has come out of the ground hot. She waves and holds up five fingers. I start up a row of vegetables with Luna and after a while, I hear, "Hi." Unlike most farmers, Lora's skin is smooth and pale. She reminds me of Snow White — her eyes are very large and her hair pulled back in a ponytail. Her wide smile reveals a dimple.

I'm Lora. I'm so sorry about yesterday, we were just overwhelmed. Today, too!

Do you mind tagging along with me as I go through my morning?

I'm from Dubuque originally. I actually ran away from home in my late teens, right after high school. I cut all ties with my family and declared myself financially independent. When I decided to go to college, I majored in English because I always loved reading and writing poetry. At Loras College in Iowa, I won a national writing contest in poetry. I managed a bed and breakfast for a few years. During that time, my best friend, Jennelle, who worked at Angelic, invited me to one of Farmer John's "Wild Hat and Croquet" parties. I met Bob there and we started dating.

John Peterson loves glitz and glamour. If you watch his film you see the pink boa that he wears. He must have had a hard time during the years he spent out here alone. When he went off to Beloit College, he and some friends started coming out to the farm, smoking marijuana and partying down, and soon the farm had a wild reputation. He made the neighbors so angry. Pretty soon all kinds of things were being withheld from John. One of them was manure. There was a family whose farm provided the manure and they stopped delivering

it to John's farm. John was so young. Pretty soon things were on the rocks and he lost the farm.

As we walk around the farm, Lora checks out the crew to make sure they have what they need for the picking and weeding. She points out the zucchini beds, the beans, the tomatoes and the rest of the vegetables to me.

John kept a narrow strip running along the eastern edge of the farm so he could feel as if at least he owned the horizon — continuing to hold on to some possibility. He went to Mexico and saw how they were doing a more traditional type of agriculture. When he came back, he started thinking about turning what was then a conventional farm into

biodynamic agriculture. And of course you know how everything seems to kind of happen at once, although it was really over a couple of years. Well, someone who was buying John's produce wholesale contacted him about starting a CSA, and a reporter came out to do a story about the farm, and after the story came out, there were a lot of calls asking John to start a CSA. John tried it and it actually started to bring the farm back. So about the same time the CSA was beginning, Bob showed up with a background in computers and accounting. He'd been with a really big accounting company.

Lora grows quiet for a moment, looking up a row of zucchini. She bends down and begins to pull some weeds from one of the vegetable beds, shaking her head.

If a bed is full of weeds the farmers look at it as messy and are less likely to keep it up. I have to apologize for this bed; it's full of weeds. I'll have to talk to the crew.

We maintain a thirty to thirty-five foot border between our conventionally grown neighbor's crop and our own.

We have u-pick sections for the shareholders *[by late 2007 there were 1350]*. At one time we supplied a number of restaurants, but we stopped when in the middle of one season, the vegetable buyer for one restaurant changed the size of tomatoes from

"softball" to "baseball." Plants just can't be changed midseason. Our shareholders purchase a share of the summer harvest and they can also choose to have a winter share — four additional boxes of storage vegetables delivered in November and December. When they sign up, they become our customer for the year — which gives us a secure market. John says when you sign up you agree to share in the farmers' experience of nature's mischief and blessings.

I started out at Angelic as the cook. I love cooking, and I still cook, but now it's along with managing the flowerbeds and getting the vegetable and fruit newsletters out. I am also doing a lot of biodynamic work. I'm in charge of human resources and hiring, and I work with the interns. There are usually about four at the farm at a time and they need a lot of management. I feel like a good farmer has to learn intuition; he must know when the air changes and when to get on his tractor. I try to train the interns' intuition. I occasionally do a cooking workshop — just because.

I'm also learning to keep bees. I have learned mostly from Gunther Hauk, a top biodynamic beekeeper who recently started the Spikenard Farm & Bee Sanctuary in central Illinois *[www.spikenardfarm. org]*. I feel like I have a special relationship with bees. When I work with them I only wear a straw hat, long pants and long sleeves — I feel it's reverent. I've only been stung twice this year. I use Rescue Remedy and Apis. At the moment there's only just enough honey for the bees. I'll harvest in springtime — once the bees have done their work.

I've also started doing biographical work with the crew and the interns. There can be disagreements and misunderstandings, so I kind of interview them and we have a dialogue about what's going on. It helps me understand them better, I think.

As we continue to walk around the farm, Lora points out the Learning Center. Inside are some "value added" products for sale like goat's milk soap, John's books and films.

Sunset Sweet Potato bisque

After boiling beets for a salad, I can't bear to pour that deep red water down the drain. So I bake a butternut squash up, thinking only about color. I decide to make a soup that will capture the dusk horizon in my soup pot.

- 1 to 2 tablespoons coconut oil
- 2 ounces butter (4 tablespoons)
- 1 large onion, coarsely chopped
- 1-inch fresh ginger root, grated
- 2 sprigs of fresh thyme
- 2 pounds butternut squash (approximately 1 medium or large squash)
- 2 medium potatoes
- 5 cups stock, vegetable stock made with beet water
- ½ cup crème fraîche, or to taste (optional, but damned yummy!)
- Fine sea salt and freshly ground pepper
- Toasted walnuts or pecans to garnish

Preheat oven to 400 degrees and roast butternut until tender (about 1 hour and 15 minutes).

In a large soup pot, melt coconut oil, and sauté onions and ginger until slightly tender, about 5 minutes. Add squash and ½ cup of stock, reduce heat to low, cover and sweat for 15 minutes.

Add remaining stock, bring to a boil, cover, reduce heat and simmer for 20 minutes. Puree with an immersion blender or food mill. (You can use a regular blender, but it's a major hassle, I think – but if that's all you've got, go for it!)

Mix in the crème fraîche, thyme, and butter. Season to taste with salt and pepper and garnish with nuts.

This can be made ahead, up to 3 days (according to the recipe). Reheat and adjust seasoning before serving. It also freezes and thaws well.

Griddle, Garlic Scapes, Tarragon, and Eggs

I always have herbs on a plate or bowl that I keep next to the stove so that I can use them in whatever I'm cooking. It helps me dream and experiment.

- 1 garlic scape
- 1 egg (farm fresh eggs have yolks that are so richly colored. The eggs from the grocer are pale in comparison.)
- 1 sprig of tarragon (strip the tiny leaves from the stem and keep them next to the stove)
- Enough coconut oil or butter to wet the pan
- A good crusty piece of farmers bread

Heat a cast iron skillet or pan on medium to high heat and add oil or butter.

Slice garlic scape into thin rounds and sauté in the center of the pan. After 1 to 2 minutes, crack the egg over the scapes (you should be able to see them through the whites).

Just before you are ready to flip, sprinkle the tarragon over the egg. Cook to desired hardness.

Red Pepper, Beet, and Tomato Soup with Crème Fraîche and Dill

- 2 tablespoons butter
- 1 onion, roughly chopped
- 1 clove of garlic
- 4 to 6 red bell peppers
- 1 small beet
- 2 to 3 medium size tomatoes
- 4 to 6 cups of vegetable stock (add just enough to cover vegetables)
- Crème fraîche
- Dill for garnish
- Sea salt

Heat butter in a lager skillet over medium heat. Add onions and cook until onions are soft and add garlic. Peel and dice beet. Add it to the skillet and cook for about 5 minutes.

Remove seeds from peppers and cut into strips. Add to skillet and cook for 2 minutes. Add diced tomatoes and cook for 2 more minutes. Add vegetable stock and cook until vegetables are all soft.

Puree and serve. Garnish with a dollop of crème fraîche and a sprig of dill.

Bob has really helped save the farm in so many ways. Did I mention that he's a CPA, and works with spreadsheets and understands the whole picture of the farm, the workers, the vegetables, John's philosophy, and how to make it work financially?

Even when John is traveling, he and Bob speak every day.

Lora has to go to the Zinniker Farm in East Troy, Wisconsin — about forty-five minutes from where we are. Luna and I pile into her little blue car. On the ride down, we talk about recipes, how one knows "home," the way working the land can change a person. She confides that she has started writing poems again, and agrees to send me a few.

When we get to the farm she introduces me to

Ruth Zinniker, then we move along into a little shed where she pours milk from a stainless steel holding tank into a glass jar.

It's one of the oldest biodynamic farms in the U.S. Ruth and Dick have recently handed it over to their kids; Mark and Petra are now running it. Biodynamics is such a life-changing way of looking at almost everything, certainly farming. I pick up raw milk here once a week. I do my shopping at the little health food store down the road where I get my cheese, bread and a few other staples.

We drive back by way of Michael Fields' Co-Op, where Lora stops to buy her weekly groceries. I duck into the store out of the rain to buy an egg-salad sandwich. While I wait for Lora, I go next

door to the Michael Fields Farm and Food Program, a beautiful campus of barns and study areas. I review literature about a nine-month program that "promotes enlivened knowledge through practical tuition-based immersion programs, short-term courses, workshops and tours." The Foundation Year is an "exploration into biodynamic and organic agriculture through theoretical and experiential learning." The Short-Term Foundation placements are for students who are balancing their education with other life responsibilities (see www.michaelfieldsaginst.org).

Almost next door to Michael Fields Farm and Food is Uriel Pharmacy, created in 1996 by Mark McKibben (nontraditional pharmacist) to meet the needs of anthroposophically oriented health practioners and their patients. They make their natural medicines using ingredients from their own biodynamic gardens (see www.steinerstorehouse.com).

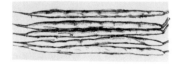

I want to stop in Milwaukee at Growing Power (www.growingpower.org/blog) — a national nonprofit organization that supports people from diverse backgrounds, and the environments in which they live, providing equal access to healthy, high-quality affordable food, but founder Will Allen is out of town.

I drive into Madison, Wisconsin, and have an early dinner at Harvest. Their summer salad of chopped snap peas, radishes, beans, and baby carrots with a light green goddess dressing takes my breath away. Tami Lax, owner/manager, gives me a menu with the evenings "splendids" and the names of all the local farms she uses.

The next morning on the road heading west, I call Shooting Star Farm, which Deborah Madison had also written about in Local Flavors. Turns out Rink DaVee's farm is not in the direction we're headed, but he has a lot to say about living sustainably, about how he feels his generation (the fortysomethings) is stepping up to the plate to make information more accessible.

for corn especially. They used it in the '40s, and my dad brought it back.

We grass feed our cows. Then for the last couple of months, we give them a little bit more grain, just to fatten them up. Organic grain, of course.

When you're buying local produce, still ask questions: How was the food grown? Using what kind of soil? What fertilizers? If it's cattle or lamb or pigs, how were they raised? Did they graze, and if so, were the grasses treated with any pesticides? Were the cows given antibiotics? And finally, how long has that meat been on the shelf?

My social life revolves around farming. Like I said, I have friends who farm. I usually have dinner with them on Thursday nights. I don't cook much. I eat sweet corn right off the cob; lettuce, tomatoes and summer sausage make a good sandwich. I use the grill a lot at night, hamburgers with lettuce and tomato. I get everything from Local Choice. I just call in couple times a week for everything I need.

Then there's weeding. Moving the grasses around helps destroy the weeds. If they get out of hand, we use a hot propane flame that kills the deep-rooted perennial weeds. A flame cultivation rig aims downward toward the row at an angle. We use it

RECIPES ■ Nicholas Zimmer

Granola

This recipe was a standard in our family. My mom would make it all the time…we had granola around for breakfast, camping trips, snacks. We all loved it!!

    10 cups oats
    ¾ cup wheat germ
    ¾ cup sunflower seeds
    ¾ cup sesame seeds
     1 cup raw spanish peanuts
    1 teaspoon salt
    1 teaspoon vanilla
    1 cup oil
    1 cup honey

Mix together and spread in a large cake pan. Bake at 350 degrees for about 30 minutes stirring often. When done add 2 cups of raisins.

Rhubarb Custard Pie

My mom always planted a huge garden. We all helped but she did almost all the planting and weeding (she liked to weed!) We helped with the picking – we didn't always enjoy it!!! She would can and freeze all summer long and we would eat it all winter. One of the first things in the spring was rhubarb and she would make great pie. She used lard in the crust . . . tasted so good.

Crust: (My Swiss grandmother's crust recipe)

Mix 1 teaspoon salt in 2 cups of flour – blend in ⅔ cup lard with a pastry blender – add ¼ cup ice cold water. Using hands mix together until forms a ball, cut in half, form into circle, and roll out (makes two crusts).

Filling

    3 eggs
    3 tablespoons milk
    1 or 2 cups sugar (less is better!)
    ¼ cup flour
    ¾ teaspoon cinnamon
    4 cups cut-up rhubarb

Heat oven to 400 degrees. Beat eggs slightly; add milk. Mix sugar, flour and cinnamon; stir in. Mix in rhubarb (or other fruit). Pour into 9-inch pastry-lined pie pan. Dot with butter. Cover with a lattice top. Bake 50 to 60 minutes, until nicely browned.

Dad's Frittata.

Oftentimes dad would cook breakfast on Sundays. He liked to go out to the garden and pick whatever was ready, sauté it in butter, stir in some beaten eggs, cook that, cover it all with cheese on top, cover the frying pan and wait for the cheese to melt – Mom called it "Dad's frittata."

In five years I'll still be here, probably farming by myself. My dad will probably be lecturing full-time. Whatever comes along. *[He shrugs and smiles.]* I might be milking a couple less cows. Once we pay our debt off. I'll graze them more, probably have extra land to graze them on. I'll still have the beef cattle and pigs, maybe a few more beef cattle, few more pigs.

I've known since I was little what the animals are for. I will take the animals to slaughter but I won't be the one to do it. Nope, not me.

A couple of years ago, my dad and I started building my house. It's not quite finished. Have to finish the basement, the decks. When it's finished it'll be a couple thousand square feet. It's logs and lots of wood inside. Wood floor. One loft bedroom. We dug a pond out back. There's pasture on it. It's called Red Hill Farm. I think it's a good place.

Ryan Hewson

Taliesin Architectural School ■ Taliesin Organic Garden ■ Spring Green, WI ■ www.taliesin.edu, www.taliesinpreservation.org

JUNE ■ *The air is thick with the hum of bees and the purr of tractors. Before going back to Taliesin, I drive down the road to a small chapel and cemetery where all of the Lloyd-Joneses are buried. There are stone benches, tall grasses and an apple tree. Among the older stones stand contemporary head-stones with detailed Wright design. So peaceful. I pull food I've gotten at Local Choice out of my backpack: cheese, lettuce and a tomato. Luna and I share a picnic.*

An hour later I meet Ryan Hewson at the Taliesin garden. Ryan, a student in his last year of the master's program at Taliesin, has run the garden for the last three years.

Ryan: I joined Americorps out of college, and was on my way to California when I stopped here and got excited about the program.

I'm interested in the idea of community, of hands-on learning the principles of Frank Lloyd Wright, of being able to use his archives.

We all get involved in the weekly chores like cleaning, taking out the trash, doing the dishes. Each of us also has a job that is with us all season. Many of us work in the gardens. We were surprised at how much work it needed. We decided to put some effort into it. A number of people were recruited to help. Jeremy Lynch, Andrew Kerr and the Zimmers all kind of shepherded us along. Our first year was a little rocky.

The second year we did really well, though, ending up with about six hundred pounds of vegetables. We also place cut flowers around here to continue the tradition of appreciating beauty, whether in a floor plan or a flower vase.

In all the gardens we have to be aware that tourists can see them from almost every direction, so we rotate the field strips. Usually Nicholas Zimmer comes in to plant the cover crop. Nicholas takes care of all the fields here organically. Having the Zimmers' help is special, and really supports our mission. They are so generous with us.

Community Gardening Day is Wednesday. Usually we get about four to five people, and a mixture of apprentices and senior fellowship members. I try to get people excited about coming out. I try to make it accessible, but seven A.M. is not for everybody. It's a great place to cure frustration, or if you like to weed, or if you want some mustard greens in your salad, or if you just want to pick some flowers.

We get our seeds from various places. People in

the area give us some, and we get some from John-ny's Seeds. We place our order in December, and they actually donate.

I suggest they check out Baker Creek Heirloom Seed Catalogue and their quarterly magazine, Heir-loom Gardener out of Missouri.

It's a three-year program for a master's. We had a gentleman from Vietnam who came over specifi-cally to study sustainability.

A few years ago, during a lightning storm, the huge oak that had provided shade for our Tea Circle blew down. The Tea Circle is another Taliesin tradi-tion. Used to be all the students would gather at 10:30 every morning for tea. Now we do it just Wednesdays at 4:30. Another little change.

I feel really comfortable here. But I enjoy the desert, too. Summers here; winters in Arizona, where we live out in these shelters that we design and I wake up and see the McDowell Mountains

and saguaro cactuses. I probably have a better view than people in Scottsdale who paid $17 million for theirs. To me, this smaller community here in Spring Green is more artistic, I think. I graduate the end of September. We all leave in September, but I will stay until October to make sure the garden is fully checked out.

We drive up the road and then wander into the woods to see the shelter Ryan is building as part of the program. It's in the middle of a cluster of sugar maples, locust and cherry trees.

Here's the ramp that gets you out on ground level, once I refill some of this dirt here that came out when I dug the foundation. This will be the walkway, then there's another ramp that goes this way. You're standing in my bedroom. I will sleep over there and look out over this view, kind of like floating above the forest floor. Greenhouse roofing material. Red oak, sustainably harvested for the

RECIPES ■ Ryan Hewson

Zippy Radish Salad

1 cup sliced radishes
¼ cup cubed Swiss cheese
1 green onion, sliced
1½ teaspoons tarragon vinegar
¼ teaspoon minced garlic
¼ teaspoon Dijon mustard
⅛ teaspoon salt
Dash pepper
4 teaspoons olive oil
Leaf lettuce, optional

In a bowl, combine the radishes, cheese and onion. In a small bowl, combine the vinegar, garlic, mustard, salt and pepper; whisk in oil until smooth. Pour over radish mixture and toss to coat. Chill until serving. Serve on a bed of lettuce if desired. Serves 2.

Sunny Summer Squash Soup

When I made this, I tasted it before adding the optional ingredients and was ready to stop there--it was simple and delicious. But I couldn't resist trying to make it a little creamier and richer, so I added the nutritional yeast and tahini (plus turmeric for color). I'll leave it up to you to decide which way you like it best.

1 large onion, chopped
3 cloves garlic, minced
1 small hot pepper, seeds removed and chopped
2 ribs celery, strings removed and chopped
2 medium (12 to 14 ounces) gold potatoes, peeled and
    cut into small dice
1½ pounds small yellow squash (or young zucchini),
    chopped
1 pinch white pepper

4 cups vegetable broth
1 teaspoon oregano
½ teaspoon turmeric (optional)
2 tablespoons nutritional yeast (optional)
1 tablespoon tahini (optional)
Salt and white pepper, to taste (optional)
Garnish: slivers of red bell pepper

Heat a large non-stick or enamel-coated pot over medium-high heat. Add the onion, reduce the heat to medium, and cover, stirring every minute or so until it begins to brown, about 5 minutes (add a little water if it starts to stick). Add the garlic and hot pepper and cook for another minute.

Add all remaining ingredients except the optional ones. Cover and cook until the potatoes are completely tender (they will mash if lightly pressed with a spoon), about 25 to 40 minutes.

Remove half of the soup and put it into a blender (I like this soup blended smoother than my hand blender can get it) and puree at high speed until completely smooth. (Be careful – hot liquids can erupt from your blender; I always remove the center cup from the lid and cover the opening with a kitchen towel.) Once it's blended, pour the soup into another pot. Add the remaining soup to the blender, along with any optional ingredients you choose to use, and blend well. Add to the other half of the soup, and simmer for about 5 minutes. Ladle into bowls, garnish with slices of red bell pepper, and serve. Makes 4 servings.

Dad's Ratatouille

Preparation time: 1 hour and 30 minutes, minimum.

1 pound yellow onions, chopped
3 cloves garlic, crushed
1 pound zucchini, chopped

walls. I wanted to be able to catch the breezes. I couldn't live in it year round. I really love doing this, love learning how to weld. I wish I hadn't used so much steel, but it's a process of learning and knowing.

In five years, I hope that I'll either be in a small firm with a partner or here, teaching. I see myself in an architectural setting that allows me to be self-directed. I'm really interested in working in kind of a collaborative environment.

1 pound yellow squash, chopped

Bell peppers with seeds removed, chopped into
½-inch square pieces:

    1 pound green bell peppers

    ½ pound red bell peppers

    ½ pound yellow bell peppers

1 pound eggplant, ½-inch cubes

1 pound fresh ripe tomatoes

¼ cup olive oil

Salt to taste

2 sprigs thyme

1 bay leaf

1 sprig rosemary

½ cup vegetable stock (or thin tomato juice)

Fresh ground pepper to taste

Preheat oven to 400 degrees.

Using a large oven-proof pan over medium-high heat, saute onions in olive oil until they begin to soften, about 5 minutes. Add garlic and reduce heat to low.

While the onions and garlic are cooking over low heat, put 2 tablespoons of olive oil in another frying pan over high heat. As soon as oil starts to smoke, quickly add enough zucchini cubes all at once to cover the bottom of the pan. Keep on cooking over high heat, stirring, until zucchini is lightly browned on all sides. Remove zucchini cubes, and add them to pan with the onions.

Repeat process until all of the zucchini cubes have been cooked. Do the same with the yellow squash. Make sure to add a little olive oil between each new batch. Continue with the bell peppers, then the eggplant cubes, adding the browned vegetables to the onion pan as soon as they are cooked.

When all the vegetables (except the tomatoes) are browned and in the pan with the onions, increase the heat to high and stir, making sure they don't stick to the bottom of the pan. Add salt to taste, thyme, bay leaf and rosemary, the vegetable stock, and stir well. Place in oven for one hour.

Boil water in a saucepan on stove. Remove stems from tomatoes, and crisscross the bottoms with a knife. Plunge into boiling water for a minute or two, until skin starts to fall away. Rinse in cold water and remove skin. Cut tomatoes in half lengthwise, remove seeds, chop coarsely, set aside.

After the vegetables have been in the oven for an hour, remove from oven, drain vegetables in a colander set over a bowl. Clean browned bits (if any) off bottom of pan with a paper towel. Return any liquid to the pan and reduce to a thick glaze over medium-high heat. Keep on adding juices to the pan as they run out of the vegetables into the bowl.

When all the juices have been reduced, return vegetables to the heavy pan. At this point the ratatouille should be moist and shiny, with very little liquid. Turn heat off. Add the chopped tomatoes and cover. If serving as a warm side dish, let the ratatouille stand for 10 minutes, just enough to cook the tomatoes. The ratatouille can be served at room temperature or refrigerated and reheated the next day.

When ready to serve, remove the bay leaf, and season to taste with salt and pepper. Serves 8.

E. Krauty's Apple Crisp

Pare and slice apples to fill an oblong cake pan ¾ full. Mix 1 cup white sugar and 1 teaspoon cinnamon and sprinkle over apples.

Cream together 1cup of brown sugar, 1 cup of flour, ¼ pound of butter, spread over apples.

Bake at 350 degrees for 45 minutes. Serves 8.

A very close friend and I are working on three architectural projects. We've opened a temporary studio called Red Squared. We only have the space until September. We plan on moving to Denver to form an architectural partnership.

Rumored news from Otter Creek Organic Farms: Gary Zimmer is setting up a foundation to work all the land at Taliesin, including the flower gardens. Soon the fields will be filled with Otter Creek's dairy cows, beef cattle, pigs, perhaps even some sheep and chickens. They will demonstrate the best organic sustainable systems and teach methods for mineralized healthy soils. They intend to have large-scale production at Talieson, with major marketing in the local community.

That afternoon I have a meal in another small town, Mazomanie, down the road from Spring Green. Since 1992 The Old Feed Mill has been owned by the Viste Family. They grind their own flour and make their own fresh wheat and rye bread. A couple of years ago, six-foot, seven-inch son Patrick came on board, and his focus is serving as much local food as possible. "Sure, I've heard of Otter Creek Organic Farm and Local Choice." He already gets Otter Creek bratwurst and other meats from Black Earth, a local butcher and meat locker.

A couple of hours later, as I drive along a back road in the heart of the lower Wisconsin State Riverway, I spot a sign that reads Muscoda: Wisconsin's Morel Capital. *What wouldn't I do for a morel? Morels are spring mushrooms that melt in your mouth. When I can find them I sauté them in butter, shallots, and a summer savory or parsley. For me, morels and rhubarb mean spring is here. I turn in and park near six trucks, each one of them piled high with brown paper bags full of luscious morel mushrooms. They are huge! A delicate creamy beige, some of them with a bulb two inches in size. They say that if I keep them in the brown bag in a cool spot, they will probably last two days, about the distance to Denver. I take three pounds.*

Ashley Lee Martin
The White Earth Reservation ■ Ogema Pine Point, Minnesota ■ www.nativeharvest.com

From La Crosse, Wisconsin, up through Minneapolis, neatly partitioned farms punctuate the highway. I stop for lunch in Minneapolis and am reminded of the summer trips my sister and I took with our mother to visit our grandmother in Salt Lake City, Utah. I remember the creamy tea we had here while we waited to re-board.

Driving northwest of Minneapolis the land becomes less green, less lush, and a whole lot flatter. Lake after lake appears and finally I stop to give Luna a swim in one of them, Otter River Lake. I hear one loon call to another, with its sweet, lonely cry.

I enter the White Earth Reservation, 1,300 square miles of prairie, where maple-basswood forest and boreal pine forest all intersect. It's named the White Earth Reservation, or Gahwahbahnikag, for the white clay that underlies part of it. It is also the land of rice: wild rice.

I call the offices of the reservation, and someone directs me to a young woman involved in the White Earth Land Recovery Project, who works at a small store and restaurant called Native Harvest. An hour later I pull up in front of a decorative, colorful teepee, and a young Native woman in a blue cotton dress greets me at the door, shaking my hand gently, averting her eyes. This is the Native adaptation to the in-your-face greeting and firm handshake my father taught me as a child.

Ashley Lee Martin: When I was very young I would go out with my grandparents on Rice Lake. Ricing is a community event; we don't do it just for the

White Earth Land Recovery

Native Harvest

MISSION:
To facilitate the recovery of the original land base
of the White Earth Indian Reservation,
while preserving and restoring traditional practices
of sound land stewardship, language fluency,
community development, and strengthening
our spiritual and cultural heritage.

money. It is an old tradition, a way of life for us.

My grandmother was always in the front of the canoe, scrunched on her knees. Then me in the middle, my grandfather pushing the canoe offshore, and then jumping in the boat behind us. My grandfather would pole toward the wild rice beds; he was at least a head taller than the stalks of rice. My grandmother would use a stick to bring the stalks over her lap and tap them with a smaller stick. The rice would fall off onto the bottom of the canoe. I can still hear the sound. On a good day they brought in hundreds of pounds of rice.

I grew up with four brothers and two sisters. I went to tribal school from kindergarten through the ninth grade, then public school from there. I also did PSEO (Post Secondary Enrollment Options) study at the local tech school. I've always liked school and reading, mostly fiction. People seem to give me books or I go to the library.

My mom still lives on Rice Lake.

Manoominikewag is the Chippewa-Ojibwe word for harvesting rice during the wild rice moon. Manoomin is the word for rice, the great gift from the creator.

Waubunanaangikwe, my ceremonial name, means "Morning Star Woman." It was given to me when I was seven years old by one of my mother's good friends. In the custom of my tribe, I can have up to four names, each one given at a time in my life of great growth or change. I feel like I am almost ready to choose someone to give me a new name.

Late December of last year, I started working here in the store. It is tribal-owned, with foods grown and harvested on the White Earth Indian Reservation according to our traditions. We have a cookbook that weaves together our language and our foods, Jiibaakweda Gimiijiminaan: "Let's Cook Our Foods." I earn eight dollars an hour clearing the tables, cooking, serving and just keeping the store together. I work Friday and Saturdays and I'm on call Sundays from eight A.M. to five P.M. I am really learning how to cook simple foods using our wild rice and our traditional recipes. They use things like squash and corn and maple syrup.

My daughter, born August 7, 2006, is named Waasamoan, which means "Lightning." She will probably be a little revolutionary. Her astrological chart has a lot of the same signs Fidel Castro has in his chart. My friend Wasey (Winona LaDuke's daughter) has a little boy my daughter's age. That's really fun for us.

When I think about who I would like to have give me my next name, I think about Winona. She knows me. She knows the traditions of our culture for sure. She is inspiring. She's a fine teacher for us. I am working with her to learn about our culture and traditions.

When I am working here in the store, Anthony, Waasamoan's dad, looks after her. In the spring I'm going to go to "the cities" to the University of Minnesota, to the college of liberal arts. I'll take Waasamoan with me. There's daycare. I want to

study political and environmental science. I want to change things on the reservation. I want to be off the grid using completely renewable energy. I want my kids and all the other kids here to have something else to do besides get into trouble. I want to be able to steer them toward good food like wild rice, corn, beans, squash and maple syrup. In the old days when we were eating that food, there was no record of diabetes. Now it's the second most common diagnosis for Native Americans. Kids drink so much soda, and eat so much candy, store bought bread, canned vegetables and pastries. I want to learn about indigenous foods. I want to eat seasonally like my grandparents did.

Having a child has completely changed the way I feel. I want my daughter to have the benefits of our culture and all of our traditions. We learn that food is medicine. The traditional practice of harvesting wild rice remains really important to our commu-

nity. We are working hard to continue to honor and protect our wild rice stands from fertilizers and herbicides.

One of the many things I have learned from working with Winona is that after Minnesota began growing paddy wild rice in 1968, it increased the yield of all wild rice to about four million pounds. That increased production allowed larger corporations like Uncle Ben's, Green Giant and General Foods to take advantage of those large amounts. Paddy rice is definitely not the same rice as wild lake rice. By 1980 the University of Minnesota had developed and cultivated a domesticated version of wild rice, which pretty much killed off indigenous varieties. By the middle of the '80s, 95 percent of the wild rice harvested was this cultivated paddy-grown version. When the huge amounts of paddy rice hit the market, the price of all wild rice fell, and knocked the Native rice right out of the market.

RECIPES ■ Ashley Lee Martin

Wild Rice Company Casserole

2 cups Native Harvest wild rice
6 cups water
2 pounds ground beef or buffalo
1 pound fresh mushrooms, sliced
½ cup celery, chopped
1 cup onion, chopped
½ cup butter
¼ cup black olives, sliced
¼ cup soy sauce
2 cups sour cream
2 teaspoons salt
¼ teaspoon pepper
¼ cup almonds, slivered
½ cup water chestnuts, sliced
Parsley sprigs (garnish)

Prepare wild rice according to basic directions and set aside. Brown the ground beef or buffalo and set aside. Sauté mushrooms, celery, and onion in butter for 5 minutes. Combine soy sauce, sour cream, salt and pepper. Add cooked wild rice, meat, mushroom mixture, water chestnuts, and olives. Add almonds, saving some for garnish. Place mixture in a lightly greased 3 quart casserole. Bake at 350 degrees for 1 hour uncovered. Add water if needed and season to taste. Stir several times. Garnish with reserved almonds and parsley. Serves 4.

Shaggy Mane Pie

4 cups large fresh shaggy mane mushrooms, caps only
4 cups fine cornmeal
1 cup cattail flour
2 tablespoons chopped fresh chives
¼ cup nut oil
4 eggs, beaten

Cut the mushroom caps into ½-inch slices, place in a pot, and almost cover with water. Bring to a boil and simmer, covered, for 10 minutes. Remove from heat and let cool in its broth. Mix together the cornmeal, cattail flour, and chives. Grease a glass baking dish or crock with some of the nut oil and alternate layering the mushrooms with the flour mixture. Cover with the eggs, drizzle the remaining nut oil over the top, and bake in a preheated 375 degree oven until set, about 40 minutes. Serves 4.

Chicken Wild Rice Soup (Manoomin Baaka'akwe Naboob)

1½ cups Native Harvest wild rice
1 large onion, diced
5 carrots, thinly sliced
2 stalks celery, diced
1 green pepper, diced
1 whole stewing chicken or chicken pieces
6 cups water
Garlic
Basil
Dill
Mustard

Mix together wild rice, onion, carrots, celery, pepper and water. Pour ingredients into stew pot with chicken on top and cook for 1 hour on stove. Turn off heat, remove chicken and carefully de-bone. Return chicken to pot, then add salt and pepper to taste, sautéed garlic, fresh basil, dill and Dijon mustard according to tastes and cook until tender. Serves 6.

Chokecherry Pudding (Asasawemin Waashkobang)

2 cups fresh, frozen, or dried chokecherries
2 to 4 cups water
Honey to taste
¼ cup flour or 2 tablespoons cornstarch or arrowroot

In a saucepan, combine chokecherries, and water to cover. Cook, stirring, over medium heat until cherries soften and render their juice. Sweeten with honey to taste. In a small bowl, combine flour and enough water to make a thin creamy mixture. Gradually stir flour into fruit mixture and simmer until thickened. Strain out seeds, if desired.

Those ricers who know about rice and are part of the White Earth Tribal council not only worry about the money, but also about the crossbreeding of the hybrid cultivated rice with the lake rice, about the impact those genetic strains will have on the lake rice. What we all worry about is the lake rice disappearing all together.

What we do here, we do with all the old equipment, the Red Clipper fanning mill, a handmade thrasher, parching drums and an old gravity table. I want my children to grow up knowing this way of life. This rice tastes much different from other rice. As Winona LaDuke says, "It tastes like a lake."

Ashley now has a second child, a son named *Aandegoons, which means "Little Crow" in Anishinaabegmowin. Her daughter, Waasamoan, will be starting Head Start in the Fall.*

Ashley is still working for the White Earth Land Recovery Project. She is co-coordinator of their Farm-to-School Program initiative, which works with the Pine Point Elementary School to provide fresh and local food for the school lunch and breakfast program. Ashley plans to return to school in the fall semester of 2010. She says her understanding and respect for fresh, local food has grown exponentially and that she wants to continue working in the food and environmental justice field during and after school.

The next day I arrive at Denver's Hotel Monaco with my morel mushrooms in hand. After I park the car and settle Luna in the room, I take them down to the chef to begin my bargaining. I offer him whatever is left over after he makes my meal. He excitedly agrees, "Dinner at seven P.M. First course with the mushrooms sautéed on their own, then a pasta dish, and then, whatever you order for a main, I'll incorporate the mushrooms." It is a splendid meal. At Kimpton Hotels (www.kimptonhotels.com) the food is mostly local and organic, they are dog friendly and they are earth friendly. Every person who works at the Kimpton Hotels and restaurants across the country is part of an effort to reduce impact on the environment. Their cleaning supplies are environmentally friendly. Paperwork is printed on recycled paper using soy-based ink. Coffee is organic, shade grown or fair trade. There is recycling of all glass, bottles, paper and cardboard. Every room makes use of energy efficient lighting, and water conservation.

Jennifer Craig
Durango Compost Company ■ Durango, Colorado ■ www.durangocompost.com

SECOND SUMMER ■ *By the time I arrive in Durango, all over the county people have started their gardens. For fertilizer, more and more gardeners are using manure from local farm animals. In New York City, some get their compost from the Bronx Zoo or even the Central Park Zoo. In New Orleans, many get their compost from nearby chicken farms. According to Jennifer Craig, co-owner of Durango Compost Company, the latest and greatest in compost comes from slimy, squirmy red wiggler worms. Jennifer is a woman who really loves her worms and her dirt. Of course, worm poop is nothing new. Darwin wrote a book about worms and their benefit to the soil.*

But here's the poop on worm dirt . . .

Jennifer: I grew up in Kutztown, PA. It was just countryside; our area didn't even have a name. I went to Brandywine Heights High School. I grew up with Mennonites all around; in fact, a Mennonite farm was right across the street from my mom's house. My dad was a mushroom farmer — cinderblock farms. For these particular mushroom houses, you put partially composted horse manure in the beds, and then seed the beds with the mushroom spores. Once you harvest a couple of crops you can take the mushroom manure out. I used to sell the mushrooms at the farmers market with my dad. He'd always weigh out a pound of mushrooms for a customer, then throw in another handful for good measure. That's how I like to operate my business.

My grandfather worked in the steel mills in Pittsburgh but in his spare time he had this greenhouse, so there's lots of agriculture and horticulture in the family. One of my uncles was a professor at Penn State in horticulture. He developed a unique geranium named Nittany Lion Red. Back then, I had two brothers. I have three now. My dad used to tell this story about how we had this big garden out back and everybody in the family would be in the garden, and I'd go back inside and lock the door and sit on the countertop eating sugar and bouillon cubes.

I studied Russian and Spanish in college at Penn State, graduated with a degree in Liberal Arts with a minor in International Agriculture. As part of that I did an internship at Rodale Institute, an internationally recognized organic farm and research center in Kutztown. After I graduated they asked me if I wanted to represent them at the 1998 International Flower and Garden Festival at Epcot in Disneyworld. For six weeks, three of us gave twenty-minute presentations throughout the day,

mostly about organic agriculture, although we were not allowed to use the term "organic." It was a Disney thing. They didn't want to offend anybody, so we had to work our way around it. A small part of the presentation was about worm composting, and that's really how I got started. I even fumbled my way through the presentation in Spanish for a South American soccer team. *Gusano* is earthworm in Spanish.

A few months later, I moved into an Ashram in upstate New York where I lived for six years. From there I moved to Berkeley for a year and a half, and finally I moved to Durango in 2006. I worked at the Durango public library, then I taught Spanish for part of the 2007–08 school year. Meanwhile I was worm composting as a hobby. In 2006, my boyfriend at the time built me a big wooden worm composter. Then I started composting big-time. By the end of the first year I had hundreds and hundreds of pounds of worm castings. I wondered

what do to with it all, and decided to sell it at the farmers market.

Initially I operated as Rocky Mountain Worm Dirt. Then Tim Wheeler, owner of Durango Coffee Company, met me at the market and asked if I wanted to turn my hobby into a business. We became partners in Durango Compost Company, and began experimenting with composting the coffee grounds from his shop. It's been a real learning process because there is no school for worm composting, and the big worm farmers in the country don't share information freely. It's like any other business; they don't want to give the results of trial and error because they don't want competition.

For worm farms (vermiculture), it's more about selling the worms because the profit margin on worms is great. On the compost facility side (vermicomposting), it's not very high at all. Some worm farms are not composting at all, but actually buying worm feed. Even though Durango Compost

Company will sell worms, our focus is on composting food waste, not raising worms.

Fishermen use red wiggler worms to bait hooks. They are like tireless eating machines used in vermicomposting — the practice of caring for worms in order to harvest their "castings" for use as a fertilizer and soil amendment. It's also the easiest way to deal with organic waste. I sell the castings at the farmers market. They have virtually no smell, unless you count a fresh earthy whiff of espresso.

If you want to compost kitchen waste and generate castings, there are several ways to go about it. The book *Worms Eat My Garbage* is a great resource, and even includes instructions for a homemade worm-composting bin. I sell a starter kit that includes a commercially available stacking worm composter (Can O Worms), a pound of worms and a how-to book. My customers will be the first to tell you that I am always available for questions, and sometimes even for house calls and worm checkups. Getting the bin going is a critical time, and too many people have called me too late. The best locations for the bin are in a basement, under the kitchen sink or in a heated garage. Inside the bins, the worms need shredded paper or cardboard bedding that must be kept as moist as a wrung-out sponge — not dripping.

The most common problem people have is that they don't feed their worms enough. Everyone is surprised at how much worms eat. They can consume their own weight in organic waste every day. Some people will take all their biodegradable kitchen scraps — vegetables and fruit, coffee grounds, tea bags and other non-animal waste, even egg shells — and blend them. Some even have a food processor dedicated strictly to food scraps for their worms. Worms will consume processed food much faster than whole pieces. I put the fruit and vegetable pulp from my juicer straight into the worm box.

In the box you need a mix of the greens and the browns, or nitrogen food and carbon bedding. Fruit and vegetable scraps are an example of the high-nitrogen "greens." Wood and paper products are the carbon-rich "browns," which provide carbon, an energy source for the entire ecosystem in the worm bin. I use shredded cardboard, shredded newspaper and shredded office paper as carbon-rich bedding for the worms. You could also use dead leaves, old straw or well-composted manure. Then you put in the worms. A box with three square feet of surface area can support up to three pounds of worms — about three thousand red wigglers. But you only need to start with one pound because they double their population every three months. They self-regulate their population based on food and space constraints.

When you water the box, its best to use a mister so you don't compact the materials. If you're using tap water, set it out overnight so the chlorine gas is out of the water. Chlorine kills the microorganisms, such as bacteria and mold, which are the workhorses of the compost process.

The bin can stay unattended for up to three weeks.

Earthworm droppings are the castings, which are the end-product of the earthworms' digestive process. The castings are full of live microorganisms, plant growth hormones and micronutrients. I always get the question, "How will I know when it's time to compost?" The rule of thumb is after about two to three months there will be enough castings, so you can start harvesting the compost.

When harvesting a homemade box, you will need to push all the material currently in the box to one side. Add fresh bedding to the empty side. Feed and water this side only. The worms will finish up on the old side and then will move over to the new side. After about a month, the compost on the old side will be ready to harvest, with only a few remaining worms to sort out.

Collecting the finished compost from a tray system is easy. You just take out the bottom tray, use the compost and put the empty tray on top. The worms work their way up through the trays, so by the time the compost is ready in the bottom, the worms will be working on the food and paper in

the middle and top trays. Depending on what you want to use the compost for, you may want to pick out any unfinished paper products and add them back into the bin. If you plan on tilling the compost into a garden, it's fine to leave in the bits of partially decomposed material.

There are all kinds of things you can do with the compost from the worm box:

Vermicompost (unscreened): Use vermicompost in addition to traditional compost to give your garden a boost of microbial life, micronutrients, plant growth hormones and hums. Also, use a generous amount before laying sod or reseeding the lawn.

Coarsely screened castings: Spread sparingly on lawns and in gardens. Make sure to water immediately after spreading castings.

Finely screened castings: Sprinkle directly around the base of houseplants and other potted plants. Castings can be used with seedlings and transplants to encourage root growth and reduce transplant shock.

Castings solution: Soak three tablespoons of vermicompost, or screened castings, or two casting tea bags (I put the screened castings in a small paper sack the size of a tea bag) in one quart of tepid dechlorinated water for twelve to twenty-four hours. (Strain if you're not using a tea bag.) Using a spray bottle, I apply the solution directly onto the foliage of house plants, including hydroponically grown plants. You can also water as usual using the castings solution instead of plain water. Using a garden sprayer, apply the solution to lawns, vegetable and flower

RECIPES ■ Jennifer Craig

Breakfast: Irish oatmeal with dried fruit and nuts

⅓ cup Irish oatmeal
Small handful dried fruit
Small handful favorite nuts (mine are almonds and
    walnuts)
1 tablespoon flaxseed oil

Put at least ⅔ cup water in a small pot and bring to a boil. Add dried fruit and nuts. Let boil for a couple minutes. Add oatmeal and stir. Turn heat to lowest setting and simmer covered for about 5 minutes. Check and stir often to avoid sticking and burning on the bottom. When the fruit, nuts and oats are soft and plump, the cereal is done. I sometimes add water during the simmering process if the oatmeal gets too thick. I don't add sweetener because the dried fruit infuses the cereal with sweetness, so I just add a spoonful of flaxseed oil. Yum!

Lunch: Leftover Grilled Chicken Wrap (No, I'm not a vegetarian)

1 large fresh tortilla
½ grilled chicken breast (or garlic hummus, depending on
    what's in the fridge)
Guacamole
Lettuce (and any other veggie like cucumbers and sprouts)

Lay tortilla on a plate. Spread guacamole down the center. Add sliced chicken and lettuce. Roll it up and enjoy. If I use hummus instead of chicken, I put lettuce on top of the guacamole and the hummus on top of the lettuce. It's not logical, but I don't want to mix the guacamole and hummus before I eat them. Lots of other vegetables could be added, like sprouts or spinach. I just use what I have on hand at the time.

Dinner: Honey-Mustard Tofu with Steamed Mixed Greens

1 block of firm tofu
1 tablespoons sesame oil
Mustard (I use yellow mustard)
Agave syrup (instead of honey. I've heard that honey
    shouldn't be cooked)
Mixed greens (spinach, chard, beet greens, radish greens,
    kale)
Ume vinegar (pickled plum vinegar)

Cut tofu into ½-inch squares. Place squares into a hot frying pan with water. Add sesame oil and cover. This avoids the

gardens, landscape plants, fruit trees and any other plant you would like to watch flourish.

The compost is good for up to two years. After that it becomes less potent, as the beneficial soil organisms either die or go dormant.

The scope of my business is three-fold. First, I sell the compost and the kits at the farmers market. I educate and answer questions. I also work with the local school district on various educational and functional worm composting projects. I've presented at garden clubs, festivals and the local college. I also work with the Durango Discovery Museum.

Second, I work with businesses that want to compost their organic waste, such as the Durango Coffee Company, as well as other restaurants and breweries. We set up a worm compost system at their location to see if the worms will consume their product.

And third is consulting for people who want to produce their own compost, including a green housing development that eventually wants to have a site to provide compost for their proposed fourteen plus acres of vegetable gardens.

The City of Durango is also looking at establishing a municipal composting program. In five years time I see myself involved in a commercial compost facility. In Boulder they actually have compost splattering that happens when wet tofu is added to hot oil. Uncover when water is simmering. Add mustard and agave to taste. Honestly, I generally don't measure anything unless I'm baking. Cook the liquid down until it is a thick sauce covering the tofu. This can be served with rice, but I often don't bother.

I wash the greens before I steam them, but if I'm cooking for myself I generally don't cut them down to bite size.

After the greens are plated I sprinkle on a very small amount of Ume vinegar.

Condiment: Fried worm bits (instead of bacon bits)

I have not made these, but a customer related a story to me about winning the Kansas State worm recipe contest many, many years ago. She made a very normal sounding gourmet soup and topped it with fried worm bits. She was very excited reminiscing about this cooking contest and her elderly father seemed quite proud.

This is how she described the cooking process:

Heat up olive oil in a pan and sauté garlic. Add worms (I assume they were alive but rinsed and patted dry. Fry until worms are very crisp. Let them cool, then crumble into small pieces like bacon bits. (I would add salt and pepper personally, I can't remember if she did or not.)

Dessert: S'mores

Graham crackers
Toasted Marshmallows
DarkChocolate (like 60 to 70 percent cacao dark)

I think most people know how to make s'mores. The difference here is the dark chocolate. It balances out the sweetness of the marshmallows. Otherwise I just skip the chocolate completely.

Castings Tea (for plants only)

1 quart room temperature de-chlorinated water (set tap water out overnight to outgas the chlorine)
1 cup finely screened worm castings
1 tablespoon kelp meal (for micro-nutrients)

Put ingredients in a used soda or water bottle. Shake well. Take cap off and let steep for at least 24 hours. Shake every so often to get oxygen into the liquid. This helps the microorganisms to multiply. Strain the castings tea with cheese cloth or window screen.

Dilute a cup of concentrate in a gallon of de-chlorinated water. Water as usual or put liquid in a spray bottle or hose-end garden sprayer and drench leaves and soil.

pickup — you put out your compost on the curb and it's picked up. In Seattle and San Francisco they have curbside pickup. The city of New York has one for backyard waste but nothing for food, yet.

Amazing thing to be able to reuse your food. And you can do this even in an apartment in the city. Friends of mine keep their worm bin under the bed,

and they don't get roaches, gnats or even smell. The trick is to keep those little wrigglers happy by feeding them appropriately and watering them. I actually freeze my compost and then take it to the farmers market, where they have barrels you can dump it in.

broken up with my live-in boyfriend, and Blake made one phone call and found me a new house. I thought, Hey, Blake really knows how to make things happen! *[Laughs]*

Blake: Then we cooked together for this reality TV show. It was brutally hard — no sleeping, we worked night and day, but our relationship was really easy. Not that much later, the opportunity came along to open a restaurant. We'd both been through Boulder and liked it. The building was empty; the prior business had gone bankrupt. We had zero money, but they let us open without paying rent for a year. The timing was perfect.

Jen: We cleaned the place up, salvaging what we could. They loaned us five grand to buy groceries, and we were able to pay them back within a couple of months.

Blake: Actually, it was three grand. We are on the grounds of the Boulder Mountain Lodge, owned by a wonderful man named Dave Mock. The Lodge is generally full, which helps us, and its good for the lodge to have a restaurant next door.

When Jen and I first started talking about a restaurant based on our shared principles and philosophies, including organics — everyone thought it was ridiculous, that we'd never be able to afford it or pull it off in this tiny Mormon town in the middle of nowhere. *[There is no cell phone reception, no ATM, no fast food.]*

The thing that we agreed on from the beginning was that if we were going to do this, the only way to conduct ourselves was to create a restaurant following the Buddhist philosophy of right livelihood, always striving for a greater and greater degree of sustainability in everything we cooked and how we lived. We knew we were quite different from most everyone we met in town, but we both agreed that we had to strike a balance without giving up who we really were.

Jen: We started by just being nice.

Blake steps away to clear to a customer's breakfast dishes and bring another round of their homemade bread and apricot jam. Much later, an older man with a walking stick comes in and announces he'd like lunch. Jen tells him that they don't serve lunch, just breakfast and dinner. He says that he's come all the way from Switzerland. Jen jumps up and after showing him to a table, says, "We'll find you something. It won't be fancy, but . . . it'll be lunch."

Blake: In 2000, local laws prevented us from serving any kind of alcohol. We knew that in order to have a profitable business, a liquor license was crucial. At our second council meeting, shortly after we opened, the alcohol permit issue came up. We explained our position in a quiet, easy way. We said that in order for us to succeed economically, we really needed one. The next day one of the council members stopped by the restaurant to say that nobody had ever presented the alcohol thing to

them in terms of the economics, so they were looking at the issue differently.

We continued to cook delicious, fresh-picked local foods and to serve rosemary limeade or herbal sun tea while we waited. Finally, after two years, the church bishop said it was time for the town to vote on the liquor license issue. Now we had to apply at the state level, which meant stacks of paperwork, fingerprinting, an FBI background check and a presentation before the Utah Department of Alcohol and Beverage Control board in Salt Lake City. We did it all, and were finally granted the first full liquor license in the history of the town.

Jen: We decided to serve only beer and wine in an effort to go halfway with the town, which didn't want a bar scene. We sell regional beer and wine.

Blake: Soon we saw that there was a need to hire more staff than the local population could provide. That meant we needed a place for staff to live. So we bought a house with eight bedrooms, which we rent to staff for a subsidized amount that helps us cover our mortgage. We got a grant from Morgan Stanley Bank for the creation of affordable workforce housing.

We provide alternative modalities and healers: an acupuncturist, a great Rolfer who works on the staff, and staff members who teach yoga. The only way a restaurant like this can work — since we all basically live together — is if people are willing to be open and not to project onto each other. We have a "harmony at all costs" rule, and a Buddhist therapist who does workshops with the staff.

Jen: For example, if one of the staff thinks I'm a jerk because I've told them that the soup is too salty, then we have a kind of go-around 'til he/she realizes that I'm not a jerk, that the soup really is too salty. I'm not saying they're a bad person. And the soup is made again.

When we first started this process, scores of people were furious at us. They had come to Boulder to change their urban lives into easier, more relaxed lives. Because of the intensity of the work environment, a lot of stuff comes up for people. And if

they're not really willing to learn new ways of dealing with things, they sort of spontaneously combust.

I glance over my shoulder and see one of the staff using what appears to be a blue vacuum the size and shape of a paper towel roll.

Blake: We also have a no-gratuitous-killing rule in the restaurant and at the farm. No one's allowed to kill anything. If you can't deal with relocating the mouse, the spider, the fly, just get someone else to do it for you. That gadget sucks up the flies, and then we can put them outside. There's a whole section in our cookbook about how we deal with serving meat. My Buddhist teacher, Chagdud Tulku Rinpoche, believes that whatever you're eating, you're causing harm — whether you're raising vegetables, flooding a garden, or eating a cow. So at least do it with full consciousness and compassionate eating.

This nutritionism — it sounds like some sort of moral elitism, another food fixation, but my teacher would say if you want to give up meat or vegetables for the benefit of all beings, that's great, just really apply yourself to it.

I have to go up to the farm to get eggs and produce for dinner. Do you want to come with me, meet my brother, give Luna a swim? We can finish our conversation before dinner tonight.

Jen: That's perfect, because I have to go prep dinner now.

After about a mile we turn off onto a narrow dirt road. We pile out, Luna barking excitedly, running right up to Nathanael Spalding, who leans against a shed with a pitchfork in his hand, looking exactly like a farmer. As if he'd known Luna all his life, he reaches down, grabs a stick near the shed and throws it right into the pond. Blake introduces us and grabs a basket Nathanael has packed with all the foods she'll need for dinner. We agree that I'll pick her up later at her house, which is up the road a bit.

Nathanael: Hey. Glad you could come. Great looking dog!

We start to walk around the acreage. Nathanael points out everything as we walk. You can tell he's proud of what he's done in the three years he's been working the farm.

I'm sure glad to be here. It's a great place to live and raise kids. People have lost sight of where food comes from. Do carrots really come from the ground? *[Laughs]* I grew up in New Hampshire. One of my first jobs was baling hay and picking strawberries and planting corn. My dad was an organic master gardener, and I helped him every summer working in his garden and greenhouse. It's definitely different having my own garden, growing my own food. I never even contemplated doing it on this scale, though.

This is what we call the Three Sisters' Garden. It's all interplanted: corn and melons shade each other and inhibit weeds; the melons and squashes climb the corn. They're harvested at different times so they don't interfere with each other. All the beans get tilled at the end of the year. They're a nitrogen fixer for the soil. Corn and squash are heavy feeders, so the beans put a lot of nutrients back into the soil. The sunflowers attract birds. The birds sit in them and scan for insects. We're a No Harm farm, so we don't use organic pesticides or step on hornworms or anything like that. We leave it up to the birds and the beneficial insects.

We flood irrigate this whole section here, it's hooked into our main irrigation system. The overflow goes into this pipe — it's all gated so I can open and shut each pipe and flood-irrigate each row as I need to. The pond is our backup irrigation. It's also great for swimming. Kids love it, dogs love it, farmers love it. It gets pretty hot down here, and I wouldn't have nearly as much help if I didn't have the pond!

We have ten varieties of potatoes, potentially six thousand pounds. Here *[he points to baskets all around the greenhouse]* are all the seeds we've saved: chard, bee plant seed, arugula, all kinds of flowers, seed potatoes, seed onions and tomato seeds which are really tricky to save.

Those horses in the field belong to the Mayor. They're racehorses, some of them champion stock. Sometimes one will start galloping and then the rest will follow — you should hear the thundering, it's just beautiful.

On a normal day I eat breakfast at the restaurant, then I go to Blake's house to feed the chickens. We feed them the compost from the restaurant. After that I come down to the farm and either weed until lunch or harvest. Three days a week we do pretty much nothing but pick beans, corn, squash, lettuce and braising mix, herbs, whatever tomatoes are ready. We dig up potatoes, pull carrots, basically picking everything that's ready.

In the afternoon, I'll work on a project like building trellises, or working on the chicken tractor. A little of this, a little of that. I had help with the chicken tractor from a guy who was a WWOOFer *[Willing Workers on Organic Farms]*.

Someday this whole area will be perennials: comfrey, chives, sorrel, arugula and dill (which reseed themselves), basil, cardoons, rhubarb, strawberries, all the tomatoes, peppers and tomatillos.

The back fields are fruit trees. Under the juniper trees are two hives of Carneolan bees, healthy, pretty much disease resistant, no mites and no chalk. Eighty to eighty-five pounds of honey in each.

I see myself here for the long haul. I'll be under this tree, which in five years' time will be pretty big! The first year I was here I tried to put up a teepee. The wind blew it down. White boys shouldn't try to set up teepees! *[Laughs]*

We buy our beef from down the road, our lamb from the farm between Blake's house and mine. Our salt is Redmond RealSalt, from one hundred and fifty million years ago when a vast sea covered North America.

RECIPES ■ Blake Spalding and Jennifer Castle

Blue-Ribbon Black-Powder Buttermilk Biscuits

A very hot oven and very cold dough collaborate and conspire to bring you the fluffiest biscuit. A food processor fitted with a steel blade will mix the butter into the dry ingredients while keeping it cold and firm. Double this batch in order to secure leftovers you'll play with in other recipes.

    3 tablespoons cornmeal
    2½ cups white flour
    1½ teaspoons salt
    ½ teaspoon baking soda
    1 teaspoon baking powder
    ½ teaspoon coarse black pepper
    1 teaspoon white sugar
    ¼ pound (1 stick) butter, chilled and cut into ½-chunks
    2 cups buttermilk (substitute 2 cups milk with 2
        teaspoons lemon juice)

Adjust oven rack to middle position and heat to 450 degrees. Grease a 9×11-inch cookie sheet or line with parchment. Sprinkle 2 tablespoons cornmeal over surface.

Place flour, salt, baking soda, baking powder, pepper and sugar in a large bowl or in the work bowl of a food processor fitted with a steel blade. Whisk together or pulse 5 to 7 times.

If making by hand, cut butter in with a pastry blender or 2 knives until the mixture resembles uneven, coarse crumbs. If using a food processor, distribute butter chunks over the dry ingredients. Pulse 10 to 12 times, then transfer to a large bowl.

Pour buttermilk over top of dough folding ingredients at edges of bowl into middle using a rubber spatula or handy plastic dough scraper. Rotate bowl one-quarter turn with each fold until dough is moistened and sticky, leaving few dry patches.

Turn dough ball out onto lightly floured counter. Lightly dust your hands with flour and gently ease dough into a square shape. With bench scraper or sharp kitchen knife, cut dough in half and stack one-half on top of the other. Repeat three times, flattening, cutting, and stacking, adding small amounts of flour if necessary to keep it from sticking.

Transfer stack to prepared cookie sheet. Sprinkle dough with remaining 1 tablespoon cornmeal. Using floured rolling pin, roll to 1 inch thick. Cut biscuits with knife or bench scraper into 2×2-inch squares. Bake until golden brown, about 15 minutes.

Arugula Pesto

During the summer, arugula takes over our garden. We view it as an invasive yet tasty weed and use as much of it as possible by grinding it into an aromatic and intense pesto, which we freeze in case of an emergency pasta sauce shortage.

    ½ pound arugula
    1½ tablespoons salt
    1 tablespoon brown sugar or honey
    1 tablespoon red wine vinegar
    4 roasted red peppers
    1 cup toasted piñons (pine nuts)
    1 cup toasted pepitas (hulled pumpkin seeds)
    1 cup olive oil

Blend everything together in a food processor, stopping to scrape sides and processing again. We like the pesto rich, salty, and oily. A few cloves of sweet roasted garlic are a nice addition.

Older arugula can be bitter; for a milder flavor replace half the arugula with fresh spinach leaves.

Spread on pizza crust and top with cheese and veggies; toss with hot pasta (ziti is a particularly good vehicle); add to sour cream for a dip. You can freeze the pesto in greased ice cube trays for easy-access portions.

Moqui Mac

As macaroni and cheese connoisseurs, we have created this, our version of the cheesy baked perfection. This is the ultimate in comfort carbo loading.

    2 tablespoons butter
    1 onion, minced
    1 tablespoon salt
    1 cup roasted corn kernels
    1 cup roasted poblano chilis, peeled, seeded and chopped
    1 cup roasted red peppers, peeled, seeded and chopped
    1 jalapeño pepper, minced

3 cups heavy cream (or half & half or milk)

2 cups pepper jack cheese, grated

2 cups chopped tomatoes with juice

1 teaspoon Dijon mustard

⅛ teaspoon each of cayenne, nutmeg

½ teaspoon each of black pepper, ground cumin

1 package (16 ounces) macaroni, cooked according to package directions

⅓ cup grated Parmesan plus ⅓ cup bread crumbs

In a large saucepan over medium-high heat, melt butter. Add onion and salt. When onion is soft, add corn, chilis, red peppers, and jalapeño and cook 10 minutes on medium heat.

Add cream and bring almost to a boil on medium heat. Cook 10 minutes.

Remove from heat and add cheese, tomatoes, mustard, and spices. Adjust salt to taste.

Heat oven to 350 degrees. Combine cheese sauce with just-cooked pasta and pour into a greased medium-size baking dish or individual crocks. Top with Parmesan and bread crumb mixture and bake for 30 to 40 minutes, till top of casserole is crusty and edges are bubbly. Let sit 10 minutes before eating.

Wicked Hot Chocolate

A very grown-up version of an old standard, with Chimayo chile and cinnamon adding considerably to the warming effect.

½ cup unsweetened cocoa powder

2 ounces unsweetened chocolate

½ cup sugar

3 cinnamon sticks

2 teaspoons Chimayo chile powder

½ teaspoon salt

5 cups whole milk

½ cup half & half

1 teaspoon vanilla extract

Mix cocoa sugar, chili, and salt into a small bowl.

In a medium saucepan, stir milk, half & half, and cinnamon sticks over low heat until mixture comes to a simmer.

Whisk in cocoa mixture and cook until cocoa is smooth and an even color and consistency. Add vanilla extract.

We serve the hot chocolate in a big mug, topped with whipped cream, a cinnamon stick and chocolate shavings.

Chocolate Chili Cream Pots

We pretty much have to keep this unbelievably rich and luscious dessert on the menu all season long, because returning diners complain if they can't order it. It's a certain cure for any emotional ill.

6 large egg yolks (we use only local farm eggs for this – substitute free-range and organic store-bought)

9 ounces good-quality sweet chocolate

2 ounces good-quality unsweetened chocolate

2 cups heavy cream

½ cup half & half

½ teaspoon salt

2 teaspoons powdered hot Chimayo chili

Whip egg yolks thoroughly in a blender. Set aside. Carefully heat chocolate, cream, and half & half together in a heavy-bottomed pot, stirring constantly until chocolate is completely melted and bubbling and mixture is a very even consistency and color. Add salt and chili powder and let simmer one minute more.

Pour the very hot chocolate mixture into a whirling blender of egg yolks and blend until thick and completely smooth. If for any reason the custard doesn't thicken up properly, pour into a heavy-bottomed saucepan and cook it on very low heat. It may temporarily break, but another quick go in the blender will fix the problem.

While chocolate is still hot, pour it into dessert cups (we use small white ramekin dishes – a little bit of this dessert goes a long way). Chill cream pot for 1 hour.

We garnish this dessert with freshly whipped cream, grated Abuelita Mexican chocolate, and edible flower petals or a whole small, dried red chili from our garden (although one time a guest ate the chili and nearly fainted . . . now servers warn the guest about the garnish, because it looks too pretty to skip).

just cram in a ton of fertilizer and every year it gets a little bit crappier and crappier and you pump a bunch of UN32 in there.

Growing in Arizona is part of a failed system. The Hohokam were here from 900 to 1400 B.C.E. They overproduced themselves out of existence. By diverting all the water from the rivers and trying to irrigate, they salinified their soil. We have a high water table, which is why we came here in the first place. By diverting the water from the rivers and irrigating with it, using the same canal systems that we do today, they elevated the water table. The salt just totally took all the fertility out of the ground.

They had to move farther and farther away from the rivers and channel the water farther and farther, using more and more fuel. The original fish were a couple of feet long. By 1400, they were only six inches.

While I was watching the encroachment, I got another idea. In 2004, my grandfather brokered the first large sale of our land. I got the developers' map and used a GPS to map out a third-scale replica of the development in an adjacent open field. My archaeologist friends helped. Then I planted it to look like the subdivision. I remembered my whole family out in the carrot field where the development is now; it was the last time we harvested carrots in that field. I'm pretty green as a farmer — three years. My father farmed for more than twenty-six years and my grandfather for forty-odd years. My mother was crying. I will be the last one to farm this ground. They'll come in and scrape all this flat. Put up houses. And we're going to have neighbors. At that I feel anger, loss and, strangely, some hope.

I have to come to terms with profiting from this transformation. Through my artworks I have been able to get a public forum, get a discussion going. When I finished "Moore Estates," replicating in plants the 250 new homes, 250 families who'll start their own histories on our ground, that's where all

that hope comes in. We're connected now. I don't want to feel that those people have forced me out. I don't want to leave it that way because I have a role in it.

"Life Cycles: Reinterpreting the American Produce" is another big project of mine. I ask questions like, "How long do you think it takes to grow a carrot? The answers are usually thirty days, forty-five days. It's really six months! Knowing where your food comes from and how long it takes to grow matters so people can understand when they're consuming too much. My thought was, What if people could go to a supermarket and see the lifecycle of a plant through time-lapse photography? How might that change the way they conceive of the food? Would they buy a smaller

bunch of lettuce, so as not let it rot in their refrigerator? When I started the CSA I had no idea what kale looked like or celery root. Here I am a farmer and I didn't know half the stuff in the grocery store. Putting a face on the farmer makes the food taste better, too. The more we know about our food, the more excited we get.

My wife is also an artist, and we're looking at getting some ground up in the Northwest, turning it into a CSA and maybe an art residency where people can come out and grow their own food and make their own work and be part of that whole structure. I think everybody needs to start growing food.

Last week my Dad and I installed the urban transplanter, a fully automated seventy-five-foot-long

Emily Capelin and Zak Randell
Vegetable Oil Vehicle ■ Durango, Colorado & the Northwest Territories ■
emily.capelin@gmail.com ■ zak.randell@gmail.com

Emily Capelin is the oldest of three kids. She has been interested in the natural world since her first river trip along the San Juan River in Utah. Emily is a recent graduate of Colorado College, a school that's all about sustainability. She and her boyfriend, Zak Randell, met their junior year. Zak had this idea of creating a biodiesel cooperative run by students.

Emily: We initially hoped to get a space on campus, to set everything up and create continuity for the future by working with retired chemistry professor Mike Morgenstern.

We got one of the two grants we applied for, which provided us with materials to begin to make biodiesel on our back porch. The neighbors thought we were crazy — there was always a lot of action on our porch, motors constantly running. Eventually we moved into a HAZMAT shed in the facilities area of campus. But suddenly we had a more personal interest in biodiesel.

Zak: I'd bought a huge inefficient diesel truck, a big Ford F-250. The good news was we didn't have to change anything in order to make the truck run on biodiesel.

Emily grew up in a family that owns a wilderness expedition camp. She spent summers hiking, biking, and rafting on the rivers and in the mountains of Colorado. Zak, from Connecticut, also has a deep knowledge of the wilderness.

Zak: During this same time, Emily and I also applied for grants to go on wilderness expeditions, and we got them. The grants covered everything, including all of our diesel fuel costs to get up North. But then I thought, Why not do the expeditions more responsibly? Get the conversion kit and convert the truck to vegetable oil.

Emily: Our friend Gordon Bassett worked with

a company in Denver called Go Green Early. We bought all the parts for the conversion from them, and then did it while we were still in school. We called Go Green a lot for help. Late April we each made one major trip to Denver to have them help us with the big things, like cutting the Ford's fuel lines and inserting the new ones.

Zak was kind of neglecting his schoolwork, reading vegetable oil blogs and blogs about biodiesel. He did a lot of research, mostly on the Internet, and I was his assistant. The truck was converted by May, just in time for the river trip.

Zak: There were six of us. We hauled up the

two rafts and all the gear. We were the "Beast of Burden" truck. We had a seventy-gallon vegetable tank, and two fifty-five-gallon barrels for storage and an oil-cleaning setup. To clean the oil, we ran it though filters so it became really, really fine.

We got the oil from behind restaurants. It came from deep fryers. When a restaurant finished with a vat, they'd pour it out into a fifty-five-gallon grease trap in the alleyway. The grease would then be picked up by a grease collector, taken away and sold as an industrial commodity — yellow grease. Before it's reused they might put thickeners in it, and corn products, and then it's fed to livestock or refined and used in cosmetics.

Emily: You need permission to take the oil away. We'd go into restaurants and ask if we could have their waste vegetable oil. The best are either Chinese or Mexican restaurants. Chinese because all the tempura — there's no waste chunks in the oil, and it's usually a pretty good grade. The dumpster behind a Chinese restaurant is usually full of

a beautiful golden oil — almost as good as new. Mexican restaurants because they're usually family-owned, so there's more of a commitment to health and cleanliness. They fry a lot of chips, so it's pretty clean oil.

Zak: We never take oil from fast food chain restaurants. That's cheap hydrogenated oil. Some places have a grease trap, so after frying up burgers, they'll scrape all the chunks into the grease barrel.

Emily: Trans fat. It clogs up our bodies. We leave those places alone.

It was always interesting talking to the chefs and the people back in the kitchen. They'd usually ask us why we wanted their oil. When we said to run our truck, they'd laugh. Sometimes the whole restaurant would empty out and come look at what we were doing. In some places out in the Yukon and British Columbia, no one had ever heard of a truck run on vegetable oil!

We drove from Durango, Colorado, all the way through Idaho, then Montana and into Canada near

For two years my family has embraced a gluten and dairy-free diet. What seemed, at first, to be a burden has become an adventurous blessing. New tastes and new smells fuel an awareness of what we eat and where it comes from. My family's neighborhood garden supplies us with a season of fresh vegetables and brings home the idea of eating local.

Breakfast: Gluten and Dairy-Free Pecan and Ginger Scones

2 cups superfine sweet rice flour

½ cup turbinado sugar plus more for sprinkling on top

¼ teaspoon salt

2 teaspoons baking powder

½ teaspoon baking soda

1 cup cold non-hydrogenated vegetable butter

2 eggs

½ cup plain rice or almond milk

¼ teaspoon rice vinegar

½ cup candied ginger, chopped

⅓ cup pecans, chopped

Preheat oven to 425 degrees. In a medium bowl, combine flour, sugar, salt, baking powder and baking soda. Add butter and cut into dry mixture until crumbs form. Stir in candied ginger and pecans.

In a small bowl whisk together eggs and milk mixed with ⅛ teaspoon of vinegar. This helps sour the milk like a buttermilk. Add to flour mixture and stir until it holds together. Pat and form into pie-shaped wedges slightly apart on an ungreased cookie sheet. Lightly sprinkle with sugar. Bake until golden brown, about 12 minutes. Best served when warm. Makes 8.

Lunch: Sautéed Stuffed Squash Blossoms with Salad

Connoisseurs of fried squash blossoms say to choose only the male flowers because the females are a bit too soft. Female flowers produce the zucchini; hence the males have a more slender stem. The texture difference seems to be minimal.

Squash blossoms (use as many as you need)

Eggs (enough of them to cover blossoms)

Gluten-free all-purpose flour (enough to dust each blossom)

Salt and pepper, to taste

Olive oil

Goat cheese

Minced garlic

In a bowl crumble goat cheese with minced garlic. Gently wash squash blossoms. Pat dry. Remove stamen or pistol inside of flower. Put a teaspoon of the goat cheese/garlic mix inside the blossom and twist the top closed. Whip up one egg and dip blossom into egg. Mix flour with salt and pepper to taste. Dust each blossom with flour. Fry lightly in heated olive oil. Take precautions for splattering!

Serve with a special salad.

Dinner: Brisket and Zucchini Latkes

Briskit

Beef brisket

Olive oil

Garlic

Rosemary

Glacier National Park. Through Alberta by Banff and Jasper National Parks, then into the southern part of the Northwest Territories, just beneath the Artic Circle. Then we drove back down to British Columbia, through the Yukon into Alaska. We were in Alaska a whole month. We went all the way to Homer on the southern tip, and then drove up to Denali National Park.

We did a ton of driving because of the vegetable oil. We didn't sleep in a bed all summer. We had food stored in these big metal river boxes. We shopped at the farmers markets and picked berries.

Zak: Blueberries and blackberries right off the bush.

One night in Alaska we had caribou. That was a real highlight. We also had fine salmon during the salmon run. We stayed with some people who caught thirty-five salmon in three hours! Their limit for the year. The salmon fishing is pretty heavily regulated.

We met all kinds of people who were into vege-

Carrots
Potatoes
Onion
Celery

Note: To cook any roast my preference is a cast iron Dutch oven set atop a low flame.

Trim the fat off as best as you can. Warm a large pan or Dutch oven. Place the trimmed brisket with the fat side down in the pan in olive oil, or an olive oil blend, with finely chopped garlic and onions. Brown on all sides, searing in the meat juices.

Add salt and a cup of dry white wine. Allow the wine to evaporate and then add 1 cup of hot water. Add organic carrots, small potatoes and celery. Cook for 4 hours. Separate out the meat and vegetables. Puree the veggies and cover the meat with veggie sauce. Slowly cook another hour until meat is tender and flakes apart. Serves a family.

**We get our organic beef from Sam and Mari Perry at Ancient Harvest Ranch in Mancos, Colorado.

Zucchini Latkes

2 cups zucchini, grated
1 cup potato, grated
2 eggs
½ cup chives, chopped
1 tablespoon rice flour
½ teaspoon kosher salt
Olive oil
Pepper to taste
Goat feta cheese (optional)

Grate zucchini and potato together. Place in a colander and sprinkle with salt.

Let drain in the kitchen sink for 20 minutes. Press out juices. Add eggs, flour and pepper. Lightly cover the bottom of a skillet with oil. Heat oil until hot but not burning. If mixture continues to bear juices, spoon out excess. Scoop ½ cup of latke mix into pan and fry until golden brown on both sides. Excellent with goat feta cheese sprinkled on top. Makes 8 3-inch latkes (pancakes).

Dessert: Lemon Almond Macaroons

1½ cups sweetened shredded coconut
1 cup almonds, sliced
½ cup turbinado sugar
½ teaspoon almond extract
1 teaspoon lemon zest
¼ teaspoon salt
4 large organic egg whites

Preheat oven to 325 degrees. Use parchment paper to line 2 baking sheets.

In a large bowl combine the shredded coconut, sliced almonds, sugar, lemon zest and the salt. Stir in the egg whites.

Drop 2 tablespoons of the mixture onto the prepared baking sheets.

Bake for 20 to 25 minutes or until the edges begin to brown. Transfer to a cooling rack immediately. Makes 2 dozen treats.

table oil. Some of them not only ran their cars and trucks off it, but their generators, their homes. Hypothetically, you can use vegetable oil for 98 percent of your fossil fuel needs. You'd have to be pretty dedicated, but it's possible.

I don't think I'll ever own a gas car again. If everyone in America drove a diesel car, we would use 30 percent less petroleum. Vegetable oil does pollute, because it also produces CO_2 — but it's a tenth of what diesel does. Consider the fact that with my F-250 I get seventeen to eighteen miles a gallon with vegetable oil. Gasoline's only twelve miles to the gallon.

Emily: Zak and I are about to take off on another adventure, this time to Latin America. First Peru, then Ecuador. We received a fellowship to work for a NGO (nongovernmental organization) seed distribution program in Ecuador. We'll be down there for five or six months. My mother used to take me on plant hikes, and I learned a lot from her.

I've always been interested in traditional medicine, ethnobotany, native plants. In Nepal last summer, Zak and I found interesting similarities between the plants of the Himalayas and those found in the Rocky Mountains. I'm intrigued by how different cultures use plants for sacred rites or a natural medicines.

As a child I spent a lot of time on the Navajo Reservation. I realize now how special it is to have access to so many Navajo, Hopi and Zuni elders. The traditional Indians are plant people. I did my senior thesis on Navajo traditional prayer and medicine. Corn pollen in particular.

In five years I see myself working in some aspect of ethnobotany. Last Thanksgiving, one of the Navajo elders told me that many plants are disappearing and there's no seed bank on the reservation, no way to really keep track of seeds or save them. Starting a seed bank would be a lifetime job. I would be able to use my interest in both history and botany. I'm excited about this upcoming trip. It will give me more information!

Alison Bailey Vercruysse
18 Rabbits ■ San Francisco, California ■ www.18rabbits.com

Alison first came to my attention a few years back. Luna and I had just gone on a long Sunday morning walk through New York's Central Park, which was piled high with snow. Colorful crosscountry skiers on the bridle path reminded me of a Currier and Ives painting. Luna loved the snow. When I threw a stick, it disappeared into the high banks and Luna disappeared after it. On the way home we stopped at Dean & Deluca for some hot chocolate, and while we waited, I spied these bright granola bar–sized packages: "18 Rabbits Delectable Granola Bar." I turned one over and read the ingredients. On a bag of granola positioned next to the bars, I read "Our Story":

"It all started down a gravel road in Farmer's Branch Texas in the kitchen of Two Lost Valley Lane. I liked to play outside with my four brothers and sisters and our rabbit, Blackjack, while Mom watched from the kitchen where she made her special granola.

"On days Mom made granola, the aroma of oats, coconut, honey and nuts wafted through the house and out the windows, and we'd all leave off playing and head inside. One day we ran off and forgot Blackjack, leaving him to a rabbit rendez-vous. Soon he had a family of 18, and our yard was hopping with more rabbits than we knew what to do with!

"I created my own recipe for 18 Rabbits granola because I like for people to feel good — the kind of good that comes from enjoying the most delicious, most nutritious food. Like the way your favorite childhood memory gives you a spring in your step, wherever it comes to you — even as you head down a busy city street far away from where you grew up. Eat some and see where it takes you. — Alison Bailey Vercruysse, Founder."

I bought the bag of granola, too.

Alison Bailey Vercruysse: My mother and my grand-mothers were a huge influence on me. Nana still lives in San Antonio and is more of a savory cook, famous for her pralines and divinity. Mama Kitty, who lived in Virginia, was the sweet cook. She made coconut cream pies and peach ice cream. Whatever she made she just whipped up out of her head, all from scratch, all wonderful.

My mom grew up in North Carolina. We spent summers there, and one of my favorite memories is going to the shrimp dock. The shrimp boats would dump everything through this wet concrete floor, and all the shrimp would tumble out. Tons and tons. And Mom and I would say, "Yes, we'll have a

them. She taught me how to negotiate with the farmer if the fruit wasn't ripe, so you could keep it in the house for a few days. We had eggplants in the garden. The rabbits made excellent fertilizer for them. For a while, I remember having eggplant almost every night for dinner. *(Laughs)* My mom's lessons helped me when I started doing my own shopping at the markets. That's how I found the purveyors for my granola.

When I first started getting serious abut all this, I went to Citizen Cake in San Francisco and asked for an apprenticeship. They were not eager to take me on because it had been so hard to acclimate past apprentices to everything in the shop. I was persistent, though, and I ended up working for them for five months.

They really tried to weed me out. We all initially think baking is such a romantic career. and can't imagine how hard it is. My second job there was to peel this huge case of quince. I had never even seen quince before, and didn't have the slightest idea how to go about peeling them. So I hand peeled them and ended up with blisters all over my thumbs. But at least I did it.

Then came the eggs, a whole case, fifteen trays with thirty eggs each. My boss wanted me to separate them into whites and yellows. I made a game out of it. I taught myself how to break an egg with one hand. I was thinking about that Audrey Hepburn movie, the one where she goes to the Cordon Bleu and she's being taught how to break an egg with one hand. Then, somehow, a bit of yolk got into the pristine whites — unrecoverable, trashed — and I had to throw the whole thing out . . . thirty-six eggs.

My next job was at Taste Catering. They all had this amazing talent in every area of food and they taught me all that they knew. It was wonderful. But that first day, the pastry chef said, "Butter, cream and sugar." So out of the fridge I got a bunch of butter, cream and sugar and put them into the mixer. Pretty simple, right? The pastry chef came over and said, "What are you doing?" I said, "Well,

few pounds," and we'd just go and scoop them up and put them in a cooler and be on our way. It was awesome.

My mom had one of the ten worst cases of asthma ever documented in the U.S. It led her to eating all natural and organic food. She experimented with everything. She even ate lion and rattlesnake — anything that was not commercially produced, because she had to be able to trace its origins. It wasn't until my mom got married and moved to Europe with my dad that she learned to cook. While she was in Germany, she learned how to make granola. She was about thirty-three.

From the time I was little my mom was pushing honey and maple syrup. We went to the farmers market in Dallas and she taught me how to pick fruits and vegetables, how to smell when they were ripe, the color, the way they felt when you held you said butter, cream and sugar." But what she'd actually meant was, "Cream the butter and sugar." Again, I had to throw the whole thing out.

Because of my business background, not only could I make different desserts with my own formulations, but I also knew how to turn it into a business. I began taking my cakes around to different cafés in the city. I used things like Pt. Reyes bleu cheese, Santa Rosa plums. I got my eggs and fruits locally. All organic, of course. Pretty soon I had five or six customers. Since I couldn't find any good scones or muffins in the area, I started concentrating on breakfast. I wrapped my inventions in folded origami paper and put inspirational messages in them. I called my operation "Divinely D'lish."

At that time I moved to a commercial kitchen south of the Market area. It was scary getting there at 4:30 in the morning. I got cornered a couple of times, and the windows were knocked out of my car. I'd never felt unsafe before. My husband advised me to just stick to packaging my own granola.

I started selling the granola at places I knew. Espresso Roma was my first customer. (They still serve it today.) Because of my Federal Reserve background, I knew about the regulations and all the legal stuff I needed to do in order to get my products into restaurants.

One day I was hiking on Mt. Tam in Mill Valley. I opened an energy bar I'd brought for the hike, and after two bites, I felt horrible, I didn't even want to continue hiking. And it wasn't the first time this had happened. I thought, I've got to create something *I* can eat. What about my own granola bar? So I went home and I made my own recipe with my own granola, and then added things to it. At first it had eggs, but they're not shelf stable. I found out that tapioca syrup could bind just as well. I blended it with the fruit and the syrup, rolled it out, packed it on to a sheet pan, baked it and then cut it up. It was so simple.

It's fun for me to find farms to work with around the country and the world, like Benina Burrough's

almond orchard. Her almonds are clean, transitioning to organic, and I love her family story.

It's all about passion and perseverance. If someone says no, you have to just keep on going. Our granola is now sold in bulk at Rainbow Grocery, and they go through two hundred pounds a month. Now I'm working with a certified organic comanufacturing company that bakes for me. Since we are wheat-free, they are extremely careful about not comingling our products with those that contain wheat.

I get up in the morning and meditate to get my mind clear. I eat before I meditate, otherwise all I think about is food. I have my granola, yogurt and tea almost every day.

We make our own bread now with whole spelt, buckwheat and flax; I much prefer eating these heartier proteins. I let the bread rise on a little chair

Jessica Prentice
Three Stone Hearth ■ Berkeley, California ■ www.threestonehearth.com

SUMMER ■ *One lush morning, I park the car at the corner of Addison and Bolivar Drive in Berkeley, then pull up a seat at the community table outside Three Stone Hearth. The table is beautifully set, including cloth napkins and a vase of petunias. Before lunch begins, Jessica Prentice introduces me to everyone at the table, including the four other owners, Porsche Combash, Misa Koketsu, Catherine Spanger and Larry Wisch.*

"The business is built around three metaphorical stones: Earth, Health and Heart," says Jessica. She is the originator of the term "locavore," which grew out of a 2005 "Eat Local Challenge" that encouraged consumers to know the distance from the farmer to their table.

Three Stone Hearth is a CSK (community supported kitchen), one step beyond a CSA (community supported agriculture). For a weekly or monthly fee, you get a box of organically grown local produce and ready-made foods that follow the dietary guidelines of Dr. Weston A. Price, the "Charles Darwin of nutrition":

- *Liberal use of traditional fats.*
- *Raw and cultured dairy products.*
- *Whole grains that have been soaked, sprouted, soured or naturally leavened.*
- *Use of only natural and unrefined sweeteners*
- *Animal products from pastured livestock*
- *Avoidance of toxic substances.*

Three Stone Hearth's weekly menu is posted on their site.

Jessica Prentice: We've been in partnership since July 2006. And we work amazingly together!

They all nod in agreement and the table erupts in a rowdy round of applause.

I grew up in the Washington, D.C., area. I got my B.A. from Brown University in 1991. In my junior year, I took a year off and went to Thailand and worked in a refugee camp. Senior year I spent at an historically black college in Mississippi. I was the only white student.

I was professionally trained as a chef at the Natural Gourmet Institute of Food and Health in New York City. I educated myself about sustainability, and was hired as the first director of education programs for the Ferry Plaza Farmers Market in San Francisco. I founded Wise Food Ways in 2004, and cofounded Locavores in 2005. My first book,

Full Moon Feast, was published in 2006 by Chelsea Green Publishing.

After lunch, the staff returns to the kitchen and puts on their aprons. Suddenly there's music and a can-can line forms. They all raise their hands and kick out their legs in time to the music. Those of us on the sidelines clap in time to the beat. There's laughing and gaiety like a scene from a Broadway musical. It's just the way a kitchen should be, full of possibilities and good cheer.

When the song ends, everyone gets back to work. Soon, there's a quiet hum of activity. Jessica shows me around the cavernous warehouse where they make the fermented drinks, where they place the boxes with the CSK portions, the office, and last, a look into the refrigerators. When we return to the kitchen, a dozen chickens are being pulled apart for stew.

All of my energy now goes into this kitchen. We try to be open to multiage participation, but it's tricky in a commercial kitchen to have kids around. Kids come along with their parents to pick up their food, so they are exposed to all of this in a quiet way. Loads of our customers have small children and are concerned about their health.

We started Three Stone Hearth with about fifty people. I'd done some catering, and some of the people I worked with joined. Then we did some cooking classes and drew more folks from there. Then we had two Full Moon Feasts. Finally, the five of us introduced ourselves in a formal announcement, explaining what we wanted to do, saying that anyone who was interested should sign up. A nice group of people came onboard, and we just built from there.

We draw our food from a group of local farmers. Much of our produce comes from Veritable Vegetables. Our menus change weekly. If you're in the area, subscribing is easy, free and carries no obligation. People go to our website and order by

Frittata with Summer Squash, Summer Onion, and Fresh Basil

3 tablespoons butter or olive oil

1 fresh white summer onion with green stem, sliced with the green stem sliced as well and kept separate

2 summer squash, cut in half lengthwise and then sliced into half moons

½ cup grated or crumbled local cheese

Leaves of ½ bunch of basil, stacked, rolled and cut into ribbons (chiffonade)

3 eggs

½ cup cream or half and half

Salt and pepper to taste

A pinch or grating of nutmeg

Heat butter or olive oil over medium-high heat in a heavy bottomed sauté pan and add onions. Sauté for a few moments. Add summer squash and sauté until tender. Mix together eggs and cream in a bowl. Add salt (be generous – adjust to taste). Add a few grindings of fresh pepper and a pinch or grating of nutmeg to mixture. When squash and onions are tender, reduce heat and pour eggs over the sauté. Add the cheese, onion greens and half of the basil to the top of the eggs, and cover.

Cook frittata covered over low heat until just set. You can also place the frittata in a pre-heated oven (300 degrees) to finish cooking it.

Slice and serve with more basil on top. Accompany frittata with a green salad, fruit salad, roasted potatoes, local sausage or other meat. Serves 2 to 4, depending on what else you are serving.

Variations:

- Add sliced or diced gypsy peppers to the sauté.
- Lay sliced tomatoes on the top of the frittata
- Add fresh corn kernels to the sauté.
- Replace basil with another fresh herb such as marjoram, scallions, or chives. Egg and Potato Salad with Green Olives and Onions

Egg and Potato with Green Olives and Onions

For the Salad:

4 hard cooked eggs, cooled

2 cooked potatoes, cooled

6 to 8 green olives

½ small red or spring onion, or a small bunch of scallions

A few sprigs parsley

For the Mayonnaise:

1 egg yolk from a farm fresh egg

½ cup olive oil

A splash of white wine vinegar

½ teaspoon prepared mustard (optional)

Salt and pepper, to taste

To Serve:

2 small heads romaine or other crisp lettuce, cut or torn into pieces

Olive oil and vinegar

Salt and pepper

A few chives, minced

Dice the eggs and potatoes into a ½ inch dice. Mince the olives, onions and parsley.

To make the mayonnaise, put the egg yolk in a bowl. Add a few drops of olive oil and whisk in. Keep adding olive oil by drips, and then in a slow steady stream, while whisking constantly, until all olive oil is incorporated in the emulsion.

Add the vinegar, mustard, and a generous pinch of salt and a grind of fresh pepper to the mayonnaise. Taste and adjust the seasoning.

Put the eggs, potatoes, olives, onions and parsley in a medium bowl. Add the mayonnaise until the salad is completely dressed. Taste and add more salt and pepper as needed.

Whisk together oil, vinegar, salt, pepper, and any leftover mayonnaise. Toss lettuce with dressing and arrange on 2 plates. Divide egg and potato salad into the middle of the greens. Sprinkle with minced chives. Serve with good bread and cheese on the side. Serves 2 to 4.

Variation: For a more classic taste, you can omit the green olives and add a few stalks of celery instead.

Cream of Carrot Soup

2 tablespoons butter or olive oil

1 to 2 white onions, diced, or 2 to 3 leeks, sliced into rounds

½ pound carrots, diced

1 bouquet garni (an herb bundle tied with string) including any or all of the following: a bay leaf, a sprig of thyme, a sprig of sage, a sprig of parsley, a rosemary stem

Chicken stock (enough to amply cover vegetables, at least a quart)

Juice and zest of one (organic) orange

1 cup yogurt, buttermilk, half-and-half, or whole milk (or ½ cup cream or crème fraîche)

Salt and pepper, to taste

Garnishes

Crème fraîche or yogurt

Minced parsley leaves, dill or scallions

A grating of nutmeg, or a grind of black pepper

Heat the butter or oil in a medium-size soup pot. Add the onions or leeks and sauté until soft. Add the carrots, orange zest, and stock to cover the vegetables by about ½ inch. Add the bouquet garni and bring the pot to a boil. Reduce heat and simmer until the carrots are soft. Turn off the heat and remove the bouquet garni. Puree the soup with an immersion blender (or in a blender), adding a bit more stock or water if it is too thick. Add the orange juice, yogurt or other dairy, and a big pinch of salt and pepper as you blend. Taste the soup and adjust the seasonings. Serve in a shallow bowl with a dollop of crème fraîche (or yogurt) and/or a sprinkling of herbs, nutmeg, or pepper.

Variation: Carrot-Ginger Soup

Replace the bouquet garni with 3 to 4 large slices of gingerroot. (Remember to remove the ginger before pureeing)

Variation: Carrot Soup with Coconut Milk and Ginger

- Use butternut squash, sweet potatoes or carrots
- Replace butter or olive oil with ghee or coconut oil if you have it
- Replace bouquet garni with 3 to 4 large slices fresh gingerroot
- Omit the orange
- Add a tablespoon or so fish sauce to the soup while it's cooking (reduce the salt)
- Replace the yogurt (or other dairy) in the puree with coconut milk (you can use the whole can)
- Garnish with a dollop of yogurt and a sprinkling of minced scallions

Summer Pot Roast

With cold San Francisco summers, this classic is wonderful year round. This is how I make mine. In summer add some fresh green beans at the last minute.

1 tablespoon tallow, lard, or other fat

1 2 to 3 pound piece of local, grass-finished beef, such as a chuck roast, round roast, or brisket, well trimmed

½ to 1 onion, diced small

2 to 3 stalks celery, diced small

1 to 2 carrots, diced small

1 teaspoon sea salt

Lots of freshly ground pepper

1 bouquet garni (an herb bundle tied with string) including a bay leaf and any or all of the following: a sprig of thyme, a sprig of sage, a sprig of parsley, a rosemary stem

1 to 4 cups beef stock, fat removed, or filtered water

¼ cup or so of red wine (optional)

Potatoes and/or carrots, cut into large chunks

½ to 1 pound green beans, stem ends cut off

Salt and pepper to taste

Crème fraîche

2 to 3 tablespoons parsley or celery leaves, minced

Heat the fat in a heavy bottomed pot that is deep enough to fit the roast with the lid covered. Have the flame at medium or medium-high. When the fat is hot, put the roast in the fat and brown on all sides, turning it in the pan as needed. When the roast is browned, remove it to a cutting board and add the onions to the fat. After a few minutes, add the celery. After a minute or two add the carrots, and then the salt and pepper.

When the vegetables have all sautéed for a few minutes, add the roast back to the pot, add the bouquet garni, then add enough beef stock, water, and/or optional wine so that the roast is about ¾ submerged in liquid. Bring the liquid to a boil and then reduce heat to a bare simmer. Cover the pot and allow to simmer about 3 hours. Once or twice during the simmering period, turn the pot roast over with a wooden spoon.

Remove the pot roast to a cutting board, take out the bouquet garni and discard. If the remaining mixture has a lot of fat floating on top, skim it off with a spoon. Using an immersion blender, puree the remaining mixture until smooth. Return the roast to the pot along with potatoes and carrots. How many vegetables depends on how much room you have in your pot and how many you want to eat or serve!

Return the pot to a simmer and cook for another 20 to 30 minutes, or until the vegetables are fork tender. The pot roast should also be very tender.

Add the green beans and most of the minced parsley or celery to the pot, reserving some for garnish. Simmer another few minutes. Taste the gravy and add more salt and pepper to taste.

I like to serve a chunk of meat surrounded by vegetables in a shallow bowl with plenty of gravy. Then I sprinkle with the remaining parsley or celery, and top with a dollop of crème fraîche. I often add a big dollop of homemade sauerkraut to the bowl as well. Serves 3 to 4 people for every pound of meat.

Calabacitas with Herbed Crema

Like a quick summer stew, this dish highlights the Bay Area's summer gems.

Calabacitas

1 ancho chili pepper, seeds and stem removed
½ cup boiling water
2 tablespoons Straus (or other local) butter
2 large leek or onion, diced
1 to 2 gypsy peppers, diced
5 medium summer squash such as crookneck, yellow zucchini or zucchini, cut in half lengthwise and sliced on the diagonal
3 ears of corn, kernels cut off of the cob
Leaves from 1 sprig fresh marjoram or oregano, minced; or 2 sage leaves, minced
½ cup chicken broth or filtered water (or more as needed)
2 medium heirloom tomatoes (or 1 large, or a few small), diced into small cubes
Salt to taste

Put the ancho chili in a bowl and pour the boiling water over it. Allow to rehydrate for 15 minutes or so, then remove from water (reserving the soaking water) and mince finely.

Heat butter in a heavy bottomed shallow pan or skillet over medium heat. Add leek or onion and sauté until translucent but not brown.

Add gypsy pepper and then squash and sauté until it just begins to brown.

Add minced ancho chili, minced marjoram, oregano or sage to pan, then immediately add corn kernels. Stir for a minute.

Add the chili soaking water (strained) plus extra broth or water and a generous pinch each of salt and pepper. Bring to a simmer. Add more liquid if it gets too dry.

Simmer for 2 to 3 minutes, then add tomatoes. Heat tomatoes through, then taste and adjust seasonings as necessary, and remove from heat.

Herbed Crema

3 scallions, a small bunch of chives, or the tender inner greens of leeks
½ bunch cilantro
½ cup Cowgirl Creamery crème fraiche

Slice scallions, chives, or leek greens into small rounds. Cut the leaves off the cilantro. Mince the scallions (or chives or leek greens) and cilantro together on a cutting board, or process in a food processor.

Stir the minced herbs into the crème fraîche

To Serve: Ladle the Calabacitas into a shallow bowl, and serve with a big dollop of herbed Crema. I like to accompany with a green salad with cold roasted chicken on top. Serves 3 to 4.

pints and quarts. Our beef stock cooks for three days. Our crackers are rustic, artisanal, made with spelt, rice flour; we have sourdough crackers, too. Twenty-somethings are really into fermented vegetables. We have lots to choose from.

Weston A. Price essentially looked at traditional diets that kept communities healthy through the ages. He traveled around the world for eleven years, studying communities that were healthy, generation after generation. He asked people what they ate, wrote it down, took it back to his laboratory and analyzed it. Price wrote a book called *Nutrition and Physical Degeneration*. Sally Fallon took his work, looked at the common denominators and created a hybrid diet that became the foundation for the Weston A. Price diet included in her *Nourishing Traditions*. There are ten thousand people in the WAP Foundation. It's really more like a movement.

Here at Three Stone Hearth, we provide nutrient dense foods, traditional fats, lacto-fermentation (sauerkraut, kimchee, kombucha, broths, soaked grains). We're concerned about soy. We're concerned about people knowing what's in their food, about ecological farming, about parents having access to information. We're interested in all kinds of holistic therapies, in real milk from pastured-raised cows. We're very concerned about the quality of water, and especially fluoride. We remove fluoride from our water. We think there are too many links between autism and fluoride. And of course, we are interested in community-supported agriculture. These are our basic principles. When you make a decision to eat this way, you place yourself outside the mainstream. But because I believe so strongly in community, I will set aside some of my concerns to enjoy a meal with friends.

In the decades ahead there is much to do in this country. Although we have built our nation on independence and freedom, in the coming years we will have to acknowledge our interdependence.

As I say in my book *Full Moon Feast*, we must balance action and relationship, vision and tradition. And may we have that delicious experience of being, at least for a moment, well fed.

and knowledge of healthy foods. People's Grocery believes in food justice, that nutritious food is a human right.] They wanted me to teach at their "Collards in Commerce" summer program. So I began teaching cooking classes in Oakland and fell in love with the Bay Area. I decided that I needed to move out here, and in 2006 that's just what I did. I'm here to stay. I also plan on purchasing property in Tennessee. There's a lot that I want to do around health, food and farming in the south.

Anna Lappé read about b-healthy! in a book— the Future 500, which chronicled youth activism throughout the United States in the early twentieth century. She saw that I lived around the corner from her in Brooklyn and emailed me. We met up for coffee. After a few conversations, I knew I wanted to write a book with her. I didn't want to be too pushy about it, but then she actually suggested it. *Grub: Ideas for an Urban Organic Kitchen* came from those meetings. We remain in close touch, not

only as friends, but because we're constantly being commissioned to write articles as a team.

I practice in the Buddhist tradition of the Vietnamese monk Thich Nhat Hanh. I mediate for fifteen to twenty minutes every morning. During the week, after I meditate, I go to the gym, then I come home and get down to work. I work from about five to eight hours a day when I'm working on a book, and that might include testing recipes or doing research.

I do a little consulting for the Bioneers (www. bioneers.org). *[Bioneers peer into the heart of living systems to understand how nature operates.]*

I have been fortunate to have a lot of mentors to guide me on this journey. I also have many peer mentors in the Food and Society Policy Fellowship Program. We had our first orientation a few weeks ago in St. Louis. We schedule monthly educational calls, monthly checkins; we're constantly engaging with each other. It's great to be in a community of people who have been doing this work for a while, who are willing to share resources and knowledge.

Traveling the country filming the PBS series *Endless Feast,* I discovered how important it is for me to support local food systems. If I go to a farmers market, I know that they're going to get the most from the dollars I spend. I know who's growing my food and that there's a sense of love and goodness that they're putting into it. Unfortunately, not everyone has access to a farmers market. In Alabama, my parents get a lot of organic food, but some is not grown nearby. When they do have availability, though, I encourage them to buy locally. December and January are lean months everywhere, even here in the Bay area. Climate chaos is affecting everything. Still, I can get just about everything I want, year round, from our markets.

Anna and I targeted *Grub* at eighteen- to thirty-five-year-olds. We wanted to write for our peers, who didn't necessarily grasp these issues. We wanted to create a book that wouldn't take itself too seriously, that was fun, accessible and practical, laying out ways for people to take action. We didn't want people to feel hopeless or angry without being able to do something about it. We moved from essays to actual steps that one can take — how to stock a pantry, for instance, or how to support local food systems. We wanted to end on a celebratory note — bad as things seemed back in 2004, we felt really hopeful. There were so many organizations and activists working to build a healthier food system.

I'm an artist, a creative person, and I think of this work as my way of expressing myself. I want to learn more about filmmaking, video, even maybe do some painting. Multimedia. And of course I'm continually writing, cooking for my family and friends. And fatherhood! That's gonna be my main job!

Flash forward six months:

PHOTO COURTESY BART NAGEL

- I got engaged, bought a beautiful home with my fiancée.
- Built three raised beds out of redwood in our front yard. I'm now growing our own food.
- I've started a new book project.

With unemployment climbing, diet-related illnesses increasing, and health care costs sky-rocketing, more and more people are looking for ways to feed themselves healthfully, simply and cheaply. I will soon prove how easy it is to cook delicious, healthy meals year round using food from one's own garden, CSA and local farmers market.

Neal Gottlieb

Three Twins Organic Ice Cream ■ St. Helena, Napa, California ■ www.threetwinsicecream.com

A WET SUMMER DAY ■ *I have been staying at my sister's house for the last two days. She steers me toward Napa and, more specifically, the Oxbow Public Market. Napa seems a little more formal than Sonoma County, a little more dressed up, a little bit older. Yellow mustard is stunning against the wet wooden slats that hold grape vines.*

At lunchtime I drive over to the market, an airy warehouse near the Napa River. There's a Tea Shop, Olive Oil Press, Rotisario, Whole Spice Shop, and a Seafood and Meat Ranch. I have a plate of cheese and olives and a glass of Benzinger's biodynamic wine at Folio Enoteca and Winery. For dessert, I stroll over to Three Twins Ice Cream. I have a spoonful of Milk and Cookies, Madagascar Vanilla, Bittersweet Chocolate and Mint Confetti before deciding on a scoop of Bittersweet Chocolate. It's some of the richest ice cream I've ever tasted. I eat it out of a compostable bowl with a corn spoon. I look up to find this young fellow laughing at my delight.

Neal Gottlieb: I'm a twin, a fraternal twin. I came first and I'm an inch taller than my brother, and I don't let him forget it. He married a twin. She's the girl on the logo.

My brother's wife, Liz, teaches at a Marin County private school. She's a biology and environmental science teacher and one of my inspirations for making the store environmentally friendly. She gave me a book called *Cradle to Cradle* by William McDonough. He talks about how consumption is okay, that it's not going away, but we need to redesign the system. He says we can't just make things with recyclable materials. We have to really design things to be recyclable, to be taken apart, so that every aspect can be reused. The book itself is plastic. He used plastic to show how the book itself can be recycled.

Neal holds up a cup.

This is sugarcane fiber, a huge commodity worldwide. Typically the sugar is pressed out, then the cane fiber is burned in the fields of some developing country, contributing to global warming, to contaminants in the air, probably contributing to a lot of asthma and who knows what else. Some people have figured out that if you steam the fiber and press it at very high pressure, you can make a value-added product that is pretty waterproof and readily compostable. Bagasse, it's called.

Neal holds up a spoon.

And this is made of potato. The straws are made from corn. Of course the best biodegradable container for ice cream is a cone. When the cones start to get stale, we take them up to our local chicken farm in Yountville and feed them to the chickens.

There are no secrets to my ice cream. I use good milk — from the Straus Family Creamery in Marin County.

I grew up in a typical suburban family, clipping coupons in New Jersey. We bought typical food from chain grocery stores. We didn't think about natural or organic. My parents were born in 1945 and grew up during the great age of chemical food. We definitely had concerns about money. I saw both my parents working very hard.

I went to a public school that had really great academics with lots of electives ranging from robotics and computer science to art classes. I was sheltered from the elitism that I found when I went to college at Cornell. I didn't know what boarding school was, or what prep school was, until I got to Cornell. There were all these kids who'd gone to Exeter and all those Eastern private schools. I found it really funny that their parents spent $100,000 to put them through high school, but we all ended up at the same place.

I had a great upbringing. My parents always had a way to support whatever we kids wanted to do. They never said no, never doubted us. When I told my mom I was moving to California she said, "No problem, it gives me someplace to visit." When I decided to join the Peace Corps she said, "No problem." They were always supportive. Same thing with starting the business. They didn't know anything about organic ice cream. As my mom still says to this day, even though she works for me, she would never buy my ice cream. She grew up with Shop Rite and coupons, and half gallons of ice cream that cost $1.99, on sale for 99 cents. She could never justify spending six dollars on a pint of ice cream for herself.

Each summer we'd go on a family vacation. We never flew anywhere. We would always drive. When I was thirteen, we took a trip starting in New Jersey, driving nonstop to Minneapolis, then up to

Seattle and down the West Coast. We ended up in San Francisco and spent three days there.

Sometime during each day of these family vacations we'd do two things: find a miniature golf course, and have some ice cream. Typically it was Dairy Queen, but if we found ourselves in the middle of nowhere, there might be a homemade ice cream shop. Certainly not organic, but we didn't know any better, and we loved it. Good family time.

There was this one day when we got going late and we didn't eat until maybe 10:30 in the morning, and we kind of skipped breakfast. The first meal of the day was actually blizzards at Dairy Queen. My mother will deny it to this day, but my brother and I swear it's true. I partially blame that incident for my going into the ice cream business.

Another story, kind of at the opposite end of the spectrum, was when we were taking a family trip in Vermont. We went up to Burlington to the Ben

RECIPES ■ Neal Gottlieb

A note for the recipes: Despite being in the food business, I am not a chef – more of an occasionally curious cook. The one truth that runs throughout of all of my flavors of ice cream is that good ingredients make good ice cream. The same is true for most, if not all types of actual cooking. Please don't kid yourself into believing anything else.Buy good ingredients and enjoy a good life.

My cooking tends to be unscripted and whimsical, which is reflected in the following recipes. They are quite forgiving and need not be followed verbatim. Play around; add some ingredients or leave out some others.

Breakfast: Pseudo Moroccan Eggs

When serving in Peace Corps Morocco, one of my favorite dishes was a tajine of a bed of tomatoes with eggs gently steamed on top, served with the ubiquitous, but always good Moroccan flat bread that was perfect for sopping up any tajine with one's (right) hand.

A couple cloves of garlic
1 small onion of any hue, chopped or thinly sliced
About 2 tablespoons olive oil, enough to coat the bottom of your pan
3 to 4 medium tomatoes, peeled and chopped
⅓ can of tomato paste (optional)
4 really good eggs, preferably fresh, organic and from a local producer
Sea salt and freshly ground pepper to taste
Raz el hanout (a Moroccan spice blend), cayenne pepper or other spices as desired

Peel tomatoes by plunging in boiling water for about 30 seconds, then rinsing in cold water. Skin will peel off easily.

Heat oil in a medium saucepan over heat, add garlic and allow to brown. Immediately add chopped/sliced onions and brown, stirring often.

Add chopped tomatoes, spices and optional tomato paste (not needed, but it adds a nice thickness/creaminess to the tomato mush). Cook uncovered over medium heat until thickened to desired consistency.

Crack eggs into a separate dish and pour on top of tomato mush. Cover and cook until yolks achieve desired consistency, about 5 to 10 minutes.

Add salt and pepper to taste.

Serve warm, preferably eaten with one's hands and some freshly baked bread. This recipe is happily modified with the addition of other veggies, such as peppers, tomatillas, green onions asparagus, or many others. Canned tomatoes (that you personally canned) can be substituted for fresh ones. Serves 2, but with a stretch it can serve 6 or more depending on the size of your skillet.

Lunch: Sesame Noodles

One of my later discoveries from the Chinese restaurants in the New Jersey of my childhood was cold sesame noodles, which is extremely simple to make, quite tasty and thanks to the nut butter, rather filling. This dish is traditionally made with peanut butter, but I make mine with almond butter for no particular reason other than the fact that it makes this dish even more delicious.

1 pound of soba noodles (though any flattish /spaghetti type pasta or noodle will suffice)
¾ cup of almond butter
3 tablespoons rice wine vinegar
3 tablespoons soy sauce
¾ cup chicken stock or water
1 clove crushed garlic
Crushed red pepper to taste
Sea salt to taste

Optional:

4 to 6 green onions, sliced
¼ cup white or black sesame seeds, toasted
½ cup peanuts or almonds, chopped
½ pound tofu or better yet, smoked tofu, chopped into small cubes
½ cup cucumber, thinly sliced
Handful of sprouts
½ cup bacon, chopped
1 can smoked oysters

Cook the noodles in boiling water that has been salted. Drain and rinse noodles with cold water.

In a separate bowl, combine almond butter, vinegar, soy sauce, stock or water, garlic, pepper and salt.

Toss noodles with sauce. Optional ingredients may be served on top or tossed in with the sauce. Starting with the base noodles and sauce, the options are really endless, so go wild!

This is great served hot, cold or somewhere in between.

Dinner: Deconstructed Thanksgiving or Anytime Turkey

While a perfectly browned turkey looks great straight out of the oven, rarely does it taste great, as the physics of the noble bird almost always lead to uninspiring dryness of certain parts . . . maybe there's a reason we only have roasted turkey once a year? Braising is a great treatment of a turkey, as the braising liquid not only keep the turkey tender, but it also imparts the flavor of whatever you choose to braise it in. I prefer a combination of chicken stock and red wine.

> 1 whole turkey, preferably one that lived a good life on a local farm
> Sprigs of various herbs including thyme, rosemary, savory
> 1 quart organic chicken stock
> 1 bottle red wine; a $5 to $10 bottle will suffice
> Assorted root vegetables: onions, turnips, beets, parsnips, carrots, celery root, potatoes to fill your braising pan
> Sea salt and freshly ground pepper to taste
> Olive oil

Quarter turkey as if you were carving a really big chicken. Leave thigh and leg quarters intact. Separate wings from breast. Discard breast. Alright, you probably don't want to actually discard the breast. Chances are that the dark meat and wings will fill your braising pan, so consider cooking it via a different means. I am going to make sausage with mine and some duck fat this year.

In two large skillets on medium heat, preferably cast iron, heat up oil and brown turkey parts, skin side first. Be sure not to crowd the turkey parts in order to allow them to brown properly. Brown in shifts as needed.

In a braising pan (with at least 3 inch high walls), make a thin bed of red onions, herbs and other vegetables, about ½- to ¾-inch deep. Place browned turkey parts on top of veggie bed. Fill area around and between turkey parts with remaining vegetables.

Pour red wine and stock into braising pan until it is about 1 inch deep.

Add braising pan to an oven preheated at 325 degrees for approximately 2½ hours, until turkey is tender and falls easily from the bone.

Remove turkey and vegetables from braising pan. Transfer braising liquid to a saucepan to reduce further and intensify the flavors.

Carve turkey, removing thin bones from wings. Braised turkey will not carve as neatly as a roast turkey, resembling pulled pork more than traditional Thanksgiving fare. Embrace this and enjoy its taste.

Your serving options are numerous here. You may keep the turkey, vegetables and braising liquid separate, or serve all together in a casserole dish.

Dessert: Port Poached Pears with Other Goodness

Poached pears look great, taste even better, are easy to make and play well with ice cream . . . a nice impressive dessert at the end of any dinner or date!

> 4 pears
> 1 cup tawny or ruby port (the good stuff is for drinking, so an inexpensive bottle works well in this recipe)
> 1 cup water
> ½ cup sugar
> 1 cinnamon stick
> Zest of 1 lemon, lime or orange
> ½ cup mixed dried fruit (raisins, cranberries, sliced apricots, etc.)

Peel pears, leaving stem intact. Slice off bottom so pears will stand freely.

Pour water and wine into the smallest saucepan that will accommodate your pears and bring to boil with sugar, citrus zest and cinnamon.

Add pears to boiling mixture, simmer covered for 20 to 25 minutes, occasionally spooning port liquid over pears to impart color. Toss in dried fruit after 10 minutes.

To plate, place 1 pear and a few tablespoons of the fruit mixture in a small pile in the bottom of a large flat-bottomed bowl. Spoon a few tablespoons of the wine mixture into the bowl. Add a scoop of Three Twins Ice Cream and serve immediately. I love the combination of hot pears with cold ice cream, but the pears may be prepared in advance and served cold.

and Jerry's factory. The week before, my brother and I had had our physicals. This was in the eighth grade, so that would make us around thirteen. I don't remember what my brother's cholesterol was, but mine was 299! I was this little pudgy kid. My mother refused to let us have ice cream at the Ben & Jerry's factory! I still remember it. We took this tour, and then at the end of it, it was ice cream time. The only thing on the menu without cholesterol was lemon ice. It wasn't even lemon sorbet, just lemon ice. I like to remind my mother of that.

Now my cholesterol is under 200. The last time I had it checked was about two years ago, right after I started the ice cream company. It was lower than it had ever been. I don't know if there's any ice cream paradox out there . . .

I moved out here in 1999 to take a job with the Gap at their corporate headquarters in San Francisco. I went to school basically studying business, public policy and government. It was a great job,

but it didn't really satisfy my inner being. That's when I joined the Peace Corps. I was in Morocco in 2002. Then in 2003, because of the war in Iraq, we were evacuated.

When I got back I wanted to find a way to combine the capitalist in me with the do-gooder. I started to think about going to business school to study entrepreneurship, learn more about green business. I applied for a fellowship from Cornell that was basically for people who were interested in business for the betterment of society, nonprofits or green businesses. I thought my Peace Corps experience would help, but I didn't get it. I decided to just go out and start the business anyway. I think it would have been a lot harder to do after business school, with six figure salaries waved in my face, and huge debt to pay back.

I looked for a retail space for about five to six months, but found that I lacked two things that landlords wanted: one was experience, the other was money. I was working with only about $60,000 cash, and maybe $10,000 or $20,000 more that I could get through loans. I had no experience at all in the world of ice cream. At that point I had actually never even made ice cream before. But I figured it's not rocket science, it's about good ingredients and learning how to use the machine properly.

I have two "normal" days a week, Wednesday and Friday. I load the truck, a Ford Ranger pickup with a freezer cap, and make deliveries — as far south as Cupertino, where I deliver to the Whole Foods we sell to, and as far north as St. Helena, to the Silverado Brew Company. We deliver throughout Marin, Alameda, San Francisco and Napa counties. At the moment I do all the bookkeeping, all the marketing, all the customer relations. Fortunately I have managers. For the first three months I had no employees. I made ice cream in the morning, then did the bookkeeping, ordering and all the other things at night. My job is always evolving. Right now we're raising about $1 million to build a factory so we can really get our pints out there. The factory will be in Petaluma. We'll share a facility with Cowgirl Creamery, another locally minded, organic company. It will feel like a real community. Cowgirl Creamery has received a lot of national attention as well as local recognition.

In five years' time, the empire groweth! I hope. I'd really like to be a national brand. I have no problem putting Baskin-Robbins out of business if it means more people are eating organic. So we have to find a way to make it a little more affordable. I think when we control more aspects of our production that will be possible. Within five years I'd like to see someone custom manufacturing our pint containers. Instead of being waxed paper, they'll be biodegradable paper containers. I'm looking forward to when the delivery vehicles are powered by renewable energy.

One of my goals is to create a nonprofit wing of the company that helps young organic entrepre-

neurs get off the ground. A real challenge that we all face is having enough resources to get going. Most young entrepreneurs just don't have the money to build out a kitchen. Three Twins could be a part of helping other people launch their organic careers, just by being an example of a successful community kitchen and providing grants for people who want to try. We'd offer advice about packaging, marketing, distribution and all those things that create the initial hardships.

We're members of 1% for the Planet, a consortium of businesses started by Yvon Chouinard, the founder of Patagonia. We agree to give away 1% of sales, not profits, to environmental nonprofits. It's amazing how that 1% adds up. Last year we gave away over $3,000. Yvon calls it his earth tax.

You can't be in the ice cream business if you don't like kids! I can't think of a better job. You get to spread happiness. And it keeps a smile on my face.

Update: Neal has grown his little empire to three stores, including a store in San Francisco's Lower Haight that opened in May 2009. He raised over $1.2 million for the Petaluma factory, which is nearing completion. Donations to environmental nonprofits, through 1% for the Planet, approached $7,000 in 2008. Neal's folks are still gainfully employed by Three Twins.

Taylor Boetticher and Toponia Miller
The Fatted Calf ■ Napa, California ■ www.fattedcalf.com

Neal Gottlieb tells me to run, not walk, over to his friend Taylor and his wife Toponia's artisanal charcuterie and butcher shop, The Fatted Calf, also in the Oxbow Public Market. Neal describes it as a nineteenth century meat market with flair. I am hoping for grass-fed lamb chops to bring back to my sister's house. Inside, all I can do is sigh at the glossy white walls that are panels of old Wedgwood stoves, the thick shelves made out of eucalyptus lined with jams, jellies and horseradish. The cold-storage display cases hold chorizo, andouille sausage, terrines, pates of duck liver, jerky. And lamb!

Taylor approaches, wearing a white apron and a welcoming smile.

Taylor: We started The Fatted Calf in March 2003. We'd been working out of a small catering kitchen in the Dogpatch neighborhood in San Francisco, down by the water. Before that I'd worked at Café Rouge for four years doing charcuterie with Marsha McBride, learning all about sustainable meats. It was a real eye-opener for me — the difference in the quality of life for the animals, how that translated into a higher quality of life for the people who ultimately wound up consuming them.

Charcuterie seemed to be a craft on a downturn; there weren't many people doing traditional salting, smoking or preserving of meats. Now it seems the pendulum is starting to swing the other way, there seems to be a big resurgence going on.

I grew up in Dallas, Texas. My mom did a lot of cooking but was by no means a professional. Since I was about sixteen I knew I wanted to cook professionally. I started after high school and really

enjoyed it. I gained insight into how the restaurant industry works. Then off to culinary school I went, the Culinary Institute in Hyde Park, New York. That's where I met my wife.

Toponia and I have been together for eleven years, and married since August 2001. We moved into this space about five weeks ago. A couple of our best workers from San Francisco actually moved up here to work with us. Community response has been incredible.

Our curing room is right here — temperature and humidity controlled. We designed the kitchen specifically for charcuterie. For the moment we have fourteen employees; seven of them fulltime.

We have nine different sources for our meats. Most of the pork comes from Heritage Foods *[Todd Wickstrom and Patrick Martins cofounded Heritage Foods, a nonprofit organization, in 2001.]* They are totally committed to everything we want in our meat. All the pigs are raised outside on pasture. They're not given any garbage, and the meat is just phenomenal.

Taylor takes me to the back of the shop and introduces me to his staff, then shows me all of his cuts of meat.

This is country rib roast. Patrick was having a hard time moving them, so we agreed to give them a shot. Now they're one of our bestsellers. Basically it's a shoulder and loin roast that we prep with a different stuffing or marinade every week. A lot of our produce comes to us from Hollister, Mariguita Farms. We got seven or eight pounds of green garlic from them last week at the farmers market and made a little relish out if it. We just cooked it down with some olive oil, a little lemon and some parsley. It's finished with a little bit of duck jelly to kind of bind it. So we're going to stuff that into a little pocket in the roast. That's the great thing about this country rib roast — it has this perfect natural pocket in between the ribs and the meat. It takes a filling or a marinade really well.

Crepinettes *[flattened sausages made of minced or ground pork, lamb, veal or chicken wrapped in*

a caul] are one of our biggest sellers. This is old-school traditional French stuff. We make a lot of different kinds, based on what's good and in season. With the wet winter behind us, we've got lots of black trumpets — so this week we've got pork crepinettes with black trumpet mushrooms. We get them all portioned out, then wrap them in these big sheets of pork. We sell them in packs of two. We make about fifty pounds of these a week.

Our sausage casing expert is Antonio. He actually moved up here from San Francisco. He's casing up Toulouse sausages right now. Everything is hand-made with a hand cranker. He just knocks them out, and it works beautifully. We're like fire ants back here. We come in and start attacking this stuff every day, because to keep this kind of thing going, and to keep it fresh and seasonal, it takes more work and thought than most people realize. Thursday's pretty much the big day for preparing for our

RECIPES ■ Taylor Boetticher

Breakfast: Chorizo and Potato Tacos

> 1 pound Mexican Chorizo
> 1½ pounds Yukon Gold potatoes
> 1 small white onion, chopped
> 2 avocados
> Chopped cilantro

Peel potatoes and cube into ½ inch squares. Cover in a pot with cold water and add 1 teaspoon of salt. Put over medium heat. Meanwhile, start the chorizo by crumbling it into a cold nonstick skillet and place over a slightly hotter flame than the potatoes. Stir frequently, and scoop out with a slotted spoon when done, leaving the fat behind. Drain potatoes when just done and pat dry.

Turn up the heat under the pan with the chorizo fat, and add potatoes.

Stir frequently until brown, then fold in reserved chorizo.

Serve in warmed tortillas, with sliced avocado, chopped onion and cilantro on top. Serves 4.

Lunch: Bucatini al' Amatriciana

> 6 ounces guanciale or pancetta, sliced thinly
> 8 cloves garlic, sliced thinly
> 1 tablespoon chili flakes
> 1 pint tomato sauce
> 1 pound bucatini pasta
> 1 cup grated Pecorino Romano

Put a large pot of water on to boil for the pasta. Start the guanciale or pancetta slowly in a heavy-bottomed saucepot with 1 ounce of water. Stir frequently and remove with a slotted spoon once it has crisped and set aside. Add the garlic to the pot and stir for 1 minute over medium heat. Add the chili flakes then immediately add tomato sauce. Bring up to a gentle simmer and taste for seasoning.

Salt the pasta water, add pasta and immediately stir. When pasta is al dente, drain and return to the pot and put back over a low flame.

Add all of the sauce, half of the guanciale and ¾ cups of

farmers market push. We pack up everything on Fridays. We do the Ferry Building *[San Francisco]* and the Berkeley farmers markets on Saturdays. We did the farmers market up here on Tuesdays last summer to introduce ourselves and our products to the people who live around here. We count on them for most of our business.

In those pots, we're making stock. We generate a lot of bones, so we make really rich stocks and then reduce them down ever further. We use them when we're cooking things like the green garlic. Sometimes we use them as binder in our pâtés. That's the essence of charcuterie — we use every scrap!

Under a full moon on my sister's deck, with a picturesque view of the Alexander Valley, we eat the lamb chops for dinner with a great bottle of pinot noir. One gets spoiled hanging around her. The next day I hit the road again, one last interview in the Sonoma area before I head south on Route 1.

the grated cheese. Stir well, then divide equally between 4 shallow pasta bowls.

Sprinkle remaining crispy guanciale over the pasta, and serve with remaining cheese. Serves 4.

Dinner: Roast Pork Loin

1 10-rib porkloin, chine removed and skin on
½ cup chopped herbs, including rosemary, sage and parsley
6 cloves crushed garlic
¼ cup olive oil
Salt and pepper to taste

2 days before cooking, peel ribs away from loin (you can have your butcher do this for you) and score the skin with a tip of a knife in a diamond pattern. Salt and pepper the roast and set aside. Mix herbs, garlic and olive oil in a mixing bowl and spread in between the ribs and loin. Tie the roast back together into its original shape, then wrap tightly in plastic and refrigerate.

Preheat oven to 375 degrees. Pull the roast out of the refrigerator to temper slightly (it will cook more evenly if not ice cold). Put the pork loin onto a roasting rack, skin side up and place in the middle of the oven. After about 30 minutes, check the color. If it is a nice golden brown, turn the oven down to 300 degrees and let it finish up slowly. Check the internal temperature in the middle of the loin after 1 hour and 15 minutes total cooking time. When the thermometer reads 140 degrees, pull the roast and turn the oven back to 375 degrees.

Remove the cooking twine and separate the ribs from the loin with the tip of your knife. Carve the ribs into individual pieces and return to the oven to crisp up while the roast rests. When the ribs are crispy, slice the loin thinly and plate. Garnish the sliced meat with one crispy rib per plate and pour any accumulated pan juices over each. This roast is very versatile and goes well with sautéed greens, polenta or risotto. Serves 10.

Tucker Hemquist

Skipstone Ranch Olive Oil ■ Geyersville, California ■ www.skipstoneranch.com

CALIFORNIA DREAMING ■ *I love olives. I eat them almost every day. In my dream life I sometimes imagine myself living in a small stone house near a stream that waters a luscious olive grove.*

My nephew Julien steered me to Tucker Hemquist, olive oil maker and beekeeper at Skipstone Ranch, an estate tucked into the steep mountainsides and rolling hills of the Alexander Valley. On the ride over, it's one splendid vineyard after another. I pass palatial homes, mostly pink in color, that remind me of Italy. I guess that's the point. Tucker said to honk when I got close. He comes out to greet me, a tall man with short cropped hair, a firm handshake and a wide smile below a mustache.

In addition to being chef, olive oil maker and permaculture guru, Tucker coordinates sustainability at Skipstone.

Tucker Hemquist: I'm originally from Minnesota. I did undergrad out East at a small liberal arts school in Pennsylvania, majoring in music performance and history. After living in Minnesota for eighteen years I moved to San Diego for a little better weather, and started working in restaurants. I moved to the Bay Area to attend culinary school, and finally settled in Sonoma County. I was attracted by a culinary scene intensely focused on using local, seasonal and sustainably farmed produce. I wanted to be more attached to my ingredients. I wanted a deep connection to the land and the ecosystem.

We stand in front of what Tucker calls his culinary garden. It stretches forever, with vegetables and herbs meticulously arranged.

This past year I designed a huge extension to the garden, and it's now all on a berm and swale

system. Much of the current garden was bare ground last year, hardpan, covered with weeds. My training is in permaculture, so there's an extreme emphasis on using water and resources efficiently, stacking functions so that one aspect of a system performs many functions within the whole. Water flows down the hillside and zigzags back and forth across the garden several times before exiting out the bottom. The design slows the water, spreading it out, letting it sink in; building up the water so it quenches the garden long into the dry season. It's all on drip, but we also do a little overhead watering, which is efficiently stored by well mulched swales. Everything is thriving.

I've been here for three years. Shortly before my arrival, Skipstone hired organic farming consultant Amigo Bob Cantisano, one of the most respected and influential figures in California organic agriculture. The vineyards are all certified organic. The garden is farmed completely free of pesti-

cides, organic or otherwise. By using biointensive planting methods *[closely spaced plantings from companion species]*, we are able to allow for crop loss due to insects and birds. I feel that all creatures have a place in the ecosystem. Using sprays, chemical or organic, upsets nature's balance. All the bed ends are planted with insectaries to bring in bees and other pollinators along with beneficial predatory insects for habitat. The surrounding area is planted with native wildflowers to provide habitat for predator birds and insects.

We donate our excess produce to the Healdsburg Food Pantry, and we've just started working with the Ceres Project, a local organization that prepares meals for families of cancer patients who are undergoing treatment. The Ceres Project has made over thirty thousand meals almost exclusively from donated food.

As a child, my life with food was simple. My parents loved to cook but the resources weren't

RECIPES ■ Tucker Hemquist

Baked Egg with Roasted Beet & Zucchini Hash and Pistachio Pesto

2 large beets
1 medium Onion, small dice
3 zucchini, large dice
2 garlic cloves, minced
4 eggs
2 cups basil
½ cup raw pistachios
Olive oil, salt and pepper to taste
Parmigiano Reggiano cheese, grated, to taste

Preheat oven to 375 degrees. Coat beets with olive oil and season with salt and pepper. Roast for 35 to 45 minutes until tender. Allow to cool slightly. Peel and cut into ½ inch cubes. Sauté onion with olive oil in a medium cast-iron pan until translucent. Add zucchini and increase to medium-high heat. Continue to cook until lightly caramelized. Toss roasted beets and garlic into zucchini mixture. Crack one egg in each quarter of the pan and cook in oven to desired egg doneness. While eggs cook, blend basil and pistachios in a food processor. With machine running, add olive oil until pesto is smooth and pourable. Salt to taste. Remove pan from oven and immediately add grated Parmigiano and pesto to taste. Serves 4.

Pulled Pork "BLT" with Avocado Mayonnaise

3 to 4 pound pork shoulder
1 tablespoon each ground cardamom, cumin, coriander, paprika, garlic, ginger, black pepper
3 tablespoons salt
2 medium onions, thinly sliced
1 cup mayonnaise
2 avocados
1 cup cilantro
1 head butter lettuce
3 to 4 large tomatoes, sliced
8 or more Ciabatta rolls

Mix spices and salt together and coat pork shoulder thoroughly. Smoke pork for 3 to 5 hours in smoker. If you don't have a smoker, add 2 tablespoons of any smoked chili powder to spice mixture and proceed with next step. Reserve any spices that don't stick to pork. Preheat oven to 200 degrees. Sauté onions and any remaining spices in olive oil in dutch oven or other deep sided pan. Add pork and 1 cup of water and cover with lid. Cook in oven for 10 to 12 hours, until meat pulls apart easily. Allow to cool for at least 30 minutes before pulling. Mix mayo, avocado and chopped cilantro until smooth. Add salt and pepper to taste. Build sandwich on toasted buns and enjoy. Serves 8 or more.

Smoked Paprika Hanger Steak with Eggplant, Israeli Couscous & Corn Pudding

2 to 3 Hanger steaks (a.k.a. Butcher's steak or Beef Onglet)
Smoke paprika, as needed
2 large eggplants
1 lemon, juiced
1 cup Israeli couscous
3 garlic cloves
½ cup mint
8 sweet corn ears

Coat steaks in paprika and set aside. Cut eggplant in ½-inch thick rounds and soak in water with juice of ½ lemon. Start couscous in olive oil in medium sauce pan over low heat until it begins to brown. Add 2 cups water, garlic and salt to taste.

great. My mom always had a beautiful garden. We ate well in the summer, and canned and froze what we could for the winter. Winter brought mostly processed and frozen foods from the supermarket — a heavy meat-and-potatoes diet.

I notice that one of their wines is called Makena. My daughter's name is Makenna.

Fahri and Jill, the owners of the Skipstone, have three children, Oliver, Makena and Melina. The two estate wines and the olive oil are named after them. Oliver's Blend is the red wine, Makena's Vineyard is the Viognier and Melina's Harvest is the olive oil. Their first olive oil harvest was the day Melina was born.

Our oil case is certified extra virgin by the COOC. Extra virgin oil must have a low acidity. Once it

Cook until al dente, 8 to 10 minutes. Cut kernels from corn and blend in blender until smooth. Strain through fine strainer. Cook in medium sauce pan on low until it thickens to a pudding consistency. Salt and pepper to taste. Preheat grill to medium-high heat. Salt and pepper beef and eggplant (separately) and coat eggplant in olive oil. Grill steak to desired doneness and lightly char eggplant on both sides. Cover meat with foil to rest off the heat. Chop eggplant and add to couscous with ½ lemon and mint. Ladle corn pudding onto a plate and top with eggplant couscous and ½-inch thick slices of steak. Serves 4.

Carmelized Apples with Honey-Mascarpone Cream and Toasted Walnuts

3 to 4 Granny Smith apples (or other tart variety)
3 tablespoons butter
2 tablespoons brown sugar
1 teaspoon vanilla
3 to 4 tablespoons honey
1 cup mascarpone
½ cup heavy cream
1 teaspoon lemon zest
1 cup walnuts, chopped
1 teaspoon ground mace
Sea salt to taste

Peel and core apples and cut each into 8 wedges. Sauté with brown sugar in butter over medium heat until lightly caramelized. Add vanilla. Mix honey, mascarpone, cream and lemon zest until smooth. Pan roast walnuts, mace and salt in dry sauté pan until lightly toasted. Toss frequently to avoid burning. Place warm apples in a bowl topped with a generous dollop of cream and top with walnuts. Serves 4.

passes that test, it's tasted by a panel that looks for defects, most of which come about as a function of poor handling. The different categories of inexpensive olive oil you see in the grocery store (virgin, light, extra light) are primarily a marketing tool. Those oils are typically made by repressing olive pomace and "cleaning" it to remove odors and colors.

We do everything possible to pick and press our oil the same day. Acidity rises the longer the olive sits once it's off the tree. We have a small operation relatively speaking — 550 trees. I'll take two bins at a time in the back of the pickup truck to the mill so they can get started.

The three basic characteristics for the taste of olive oil are fruitiness, bitterness and pungency. Fruitiness is the flavor of the olive. Grassiness, nuttiness, floral and green apple are just a few of the descriptors of an olive oil's fruitiness. The bitterness is what you feel in your mouth — the pucker factor, if you will. And the pungency is the throat feel, the way it lingers down the back of the throat. Does it last long? Does it burn? Tasting olive oil in its purest form is done with a tinted glass, because despite the common misconception, color is no indicator of quality. The most prized oil has a nice balance of aroma, fruitiness, bitterness, and pungency.

Our olives are primarily Manzanillo, which is a Spanish olive with a floral, buttery, nutty flavor. Our oil maintains a very delicate balance between a floral, nutty flavor and slight grassiness, with a delicate pungency on the finish. It's perfect for many applications because its flavors don't overwhelm other ingredients. It is good to have a few different olive oils on hand to cook with, because there are so many different flavor profiles. They all work well in different preparations.

Olives are fairly easy to cultivate. The biggest challenge with manzanillo is you really have only about a week or two to pick when the flavors are perfect. If you pick too early, the pungency and bitterness are overwhelming. Too late, and the flavor is bland.

Artisan oils out of California are more expensive, but much more diverse and dynamic in flavor than most of those imported from Europe and North Africa. Labor costs for picking olives are astronomical. We hand-pick everything to protect the delicate fruit. Certainly not for efficiency. We do it for love.

Like most fruit trees, olives are very heavily alternate-year bearing. This is supposed to be our "on" year, but this May and June the weather was

abnormally cold. We had an amazing bloom, lots of flowers, but a very small fruit set. All the olive producers I talked to say the same thing. You need a certain temperature for pollination and we just didn't get it this year. That's farming!

Part of our sustainability goal is to be able to have everything happening here. They've started preliminary plans for a winery on site. We have a Class B fault line running right through our property, which makes development very difficult. However, it's created amazing diversity at the site. We've done extensive soil studies and determined that there are over thirty different soil designations, completely different growing conditions within the acreage of the vineyard, giving our winemaker a huge palette to work with in blending. The vineyard has rich nutrient soil, really loamy. It's producing amazing wines. The vines are stressed, which is how you make exceptional wine. The terraces are twenty-year-old, grandfathered-in vines. You can't put terraces like this in anymore because of erosion concerns.

We fluctuate between three hundred and five hundred cases of wine every year. We've replanted an area, and when that's in full tilt we'll get up to one thousand cases. All the grapes and berries are sorted, so we're only using perfectly ripe berry fruit. This, as well as the garden and the olive orchard, is all really labor intensive. But it goes with our philosophy of supreme quality and sustainability with all of our estate products.

I live in the Forestville-Sebastopol area on two acres with my partner, Julia, our son, Isaiah, and five other people. We are food-foresting the entire property, meaning we plant first and foremost with the idea of feeding ourselves entirely from the property. My life is defiantly communal.

My training in permaculture tells me that after you set foot on a piece of property you shouldn't do anything for a year but observe the land. Observe sun patterns, wind patterns, water patterns, migratory patterns of birds and what insects you have on the property. Those are all the things that make up the property. They've been there longer than you have, and can best tell you what to do as a steward of the land.

When I first came here, I did very little the first year. I observed the blank canvas. I built a couple of garden beds and planted a few trees. Most of the trees I had to move, or they died because they weren't in the right place. That was a good lesson. Being antsy is not going to get you anywhere. Having the land speak to you and tell you what to do is what you need. I count Brock Dolman, the permaculture teacher and water rights activist, among the most influential people in my life. Brock taught me to always look through a lens of complete interconnectedness. What you do here is going to affect this plant over there, this animal over here, these microbes. Thich Nhat Hanh has a quote that is a favorite of mine: "We are here to awaken from the illusion of our separateness."

Carolyn Swanson
Passion Purveyors ■ Pacific Grove, California ■ www.passionpurveyors.com

I rise early. It's already warm and I'm in the heart of Monterey, California. I take Luna walking on one of my favorite stretches of Point Lobos. As we continue along the cliffs, I catch sight of a plastic water bottle stuck under a small rock. Then another one. Every piece of plastic that's ever been made still exists in some form. Plastic is a polymer so dense nothing on earth can break it down.

Carolyn Swanson grew up around good food and has worked in the restaurant business for much of her life. Several years ago Carolyn decided to start her own business using products made from renewable sources such as corn, sugar cane, and potatoes, 100 percent compostable, for restaurants.

Carolyn Jean Swanson: I'm named after my mom's favorite Catholic nun. I was born and raised in California. When I turned sixteen my family moved to Washington State for my dad's job. I have one older sister and a younger brother. We're all five years apart. I guess you could say that my parents are very organized. I finished high school and attended Washington State University. There I met my husband, Brandon. My degree is in statistics and operations management, and his is in hospitality management. I knew with those degrees we could work so many places, live in beautiful areas. When we graduated we decided to move to Monterey, California, where Brandon was offered a job at a premier golf resort.

My mother's parents (Tip and Grandma) were German, and food was strictly a necessity for them. Because Tip grew up so poor, he and Grandma enjoyed simple foods, like pasta, meat and sandwiches. My Uncle Steve talks about a pasta dish he had as a child. The "recipe" goes like this: boil pasta, then drain. Cook ground beef, then add a can of tomato sauce and enough water to make the meat float. Pour over the pasta. Serve in a bowl.

The bowl was key, because the dish simply had too much liquid in it to be served on a plate! This soup spaghetti is probably the reason I have more memories of going out to eat with this side of the family.

My father's Greek parents, Yiaya and Papou, were the exact opposite. Papou and Yiaya were always cooking. Sometimes it was a simple roast chicken with oregano and lemon, sometimes it was complicated delicacies like spanakopita (spinach pie) or skordalia, a highly potent garlic sauce (think hummus, but made entirely of garlic and potatoes for thickness). They cooked as if each meal was their last. And we would all help. We couldn't leave their house without bags and bags of leftovers. Papou

came here from Greece in 1935. He had nothing, not even the native language. He worked for years for a small foodservice distribution company, then opened his own restaurant. A photograph of Papou with his two employees hangs in my kitchen. If you look closely, you can even read the menu. A tuna sandwich was only 25 cents! I love that about food and restaurants — you can come with nothing, work hard and become something. Magic! I learned so much about food from both sides of my family. From Tip and Grandma, I learned that food is a necessity, that it's not to be taken for granted because it might not always be there. From Yiaya and Papou, I learned that food is celebratory and brings people together.

I love cooking. My husband and I cook together all the time. A lot of our ingredients come from a local community supported agriculture program (CSA). Every Friday morning as we leave for work,

we put a check under our doormat. When we come home, there's a box of delicious locally grown organic fruits and vegetables from JP Organics. This past week we got two baskets of strawberries, a basket of raspberries, basil, cilantro, beets and a beautiful squash.

We also frequent the local farmers markets year-round. There's one almost every night of the week. Sometimes, when I get my box of veggies, if I'm on my way home from the market with farm fresh eggs, I stop to think about it and almost cry. Food is precious. I realized I needed to do something that would help preserve it because it had brought so much to me, to the people I love. I knew I wanted to make my living helping the food industry, I just had to figure out how.

I always wanted to have my own business. As a kid I had a rock store. I would collect rocks from our yard, clean and sort them, then sell them to my sister and our neighbors. There was no real money involved, just displays, customer service and fake phone calls that I answered on an old broken phone. When I wasn't working in the "store" I would "make" food out of homemade bread dough for a pretend restaurant, little pizzas and pastas.

Through school and as an adult, I've worked in several restaurants. One of my favorites was Clint Eastwood's Restaurant at Mission Ranch. If you've never heard of it, it's a fun, quirky place. Once the sun goes down, "It's a Wonderful World" and obscure operas are belted out by locals and visitors in the main dining room at the piano bar. The California ranch style food is all made from scratch. I loved visiting with the cooks at their stations, helping to chop and season food until the dinner rush came in and I went out to serve. It was a magical place for me.

Every restaurant has its own personality, recipes, special characters, unique vibe. They are alive and fragile. They easily become a nightmare if the owner has even the slightest delusion of grandeur. I began to think about how I could bring something to each of these restaurants that they couldn't do for themselves. Something that would make their lives easier, their businesses stronger, and benefit the communities that support them.

A friend of mine had this little place where she'd make soup from scratch. She told me that most soups come to restaurants in a large, thick plastic bag. The bag is either boiled, or microwaved, or the contents are placed in a huge soup pot and kept on heat all day. This is done for efficiency, consistency and to keep the soup safe from contaminants. Most people think soup is made on site with leftover pieces of meat and vegetables from meals. This would certainly be a great way to create less waste and more profit. However, the majority of restaurants don't make much of the food they serve; they simply reheat it. It's not fresh, and not nutritious.

I thought about that simple plastic bag made only to transport loveless, premade soup. Another problem started to unfold in my head: Where *did* all the

food scraps that could be turned into soup go? What about the packaging the soup came in? How about the packaging that restaurants send their soup out in? I started to realize that although the quality of food may be an issue in some restaurants, the waste created by food service is an issue in *every* restaurant! If a simple menu item like soup had such a huge carbon footprint, we had a problem.

That was the moment a second passion was born to me, and that passion was waste. I saw it everywhere! I found myself looking in trash cans along the sidewalk. I'd drive down the road and see plastic bottles in the gutters. I noticed lights being left on all day regardless of need, water usage without low-flow nozzles, food scraps going to the landfill instead of being composted. So here I was with my newfound sense of direction. I loved restaurants, and I knew they were plagued by waste.

One day, I was talking to a café owner and she showed me a spoon that she said was made from corn and potato starch. "It will break down and go

RECIPES ■ Carolyn Swanson

Breakfast: Crustless Quiche

When we get our CSA (community sustained agriculture) box I am faced with veggies that need to be used quickly to preserve their perfect nutrition. What to do with a myriad of veggies? I love making this crustless quiche. It's super easy and good for cleaning out the fridge! Since the dish is baked in the oven they develop a texture like rich, savory custard. The potatoes and eggs have to stay constant – but you can use any veggies and any cheese you have on hand.

- 2 tablespoons of olive oil
- 2 large potatoes
- 5 large eggs
- 4 cups fresh veggies (broccoli, spinach, cauliflower, toma-toes, zucchini, eggplant, anything!)
- 1 clove of garlic
- 1 handful of fresh basil, or a few large pinches of fresh Greek oregano plus a pinch for garnish
- 2 ounces feta cheese

Preheat oven to 350 degrees. Using a mandolin – slice potatoes as thin as possible. Heat a large skillet (that you can place in the oven with a tight fitting lid) on the stovetop with olive oil at medium. Add the potato slices one at a time to create an even layer of crust on the bottom. Season with sea salt and freshly cracked pepper. Let the potatoes start to crisp (about 7 minutes).

Meanwhile, chop the vegetables into same size pieces so they will cook evenly. Mince the garlic. Whip the eggs with 4 teaspoons of water. First place the herbs, then the chopped vegetables onto the potato crust. Season with sea salt and freshly cracked pepper. Slowly pour the egg mixture over the veggies. Sprinkle with cheese.

Cover and bake for 20 to 30 minutes depending on your vegetables and oven. It's done when the middle is ever so slightly wiggly. Let cool with lid on for 10 minutes (it will finish cooking here). Garnish with a bit of leftover herbs. Serves 4.

Lunch: Confetti Salad

This salad eats like a meal – filling but also good for you! A well balanced, colorful mix of my own interpretation of the Italian caprese salad (tomato, fresh mozzarella and basil). The best in summer. I usually bring this to any event that requires us to bring a side dish. The key is to make everything consistently small – so that it looks like a bowl of colorful confetti.

- 3 slices whole wheat bread (preferably stale)
- 2 pints cherry tomatoes
- 1 large ball of fresh mozzarella
- 4 Persian or 1 English cucumber
- 12 large basil leaves
- ½ cup of dry toasted pine nuts
- 8 ounces crumbled feta cheese
- Olive oil
- White balsamic vinegar

Heat oven or toaster oven to 350 degrees. Cut bread into tiny ½-inch cubes. Toss with 3 tablespoons olive oil, 1 tbsp white balsamic vinegar, sea salt and freshly cracked pepper. Bake until golden brown and crunchy.

In the meantime, chop tomatoes in half. Cut fresh mozzarella and cucumber into ½-inch cubes. Place all basil leaves on top of one another, roll like a cigar and slice thinly (known as chiffounade).

In a small bowl, whisk together 4 tablespoons olive oil, 1¼ teaspoon white balsamic vinegar and sea salt and freshly cracked pepper for salad dressing. Set aside. Sometimes I double the amount of dressing – depending on how dressed you like it. Serves 4.

Dinner: Secret Rack of lamb

My girlfriend, Crystal, first introduced me to this lamb preparation. I love lamb and it is a staple in Greek Cuisine. This preparation makes even the skittish enjoy the succulent meat. The flavors compliment each other so well; there is not even a hint of gaminess to be found. We never told people how to make this, until now – it's better than any restaurant preparation we have ever had.

- 2 racks of lamb (approximately 8 ribs each)
- 4 cloves of garlic
- 3 sprigs of fresh rosemary (must be fresh)
- 3 tablespoons Dijon mustard

1½ cups of bread crumbs
Olive oil

Let the lamb come to room temperature before you begin. Preheat oven to 450 degrees. Mince garlic and rosemary. In a large bowl, toss bread crumbs with garlic and rosemary. Drizzle olive oil into bread crumb mixture until it resembles damp sand. Not too oily, but enough to loosely bind the mix together when you squeeze it in your palm.

With bare, clean hands, rub every crevice of the lamb meat with dijon mustard. Act as if it's sunscreen and you are going to the beach all day – cover every part with a thin layer. You should be able to visibly see the layer of dijon mustard.

Push the bread crumb mixture onto the meat so that you have a ¼-inch layer of bread crumbs all around. Heat a skillet that can be placed in the oven with 3 tablespoons of olive oil. Sear both racks of lamb on both sides until golden and then immediately place in the heated oven with the bones facing up. Cook for 22 minutes for medium rare.

In a large bowl, toss all ingredients except croutons together. Dress. At time of service, sprinkle croutons on top of salad. Serves 4.

Dessert: Three's My Lucky Number
My Aunt Tina, her Greek name is Athena, first showed me this strange yet addictive dessert. You need three ingredients and a willingness to try something new.

1 pint of organic strawberries
3 tablespoons sour cream
3 tablespoons brown sugar

Simply wash and stem the strawberries. Place sour cream and brown sugar in separate, shallow bowls.

Dip dry, clean strawberry in sour cream, then brown sugar.

Enjoy! This tastes like cheesecake to me. What does it taste like to you?

back into the earth," she said. I thought to myself: Cutlery made from renewable resources, and disappears without a trace! My lightbulb moment. That one spoon opened the door to a world of restaurant service I had never even imagined.

Shortly after that, Passion Purveyors, the Green Goods distributor, was born. Our mission — helping local food servicers produce less waste and reduce their carbon footprint. I sought out every manufacturer of compostable products I could find. I learned that those compostable spoons were certified to break down in 180 days in a compost environment — heat, humidity and time. I also found out that it wasn't just spoons, but almost any food service product that you would want in a restaurant. I ordered samples, learned which pieces were best for which applications. Some were plant-based polymers that aren't heat stable — fine for cold drinks, but the second you put them into a warm liquid, they warp and melt. Soon I was ready to take my ideas to local food service outlets. I knew a good restaurant owner would care about the environment as well as the food being served. However, since a restaurant is a business, each product had to be cost effective and perform to the high standards of each chef. How could I sell something that was more expensive than what the restaurants were already using?

I decided to pair the sale of these goods with all the "greening" services I could find. Services that would save the restaurants money as well as reduce waste. I found a third-party funded program that would come in and update lighting systems, including new CFL *[compact flourescent light]* bulbs, fixtures, and switches with motion sensors, along with updating fluorescent light ballasts, making less electricity produce more light. I discovered a program that would teach restaurants how to clean and maintain the coils in their refrigerators, freezers and air conditioning units. These changes would help save the restaurants money on their power bills. I could bring them compostable goods, but also give them important information. For instance,

1. Only 3.5% of petroleum plastic is recycled in any way. Very few plastics are recycled into the same type of container or product that they were originally. Usually, recycled merely means collected, not reprocessed into useful products.

2. The "chasing arrows" symbols only denote what type of plastic items are made from. Plastic manufacturers adopted the symbol over the protests of environmentalists, and are now being challenged in court by several cities over its implications.

I would teach them about things like polystyrene (commonly known as Styrofoam), which is actually a plastic product made from petroleum. No organism on earth can break it down because it's too dense. It truly will never go away. As Passion Purveyors gained accounts and I continued to grow my business, I learned that some people were more interested in listening than others, but I felt like I was making a difference.

As I became more passionate about waste issues in restaurants, I found that other local businesses and even residents had needs and questions. People would ask: "What can I do?" Fortunately, I have lots to say. I found myself helping more than just my beloved restaurants. Best of all, I learned it was not a secret. Anyone could find these resources. They're in *every* community.

One of the most frequent questions people ask is why compostable packaging is even necessary. Why not just recycle the current packaging? This is a good question because it shows the absolute disconnect we have with the waste we create.

Around the Monterey Peninsula there's a polystyrene ban that several coastal cities are in the process of passing. The ordinance will ban the use of polystyrene in restaurants. These cities realize that changing methods in local restaurants is one of the keys to reducing waste in the community. What keeps me passionate is the realization that the waste we create actually comes back to us in our food! The food that I learned as a child to celebrate and cherish.

My vision for Passion Purveyors is an evolving model, a community-minded supply company, to be used in every region. Creating less waste doesn't always have to mean focusing on trash. There are so many other ways to prevent waste by becoming more focused locally and thinking more sustainably.

I'll be traveling to Brazil for a month in 2010 to study their sustainable food practices and waste management systems. I'm also excited about learning what other cultures are doing to create less waste, reduce their carbon footprint. One of the biggest mistakes anyone can make is to assume that they have all the answers, so, I will travel with a fresh eye and an open mind. Look for updates on our website: www.passionpurveyors.com.

Benina Marie Burroughs
Almond Farmer ■ Merced County, California ■ www.vistaalmonds.com

AUGUST ■ *The pollination of California's almonds is the largest annual managed pollination event in the world. Close to one million hives, nearly half of all beehives in the U.S., are trucked to almond groves between the end of November and February. Two thousand of those beehives are hauled in the huge semi trucks of Newswander Brothers to the 950-acre almond orchard managed by Benina Burroughs.*

Burroughs farmers go back five generations, to the time when Benina's great-great-grandfather came to California from Illinois to find his future in milk.

One hundred years later, Benina and two of her siblings, Christina and Zeb, partner with their parents, Ward and Rose, on two thousand acres in the northern San Joaquin Valley. It falls to Benina to manage Vista Almond Company. She's in the process of transitioning 250 acres of groves to organic — with the rest soon to follow.

At the top of a long drive, through beautiful old oaks and cottonwoods, lies a white farmhouse. Benina waves as the front door slams behind her. After shaking hands, I tell her how much I like her name and she blushes. She's named after the daughter of a Ute Indian and a French soldier.

Benina wants to show me her garden. We walk away from the house toward an overgrown stretch of land.

Benina Marie Burroughs: I grow vegetables for everyone on the farm, employees included. I've decided to charge a small amount, $5 a week, to everybody. I want them to eat well, but I want them to realize that it's not free — I don't want them to take it for granted.

We once had fruit trees all over the almond groves, but I wanted them closer. We moved some of the trees up here. These are Sommerfeld apples — a Gala-Fuji cross. I hope next year they'll produce fruit. My melons last year were delicious. Ambrosia. This tree is an apricot and this one's a nectarine. I'm thinking of planting olive trees; olive oil would be great! I want to plant pomegranates. Wait 'til you see my mother's. Then I'll have dried fruit to go with the nuts. I'd like to have an herb garden, supply our local restaurants. And eventually, with all the milk from both the dairies *[run by her siblings]*, I'd like to make artisanal cheese.

I originally wanted to work the dairy but my sister beat me to it. After I graduated (from Cal Poly) in 2001, I planned to go away and work for someone else for a couple of years. In 2002 my dad hurt his back, so he asked me to come back and help out. At the time we still had beef cattle; I slowly started working with the beef cattle and the almonds. We pretty much got out of beef entirely just before the whole mad cow thing in 2003. Do you want a tour of the almonds?

I pile into her truck and we take off down the hill. As we drive along a curvy dirt road toward the almond groves, she points out her uncle's conven-

RECIPES ■ Benina Burroughs

Chicken Curry

    3 tablespoons olive oil
    1 small onion, chopped
    2 cloves garlic, minced
    3 tablespoons curry powder
    1 teaspoon ground cinnamon
    1 teaspoon paprika
    1 bay leaf
    ½ teaspoon grated fresh ginger root
    ½ teaspoon white sugar
    salt to taste
    2 skinless, boneless chicken breast halves, cut into bite-
        size pieces
    1 tablespoon tomato paste
    1 cup plain yogurt
    ½ cup coconut milk
    ½ lemon, juiced
    ½ teaspoon cayenne pepper

Heat olive oil in a skillet over medium heat. Saute onion until lightly browned. Stir in garlic, curry powder, cinnamon, paprika, bay leaf, ginger, sugar and salt. Continue stirring for 2 minutes. Add chicken pieces, tomato paste, yogurt, and coconut milk. Bring to a boil, reduce heat, and simmer for 20 to 25 minutes. Remove bay leaf, and stir in lemon juice and cayenne pepper. Simmer 5 more minutes. Serves 2.

Almond Pie Crust from Ama

This is a wonderful pie crust, healthy and can be made with no sugar or salt. We use for all our cheesecakes and cream cheese pies. It is divine for a chocolate pie. For a large party, double the recipe and use in a 9×13-inch pan.

    1 cup of whole natural Vista almonds
    1 stick of Organic Valley butter
    1 cup of flour (may use oat, wheat, rice or barley)
    1 tablespoon of sweetener (honey, brown sugar or sugar)
    1 teaspoon of vanilla (optional)

Process nuts in a food processor just until chopped. Add flour and blend. Add cut butter – process until blended add optional ingredients. Spread the mix into pie pan and press to cover the bottom and sides. Bake for 15 minutes in oven at 350 degrees. Let cool. Pour in filling – use in place of graham cracker crust.

---

tional farm. We pass a field of sorghum and a pasture of horses.

Our properties used to be together, but because of the differences in the way we wanted to farm, my uncle and dad split them up. My parents didn't want us to go through the same kind of unpleasant splits they went through with their father and grandfather.

We cross over a wide creek.

When we were young we would ride either our horses or bikes along this creek to catch crawdads. This whole area used to be farm fields, corn or alfalfa or whatever. Then on the other side of the ranch it was wide open. We would just have the cattle out there. We never went to Hawaii or any place exciting on vacations. We would go on pack trips on horses into the Sierras. Camp out. Those are our chickens. *[Benina points to a bunch of* open-ended coops.] That's my grandfather's house, all made of river rock. He's eighty-six and we had to take his car away last week. But I saw him driving and I had to tattle.

My sister's calves are raised over there in those red sheds, fourteen calves per pen. That's her organic dairy. She's been up here since 2000. Over there's my uncle's conventional dairy, and my brother's organic dairy's to the west. The almond grove kind of borders on all of them. Having the dairies here is awesome. When they move the cows onto fresh grass, you can actually hear them munching. Gives you a good feeling. When my great-great-grandfather dairied, milk came in glass bottles. My mom still has lots. She sold some as a fundraiser — $10 a bottle to raise money for a school she started for dyslexics. Both my brothers are dyslexic.

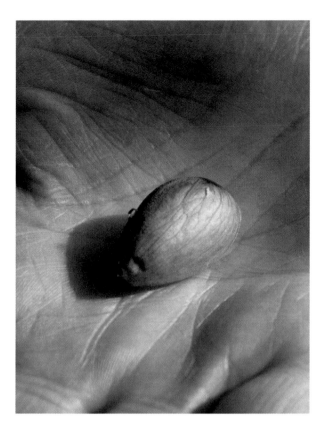

Up one hill, down another, then I see the almond trees.

Those won't be conventional forever. I can't transition all of them at once because I have to maintain my overhead. But I don't want to put anything that's not natural into the ground for all kinds of reasons, including employee safety. We just had Joel Salatin and Jerry Brunetti come up here during SlowFoodNation. I was so inspired. I can't wait to implement all this stuff! But with almonds, what I do today I don't see results for a year, sometimes three to four. Soon as you change a cow's feed, you can tell if milk production goes up.

She points to small wooden boxes that sit on top of long poles stuck into the ground.

Even before I began transitioning to organic, I was up against my sister's and brother's organic ground. I wasn't going to do anything that didn't use organic methods to get rid of squirrels and rodents. Those are owl boxes. They are house barn owls that prey on small rodents like squirrels, gophers and rabbits.

Those rows of grass and other ground covers are mowed at alternate times to sustain some habitat for beneficial insects. We make our own organic compost from dry manure and almond huller trash, which comes from trees that have died. I love what we're doing here. I love the changes that we're already starting, like composting.

Acre after acre of almonds . . .

Water is an issue for us. Second year without much rain. All we have are wells. Irrigation is required for almond production and water is pumped from the ground into microsprinklers or double-drip irrigation systems. We're not in any irrigation district. There is a corner piece of the property along one of the districts, so we're able to get some, but not very often. Some of our neighbors said their wells dropped thirty feet. We have a dry creek — called Dry Creek, which mainly runs during big rainstorms. My brother uses it to irrigate some of his pastures. We don't pump out of any rivers.

Some of our trees are as young as third leaf (have

ALL ABOUT ALMONDS ■ Benina Burroughs

Almonds are a heart-smart ingredient and snack that offers many nutrients. A one-ounce, 160-calorie handful of almonds (about 23 almonds) provides protein (6 grams) and fiber (3 grams) and is an excellent source of vitamin E and magnesium. Plus, one ounce of almonds offers potassium (200 milligrams), calcium (75 milligrams) and iron (1.0 milligrams). To include an ounce of almonds in your daily diet, add them to dishes and snack on almonds throughout the day. Visit www.AlmondsAreIn.com for more recipes using almonds and additional information about almonds and nutrition.

Recommendations for Storage:
- Store in refrigerator in glass containers
- Avoid exposure to strong odors as almonds can absorb odors of other materials if exposed for prolonged periods.
- Protect from insects/ pests.
- Roasted products must be protected from oxygen. Nitrogen flushing and/ or vacuum packaging are two options.
- If kept under cold storage conditions (<5°C and <65 percent relative humidity), whole natural almonds can be stored for about two years with no significant loss in quality.
- Rotate stock.

Almonds are perhaps one of the most versatile nuts in the world. Whatever the meal course, and whatever the ethnic cuisine, there's bound to be an almond form or culinary technique to fit. Whether you're using almonds for their flavor, crunch, or thickening properties, here are some guidelines and suggestions on using all the different available forms to their best advantage.

Whole Natural Almonds: This form is versatile, and is suitable for all-around use. Try it in cocktail mixes, such as Sweet 'N Spicy Almonds. This recipe uses a technique in which egg whites are whisked and combined with seasonings; the almonds are then coated with this mixture, laid out on a baking sheet and baked until crispy. Other techniques include coating the almonds in simple syrup and seasonings, and then baking them; or sautéing them with seasonings in a touch of oil or butter. Serve roasted whole natural almonds and dried fruit with cheese as a pre- or post-dinner snack.

Whole Blanched Almonds: This form works well as an attractive garnish, either as is or roasted to bring out its flavor and color. It's beautiful for color contrast on cakes, cookies and other sweets, or it can easily be ground for pastes or for thickening. Grind them in a blender or food processor as part of soups, sauces or vinaigrettes to add body and nutrition. Place them on top of sugar cookies just before baking – either one by itself, or two in the shape of a heart, or five in the shape of a star.

Roasted Almonds: Roasting almonds before serving them brings out their toasty crunch, flavorful oil and their golden brown color. To roast almonds, place them on a baking sheet in a preheated 350 degree oven for 10 minutes, or until golden brown and fragrant; stir once or twice to ensure even browning. Almonds will continue to roast slightly after removed from oven.

Sliced Natural Almonds: This form is well-suited for fruit salad, green salad, in hot or cold vegetables, in granola and in soup. Try a creamy vegetable soup with a sprinkle of roasted, sliced natural almonds for crunch and flavor. Or make a granola by bringing a touch of butter to a simmer

produced three sets of leaves, are three years old) all the way up to twenty-one years.

Here's how pollination works: The Newswander Brothers truck their hives down here in late November or early December. The queen doesn't lay eggs when it's cool, so the worker bees are kind of dormant, cuddled up to each other. After they arrive, the hives are set out on the perimeter of the almond fields until spring. It's warmer here, so they fly around a bit and forage. They eat honey from the hive, generate heat and try to get outside for "cleansing" flights. Come February, Mike Newswander returns and goes through each of the hives, removing bees that might have died over the winter. If a hive becomes too small, they're combined. Then, two and a half hives per acre are placed throughout the grove. The bloom starts in February and lasts two to three weeks. It's spectacular, white all over and steeping it with some orange zest; then stir in sliced natural almonds, oatmeal and dried cherries. Spread it on a baking sheet and bake.

Sliced Blanched Almonds: This form is attractive on decorated frosted desserts or as sprinkled on muffins or other pastries before they're baked. Make a spinach salad containing sliced blanched almonds, orange segments and red onion. Spread celery sticks with flavored cream cheese, and sprinkle some sliced blanched almonds on top for extra flavor and an additional layer of crunch.

Slivered Blanched Almonds: For stir-fries and grain dishes, this form holds its shape without breaking, to give some nice crunch and flavor. For one-pan meal preparation, try roasting slivered blanched almonds in a dry wok. Then dump them into a saucer, and stir-fry some meat, vegetables and sauce in the wok. Return the almonds to the pan and stir before serving. Try slivered blanched almonds in a rice pilaf or in couscous, with small-diced zucchini, red bell pepper and feta cheese. Top baked chicken breasts with sautéed mushrooms and a sprinkle of slivered blanched almonds.

Diced Natural Almonds: This form works well for stuffings and coatings. Many bread bakers include it in their whole grain bread dough. Coat fish fillets with milk, then with a mixture of diced natural almonds and Italian bread crumbs before baking. Stir diced natural almonds into whisked egg before making an omelet, for extra texture and nutrition.

Diced Blanched Almonds: This form works well for stuffings and coatings when a light, delicate appearance is needed. Press diced natural almonds around the sides of a cake, for a homey, crunchy rim. Include diced blanched almonds in pancake batter, and serve the pancakes with fruit such as peaches or raspberries.

Almond Milk: Found in a box near the soymilk at the supermarket, this form is delicious in coffee or in smoothies. Some pastry chefs sweeten it and make almond milk sherbet. Blend together almond milk, fruit and ice cubes or frozen yogurt to make a delicious smoothie. Make hot chocolate using almond milk instead of plain milk.

Almond Oil: Found in a bottle near the olive oils and flavored oils at the supermarket, this delicately flavored oil can be used in the same way as olive, vegetable and canola oil. Use it to enhance vinaigrettes, sauces and baked goods with a distinctive, subtle almond flavor. Make a creamy Lemon-Almond Vinaigrette by whisking together ½ cup almond oil, 2 tablespoons each of fresh lemon juice, light sour cream and honey. Season with salt and pepper. Replace olive oil with almond oil in a hummus recipe. Add toasted almonds to the hummus for more toasted almond flavor and serve with fresh veggies or pita bread.

Green Almonds: Available in limited supply in spring, green almonds are a true delicacy. These young, small, ivory almonds are still inside their fuzzy green hull. Cut the almond hull along the seam with a paring knife, and use the fresh, herbaceous-tasting nuts inside as part of a composed salad, or nibbled plain with a bit of sea salt.

To toast: toss until brown (2 to 3 minutes) in a non-stick pan over a high heat.

To blanch: drop them into a boiling water 2 to 3 minutes. Then rinse under cold water. With a pinch, the skins will easily, slip off.

the trees and on the ground, like fallen snow. And the smell is wonderful. The bees work like mad pollinating one variety of almond tree after another. End of March or first of April, the Newswander Brothers return, gather up their hives and go back to Idaho, where the bees rest. Summer's the time for honey production.

Harvest starts in August and runs through October. We have a wide array of almond varieties — Nonpareil, Fritz, Monterey, Padre, Butte, Ruby, Mission, Carmel, Sonora and Livingston. We need multiple varieties so the bees can cross-pollinate. Also, with different varieties, we don't have everything coming in at once. When the trees are ready, a machine goes down the rows and shakes each one of them individually. We've harvested the Nonpareil and we're getting ready to shake the Monterey.

Benina leans down and gathers up a handful of

almonds. She breaks one open and pops the nut into her mouth.

Taste one. They're kind of chewy. A little watery. You want the shells to be dried out like this. Some of them are still a little wet since we had a light rain last night. These trees are starting to get a bit stressed — we're holding back the water because we don't want them to be too wet when they're shaken, because they can mold — so we try to keep them dry.

After shaking, the almonds are left on the ground for about seven to ten days, depending on how green they are. Then they're swept into windrows in the middle of the row and picked up. Farmers pronounce almond without the "l" — a-mond, because they say that the nuts have had the "l" shaken out of them. *[Laughs.]* This is when the shell can be broken, when there's a chance bacteria could penetrate. If you have good management practices, if you've applied the manure early in the season, it should be fine. Due to a few cases of salmonella, the Almond Board passed a law in 2007 regarding pasteurization. Now we can't ship raw almonds. You can buy them at the farmer's market, or sell them directly from your own farm, but if you ship them to supermarkets, they must be pasteurized. Some farmers use polypropylene oxide and others use heat, steam vacuum or roasting. Alison (18 Rabbits) purchases those certified organic and heat-steamed for her granola products. In the markets, you can buy unpastuerized almonds from Spain or some other foreign countries — just not from the U.S. How crazy is that?

I've devised this system of watering where, as you can see, the sprinklers are wound through the trees facing upside down, watering the trees and grass from above. The sprinklers have good pressure and only open when there's water, as opposed to others I've tried that stay open all the time, allowing bugs to crawl into them and plug them up.

I'm trying to see how these organic trees do without so much water. They're still in good green shape and this block hasn't had water for a month. I'm proud of them.

Benina asks if I'd like to meet her parents. On the drive over, I ask Benina what she does for fun.

Fun. Well, there's my garden. I'm president of our local chapter of California Women for Agriculture. We do a two-day safety camp for third graders in May each year. I started the Young Farmers and Ranchers group up here in Merced. I guess you could say those things are fun.

Benina stoops to retrieve something from the ground—one of last fall's lush pomegranates.

Her father, Ward Burroughs, stands outside his single-level brick ranch house. He's six feet tall at least. He greets us at the door in jeans, cowboy boots and a wide-rimmed, white cowboy hat. Behind him, Rose seems half his size. They invite us in. Ward brings me a glass of water and a bowl of almonds for the table.

Rose tells me they met at Cal Poly, where all four of their children later went to school. They have been married for thirty-six years.

Rose: Ward and I have lots of experience dealing with family throughout time. What we wanted to do was prevent some of the hardships that we had when you have one big family partnership. We have four separate partnerships with each of our children. We're thrilled that we now have three organic farms. Our greatest legacy is not only what we can see right now happening for our children, but what we see happening for our grandchildren. It's not just a way of farming; it's a way of living.

Ward: My brother wanted to continue his conventional farm. The biggest problem is saving the equity in the business. We were lucky that our father set it up so that we could do this and we have done it amicably. It was a win-win situation.

Rose: Right now, depending on the year, California ranks fifth or sixth worldwide in ag production. At the rate we're losing land, they estimate that by 2040 we will not have enough land left in California to feed just the people who live in the state.

When we first moved out here thirty years ago, it was like looking back in time two hundred years. There were no power poles. There were three wind-

mills. No ag development. You could see all the way to Half Dome.

Ward: Most of the time you could see the Sierras. Now, you can only see them in the wintertime. Sure, part of it's the air quality, but its also just because of the pressure you get with more and more people, people coming out and developing the land, losing farm acreage.

Rose: About fifteen years ago the ranchettes started. It's a very nice opportunity for someone with lots of money who wants to retire. It's my opinion that the best prime ag land should not be used for houses.

Sometimes families don't have a choice. There are many, many stories of people that when their parents die, the inheritance tax is so high that the only way they can pay the taxes is to sell the land.

I ask if the State taxes it at the highest and best use, meaning subdivided. So that instead of $1,000 an acre for farming, it's $20,000 an acre for subdivisions.

Rose nods in agreement.

The pendulum has swung back and forth through history. Right now you have this kind of individualism that allows for little ranchettes. We're not looking at the whole — our existence here on this planet, and using the best fertile soil for the best quality food, when that makes the best quality of life.

We talk about Proposition 2 — a state bill to allow farm animals to be held in tight places where they can neither lie down nor turn around.

Benina: The Salatins and the Zimmers have the right idea about that: Chickens should graze grass. My sister is doing it with her chickens, selling all her eggs. She has sixty people on the waiting list since she signed up with a friend of ours who's doing a CSA.

Rose: We have to be careful not to regulate so stringently that we completely abolish production. We need sound science to base our decisions on.

Ward: We need to make sure that as many of these sustainable practices as possible are introduced so

that farmers can see the benefit of them. You're not going to force anything down anybody's throat. This organic dairy was started because it could be financially sustainable and still improve our world. Everything has to be sustainable, including the finances. Benina's applying methods like using compost, trying to incorporate some new ideas in the almonds, in the orchards; make it more than just a monoculture.

Rose: Our greatest accomplishment is having children who have the same interests that we do in terms of being in the ag business and having stewardship of the land. Benina's doing a tremendous amount of relationship building. She takes care of her employees, making sure they have the right equipment, that it's working properly and that their houses are well kept up. She started some savings and retirement practices. She plans picnics, soccer parties, takes her employees deep-sea fishing, to baseball games, Friday night barbecues. As a woman in ag, Benina has had her challenges.

Benina nods.

Benina: Just recently I was trying to get some materials to develop a mower that fits on the front of a tractor that can mow under my hoses up in the orchard. My foreman, who is not really a book learner, either, but he's really good with his hands, described what he needed. When I went in to order the rams, I described it as he had to me. The sales guy wanted specific measurements. I told him I didn't have exact measurements. Instead of being helpful and saying, "Okay, do we need to come out" or "Let's take some measurements," he pulled out his big old stack of papers and pointed at the piles and said, "here's all your options."

Ward: There have been times people have tried to circumvent her and come to me. I just reroute them and tell them to talk to Benina. "Ward, your daughter called and we couldn't understand what she wanted, do you want to clarify." I tell them, you need to call Benina.

Benina: If I were a man, they'd call me tough. But since I'm a woman, they say other things.

I'm going to *Terra Madre* — The Slow Food Conference in Turin, Italy. Since I'm single, I am the one in the family nominated to go.

Rose: This is my favorite story about Benina. She was four years old, and very independent. One time she got into trouble and I told her she had to stay home. As we were driving out of the driveway, she came out on the porch, hands on hips and said, "It's not my fault, I got bad blood on both sides of my family!"

Benina: If you knew their fathers, you would understand!

Update: Benina was married at the end of 2009.

SECOND FALL ■ *Late September in Durango, I start to gather things in piles for our trip back to New York City. It never seems to get easier to close up the house. Once again I'm caught in the hireth of leaving, the pull toward New York City, the tear away from Colorado.*

I've sent Lora Krogman (Angelic Organics, Illinois) several emails. It seems out of character for her not to respond. I know it's still the height of her busy season, but I decide to call her. I want to visit her on my way back to New York City. A woman with an unfamiliar voice answers the phone. She doesn't immediately respond when I ask for Lora, but after a beat or two, she says to hold on. I explain to another woman who picks up the phone about my project, and Lora. "I know Lora was very excited. I'm terribly sorry, but on September 14, Lora was involved in a fatal car accident and . . . she, she, died at the scene. I thought we had gone through all her emails and her phone book. I'm so sorry you weren't notified."

I drive until I hit Lawrence, Kansas.

Hillary Brown
Owner of Local Burger ■ Lawrence, Kansas ■ www.localburger.com

Hillary: Throughout my life I was plagued by chronic muscle pain, ear infections, mood swings, ADD, migraines and an overall general weakness. When I was in my early thirties I saw a naturopathic physician. He performed numerous lab tests that revealed food allergies and intolerances as well as thyroid dysfunction. He prescribed amino-acid therapy and probiotics. I quickly removed all the foods that I was reacting to from my diet.

Within a short amount of time I felt better than I ever had before. I began to do a tremendous amount of research on food and health. It was such a gift to finally begin to feel like myself again and start to learn about the connections between our food system, the environment, our economy, our culture and our health.

In September of 2005 I opened Local Burger. Local Burger is clean, real food free of unnatural additives and preservatives. Our meats are local and "beyond organic." Livestock such as buffalo, elk, beef and lamb are grass-fed only. Pork and turkey are pasture raised and heritage breeds. Our entire menu is gluten free, except for the locally made wheat bun. We also offer a locally made gluten-free bun for our hamburgers, and buffalo dogs that are just delicious.

Local Burger is committed to making food that helps people feel good physically and mentally, and serving the growing population of people with food allergies and intolerances.

In January of 2007 Local Burger did an experiment called "Localize Me." For thirty days we fed a guy only Local Burger. The results were astound-

ing! Dr. David Dunlap performed all the testing that we did at the beginning, middle and end of the experiment (see table).

Local Burger was fortunate to have Sundance Channel air some of the experiment in their series *Big Ideas for a Small Planet.*

I also stop in Mansfield, Missouri, at the Baker Creek Heirloom Seed Company.

	Weight	Blood Pressure	Pulse	Cholesterol	Testosterone	Insulin
Before	295	152/110	76	287	366	12.3
After	276	118/88	64	166	513	5.8

Jeremiath and Emilee Gettle

Baker Creek Heirloom Seed Company ■ Mansfield, Missouri ■ www.rareseeds.com

When I first visited Northern California and interviewed Jamie Peterson, he told me about Baker Creek Seed Company. He was standing ankle deep in the middle of his lush summer garden in Healdsburg, California, pointing out heirloom tomatoes, squash, and melons, all of which grew from Jeremiath Gettle's seeds.

"Apparently he's been saving seeds since he was four years old," Jamie said. He handed me the latest 120-page glossy Baker Creek Heirloom Seed catalog. "You gotta meet him, he lives somewhere in the middle of nowhere. Missouri, I think."

I drive toward Bakersville where Jere Gettle and his wife, Emilee, live on an original 1850s homestead and produce farm. It's also a replica of a pioneer town. I know from reading their quarterly magazine, The Heirloom Gardner, *that they began building the town mid-winter 2007. I'm not prepared for the lushness of the fields, the myriad colors of autumn.*

Jeremiath Gettle is also a bit of a surprise, with his boyish manner and unabashed excitement, his ear-to-ear grin. He greets me all dressed up in cowboy clothes in front of his white picket fence. The hand-hewn woodwork of the structures that make up the village is stunning, each building filled with antique furniture collected through the years. Fenced-in areas hold heritage chickens, ducks, geese, pheasants, pigeons, turkeys, a few rare sheep, rabbits and swans. There are piles of heirloom fruits, vegetable produce and a storeroom full of alphabetized seed packets. He's a modern-day Noah with Bakersville as his ark.

Jeremiath Gettle: I feel so thankful to be able to work at my dream job. I've been collecting seeds since I was little. When I was three or four I planted lemon cucumbers, scalloped squash and yellow pear tomatoes. I always had a little space in my parents' garden for my own plants. Each year I would plant everything I could find in the catalogs, but there wasn't a lot at the time. At sixteen I joined Seed Savers Exchange. That's when I really got into collecting unusual varieties, ten thousand seeds offered by their members.

I started my own catalog at seventeen. It was black and white. I sent out my first bunch to 550 gardeners, filling all the orders myself in my bedroom. Now my seeds come from everywhere. People bring them to me, saying, "Here's some seed for you," or "My great-great-grandma brought these over from Germany and we're afraid we might lose them." I also find seeds wherever we travel; so far I've been to Thailand, Cambodia, Burma, Mexico, Guate-

mala, and Belize. I look for seeds on the Internet. People find us online and send batches from different countries.

Heirloom seeds are seeds with a history passed down from generation to generation. There's a difference in opinion about how old an heirloom seed needs to be, but basically it's just one that has been passed down. The oldest varieties are more nutritious: they have a higher level of protein and vitamins along with micronutrients. The more diversity you have when you're growing a crop, the stronger it will be.

When we get seeds, we grow them here in our gardens, or send them to one of the many farms in the area, or farms in a couple of different states that help us out. Many of the farmers are Amish or Mennonite, or just seed collectors, even hobbyists with large gardens who just want to see the varieties preserved.

If the seeds grow true each year, we know they

RECIPES ■ Jeremiath Gettle

BREAKFAST: Vegan Waffles

We have these several times a week. We are always on the run and this recipe is quick and easy. If you have extras toss them in the freezer.

2¼ cups high gluten flour
½ cup quick oats
1½ teaspoons egg replacer
1 teaspoon salt
1 teaspoon cinnamon
½ teaspoon baking soda
2 teaspoons baking powder
2 tablespoons olive oil
1 13.5 ounce can coconut milk
2 tablespoons local honey
1 teaspoon vanilla extract
1 cup water

Preheat waffle iron to highest temperature. Combine all ingredients and pour into a lightly greased waffle iron. Serve hot with maple syrup or fruit that is in season. Recipe makes about 12 waffles.

LUNCH: Breaded Baked Tofu and Vegetables

1½ cups matzoh meal
1 cup yellow corn meal
1 tablespoon paprika
1 tablespoon parsley flakes
2 teaspoon salt
Dash of cayenne
Vegenaise (mayonnaise replacement)
1 box extra firm tofu

Preheat oven to 425 degrees. Combine all breading ingredients in a 9×9-inch pan. Slice tofu lengthwise, about ¼ inch thick. Spread veganise on all sides and roll in breading. I like to lightly press the breading into the veganise coated tofu. Place on lightly greased cookie sheet and bake for 30 minutes, flipping halfway through baking time or when lightly browned.

Use the same technique with sliced veggies for a great side dish. I like to use eggplants and summer squash. Serve with homemade bread. Serves 4.

DINNER: Vegan Tempura & Jasmine Rice

This recipe is really great to use with all sorts of vegetables. We especially enjoy sweet carrots, green beans, cauliflower, eggplants and summer squash. Okra is great too! Thinly slice or break apart the veggies and following the batter instructions below.

2½ cups flour
2¼ cups cold water
1½ tablespoons egg replacer
Dash of salt
3 to 4 cups oil for frying

Combine all ingredients until mixture is smooth. Oil temperature should be between 325 to 350 degrees. Dip vegetables in batter and gently drop into hot oil. Fry until golden brown and slightly puffy. They should rise to the surface. Transfer to paper towels to drain. Serve with jasmine rice and your favorite dipping sauce. Tamari is traditional.

DESSERT: Sweet Dumpling Squash with Apple Stuffing

10 sweet dumplings
5 medium Fuji apples, peeled and cubed
½ cup turbinado sugar
½ cup sucanut (or brown sugar)
¾ cup chopped walnuts
¾ cup dried, sweetened cranberries
½ cup melted margarine
2 tablespoons cinnamon
1 teaspoon nutmeg

Preheat oven to 350 degrees. Cut tops off squash, being careful not to break the stem. Clean out seeds. Place cut side down in a 9×13-inch pan filled with ¼-inch water. Cover with foil. Place the sweet dumpling tops in a pie plate filled with ¼-inch water and cover with foil as well. Bake both for 30 minutes. While the squash is baking, in a large bowl toss together apples, turbinado, sucanut, walnuts, cranberries, melted margarine, cinnamon and nutmeg. Remove squash from the oven and drain water. Set squash tops aside. Place the sweet dumplings cut side up in the pan and stuff with apple mixture. Cover with foil and bake for another 30 minutes. Serve the sweet dumplings with their stemmed tops as a garnish.

are open pollinated, or heirloom. If they don't come back true, they're hybrids.

There's no real way to confirm a seed's history other than by stories I'm told that have passed down through a family.

Last year was an exceptional season for us and for many of our growers. That meant lots of new seed varieties for our catalog. It was my best gardening season in many years, with a nearly perfect amount of rain and sunshine. I was able to harvest almost every crop we planted, which totaled almost two hundred. I'm always so excited to taste the many new types of plants we grow each year. This time around my favorites were great varieties of Angled and Sponge gourds that my colleague, Andrew Kaiser, brought back from Thailand. They made such beautiful vines and flowers, not to mention the great tasting, squashlike fruit that grew to an amazing length.

This year I'm expanding our trial gardens and

I am going to plant more demonstration gardens. The diversity out there amazes me. I feel so thankful to walk into my gardens and harvest vegetables grown by the likes of Thomas Jefferson or Luther Burbank.

This year we printed 150,000 copies of our seed catalog. People are tired of all the commercial food on the grocery store shelves, full of gene-altering or radiation, dyes, pesticides, hormones and artificial everything. It's a new day in America when the mainstream is proclaiming the virtues of local, green and heritage food. It's happening all over our country.

Speaking of food safety and genetic purity, we've been doing major and extensive GMO testing on all of our corn varieties and we only carry corn seeds that test GMO-free.

Emilee and I wanted to develop a living history village and farm, right here at our historic homestead. We started by building an old-time mercantile with the help of some of the local Amish builders. Next, we built an apothecary, a native stone oven, a new music barn, a jail, a brick herb garden and many new heirloom poultry houses. Recently, we've added a seed industry museum, a blacksmith shop, livestock pens, a gristmill and bakery, a restaurant that features local food and some new gardens. We are trying to bring back simpler times and demonstrate life in a small 1940s village. Our goal is to educate people about our rural heritage, to teach about our crops and gardens, about cooking and food preservation, about traditional animals, craftsmanship and music.

Our May Spring Planting Festival attracts six thousand people in a two-day mega-event of Ozark life. During the festival, our four-thousand-square-foot restaurant serves food grown locally. We do eleven smaller monthly festivals the first Sunday of each month. Vendors come from all over, setting up their booths of organic produce or crafts. We have speakers, musicians on the stages playing great Ozark tunes. Picking and yodeling!

I always look forward to spring, particularly after a long, snowy winter. I can't wait to get my hands in the rich soil again, to hear the mockingbirds and whippoorwills sing, to go into the bright meadows and gather delicious poke greens and morel mushrooms, to walk along a crystal clear stream and catch gleaming trout. Maybe I'll even catch another glimpse of that beautiful black panther that stalks the Ozark forest.

More and more people are interested in gardening. People want to get back to how grandma and grandpa did things. Have you seen our online garden forum, www.idigmygarden.com? Check it out. Our seed catalog comes out once a year.

I've had lots of mentors. As far as the seeds go, Kent Whealy, who founded Seed Savers Exchange, and Glenn Drowns from Sandhill Preservation Center. Older seed companies that got me interested — Gurney's, Henry Fields and Tomato Growers Supply Company. Early on, there was a lady in Australia who sent me a lot of information. And I'm in touch with an Iraqi man who recently sent me some seeds, along with a letter about what's been going on with seeds in Iraq since the occupation began. He told me the tomato seeds he was sending were the last of the old varieties.

My parents live right across the river. My mom makes the bread in our bakery and illustrates the catalog and magazine. Emilee's parents are only four hours away. We still don't watch a lot of TV. We have all our meals together every night. Life is good. Really good.

After Baker's creek, I head far north.

Tod Murphy
The Farmers Diner ■ Quechee, Vermont ■ www.farmersdiner.com

END OF SEPTEMBER ■ *The first time I ate in the Farmers Diner was back in 2002, not long after Tod opened on North Main Street in Barre, Vermont, a working-class town. I came upon the diner by chance while I was knee-deep in a cookbook I was compiling for kids. Tod came over to where I was sitting at the counter on a shiny chrome stool, and after introducing himself, introduced each item on my plate. He gave me the name of each farmer and farm. Turned out all the food was within one hour's drive. I was stunned by the quality, and surprised that I'd spent less than $10, but was stuffed.*

Now the Farmers Diner is in Quechee, Vermont, just off Route 4, in a restored 1946 diner transported from Worcester, Massachusetts. Tod's been described as "a short–order revolutionary" by one writer. Another states, "Murphy's Law: Buy Local, Eat Local, and Prosper." Barbara Kingsolver, in Animal, Vegetable, Miracle *declares that the Farmers Diner is a restaurant for folks who want to fill up with a burger that does not come with a side of feedlot remorse.*

While Gene Pitney's "Town Without Pity" plays on the jukebox, I eat a hush puppy, one of the house specialties.

Things have changed for Tod. He says he found the ideal business partner in Denise. We sit down in a booth and order pancakes made with local flour and eggs, local syrup, and some of the local smoked and cured bacon.

Tod Murphy: I grew up on a dairy farm in Connecticut. When I was a kid, my great-grandmother told me how they used to drive into town on Saturdays to sell eggs and butter to stores.

When I first went looking for investors, there were lots of people who liked the idea of a diner with local food, but nobody believed it would work until I gathered my suppliers. At the time that was no small deal. But I found them:

Vegetables (in season)
Cornmeal: Butterworks Farm, Westfield, VT
Organic tomatoes: Long Wind Farm, Thetford, VT

Dairy
Chedder, cottage cheese, sour cream, butter:
　　Cabot Creamery, Cabot, VT
Eggs: Rocky Ridge Farm, Salisbury, VT
Swiss cheese: Boggy Meadow Farm, Walpole, NH
Goat chevre: Vermont Butter & Cheese, Websterville, VT
Organic ice cream: Rock Bottom Farm, Strafford, VT
Milk: Thomas Dairy, Rutland, VT

Meats
Bacon, ham, sausage: Vermont Smoke & Cure, South Barre, VT
Hamburger, Corned beef: PT Farms, St. Johnsbury, VT

Cereals
Granola: Nutty Stephs, Montpelier, VT
Breads, flours, pasta: La Panciata, Northfield, VT; Butterworks Farm, Westfield, VT; King Arthur Flour, Norwich, VT

Maple syrup: Sweet Retreat, Northfield, VT
Tea: Vermont Liberty Tea, Waitsfield, VT
Honey: Champlain Valley Apiaries, Middlebury, VT

I wanted to make local food a reality for people who weren't yuppies or hippies or even gourmands.

The Farmers Diner started with $240,000 of capital. I made my pitch to friends and to the "Investors Circle," a venture-capital group with over $130 million invested in early-stage, socially responsible businesses. The group looks for projects they think will create long-term value for society, and for entrepreneurs with lots of energy!

Since the diner was going to serve breakfast, I needed bacon, sausage and ham. I was not about to use pigs from the huge agri-commodity farms where thousands of pigs are on top of one another. I wanted pigs from the kind of farm that was everywhere in the 1950s, with thirty to seventy breeding sows. A family farm.

John and Janie Putnam, who provide cheese for the diner's macaroni and cheese, had been complaining about their wasted whey. Their fifteen-year-old son, Andrew, was looking for a part-time job. Tod suggested that he get some piglets to take care of, and promised to later buy them all.

It turned out that I also was going to need a place to process the local pigs since I couldn't find a processor in the state who would do it.

Tod then bought Vermont Smoke & Cure, one of the smallest U.S.D.A. inspected meat-processing facilities in the country.

At first, we were too small. We had fifty seats,

the kitchen was cramped and we didn't have room for larger prep equipment. We actually sliced all the potatoes by hand. We now have one hundred seats with room to move outside during the summer. The kitchen is bigger and we have a machine for slicing potatoes.

We buy some of our flour from King Arthur, out in the Midwest. Some from Butterworks Farm up near the Canadian border. Jack and Anne Lazor do yogurt, cornmeal, dried beans and whole grain flour.

Food in the diner is well priced. Our goal is to be within 10 percent of the norm, but even at 15 or 20 percent, we'd still be a good value.

A regular diner has a food cost of 18 to 20 percent; ours is about 28 to 29 percent, so we know we're not making as much money as a regular diner. People understand that, that there's a longer return on investment.

Eggs are a good way to make up some of the

difference. It still costs us more to do a plate of eggs than a regular diner, but it's not as noticeable as when you get down to dinner, with a twelve-ounce steak. You've got a bigger price difference to deal with there.

In the winter we're open every day until 3:00, serving breakfast and lunch. Beginning in June we stay open for dinner 'til eight P.M. At the end of October, when the foliage ends, we cut back to just breakfast and lunch.

My idea for real growth and expansion is to go into a market area and create pods of diners. Each pod would pull from the same farmers, business leaders, investors, citizens and service channels. We're opening a second diner in Middlebury, Vermont, and thinking about opening one in Williston. This will allow Farmers Diner to leverage its core business processes, technology and management expertise across multiple locations with significant economies of scale. This will allow us to increase benefits to employees, continue to pay profitable prices to local farmers and provide a return to our investors.

For our next restaurant in Middlebury, we've raised a little more than half of our startup capital from the people of Middlebury, as a local investment opportunity. It's done as a convertible loan we pay back over seven years. But if someone decides, "Hey, this is really great, we'd like to be part of the company," they can convert the loan into ownership.

We went to the Methodist church in town and had a "Come Meet Us Dinner" to tell people what we're about and to let them try out the food. About seventy people were interested, and about twenty people signed up. The minimum investment is $5,000. But if someone can invest $1,000, they get $1,250 return in food credit at the restaurant.

Some folks in the Bay area are very interested in doing a Farmers Diner. They found us through

RECIPES ■ Tod Murphy

Polenta Fries

1 quart milk
1 tablespoon chopped garlic
24 ounces local cornmeal
1 teaspoon thyme
2 teaspoons kosher salt
1 teaspoon black pepper
1 cup grated parmesan cheese

Combine all ingredients except cornmeal and parmesan cheese, bring to a simmer. Whisk in cornmeal and return to a simmer. Cook over very low heat stirring frequently for 20 minutes. Stir in parmesan cheese, remove from heat. Press mixture on to a cookie sheet lined with wax paper. Spread mixture to one inch thickness. Place in fridge to cool. When cool slice polenta into fries 1 inch wide by 4 inches long. Cook until golden in fry oil of your choice.

reading Barbara Kingsolver, and after watching their community go from farms to homes for multi-millionaire baseball players and basketball players. We'd provide recipe books and our steps in service, and they'd add whatever's unique to their area, including local foods and recipes. In the San Francisco area that might mean an Asian influence.

My kids help out. Seamus loves hosting. He's twelve. He loves it when the urban folks, who sometimes seem to have a high sense of self-importance, come in. He's willing to tell them, "Hey, this is Vermont. Relax a little." Grace, who's ten, likes working catered events. A bus'll come in and we've pre-sold meals, so we're doing assembly. Grace likes to help with that, with organizing the plates and placing them. Like any startup, the family makes sacrifices. Denise and I enjoy finding opportunities for the kids to participate. This summer Seamus will actually be an employee. As soon as school ends, we'll have him every other week. He really wants to do the prep. He likes making batters. He won't be using the machinery, but he'll be weighing things. There's a real sense of accomplishment. He likes the tips, so occasionally he'll bus tables.

We don't usually have interns, although we did have one from Cornell's hotel management school. They're kids. They have a hard time 'cause it's not like working in a regular restaurant. Things move more quickly, and you have a different breed of diner, a different breed of animal in the kitchen. It's three guys on the line, plates going out in ten to twelve minutes. If it's a busy Sunday, and you've got four groups of eight to nine people, then somebody's going to be backed up at twenty minutes. That's about the tolerance level people have for waiting. That's entirely different from fine dining with multiple courses, they're pushing those plates out, and you've got eight to twelve guys in the kitchen working their stations.

We should be allowing people to invest in local business in really simple ways. If you invest ten grand in a Vermont business, you should be able to write $5,000 off over the next five years on your taxes. That's a no-brainer. A little restaurant like ours, we needed to raise $150,000 in the local community. If we do that, it's a million-dollar impact. That means we're buying $300,000 worth of products from the local community. We're employing twenty people. Because we're buying local products, the local produce company needs to hire another driver. The state should see the economic benefit. All these folks are on the tax rolls. It's not rocket science.

Next stop — The Mountain School, Vershire, Vermont.

Alden Smith and Melissa Anne Hopkins Smith
The Mountain School ■ Vershire, Vermont ■ www.mountainschool.org

OCTOBER ■ *The Mountain School is a coed semester school offering a high-caliber academic program alongside total immersion in all the activities required to manage an organic farm.*

As an English teacher there, Alden Smith introduced his students to the environmental and nature writers such as Wordsworth, Thoreau, Cather, Frost and Tolstoy.

Although he still teaches, Alden is now the director of the Mountain School. He's married to the admissions director, Melissa (Missy) Anne Hopkins Smith, and they have a baby girl, Ellicott Amalie. They live in Derby House, right in the middle of the campus. They are close to the dining hall and available to the staff and student body pretty much 24/7.

Alden: We met in July of 2006. It was pretty much a done deal. I knew right away, and I think Missy did too.

Missy laughs and nods. We sit in the living room of their home, which is filled with Missy's art and lots of wood and antiques.

Missy: I had a little farm over in Middlebury that I'd started a couple of years before called Whistling Chick Farm. I raised different kinds of chickens, for the eggs mostly. Occasionally the roosters were meat poultry. For about three years, I raised ducks.

I didn't grow up in a farming family. My mom says the stork dropped me off at the wrong house! She's a high-heels kind of city woman, grew up just outside of New York City. My mom always let me grow vegetables and flowers in our backyard. My grandfather grew up at White Haul, a farm in Howard County. He and one of his brothers had a beautiful vegetable garden, and during the summer, as the oldest grandchild, I was the only one allowed in that garden. I harvested with my grandfather every night before dinner. I think that sort of instilled in me my passion for the land. I

PHOTO COURTESY MISSY HOPKINS SMITH

would spend three weeks to a month with him. My grandmother spent summers with her sister and her sister's husband.

For seven years, while coaching lacrosse and field hockey at Middlebury College, I volunteered at the college's new, student-run organic garden.

Alden: I grew up in Nashville, Tennessee. My grandfather had a farm out in the country called Spring Hill. It's now the site of a Saturn auto plant. But when I was a kid it was wide open country. We used to go out there on weekends. Our parents did all the work while we kids messed around. I got no practical training for farming as a child, but just being there — fishing for brim, loading vegetables into the car, seeing the trains go by — got hold of

me. I still have a lot of nostalgia for those days on the Spring Hill Farm.

I didn't really get interested in food as an important or pleasurable issue until after college. My interest really grew as I got to know this place.

I've been here ten years. I taught for five years at Choate. During that time, I spent summers studying for my masters at Middlebury College. I studied the landscape of Vermont and got interested in food and farming.

The other way I've come to know food is as a hunter. I grew up hunting birds with my dad. Ducks mostly. Since moving here, I've gotten into different kinds of hunting, especially turkeys and deer. I do it because it's fun, because it's such an intense connection to food, and a way to eat right from the landscape.

I'm a different kind of gardener than Missy. While she grows vegetables and flowers, I head out into the woods, releasing apple trees by cutting the hardwoods around them, creating places for wildlife habitat. Hunting wild game is my favorite kind of harvest. The two of us have been a little bit harvest crazy this fall, though — I mean, we have a freezer full of wild turkeys, and Missy's roosters that we slaughtered before . . .

Alden pauses.

Missy: *[finishes his sentence]* . . . I moved here. Every spring over in Middlebury, when I got new hens, inevitably they weren't sexed perfectly, so I'd have X number of roosters every year. I liked having a couple of roosters even though they do fight. They're territorial and each one wants to rule the roost. Mine actually got along pretty well. When it came time to move over to Vershire, we decided to move my hens in with the Mountain School's flock. I knew I couldn't bring the roosters. I knew I could only bring one. The rest we slaughtered, together, using a block.

Alden: We did it last year with ducks. In the fall we harvested her ducks, which was interesting to me because I'd always hunted wild ducks. Missy

RECIPES ■ Alden Smith and Melissa Hopkins Smith

Breakfast: French Toast & Bacon

 1 pound bacon
 1 loaf of great bread (my favorite is brioche) cut into ½ inch slices
 1 heaping teaspoon vanilla bean paste
 ¼ cup of whole milk
 2 teaspoons cinnamon
 6 farm fresh eggs

Bake the bacon on a cookie sheet with sides at 450 degrees for 7 minutes, being cautious with the grease. Mix the bean paste, milk, cinnamon and eggs in a bowl. Butter griddle or frying pan set at medium-high cook until crispy. Serve with warmed maple syrup! Serves 4 to 6.

Lunch: Pizza and salad

We keep salads simple in our house. We love arugula with some seasonal berries on top. We keep our dressing simple with equal parts oil, vinegar and maple syrup. We switch up the vinegar and oil on occasion although our top pick is olive oil and pear vinegar.

Pizza:

We like to adorn with wild mushrooms – morels in the spring, suillius and dryad's saddle in the summer, chanterelles and puffballs in the fall. Baby beets also bring the perfect sweetness. In the winter we keep it simple with canned tomatoes from our summer garden and fresh mozzarella.

Crust:

 1¾ teaspoons dry active yeast or 2 tablespoons of wet bakers block of yeast
 2 cups water
 Add 2 tablespoons olive oil
 1 tablespoon sugar
 1 teaspoon coarse salt

Mix and let sit 7 minutes. Add to dry ingredients that have already been mixed with dough hook in mixer. Knead in machine 10 minutes, then knead by hand 10 minutes adding flour as necessary to keep your hands dough free. Cut into 4 equal discs. Place on oiled cookie sheet. Cover with clear plastic wrap. Let rise in fridge for at least 4 hours and up to a few days. Stretch dough carefully onto a piece of baking parchment sprinkled with cornmeal. Stretch from sides – not the middle – to avoid holes in your flatbread pizza dough. Add fresh tomatoes, mozzarella, and anything else you want! Bake on pizza stone in your oven at the highest temperature your oven can handle for 7 to 10 minutes until crust is golden and crispy.

Dinner: Roasted Wild Duck

Brine duck with ¼ cup brown sugar, ¼ cup salt overnight.
 Take it out of brine and pat dry. Let dry at least 1 hour.
 Fill cavity with sage and garlic and a small onion. Salt and pepper the bird.
 Cook uncovered at 425 degrees for 15 minutes then baste duck with orange garlic port reduction sauce and finish duck

had named all her ducks. But the roosters were even harder because they had been with her for years — not just for the growing season. It was really emotional. We put it off for as long as we could. When we eat one, when we prepare one for guests, it means a lot.

Missy: In the freezer, each package is named. I couldn't imagine not doing that after de-feathering them, getting them ready. It means something. Eating them as food is just a different kind of experience. We really know our food.

Alden: It's easier with the carrots and beets.

A big part of our relationship and our marriage will clearly be hunting and harvesting. That includes animals we raise and wild animals. So what we eat will be from the best possible source. Ideally we wouldn't need to buy meat, or at least not much. We're both committed to sustainability.

My teaching has shifted some since our daughter arrived. I'm more focused on our separateness from each other — barriers between us, how we try to get along in spite of them. The difficulty of imagining the world from someone else's point of view. For three to four weeks this year our theme will be at 350 degrees until juices run clear and the thermometer in thigh reaches 167 degrees. Take juices, add another tablespoon of butter and 1 teaspoon of flour for gravy. We like to take sharp kitchen shears and cut the duck in the half. Serve with wild rice and roasted root vegetables.

Orange Garlic Port Reduction Sauce:

4 cloves garlic, minced with zester
2 tablespoons cointreau
2 tablespoons grand marnier
¼ cup fresh squeezed orange juice
½ teaspoon orange zest
⅛ cup port wine
¼ cup Duck Demi (highly concentrated broth I make from duck carcasses, but boullion works too)
2 tablespoons butter

Roasted Root vegetables:

Dice carrots, parsnips, beets, celery, onion, turnips (and any others you like and have on hand). Mix with 2 tablespoons olive oil and 2 tablespoons maple syrup. Salt and pepper to taste. Spread on cookie sheet and roast at 350 degrees about 25 minutes.

Desert: Apple or Pear Crostata

My favorite Fall Dessert

Slice and core 4 apples or 4 pears
½ teaspoon orange zest and a little fresh sqeezed orange juice
½ teaspoon cinnamon (and a pinch of nutmeg and a pinch of allspice)

For crust:
2 cups flour
¼ cup sugar
½ teaspoon salt

Mix dry ingredients. Then add 2 sticks diced butter (dice it then put it in the freezer to harden). Pulse in food processor while adding ice water about ¼ cup (sometimes a bit more). Work quickly. (Can put in fridge to cool again for 30 minutes or up to 2 days.) Roll out dough into a circle on a piece of parchment paper. Place apples in the middle. Gently fold over the sides about an inch. Top with the crumble.

Crumble:
¼ cup flour
¼ cup sugar
½ teaspoon cinnamon
½ stick of butter, diced

Pulse in processor then crumble together in your fingers onto the apples in the crust. YUM.

Bake 25 minutes at 450 degrees.

When I make the pear crostata I drop the spices out of the filling and I use lemon and lime zest instead of the orange.

rural immigration. We'll read the works of Annie Proulx, Flannery O'Connor, Noel Perrin, Jhumpa Lahiri– authors who write about people who have difficult relationships with the natives of a place. How they manage to live in that place alongside those difficulties, either overcome them or don't. I still teach Wordsworth, Annie Dillard and Thoreau.

I just got back from a trip with three kids who signed up for my wildlife tracking activity. We saw a mink up close. It came out of its hole, put its nose in the air, smelled us, then scooted away.

Earlier today we were tracking a moose — we walked through its bedding area, found a bed, but no moose.

I don't talk a lot about hunting with my students. Only if asked. When they see me walk back on campus with a turkey in my hand it could be confusing. It's a curious thing to love an animal, then take its life.

As director, I have a hand in pretty much everything that happens at the Mountain School. Along with teaching English, I live in a dormitory, work on the farm and participate in all student activities, even on weekends. I also manage the board, raise

money, design the strategic plan, and anything else that seems like it will improve our school over time.

We recruit students all over the country. This is the time of year I work for my wife — the director of admissions. She tells me where I have to go. This season it's New York, Baltimore, D.C., and Nashville. Other faculty members will go to Cleveland, Boston and Seattle. Over two hundred schools across the United Stated have sent us students.

Since Ella was born, we stay closer to home, keep the woodstove going, take greater care with all we do. Our dogs love that we're home more often, the pack all together. Having Ella in our lives confirms that we belong to a place that nourishes us. She'll eat from our gardens, our livestock, wild mushrooms, deer, ducks.

We walk quietly around the campus. There's a group of kids playing basketball. In the front green- *house, Alden points out the pumpkins and squash recently harvested by the kids. Missy and Alden both stop to pick up a handful of squashes lying on a ledge. Missy starts juggling first.*

Missy: Juggling was one of the exercises I gave my goalies at Middlebury.

Alden laughs.

Alden: For many of these kids, this is the first real separation, first real independence from their families, from where they've grown up. Some of them gain something that their parents have been living all along. This program is able to reinforce it, because it's not coming from the parent. The kids really get it.

Of course, a lot of the students come from families with values that are quite different from what they experience here. So then this is new exposure for them, it broadens their horizons.

Eliza Jamison

Rockland, Maine ■ www.primorestaurant.com, www.jamisonfarm.com

OCTOBER ■ *Eliza Jamison comes from a food family. She grew up the youngest of three children on the Jamison lamb farm outside of Pittsburg, in Latrobe, Pennsylvania. Eliza loves horses and remembers Kanga as her favorite lamb. When Eliza was thirteen, her parents bought a processing plant where they would slaughter and process fifty to one hundred lambs a week.*

Eliza Jamison: It's kind of weird going to a slaughterhouse when you're thirteen. Killing a pig or a lamb, you see it, you hear it. It was hard. Now it doesn't matter. After a while, I stopped being attached to the sheep. Now I keep myself at a distance. Back then, kids in school would tease me and I felt like I didn't fit in. Also, we ate lamb eight days a week.

We made our own bread, and cookies too. I'm a picky eater. I don't eat lamb. I can't call myself a vegetarian because I don't really eat vegetables. Maybe because I'm always around so much food, I don't have much time to sit down and eat. But I love bread. I take it home from the restaurant.

When I was a kid I did 4-H. My brother wanted to do it first. He's the oldest — nine years older than me. He had capons and dairy goats. Then when it came time for me, we got the lambs. A few at a time. Some of the lambs hung around for a while, like Kanga. So I did kind of get attached.

All of us went to boarding school. I went to Northfield Mount Hermon. Afterward, I went to William and Jefferson College *[like her parents]*, but I didn't last long there. I took a few years off, then ended up at the CIA (Culinary Institute of America) for twenty-two months. Before I chose the CIA we checked other schools out. We went up to Boston and talked to Julia Child, a good friend of my mom's. We had breakfast with her. Instead of coffee that morning, she opened up a bottle of

champagne. My parents know a lot of chefs — Jean-Louis Palladin was a good friend, Bill Telepan, Daniel Boulud — and many more. To me they're just family friends, no big deal.

At the time, I wasn't really interested in the food industry. I wanted nothing to do with it. It was my parent's thing. I wanted to get far away from it.

At the CIA Eliza did her externship at Café Boulud in New York City; Andrew Carmellini was the chef. After graduation she worked in some of the finest kitchens in New York. She was hired by chefs Jean-Louis Palladin, Bill Telepan and Eric Ribert.

After I left New York, I interned for Browne Trading.

Browne Trading provides select restaurants and home kitchens with the freshest fish from New England, other parts of the U.S., and from around the world. They have the finest offerings of domestic, farmed and wild caviars.

I'd gotten a Jean-Louis Palladin Foundation Award for the internship at Browne Trading.

Jean-Louis Palladin never accepted anything but the best ingredients for his kitchen. He encouraged vegetable farmers and livestock producers to use the purest methods of production. He sought out fishermen with line-caught products brought in on day boats. He supported anyone who was as passionate as he was about quality.

The Foundation rewards passion for the best ingredients in the next generation of cooks. The program is designed for working cooks and chefs with a minimum of three years' kitchen experience. Each award provides the winner with an opportunity to learn through hands-on experience about how first-rate ingredients are produced and how sourcing those ingredients benefits cuisine.

During my internship, I was expected to keep a journal of my two-week experiences. Here's what I wrote:

> It seemed a little bit unexpected. The idea of going to Browne Trading seemed to be quite an uncanny choice for someone with my wealth of lamb experiences. Even so, choosing this adventure seemed to end up being quite fitting for a farm girl.
>
> The first day at Browne was a wash, so to speak. The thirty-knot winds and fifteen-foot waves anywhere in Portland kept me in the enclosed area, referred to as the caviar room. Who would have thought that there would be an entire room designed for the soul purpose of receiving, repackaging and distributing caviar?

Luckily for me, upon arrival at Browne, I met Richard, who is in charge of the caviar room and has a wealth of knowledge in reference to all the different types and packages of caviar. The first task was pre-packaging paddlefish roe (American caviar) into one-ounce glass jars. Seems easy enough, right? The daunting task was to waste nothing when transferring from the large vat (five-pound container) to the little jars, while using a misshapen rubber spatula. Who knew there would be that much frozen roe anywhere? The paddlefish season had not yet begun this year, so the packages were the last of the previous year's harvest.

Who knows or has ever heard of Azerbaijan? I, myself, had no idea a country with that name even existed. It is a small country on the Caspian Sea sandwiched between Russia and Iran. Since Russian caviar cannot be imported at this point, Browne uses caviar from Azerbaijan, which is delicious anyway.

The selection of caviars that Browne Trading carries is quite diverse. Of course, there is the private stock, which was designated and reserved for Daniel Boulud. Next, is the line of Browne Trading caviars, which are the product of Azerbaijan. And then there are the coveted Iranian caviars. The Caviar Astara is distributed exclusively by Browne Trading.

I had to taste each of these different varieties while I was helping package the caviars to learn the grading criteria.

There is, however, much more to Browne Trading than just lab coats, hairnets and spooning eggs in the caviar room. From searching for scallops to harvesting seaweed and butchering all kinds of fish, something new every day, but the caviar room was a real initiation into the world of

fish and where it all comes from for a farm girl from Western Pennsylvania.

For the last four seasons Eliza has worked as a line cook for Melissa Kelly and Price Kushner, who own Primo — a world-class restaurant in Rockland, Maine. The restaurant is surrounded by four acres that include two greenhouses, an herb garden, vegetable fields, a pen full of Tamworth pigs and a root cellar.

When I first started, I didn't think I was very good at what I did. I'd never worked "sauté." All I'd ever done was poach fish — and for a year at Le Bernardin, that's all I did. But it turns out I can do this. I think it's mostly that I'm organized. In the kitchen I take organization to a new level. Everything outside of the kitchen is disorganized. My room is a mess, my apartment is a mess, everything. I go to work and it's totally different. There's a system to everything at work. I sharpen my knives every morning. My clogs

RECIPES ■ Eliza Jamison (With John and Sukey)

Scones:

- 2 cups all-purpose flour
- ¼ cup sugar
- 1 teaspoon baking powder
- ¼ teaspoon baking soda
- ¼ teaspoon salt
- ½ cup butter, cold and diced
- ⅔ cup buttermilk
- 1 tablespoon Lemon Zest

Combine dry ingredients and lemon zest in a bowl. Cut in butter until mixture is pea meal size. Add buttermilk and fold until just combined. Turn out onto floured surface, knead ten times and shape into a disc. Roll out disc to ½-inch thick rectangle. Cut six triangles out of dough. Transfer to a non stick baking sheet. Brush with 2 ounces melted butter and sprinkle with ¼ cup of coarse sugar.

Bake at 425 degrees for 10 to 12 minutes or until golden brown.

Serve warm with seasonal fruit spread or honey.

Lamb Burgers with Caramelized Shallots and Blue Cheese:

- 4 semi-hard buns
- 1 pound ground lamb
- 2½ teaspoons fresh rosemary, chopped (1¼ teaspoons if using dried rosemary, crushed)
- ½ teaspoon Sriracha sauce, or any other hot chili condiment
- 1 teaspoon kosher salt
- ½ teaspoon coarse black pepper

Combine lamb and seasoning in a bowl and mix until just combined. Shape into four burgers and place on a hot grill for approximately 3 to 4 minutes per side. Let rest and place on bun and top with caramelized shallot and blue cheese spread.

Caramelized Shallots and Blue Cheese Spread:

- ½ cup shallots, thinly sliced
- 1 teaspoon vegetable oil
- 1 tablespoon heavy cream
- 3 tablespoons crumbled blue cheese
- ¼ cup plain yogurt

Place shallots and oil in pan over medium-low heat. Season with salt and pepper. Cook low and slow for about 15 minutes until shallots are soft and golden brown. Place in food processor with remaining ingredients. Season with salt and coarse pepper to taste.

Oven Roasted Hake with Grilled Zucchini Salad and Tomato Caper Relish:

- 2 fillets hake, skinless (or any other white flaky fish)
- 1 medium sized zucchini, sliced ½ inch thick lengthwise
- ¼ cup ricotta salata, ¼ inch dice
- Juice of 1 lemon
- 2 tablespoons basil, chiffonade
- 2 tablespoons extra virgin olive oil
- Salt and pepper to taste

Season zucchini with olive oil salt and pepper. Place on preheated grill for 1 to 2 minutes per side. Place on cutting board. Cut zucchini into strips and then dice into ½ inch cubes. Combine with ricotta salata, lemon juice and season. When properly seasoned fold in chiffonade basil. Season hake on both sides with salt and pepper. Place pan over high heat. Put 2 tablespoons of oil in pan. When smoking hot, place fillets in pan. Put in 450 degree oven for 8 to 10 minutes. When cooked, flip fillets and brush lightly with butter. Plate fish with grilled zucchini salad and top with tomato caper relish (recipe follows).

are always clean. My cubby, where everything is kept, is always totally arranged. Of course it doesn't matter how organized I am if the food's not seasoned properly, or if it's either undercooked or overcooked.

Eliza went to Patagonia during the restaurant's off-season, four months of work at a fly-fishing lodge.

She cooked three meals a day for eight people a week, sometimes more — depending how long they stayed.

Fly fishing right off the river. My Spanish is now almost fluent. I loved the scenery, the landscape. I hiked a glacier, swam in the river. The week after I left, a volcano erupted — it had been dormant

Tomato Caper Relish:

½ red onion, finely diced
1 cup heirloom tomato, small dice
1 tablespoon capers, coarsely chopped
1 tablespoon flat leaf parsley, chopped
Juice of 1 lemon
1 tablespoon extra virgin olive oil
Salt and pepper to taste

Combine all ingredients in bowl, season to taste and spoon over fish. Tomato caper relish can be made a few hours in advance.

Delicious Lamb Shanks:

1 shank per serving
For 4 servings, can be doubled

¼ cup olive oil
4 lamb shanks
1 cup onion, chopped
1 cup carrot, chopped
1 cup celery, chopped
3 sprigs fresh thyme or 1 tablespoon dried
3 sprigs fresh sage or 1 tablespoon dried
1 teaspoon cinnamon
¼ teaspoon nutmeg
Salt and pepper to taste
2 tablespoons gin
2 tablespoon tomato paste
2 cups white wine
Lamb or chicken stock to cover (about 1 quart)

Place oil and shanks in large oven pan. Brown shanks over high heat on all sides. Add onion, carrot, celery to brown lightly. Add gin and let cook down. Add wine, stock to cover, tomato paste, herbs and spices, salt and pepper. Bring to boil, then place pan in preheated oven (325 degrees) and allow to simmer for 2 to 3 hours, until very tender.

Remove lamb from broth, strain broth and cook down for added thickness. Meat can be removed from bones or served on the bone with rice, couscous or polenta.

Perfect Pecan Pie:
Pie Crust

2 cups all-purpose flour
¼ teaspoon salt
⅓ cup vegetable shortening
⅓ cup unsalted butter, diced and cold
¼ cup ice water

Cut butter and shortening into flour and salt mixture until the mixture is mealy in texture. Add water gradually until the dough just comes together. Turn out of bowl and wrap tightly in plastic wrap. Let rest 1 hour or even overnight.

Pecan Pie Filling:

1 9-inch pie crust
For filling:
1 cup light brown sugar
3 eggs
½ teaspoon salt
⅓ cup melted butter
1 cup light agave nectar
1½ cups pecans, coarsely chopped
2½ tablespoons bourbon or vanilla extract

Pre-bake pie crust for five minutes at 400 degrees, lined with aluminum and weighted with dried beans. Whisk eggs, butter and salt together briskly until frothy. Fold in butter, corn syrup, pecans and bourbon. Pour into pre-baked pie shell and bake immediately. 375 degrees for approximately 45 minutes to an hour, or until center is set.

for 450 years. The whole town of Chaiten washed away; a river runs through the middle of it. Everybody was evacuated.

But now I'm back here in Maine, and this afternoon I'm going to blanch vegetables, make some mashed potatoes and check Melissa's prep list.

Melissa sets everything out in the morning. She puts all the protein in our boxes, does some of the prep and then she goes to the farmers market.

Of all the things I do, butchering is my favorite — being inside a cow or fish. I butchered fish early Saturday, and then a half of a cow. The pigs will be

butchered in November. Last year I left at the end of the season, which was before they were slaughtered. This year I will stay through November, help butcher them, and then I'll go to help out in Tucson, at Melissa and Price's restaurant there. Then I'll go to Italy or I'll do something until I'm needed here, in the spring.

I'm learning people skills. I have to be more patient with everyone because this new crew, they're all green. It's hard because I normally just cook, and now I have to be sociable, nice and patient. These are things that don't come easily to me. But I love this place. It's pretty sweet digs. I get lots of hours. I'll do almost anything as long as I'm in the kitchen and working with good food. I think, I hope, I'm good at what I do. I have no idea what my future will be. I am all about today – I don't worry about tomorrow, until the late afternoon of today.

I have chosen my career over everything else, at least for now. I'm good for about four months, and then I like to move on. Same career, just a different place. My mother has a photo of me with a cow bell around my neck, so she could keep track of me. Melissa Hill says she'd like to put one on me now.

Zachary Stotz
Backshore Road, Round Pond, Maine

OCTOBER ■ *I remember when I was a girl we had a house on Trent Street in Washington, D.C. My father often went up to Boston to teach a class at Harvard Business School. On his way back, at Logan airport, he would stop for lobsters. When he landed in D.C. he would call my mother and say, "Turn the heat up on that lobster pot. I'll be home in half an hour." My sister and I would wait by the front door for the sound of his key. We'd pull open the door and watch as our dad lifted each lobster out of the sturdy carrying case. We'd examine their mottled brown shells, all the tiny orange flecks, their huge, waving claws plugged with wooden pegs.*

"Caught this morning. Water boiling?"

"Rip-roaring," my mom would say.

"Did you add salt?" Lighted cigarette hanging from the corner of his mouth.

In the kitchen, I'd hold my breath. I couldn't bear their high-pitched screams as my father put them into the roiling water.

For our morning walk, Luna and I go around a jagged granite ledge at the end of Clark Island Road. Luna has a swim in one of the hidden quarry pools.

After breakfast, we start back to New York City. I hope to stop somewhere along the way to pick up some lobsters. Seventeen miles down the narrow coastal road, I see a sign for Round Pond. *The name rings a bell. Let's just say I have a feeling.*

I park near the Round Pond Harbor pier. The sky is a deep blue with a few scattered clouds. The wind is blowing. Someone once said the life of a lobsterman is like that of a cowboy.

"How many?" the fisherman behind the counter asks, a smile half hidden within the deep lines on his craggy face. "Four," I say, and "I'm looking for a young lobsterman for a project I'm working on." "Your lucky day," he says, pointing towards the water and the pier. *"Zachary Stotz. He's the one with the new boat. Well, pretty new."*

Zachary is cleaning his boat — which turns out to be two years old. They say that the relationship between a fisherman and his boat is like a marriage. Zachary Stotz has lived on Round Pond all his life. He admits he's crazy about lobstering.

Zachary: I've been doing this since I was about seven, so that's about eighteen years! The dynamic between my father and me was always that he was teaching me, and I was resisting. Now I'm thankful for his lessons. I learned a lot from him.

I live just on the other side of that house beyond the pier. *[He points at a cluster of wooden shingled*

houses.] Now, most of the other houses are summer homes. I went to Bristol Elementary and Lincoln Academy. I've been preparing for this work all my life. I like to think I'll be doing it forever, although this past year was kind of a grind. The lobsters haven't trapped as well as they have in the past. That's Mother Nature. But I did really well the last couple of years. I don't think there are any fewer lobsters. I just think there are more lobstermen. This dock and the dock over there are competing docks. When you're starting out, you have to either work with a guy who's established in the harbor, or be a family member.

Whoever has the most traps in place first has the advantage. Still, when we're out there, we all look out for one another. Even when we're not from the same harbor, we have to. There's an element of danger in what we do.

We leave the dock about 4:30 in the morning. We usually put in a twelve-hour day. We come back in about 4:00 P.M. This time of year we're fishing offshore a ways, so we have an hour commute by boat. It's a long day this time of year. Summertime, it can be a lot shorter day. We're just fishing outside of the harbor, and in the bays. Some of the guys in the harbor go thirty to forty miles out.

I don't go out anymore with my father. He's got his boat and his gang, and I've got my boat and my gang. The orange and black buoys are mine. Each buoy is attached by a long length of line called the potwarp that's attached to one trap, sometimes more.

I love the freedom of lobstering. I love the hours, the fresh air and being on the water. I don't answer to anybody. I'm my own harshest critic. If I don't go out, I feel guilty. I fish five days a week. My week is usually three days on and a day off, three days on and a day off. It has to do with the time of year and the weather. In the summertime the weather isn't much of a factor. In the spring and fall we get

RECIPES ■ Zachary Stotz

Lobster Stew

4 lobsters
Dry sherry
1 stick butter
4 ounces cream cheese, softened
Whole milk
Salt
Pepper

Boil 4 lobsters for 15 minutes. Pick out meat, reserving shell liquor for stew base. Soak meat in just enough dry sherry to cover for ½ hour. In a heavy pan over medium/low heat, melt 1 stick of butter, whisk in 4 ounces softened cream cheese 'til smooth, whisk in shell liquor. Add lobster and ½ cup of the sherry in which it soaked. Heat and add as much whole milk as necessary to have a meaty stew. Salt and pepper to taste. Serves 6.

Apple Crisp

12 or more apples, peeled and sliced (not too thin)
Topping:
1 cup graham cracker crumbs
1 cup pecans, chopped
1 stick butter
1 tablespoon flour
1 tablespoon orange zest
1 cup brown sugar
¼ cup white sugar
Dash salt
½ teaspoon cinnamon
½ teaspoon nutmeg
½ cup melted butter

Mix all topping ingredients together. Butter 9×13-inch baking dish, then layer peeled and sliced apples. Bake apples at 350 degrees for 15 minutes. Put on topping and bake additional 25 minutes.

rougher weather. Today would've been choppy. Because of the weather yesterday, I took the day off. Some would have fished yesterday, for sure.

For bait I use herring, porgies, redfish. The guy that buys the lobsters from us also deals with the bait dealers. They come down weekly, delivering pallets of frozen bait. It's a pretty big business, the bait business. The smaller shack up there, next to where you bought your lobsters, is the bait shack. The other building is a kind of seafood processing plant.

A lot of my friends went off to college. There's a core group of five or six that I'm still in contact with. Sometimes I feel like I spend too much time lobstering and not enough time being twenty-five. I feel a lot of responsibility. And I have debt because of this new boat.

Lobstermen always have a lot of stories. My worst experience happened when I was about fourteen. I was coming up on the age where I thought I knew what I was doing. I was still hand-hauling. I was alone. I didn't have a sternman yet. I was leaning over the side and I fell out of my skiff. Had on my boots and all my other gear. The first thing I did was shed my extra weight, which was hard. Then I swam back to my skiff, climbed in, and went on my merry way. It was an eye-opener for me. Now I usually have a stern man with me. It makes the work easier. We're able to do more, and I guess we look after each other.

Hundreds of thousands of lobster traps are fished in Maine waters each year. There are roughly seven thousand license holders with a trap limit of eight hundred per license. I've got a little over six hundred traps out there. That's pretty average. We hope by limiting the number of traps, the lobster won't be overfished. So far it's been a renewable resource for all of us. We rotate the days we haul, about two hundred per day. Then we take a day off. Then we start in again. We generally haul the traps about four nights after we put them in. My traps usually have lobsters in them when I pull them out.

increase as the current charters add grades and newly approved charters open. (Charter schools, which are quasipublic schools, operate independently, making their own decisions on hiring, spending and curriculum.) These schools have shown results, bringing low grades and achievement scores to a higher level.

During my ten-day stay in New Orleans, I intend to meet with those folks who are most concerned with seeing to it that fresh, healthy food is made available. They include:

***Emery Van Hook**, who recently moved home to New Orleans from New York City. She's director of markets at marketumbrella.org, and heavily involved with the Crescent City Farm Market.*

***Tom Farley,** director of Tulane University's Department of Community Health Sciences and director of the university's Prevention Research Center. Following Hurricane Katrina, he became involved in trying to rebuild the city's public health infrastructure. Tom wrote the fine book* Prescription for a Healthy Nation.

***Vanessa Ulmer** and **Sarah Custer**, both colleagues of Tom's at the Tulane School of Public Health, and involved in the rebuilding.*

***Grant Estrade,** who runs Laughing Buddha Nursery provides an example of how to put together and manage a backyard organic garden. He's another lover of New Orleans looking to put the infrastructure for food back together in a different way.*

***April Nuejean,** head chef at the **Edible Schoolyard of New Orleans** at the Samuel Green Charter School.*

Late morning, I take the St. Charles streetcar out to the Garden District to have an early lunch before heading over to the Edible Schoolyard. The trolley has wooden seats and wide-open windows. I breathe in the scent of lilacs as we pass by gracious mansions with iron gate work and sprawling front porches.

April Neujean
Head Garden Teacher ■ The Edible Schoolyard ■ New Orleans ■ www.esynola.org

Alice Waters created the concept of Edible School-yards to teach children about healthy eating. According to Donna Cavato, director of the Edible Schoolyard New Orleans at Samuel J. Green Charter School, "Before Hurricane Katrina, Green was just another failed New Orleans middle public school. It had a twenty-year history of low performance. It was surrounded by barbed-wired fences, concrete everywhere, boarded-up buildings where the playground should have been. What little soil there was on the campus had lead contamination."

Folks involved in the Edible Schoolyard project tore up the concrete, pulled out the soil, and replaced it with river sand and topsoil. They built the garden on top of everything. Chef April Neujean is head garden teacher. Kelly Regan is a volunteer and community coordinator.

April Neujean: I came down in March of '07 with the Culinary Corps and a group of chefs, primarily out of New York, who had come down earlier to do service work after Katrina.

I was lucky enough to be on the first trip down here for a week of service around the city related to food. I did surveys at the farmers market, which was just getting up and running again. I helped them figure out how they could best serve the community. We worked for Emergency Communities, a community center and food kitchen in the Lower Ninth Ward. Our last day of service was here at the Edible Schoolyard.

Originally, ESY-NOLA was just Donna Cavato, a few raised beds, some simple benches, and the kids gathering under a tree. That's all there was when I first came. I said that first day, "If I could do this every day for the rest of my life, it would be my dream job."

Then I found out they were looking to hire a chef. They thought it was still a couple of years away, at

least after their garden was in. I kept in contact with Donna and was willing to relocate. Two months after my first visit, I came back, signed a lease in this neighborhood and formally interviewed for the job, hoping it would all work out. Two months after that, I was back here permanently.

My job here means that I wear a number of different hats. I teach all of our seasonal cooking classes through the Edible Schoolyard. The kids come through in different rotations depending on the age group. They spend lots of time in the garden. They've planted everything you see. And while they're planting and watering and fertilizing and harvesting, all the activities tie back to their classroom lessons. So a lesson about a garden bed might actually be a measurement lesson to reinforce what's happening in the classroom. Or it could be something about math — grouping and counting while they're sorting seeds.

We have a third acre here that wraps around the school. Everything is organic. In the garden science class, all the food out here is tied to their Louisiana State Standards for science. They learn about the difference between organic and conventional. Why we choose to do everything organic. There's a small garden area for the kindergarteners, the Butterfly Garden, where they learn about the lifecycle of a butterfly.

You can see we've expanded the gardens vertically as well as horizontally. *[April points to the top of one of the roofs which is covered with plants.]* The building where the kids have gathered is our outdoor classroom. It has the largest green living roof in the region. We have grapevines. The arbors will eventually be covered and form a natural curtain for the classroom.

All of this happened over the last year and a half (2007–08). All of the construction was done over the summer. The plantings started last year. There's a little over two hundred plants, native Louisiana plants, and second- through eighth-graders planted all of them. One day there were trays on the ground. The next, we had a company come with a big Genie to put it all up on the roof. It has its own irrigation system that gets routed to our wetlands area. Dana, our head gardener, checks on it periodically, and it seems to get enough water from rainfall. The drainage keeps it moist. The plants are thriving.

Today we had a class with second-graders. We made nasturtium pesto ravioli with a tomato cream sauce. All the nasturtiums came from our garden. We used the leaves this week. Next week we'll use the flowers when we make a nasturtium risotto with the third grade. We've been eating kale, collards and spinach, so the kids are getting a wide variety of greens. We don't have to focus on how nutritious

> **TIP** ■ I learned recently that if you freeze your leftovers, the room they take up in the freezer saves on electricity. Then you can bring your frozen compost to the farmers market and add it to their pile.

it is for them; our approach is holistic. We expose the kids to a variety of great food during the peak season. We don't want them to feel bad about what they might be eating outside our classes.

The outdoor classroom is utilized every day, even in the rain. The lower garden is like something one could duplicate in a neighborhood urban garden. The teachers do a lot of lessons on why one design is beneficial for backyards and another is more beneficial for larger production.

We often have leftovers from our pickings, and we'll actually go and drop things off to folks in the neighborhood. We do giveaways to the parents when they come to pick their kids up. We teach them how to go out and pick their own food. We do a community day — Open Garden Day — once a week, which Kelly organizes. On Saturdays, we stop being a school garden and we turn into a community garden. Anyone can come and work. It's a good day for volunteers to come through. That's when we do a lot of our tours. Part of the day is garden work, and the other part is doing lunch. So we have a food station, mostly run by kids and me. We take whatever we haven't been able to use in the classes and turn that into lunch for everybody.

We've done two neighborhood markets so far — the first of each month — and we're starting to do that as a monthly project. There's a market on Ferret Street, just a couple of blocks away. The kids get an idea of commerce; then in class they talk about how much we should price things. They learn about labor costs and material costs, about how to include these costs in their final price.

Denise is teaching everyone how to compost —

and people in the neighborhood are dropping their compost off. We don't put in any protein, fat or sugar, so we haven't attracted any rodents.

The kids are building a rain garden. They're learning about erosion in their science class. We noticed we had an erosion problem out here. They got together and thought of solutions for how to fix it. What came about was this rain garden. We're digging a hole and filling it with gravel and sand to keep the water from overflowing into the garden. When the water falls from the roof it falls straight in, so now it won't flood the garden.

We think chickens and bunnies are in our future. I know that we've done some work with Laughing Buddha Nursery, so perhaps that's where we'll get the chickens.

Our next phase is actually to put in a state-of-the-art teaching kitchen. Right now, we're cooking in our classroom. As the kids go through the garden, they end every rotation with a cooking class. In our seasonal cooking class we use everything we can from the garden.

We start at 7:30 A.M. The kids are here until five P.M. Built into that day is a universal breakfast program, so every child receives a free breakfast, regardless of their income. On top of the academics, they've got lots of enrichment programs, like learning about Mardi Gras Indians, beading, a yoga or dance class. They come through the garden in the morning, then there's P.E. In the afternoon, from 3:30 to 5:00 P.M., everybody gets a snack. Breakfast, lunch and a snack at this school.

The other hat I wear is as food and nutrition services coordinator for our two schools, grades K through 8, and 9 through 12. I work on cafeteria reform. Our goal is to serve the same type of food, with the same type of experience in the cafeteria that the kids are now becoming accustomed to through the Edible Schoolyard. What we get from our food service provider are things that come

Eggplant Caponata on Crostini

    3 tablespoons olive oil
    2 medium onions, diced
    2 cloves garlic, minced
    2 tablespoons diced jalapeno, hot wax, or other garden
        variety pepper
    4 medium or 6 small eggplant, diced
    4 tomatoes, seeded and diced
    ¾ cup olive salad
    1 can tomato paste
    ¼ cup honey
    ½ cup red wine vinegar
    ½ teaspoon salt
    ¼ teaspoon pepper
    2 bags crostini

In a large skillet, cook the onions in olive oil over medium heat until they are soft and translucent, about 10 minutes Add the garlic, peppers, eggplant, tomatoes and olive salad. Continue to cook over medium heat until the eggplant is soft and cooked through, about 6 to 8 minutes. Stir in the tomato paste, honey and red wine vinegar and cook over low heat until sauce is warmed and thick, about 5 minutes. Season with salt and pepper. Taste and adjust seasoning as necessary. Spoon a tablespoon of caponata onto each crostini and serve. Serves 20 appetizer portions.

Job Breakdown:

- Turn eggplant planks into diced cubes (2 fourth grade students)
- Saute onions in skillet (1 student)
- Seed tomatoes (1 to 2 students)
- Dice and add tomatoes (1 fourth grade students)
- Dice and add peppers (1 fourth grade student)
- Measure and add olive salad (1 student)
- Scoop in tomato paste (1 student)
- Measure and add honey (1 student)
- Measure and add vinegar (1 student)
- Measure and add salt and pepper (2 students)
- Take turns stirring at stove (all)
- Transfer caponata to large bowl (table leader)
- Spoon caponata onto crostini (all)
- Clean up station (all)
- Put around chairs (all)
- Spread out tablecloth and place flower bouquets on table (2 students)
- Pass out plates (1 student)
- Pass out napkins (1 student)
- Pass out forks (1 student)
- Pass out cups (1 student)
- Pour water (table leader)
- Serve dishes (table leader)

in large quantities, that don't need to be cooked, ready-made food. In most schools, the ovens went out years ago.

One of my big missions this year was to create a wellness policy for our school. It states that we won't serve any competing foods. We'll never have vending machines. We don't sell candy for fundraisers. We don't use candy or food as incentives in the classrooms. The kids know if they bring anything like that on campus, it's going straight into the garbage can. The school has always supported this kind of mission, but we've really cracked down because the teachers need help. The Edible Schoolyard has been able to help facilitate this change. The wellness policy helps, too. If the kids bring in McDonald's or chips, candy, whatever, I say, "Please tell your mom not to waste her money." Our philosophy has always been that there's no good food, there's no bad food. But when you're in school, we're going to eat things that help us be better learners.

Alice Waters came back last year for her first really big visit to see what's happened since she gave away her baby. We were all really nervous, but we got her blessing. She was really happy with what we'd accomplished. Their program in Berkeley is only a middle-school program. Doing this in lower school is a first. There are other lower-school kitchen and gardening programs, especially in California, but this is the first time for Edible Schoolyard.

- Napkin trick (all)
- "I am Glad" song (all)
- Eat (all – when all are served)
- Wonderful conversation (all)
- Clean up/garbage (table leader)
- Take off aprons (all)
- Collect aprons (table leader)
- Push in chairs and line up (all)
- Additional clean up if time allows (all)

Nasturtium Pesto Ravioli with Tomato Cream Sauce

Ingredients for Ravioli:

1 7 ounce container ricotta cheese

1 large egg

1 cup olive oil

2 cups nasturtium leaves, finely chopped

1 tablespoon fresh parsley

3 cloves garlic, minced

1 half lemon, juiced

¼ cup pecans, crushed

1 teaspoon salt

½ teaspoon black pepper

⅓ cup grated parmesan cheese, plus more for garnish

½ package wonton wrappers (30)

Ingredients for Sauce:

2 tablespoons olive oil

2 cloves garlic, minced

¼ teaspoon crushed red pepper flakes

2 cans crushed tomatoes

1 teaspoon sugar

1 cup heavy cream

1 tablespoon fresh oregano

½ bunch chives, thinly sliced

In a medium bowl, mix together all ingredients for ravioli filling until thoroughly combined. Lay out wonton wrappers in a row of diamonds (point facing you). Place half a tablespoon of filling in the center of each ravioli. Moisten your fingertips with water and trace around the outside edge of the wrapper. Bring the top point down to meet the bottom point, forming a triangle. Run your fingers along the edge to ensure a tight seal. Bring a large pot of salted water to a boil. Cook the ravioli in batches until they float, 3 to 4 minutes.

In the meantime, in a saucepan, heat olive oil over medium heat. Add garlic and crushed red pepper and stir for 1 minute. Add crushed tomatoes, sugar, heavy cream and oregano. Cook for about 5 minutes. Add chives and cook for another 3 minutes.

Arrange ravioli on plates. Top each plate with a ladle of sauce and a sprinkle of parmesan cheese. Serves 6 to 8.

April takes me on a tour of the indoor facilities. She points to a bulletin board filled with photos of the kids with Rachael Ray, articles from Good Housekeeping, Wine Spectator, *and* Scholastic *magazine. The cafeteria is spacious, light and clean, with a flower and a water pitcher on each table.*

Our next big step for the kids will be the cafeteria. When they come back in the fall, if we get the funding, we'll have replaced all the tables and chairs with real dining tables and chairs. We'll have tablecloths and be using lovely new lighting. We'll have painted the industrial piping so it fades out of view, although it is very theatrical! Everything will be done as green as possible. We'll get rid of the styrofoam and have plates and silverware. We want to teach dining manners, how to have an appropriate conversation, how to take care of each other at the table. We'll put napkins on our laps. We will pass the food and say please and thank you!

Our classroom and office space is where almost everything happens when we're not out in the garden. It's where we do all our cooking, until we build our big beautiful kitchen. Our mission is to turn back the clock, take our food back from the large companies that now provide the ready-made food. Begin to incorporate the same kind of care into what we feed the kids for lunch, as we talk about in the garden. Letting the kids know that food doesn't magically appear on their plates. It comes from somewhere before it gets to us. I've been able

to work with our providers. Now, because of our wellness policy, I can actually say that a particular menu doesn't work for us. We'd like to see more food from Louisiana on the menu. Baby steps.

There are so many great lessons tied to food; not only history and culture, but also table manners, socialization. It became really clear early on that we couldn't just change the food, we had to change the entire environment, including where the food was made and eaten. And the kids were ready for it. We've slowly been working on changing the food. We have fresh fruit every day. We've eliminated all canned and processed food. Our cafeteria staff is being trained to do more scratch cooking. We have a salad bar. We're buying more and more whole grains, brown rice. We're introducing a more local and organic diet.

Some kids are bussed from up to an hour away. A lot of the areas where they live don't have grocery stores. Most of their food comes from fast-food restaurants or corner convenience stores. There are lots of folks in the city working to get more fresh fruits and vegetables into the corner stores so there's more access. Access is a huge issue for our families. We're trying to fill the gap any way we can, by providing access to our garden, using fresh fruits and veggies in the cafeteria. Then at least we know that when the kids are here, we're feeding them as best we can.

We're getting ready to do our first family nutrition night. I feel like my job is to get the kids to like vegetables. The parent's job is, once they like them, to go buy vegetables and start cooking them at home.

The kids come to us with deep issues. Post-traumatic stress disorder from the storm, from everyday violence in their neighborhood. This is a healing place. You have to heal them first. Then, you know, baby steps. You make them feel loved and cared for. Then they improve academically.

Here at ESY-NOLA we're starting to take some more formalized data. Kelly was part of getting Tulane to come with surveys, interview the kids, just to find out how this kind of programming is impacting their daily habits. What we've found is that last year, the third-graders had the most exposure to the gardening program. And they scored, they outperformed the state on their science test. We'd like to think it's because of our program.

We've had our highest parent engagement through Edible Schoolyard, with our open houses. You don't need a college degree to be a good cook. And everyone in New Orleans loves food! The same with gardening. The garden is not a place to feel intimidated. Everyone is valued here. We want to share our recipes. We want to hear how they make gumbo.

We're beginning to upgrade our kitchen equipment. We bought a second steam oven this year. We'll be putting in walk-in refrigerators and freezers. We'll put in a stove — we don't have a stove. We'll have a washing station so we can have more fresh produce. We're dreaming big. Eventually our goal is to purchase food from local farms for our cafeteria fare. We're in our early years. Someday we're going to have a full composting kitchen in the back.

I think the Edible Schoolyard will become a model for other schools. Then we'd love to dedicate some of our time to sharing what we've been able to do. Schools constantly come to us to learn how we do what we do. We barely know ourselves. We're still so new. We want to formalize our curriculum, making sure it's really tied to Louisiana standards, so it's something that other schools want to replicate. Its great to be creative, but we want to make sure that it's as enriching and educational as possible.

By creating demand from the ground up, it's our intention that school-based food and snack programs will reflect the values of "wholesome, nutritious and delicious" — fueling our children in mind, body and spirit. As Alice Waters says, we want to leave the land and everything we touch in better shape than we found it.

Grant Estrade
Laughing Buddha Nursery ■ Metairie, New Orleans ■ www.laughingbuddhanursery.com

To get to the Laughing Buddha Nursery, I rent a car and drive five miles out of the French Quarter on a four-lane highway. I drive past cemeteries with crypts the size of large houses and more white FEMA trailer parks. Metairie is the first suburb outside of New Orleans on the south shore of Lake Pontchartain. "Metairie" comes from the French word for farm. Grant Estrade started the nursery in 2003 as a garden-supply shop. He is an entrepreneur who grew up in a family where there was always a vegetable garden and he loved playing around in the dirt. There was no one else around selling organic gardening supplies or edibles on a sustainable, organic landscape, so he filled a niche.

Grant Estrade: I'm a total product of private schooling; I say this because I find that many people see farming as an inferior career to pursue, but I see it as a specialized skill that needs to be encouraged. I went to Christian Brothers School and Jesuit High School, and then I went on to the University of New Orleans. I grew up in New Orleans; my parents grew up here and then did the white-flight thing to the suburbs.

I started out studying biology, but didn't like it because it was a prep for medical school. I wanted to get dirty and do field stuff. I would have been better off in an environmental science or an ecology type program. So I switched degrees after a year or two to philosophy, and then started picking up sociology. I dropped out of college with six credit hours left to start Laughing Buddha Nursery; a move that my parents were not happy with in the least, but nonetheless supported. When I finish, I'll have degrees in sociology and philosophy. I'll have to go back because eventually I want to teach — earlier today I was at a garden club meeting where I teach once a month, and it is an important part of this business for me, spreading awareness of what we're doing here in the shop and why. I want to do more and more teaching.

I'm an Eagle Scout. I went through the entire Boy Scout program, and I'm still involved in Boy Scouts. I have two older brothers, twins, and we were rough with each other. We fought, we made up and we threw each other around. As a kid I enjoyed outdoor stuff in general. I worked in a pet store; I bred my own snakes and loved aquariums. I never really made a good employee, though. I say what's on my mind, and when I come up with a way I think things should be done, that's the way I do it. I would not do well in a corporate environment because I don't like sitting around. I don't like bureaucracy. After studying capitalism in sociology, and the ins and outs of it, I figured that starting my own business was the way to go.

I got a loan from my parents, worked full-time, seven days a week at the shop and five nights a week bartending. That's how it started. Then my parents gave me the rest of my college money from the college tuition fund to put as part of the down payment on this building. I started off very, very small. I had done some research and there wasn't anybody doing this work, selling organic garden supplies and edible plants. I opened the business and then I actually got caught up in the stuff I was telling people, if that makes sense. And then, being exposed to permaculture, permanent agriculture according to Bill Mollison [an Australian known as the father of permaculture], going through class with that and reading books, I just really got into it. Business started coming in, and I reinvested every dollar back into the business. And now we have plants for sale, we have grown all our own vegetables and herbs that we sell. The main crux of this business is getting the consumer — who has a backyard — to start growing his or her own food. That's how the store is set up, from the soil to the seeds and the classes that we teach.

What I've begun to notice with kids is that sometimes they have no connection to their food supply. We have kids who come in here and see the broccoli growing and they're like, "What's that?" Where we get our food from has changed so much in the last fifty years. I grew up getting carrots, tomatoes and blackberries from the backyard. But most of my contemporaries got their food from the grocery store. I asked my mom where she would go for food when she was my age and she said if she wanted meat, she went to a freestanding butcher shop. He would have live chickens that he was going to slaughter, fresh. My grandmother grew up on a farm right around here, and she went into the yard for her food.

People have really lost their connection with their food. They've lost the connection with seasonal ingredients, where their food comes from and what

it's supposed to taste like. That's my biggest eye-opener with this business, and what I'm concentrating on when I talk to people. "Yes, you can grow your own food, and even raise your own meat if you want."

When Katrina hit, I'd been open about a year and a half. I was tempted to just close up shop, but my past experience taught me that if I give up on something I feel bad. We had a lot of wind damage out here but no flooding. One more inch and we would have been flooded. Nobody was buying garden supplies after Katrina, but SBA loans and insurance money held us until people started coming around, and we've been growing ever since. It took us a solid year of hard work to get back on our feet, and then we bought some equipment and started selling soil. I got some chickens and started selling eggs at the farmers market.

This yard mimics my backyard. We're doing our own composting, mixing our own soils. Soil has been very important to rebuilding New Orleans. We have a harvester; the vermicomposting has been excellent for us. The castings are grade-A compost. It's a specialty gardening thing, really good in seed-starting mixes. We're doing all of our own worm composting at the store until we can move them someplace else, to the farm I'm starting. Same with the vermicompost, all raised locally. We are rerouting waste that would normally go to landfills, and actually making a marketable product out of it.

There's nothing that makes me so comfortable as when I'm by myself doing an agrarian activity. So about two years ago, I bought three acres of property and started up another business called Local Cool Farms, growing produce to sell to restaurants. I'm not going to take out loans on that, but as I have cash we kind of put it into the new project. It's a spin on global warming — fun name, huh! We'll have livestock out there and basically do what we're doing here, only on a larger scale.

We try to be as green as possible in our business structure. Our delivery truck runs on vegetable oil from restaurants. We make biodiesel for the tractors

changed everything, made those who disbelieved open their minds, and people were willing to think about the real possibility of global warming and what else might be out there that could help us move through this hard time.

Recently I had it out with a nonprofit. I said I believed that we're not going to accomplish anything by trying to feed a bunch of poor people organic food. That comes later. We're trying to start a movement, and the people that we need to convince in this moment are those people with connections, who have money and are willing to support the overhead of a new venture. Obviously I was being pissy due to being passed over with support that went to another group, but I said, if you really want to do this, we have to hit higher end restaurants and sell to people who can afford it — and it will trickle down. We have limited resources at the moment, so give them to the movers and shakers and trust that it will eventually get to everyone. Walmart is selling organic products that they're getting from who

knows where, and Whole Foods store brand frozen broccoli was grown in Asia — they are missing the point of the whole movement.

I am always available to the nonprofits but we need to be a multipronged entity. You go after these people for this reason, you go after those people for that reason and so on. As long as I make my ends meet, I can offer myself up as a volunteer and go talk to a garden club or a school.

In my spare time I do jujitsu. I've been doing it for ten years now. I work on my higher-level stuff and teach twice a week. Religiously. I read a lot of Eastern philosophy. I still bartend two nights a week, which is a nice supplemental income and I'm still involved with the Boy Scouts. I participate in triathlons. I love to cook. I make soap out of the leftover oil.

My primary goal is very specific: It's about creating a connection for people to where their food supply is coming from.

Emery Van Hook
Director of the Crescent City Market and ■ www.marketumbrella.org

The Crescent City Farmers Market is about a fifteen-minute walk from the French Quarter, if you do it with intention. It's on the corner of Magazine and Girod. A magnificent, colorful mural wraps around the back and side walls.

On the afternoon of my interview with Emery, I arrive at 4:45 P.M. precisely. The sun is just heading down over the horizon. Wearing white pedal pushers, her dark hair framing her face, Emery rushes across the street to meet me. We walk up the block and sit on the steps of a church.

Emery: I grew up cooking. My mom's mom is from here and my dad's from here. My mother has a Sicilian background. I grew up in the kitchen with both my mother and grandmother. It's part of life, growing up in New Orleans. Food is everywhere.

I was a literature major in college. After I graduated, I came back and started working for an independent restaurant group doing concept development and community outreach projects. For one project, I was working with some people in New York. The event was here but the people were there. I was reading a lot of bios, and I saw that one of the people involved had done a master's in food studies at NYU. I'd been thinking about going back to graduate school. I wasn't certain if I wanted to do business or journalism, but I knew whatever I did it would be food related. I applied to NYU and was accepted. That summer I gave notice here. By then I'd been with this restaurant group for seven years.

The Friday before Katrina was my last day at my job. There was a going-away party planned for me on that Saturday night. All over people were beginning to evacuate. I had some friends who'd come into town for the party. Believe it or not, we'd gone ahead with it. The next morning I woke up and saw the storm in the Gulf, and called my parents, who live a little bit west of the city. In all their years here

they'd never evacuated. I got hold of my brother and we went out to where they live. At that point the mayor called a mandatory evacuation for everyone. We threw some things in the car and drove to Houston, where my sister lives. Usually a five-hour drive, it ended up taking nineteen hours.

We stayed in Houston as the storm came through. We knew we couldn't get back to the city. I had already signed a lease up in New York and was set to start school. I'd already quit my job. I made a decision that the only thing to do was to go. So I moved to New York. For the first six months, I came back about every month. I had a house here. The second floor had been shredded by all the mini tornadoes that touched down around things, like Mimi at the Market — where we bring school groups through — or low-income senior groups, we introduce them to the market, what's fresh, what's healthy. We started a club for kid shoppers under fourteen called the Marketeers Club. We do activities with them on the first Saturday of the month. Right now we're doing healthy cooking demos, showing them how to make pizza with whole-wheat flour. They shop for fresh local toppings with their parents.

We do a lot of outreach to senior centers. We give out this farmers market bingo game where the common denominator is food, showing what's seasonal and what's nutritious. Then we go to the centers and play bingo with them. That's to increase redemption for the farmers market nutrition program. They get vouchers for $20. We'll match with an additional $20 *[from private funding]* if they spend it all.

Being innovative, that's what I like about this job. Taking a different approach to things. And working with the farmers, helping them expand their product line, stretching their season into different varieties and backing that up with chef support. We do a lot of foraging work, trying to get local products into the market. Having a restaurant background, I really enjoy introducing chefs to producers. I love when the farmers hear that their items are on someone's menu, or they meet one of the chefs, or hear that their food was featured.

We do something called the White Boot Brigade *[named for the distinctive rubber boots worn by the commercial fishers]*. We started years ago, taking Louisiana shrimpers and partnering them with farmers markets. I think about 80 percent of the shrimp coming into the U.S. are imported. Recently, we partnered with Sankofa Marketplace *[an open-air market in the Lower Ninth where folks get together to exchange information, enjoy live jazz and fresh foods]*. We introduced the shrimpers to the market place and people. In exchange they've agreed to certain sustainable harvesting techniques and practices. That can be anything from collecting oil from restaurants in the French Quarter, and making biodiesel for their boats and other vehicles. Another shrimper has installed a deck freezer. Whatever he catches he immediately freezes; that way he's not burning gas coming in and out. They've also committed to reducing bi-catch — anything else they might pick up as they troll for shrimp.

We have a program on marketumbrella.org, featured on YouTube, called Go Fish on Film. That's something where someone like Lance Nacio, the shrimper with the deck freezer, will explain what he's done and all that's involved so that other shrimpers can replicate. We did a series that showed all of us setting up market and breaking it down, things like that.

There's so much potential in this city. I can't imagine living anywhere else. During the storm, while I was in school, all I could think about was coming home. I feel we're at the beginning of a movement here. The storms gave us a blank slate. If something's completely broken, it causes you to think about how you want to rebuild it. Our farmers are resilient. They have to go through storm after storm after storm. Evacuating, losing everything, boats getting flooded out and coming back again. There's something about this town.

I want a role in rebuilding New Orleans, from the restaurant community to the grocery stores that need to be rebuilt in the neighborhoods. What I love about our markets is that they're free. And they're open to the public. They bring together urban and rural, rich people and poor people, people from all around the city. Everybody in this town loves to talk about their recipe for this, their mom's recipe for that, and where they went to eat. People are just so food obsessed. It's the conversation. It's a common denominator for everybody.

Vanessa Ulmer
Tulane University School of Public Health ■ www.sph.tulane.edu

Vanessa Ulmer and Sarah Custer are both involved in the day-to-day tasks of Tulane University's Prevention Research Center. They implement strategies to bring grocery stores, farmers markets, urban gardens and other healthy-food retailers into underserved areas of New Orleans.

Vanessa studied policy analysis at Cornell University (1998–2002). She then spent a year in Washington, D.C., working on international trade policy. Following that, a year teaching in Nicaragua, then back to D.C. working for the German Marshall Fund doing trade and development policy work.

Vanessa Ulmer: Cornell has always been fairly cutting edge. It had a very strong farmers market even when I was there. They have been doing more and more to get local food into the dining halls. And there's a student-run farm on campus. I don't know much about growing, but what you could do as a student was to show up, weed, dig, whatever. You would record how many hours you volunteered, and then you could trade in your hours for produce from the farm. So I did that, which was really fun. And it required no skills, just the ability to have someone tell you what was a weed and what was a plant.

After Nicaragua, I went back to Washington. Essentially one of the bosses from my first job switched organizations while I was in Nicaragua. When I got back he hired me in this new organization. Although I learned a lot, I didn't really believe that working toward a small kind of textural change in a trade agreement would really help farmers on the ground in Africa, ostensibly the people that we were trying to serve. One of my supervisors pointed out that a lot of what we were doing was just trying to prevent really bad policy. We were not necessarily going to get good policy, but we'd prevent things that just shut down opportunities for poor farm-

ers, that stopped them from selling what they grew. I wanted to do something that felt more tangible, something I was more connected to, where I could see results more quickly.

Before coming here, I was with my husband at Oxford, England for a year. He had a fellowship to study for his master's degree. I was able to secure a one-year master's program for myself. My husband had grown up in New Orleans. When Katrina hit, despite the fact that he had another job offer on the table, he decided he wanted to come back here. So even before we had jobs, we returned. I finished my thesis here and began working for The Prevention Research Center.

For a while now, I've been spending most of my time working with the City of New Orleans

RECIPES ■ Vanessa Ulmer

Breakfast: I like breakfast to be healthy and quick – which for me means oatmeal, cereal, or yogurt – all of which I enjoy topped with seasonal fruit, bananas, or raisins and slivered almonds. No recipes required.

Lunch: Cucumber, Tomato and Feta Salad
During the summer in Louisiana, cold salads taste great in the heat, and Creole tomatoes and cukes are in season. Enjoy this salad with hummus and a good whole wheat bread or pita.

- 2 medium cucumbers
- 1 tomato
- 2 ounces of feta cheese
- 2 tablespoons of red wine vinegar
- 1 teaspoon of sugar
- Spices: salt and pepper; dash of hot sauce; chopped fresh dill, parsley, or basil (optional)

Peel the cucumbers in alternating strips so they're striped, with half the peel left on. (Taste first, and if there's any bitterness, peel the cucumbers fully.) Cut the cucumbers into thin slices.

In a bowl, combine the vinegar, sugar, a dash of hot sauce, a scant pinch of salt (¼ teaspoon or less – the feta will add salt), and black pepper to taste. Add the cucumbers and toss well. Refrigerate for an hour or overnight if you have the time.

Just before serving, chop the tomato, the feta cheese, and about a tablespoon of either fresh dill, parsley, or basil (you may want to skip the hot sauce if using basil), and then toss gently together with the cucumbers. Adjust the seasonings to taste, and enjoy. Serves 2 or more.

Dinner: Summer Squash and Cannellini Bean Saute
I like to use a mix of zucchini and yellow summer squash for this recipe, and serve it over brown rice, quinoa or whole wheat penne sprinkled with grated parmesan cheese.

- 4 medium zucchini and/or summer squash
- 1 to 2 medium tomatoes, chopped
- 1 can of cannellini beans, rinsed (or substitute another white bean or chickpeas)
- 1 tablespoon olive oil
- 2 cloves of garlic, finely chopped
- ¼ teaspoon salt
- Pepper to taste
- Grated parmesan cheese (optional)

Cut the zucchini and squash lengthwise, then crosswise into ⅓-inch thick half moons. Set aside.

In a large sauté pan, sauté the garlic in olive oil for about 30 seconds, stirring constantly so the garlic becomes fragrant but does not brown. Add the chopped tomato and the rinsed canned cannellini beans, sprinkle with salt and pepper to taste, and sauté for several minutes over medium-high heat. The tomato mixture should become juicy; add a splash of water as needed.

Add the sliced zucchini and squash to the sauté pan, stirring to mix well with the tomatoes. Cover loosely and cook over medium-high heat until tender, about 8 to 10 minutes, stirring occasionally. Add a splash of water as needed to prevent the vegetables from sticking to the pan.

Serve immediately. Sprinkle with grated parmesan cheese if desired. Serves 4.

Dessert: I don't enjoy baking and I find it hard to improve upon my favorite desserts – fresh seasonal fruit or a few squares of quality dark chocolate. Again, no recipes required.

on a proposed grant and loan program to provide financing for supermarkets and grocery stores. We want to open them in areas of the city where you can't get access to fresh fruits and vegetables and other healthy foods. This project would have an advocacy role. The Food Policy Advisory Committee presented this recommendation to the city. Then we started talking to people about the importance of such a program, and what it would look like.

The FPAC has really been more of what's called a grasstops project, made up of people who are actually in city government, people who can make decisions. We've made an effort to have a cross-section of stakeholders. We have very strong representation from the grocery-store sector for this initial set of recommendations. We also have civic leaders from a variety of nonprofits, and have the public sector represented.

At the state level we have the "Healthy Food Retail Study Group." Again, the idea is to bring a cross-section of stakeholders to the table. This study group focuses very narrowly on access to food retail and getting expert speakers to share their knowledge with the group, discussing and creating recommendations for a statewide program. I'm presently writing up the report for that study group. Even in this financial climate, we've gotten enthusiastic response from some key senators signaling that they think they can make funding available for this type of work.

There are three programs that we're working on with the city: the community gardens program, grocery stores, and community markets. Seven million dollars has been allocated to the grocery sector. It's going to be structured as a partnership between the City of New Orleans, a community development lender, and a nonprofit with expertise in access to food or public heath in some way. It will have a competitive application process, with retailers submitting applications. We would first screen for eligibility — that it's actually a grocery store and that it's going to sell healthy food. We don't want to fund liquor or convenience stores. And we make sure it's located in an underserved area. That's where the nonprofit partner with expertise in food access comes in.

Then there's the Lot Next Door project. If there's a vacant lot next door to you, you can buy it, turn it into a garden. We're having conversations about tenure over the lot, what's going to happen in five years. The idea of using these lots as temporary sites for food production seems ineffective, because there's a lot of investment in amending the soil, making sure it's safe, making sure it's productive for crops. If it's a community garden, the social infrastructure and support you need to build it and keep it maintained are huge. So we've really emphasized that food production as a short-term use of vacant land is not the way to go. Other folks are talking about sunflower gardens as short-term use of vacant land. Sunflowers help take the lead out of the land. That's fine, but it's not food. Food is a different thing all together.

If we're talking about providing sites where there is some security over the land tenure, how do we do that? In other cities where it's been done successfully, there are often very strong land trusts that are partners, which makes it easy for the city. We're not there yet. The city needs to feel comfortable if it's going to hand over land for more of a public-purpose-type garden that an organization will be responsible for maintaining.

In my work, health and food access for low-income people comes first, then thinking about how can we encourage and promote local agriculture. From where I sit at the Prevention Research Center, that's a close second.

Sarah Custer
Bill Emerson National Hunger Fellowship ■ www.hungercenter.org

Sarah Custer: When I graduated from McGill University in Montreal, I really wanted to work in an urban area looking at the issues of food access and quality. I received a Bill Emerson National Hunger Fellowship *[a social justice program that trains, inspires and sustains leaders]*. When you're accepted, you don't know where you will be placed, but you spend the first six months in a host field community. There are twenty fellows. Two of us are here in New Orleans.

Before the fellowship, I was really more interested in international issues and food policy in terms of trade. Now I'm questioning that. There's a lot of work to be done here.

I feel like I have some kind of personal responsibility in terms of East Africa, because that's where most of my family is from. My mom is Ethiopian.

She grew up there and moved to Italy when she was eighteen. She had a scholarship to go to college in Italy. My father's Somalian. His mother is Somalian and his father is Italian. My dad went to the same college as my mother. Further down the line my dad had a job that required him to travel. He worked for an Italian telecom company. When I was born he was working in Saudi Arabia, so I spent the first six years of my life there. After that, we moved to New Jersey, where my mom has family. I have two older sisters who were born in Rome; one is nine years older, the other twelve years older. The school in Rome was not very good for either of them. That's why we moved to New Jersey. We lived there until my father got transferred back to Italy, just outside of Rome. We had a little garden where we grew our own tomatoes.

RECIPES ■ Sarah Custer

BREAKFAST: Pumpkin Butter Pancakes

I recently acquired a big jar of pumpkin butter, and although I thoroughly enjoyed eating it on toast, I decided to experiment with it. These pancakes came out really good, especially with fresh fruit, walnuts, and pure maple syrup.

> 1 cup whole wheat flour
> ½ cup unbleached all-purpose flour
> 3 teaspoons baking powder
> 1 teaspoon cinnamon
> 1 teaspoon nutmeg
> 1 teaspoon salt
> ½ cup milk
> 1 egg
> 3 tablespoons pumpkin butter
> 2 tablespoons vegetable oil

In a large bowl, sift together the flour, baking powder, spices and salt. Pour in the milk, egg, pumpkin butter and vegetable oil; mix just enough until smooth.

Heat a lightly greased pan over medium heat. Scoop about ⅓ cup of the batter onto the pan for each pancake. Brown on both sides and serve! Serves 2 to 4.

LUNCH: Maltagliati e Funghi Porcini (Porcini Mushrooms and Maltagliati)

Sometimes my uncle and I would really score and find a bunch of porcini mushrooms in the woods outside of Rome. This is my take on one of the dishes we would make with them. It calls for maltagliati, but you can substitute pappardelle, fettuccine, or your favorite kind of broad pasta.

> ¼ cup extra virgin olive oil
> 5 to 6 porcini mushrooms, sliced
> 2 cloves garlic, minced
> Salt and pepper to taste
> ⅔ cup heavy cream
> 2 tablespoons parmigiano Reggiano
> ⅓ cup white wine
> 1 teaspoon nutmeg
> 1 pound maltagliati

Heat oil in a large skillet and sauté mushrooms and garlic, and season with salt and pepper. Add cream, parmigiano, wine and nutmeg to mushrooms and cook for another 5

minutes. Meanwhile, bring a large pot of salted water to boil and cook pasta until it is al dente. Toss drained pasta with mushroom sauce, serve, and add parmigiano and freshly ground pepper to taste. Serves 2 to 4.

DINNER: Vegetarian Gumbo

I always loved okra, and living in New Orleans it is everywhere! This is a vegetarian recipe, but for a more authentic version, add Andouille sausage, chicken or shellfish.

The word "gumbo" comes from the Bantu word for okra – *kigombo*. This is just one of the ways in which African culture and history is present in many aspects of New Orleans life.

> 2 tablespoon olive oil
> 3 cloves garlic, chopped
> 1 onion, diced
> 2 stalks celery
> 1 green bell pepper, diced
> 1 (28 ounce) can diced tomatoes
> 1 (16 ounce) can red beans or kidney beans
> 1 cup vegetable broth
> ½ pound of okra, cut
> 1 teaspoon oregano
> Salt and pepper to taste
> Cayenne pepper or hot sauce, if desired
> Gumbo filé powder, if available
> 3 cups cooked brown rice

Heat oil in large pot. Sauté garlic, onion, celery and pepper for 5 minutes, then add tomatoes, beans, broth, okra and seasoning. Boil for about 30 minutes. Stir in gumbo filé and serve over warm rice. Serves 4.

DESSERT: Vegan Ginger-Walnut-Coconut-Carrot Cake

This is a recipe that we used for one of the McGill Organic Campus' cooking workshops. I'm not a vegan, and wouldn't even call myself a vegetarian (I prefer "flexatarian" as I do on occasion eat meat), but this recipe will prove those who think "yummy vegan dessert" is an oxymoron wrong!

> 2 cups unbleached all-purpose flour
> 1 tablespoons baking powder
> 1 teaspoon baking soda
> ¾ teaspoon salt

2 teaspoons ground cinnamon
½ teaspoon ground nutmeg
1 cup pineapple juice
½ cup canola oil
¾ cup sugar
½ cup pure maple syrup
2 teaspoons vanilla extract
1 cup walnuts, chopped
¼ cup crystallized ginger, chopped
1 cup unsweetened shredded coconut
2 cups carrots, grated

Preheat oven 350 degrees and grease two 8-inch round cake pans, 9×13-inch pan, or 24 muffin tins.

In a large bowl sift together flour, baking powder, baking soda, salt and spices.

In a separate bowl, mix together the pineapple juice, oil, sugar, maple syrup and vanilla. Add the dry ingredients to the wet in batches, and combine well. Fold in the walnuts, ginger, coconut and carrots.

Divide the batter evenly among the pans and bake 40 to 45 minutes for the 8-inch or 9-inch pans and 15 to 20 minutes for the muffins. Let cool in pans and ice with coconut icing.

Coconut Icing

¼ cup non-hydrogenated margarine, at room temperature
¼ cup coconut milk
1 teaspoon vanilla extract
2 cups confectioners' icing sugar
1 cup unsweetened coconut

Cream the margarine until light and fluffy. Add the coconut milk and vanilla and combine. Add the sifted confectioners' sugar and mix until smooth. Add the unsweetened coconut and combine. Refrigerate until ready to use.

In the fall, after it rained, my uncle would take me mushroom hunting.

I really enjoy cooking. Growing up, we always had a kind of international cuisine. My mom would cook Ethiopian food, my dad would make rice in the traditional Somalian way, and then, lots of Italian food.

After Italy, my father was transferred to Cuba. We lived in a town called Siboney. I loved it — the culture, the food. We had our own garden. We had chickens, too. It was mostly out of necessity that we got the chickens, after a hurricane when there were no more eggs — well that's not entirely true. There were eggs in the supermarkets, but they were only sold to the diplomats. So we got some chickens and we had our eggs and our vegetable patch. Our dogs tended to eat the vegetables. *[Laughs]* We had one dog, then suddenly there was another one, then one of our dogs had puppies. At one time we had eight dogs.

At McGill I originally studied African studies and international development. I ended up doing an honors program in international development, a major in economics and a minor in political science. I was also involved in the organic campus. Kind of a buying club. We had this farmer who lived about an hour outside of town, near Ottawa. He would come every week and bring a basket of vegetables. You would place your order the week before, $10 to $15. We had a lot of Jerusalem artichokes, potatoes and cabbage. We integrated them into what we were already eating.

During the summers, I would usually come back to New Jersey. I worked for an organization called Global Policy, based in New York City. They looked at issues of United Nations reform, making it more accountable and transparent. Issues of social justice. One summer I did AmeriCorps Direct and worked for the New York City Coalition Against Hunger. Once a week we worked at the Long Island City CSA, helping to coordinate, getting people to sign up, organizing events for members, compiling the newsletter, recipes. We delivered vegetables to seniors.

We worked on a USDA market basket study,

looking at what's available in a particular neighborhood. The neighborhoods I worked in were on the Lower East Side of Manhattan, two areas of Brooklyn and one area of Queens. We looked at what was available within a ten minute walking radius of a farmers market — comparing prices and the quality of the food surrounding the market to see how competitive they were, if they catered to the needs of the community. We went into every single store and checked the quality, the prices, what they had. Sometimes the storeowners were not happy about it and told us to leave. We had to be okay with that.

As I found myself in these jobs, my interest began to grow. I really think it's a question of social justice, being able to eat healthy food. It doesn't matter if you're wealthy or not. It's a human rights issue. That's what I really want to work on: food, hunger issues, trade problems, fair trade.

With this fellowship I've been working very closely with Vanessa Ulmer. We've been looking at issues of access to healthy food in neighborhoods here in New Orleans. We're working with the city and state to implement financing programs for grocery stores, farmers markets and community gardens. For example, grocery stores that have not been able to reopen after the hurricanes in certain neighborhoods because they didn't have financing. There's an empty lot program. There are a lot of empty lots, and people don't want to have an empty lot next door to them. The question really is, how do you transfer vacant lots to community gardens; how do you assemble larger tracts of land for more intensive urban agriculture?

All the fellows have to write a hunger-free community report. It can be anything from a documentary to a collection of data. I've been working on a tool kit for neighborhood organizations that want to work with corner stores in their neighborhoods to bring healthy options. It looks at what neighborhood groups can do. And strategies — I've spoken to a lot of folks from the Healthy Corner Stores Network. We're tracking all kinds of possibilities, including costs.

My last day here is next week, Thursday. I don't want to leave yet — because of Mardi Gras. I feel like I'm just beginning to learn and understand. The Bill Emerson Fellows Program is a really great program, and I don't want to give that up. My next stint is in Washington, D.C., with the Alliance to End Hunger. I'm looking forward to being there.

THIRD SPRING ■ *The crocuses and bluebells are first up in Central Park. Daffodils and tulips poke through, too. I can hardly wait for the first show of apple blossoms, but that's a couple of weeks off. I transcribe the interviews from New Orleans. I've been doing research on some possible profiles in North Carolina and Virginia.*

I drive down from New York City. Luna's always happy to be included. I spend the first three nights with an old friend and colleague in North Carolina who's just finishing up a cookbook. We go on hikes, and she and her husband join me for dinners at local restaurants.

Cullen Owen

Spinning Spider Creamery ■ Marshall, North Carolina ■ www.spinningspidercreamery.com

MARCH ■ *Half an hour from Asheville, along the narrow back roads of some of the most splendid green stretches of countryside, is Spinning Spider Creamery. Nestled between the Smokies and the Blue Ridge Mountains, it's a microdairy set in among beech, American elm, bitternut hickory and white cedar trees. From Bailey Mountain, where the barn is perched, there are spectacular views of pristine farmland, with a few chickens sprinkled about, and white Saanen goats.*

Usually the parents define the makings of a farm and its farm life. But for the Owens, it wasn't until Cullen, aged ten, got involved with the 4-H Club, and received the gift of a goat that the seed for the family business took hold.

Cullen, now nineteen, is finishing up his associate's degree in science at A-B Tech. He plans to start at the University of North Carolina in Asheville, majoring in biology. Right now, he's really running the milking show at the farm.

Cullen Owen: After I learned about the Dairy Chain Project, I got in line for it. In 1999, I moved to the front of the line and secured a baby goat. By the time I was twelve years old, I'd raised it up, bred it. When one of its babies was old enough, as the project detailed, I turned the kid over to another 4-H'er, keeping the daisy chain going.

The mama of the goat I raised turned out to be second in the Nationals that year. I definitely feel that the quality of that first goat, the sense of ownership it gave me, built my confidence. Soon I was managing five goats here on the farm and getting five gallons of milk a day. Goats have this horrible ability to multiply.

Cullen's laugh echoes off the milking room walls.

We needed another refrigerator. In fact, two. Suddenly, we were looking for other things to do with all the milk. My mom started making cheese.

There was a tailgate market nearby, and our cheese began selling out. Pretty soon we were writing a business plan to Mountain Micro Enterprise Fund in Asheville. We were milking twenty to twenty-five goats. Since my parents were already tied down, we went for full licensing, and Spinning Spider Creamery was born.

The milking room is the heart of the dairy and where I spend at least two hours twice a day — one in the early morning and again, late afternoon. I like the continuous rhythm, *hiss-thump, hiss-thump,* the sound of the milking machine. Kind of like the double-time of contra-dance music, which I love. I play it while I milk. I also like British folk/ rock, specifically Jethro Tull, Richard Thompson and the more classic rockers, like David Bowie and The Who.

Cullen opens a side door and eight white Saanen goats file in, each moving swiftly to its stall — a lineup of eight tushies ready to be relieved of their milk.

I clean each of their teats with iodine. Then I attach these rubber hoses that automatically suck the milk into the narrow stainless steel piping. The raw milk's pulled down into the bulk tank, where it's chilled and then stored. In the first years of having the goats, we milked by hand. Once we had more than fifteen goats, our hands took a beating. People who milk for years usually end up getting carpal tunnel. It's cheaper to buy the machine than to pay for the surgery.

It takes me about ten to fifteen minutes per group of eight; about two hours to milk all seventy goats, which is what we have now. It's a really clean system. Nothing touches the milk as it makes its way through the stainless steel piping. Meet Sylvie, Fiona, Echo, Kambera, Kersey, Sukie, Wisteria and Maggie. They're really sociable animals with distinctly different personalities. Sometimes they're stubborn, sometimes moody. They're also curious

and playful. Some of them even seem to have a sense of humor.

After I milk the goats they're put out on the pasture — which this time of year is cool and green. We've had a lot of rain. Their work for the day is to munch the grass. Sylas *[middle brother]* puts out grain for them to eat. Goats are ruminants, cud-chewing animals. They take in large quantities of food in a very short period of time, swallowing with not much chewing. Then, during a resting period, they chew again, making the pieces smaller. They work through their food quickly and put it out as milk. Not a bad life.

Cullen flashes another million-dollar smile.

After the second milking, the goats go to their pens for the night. We have two guard dogs that keep watch over them. They live in the pasture with them, protecting them from coyotes — actually, anything threatening that might come into the area, including a neighbor's dog. That's happened.

Thank goodness I left Luna in the car!

I'm also the backup cheese maker to my mom. During the summer, when school is out, I spend more and more time in the cheese kitchen. I haul the milk from the bulk tank, where it's stored, bucket by bucket into the cheese kitchen. The milk goes immediately into the vat where the actual cheese making begins. I've always loved working with the goats. The cheese making is really just as interesting. It takes a skill, there's an art form to it. At the same time there's this really cool science — an interesting blend, and in the end, you get to eat it. Yeah, these are good results. The fridge in the cheese kitchen has a shelf that everyone in the family is allowed to snack from — leftover samples, some of the best cheese, although maybe not picture-perfect, but so good.

A couple of years ago, I wanted to spend a month in Finland. It was one of two places that the 4-H Club offered for a semester abroad. Since my

RECIPES ■ Cullen Owen

Breakfast: Yoghurt with Granola

A favorite is our yogurt with granola from Farm and Sparrow, a local brick oven baker. Top it with fresh berries, in season, or dried fruit when berries aren't available. Add a cup of coffee and the meal is complete. Our yogurt is a thick Greek style, lightly drained with live cultures and probiotics.

Lunch: Simple Quesadilla

Heat a flour tortilla on a skillet topped with drained, cooked black beans, shredded Pepper McChesney (our pepper cheddar raw milk goat cheese), fresh cilantro, thinly sliced tomato and a second tortilla on top. Flip when one side is browned and the cheese begins to melt. We always keep ingredients for this fast, simple lunch on hand.

Dinner:

A steak on the grill topped with crumbled Black Mountain Bleu cheese. On the side, a baked potato and salad with warmed Chevre. Another option on the side is Braised Greens with Feta.

Stuffed Jalapeño Peppers

Jalapeño peppers
Thinly sliced bacon
Fresh Chevre (plain, herbed or we've even used our
   curried ginger chevre)

Fry bacon until just barely crisp. Set aside. Wash and cut peppers in half length-wise. Remove seeds and membranes. Blanche lightly by dipping in boiling water or microwaving one minute. Fill pepper halves with fresh chevre. Top with a 1- to 2-inch slice of fried bacon. Broil for a few minutes until cheese is warmed through.

Salad with Warmed Chevre

1 8 ounce log goat cheese (hand roll it into a log if it's in
   a tub)
Vegetable spray
1 egg
2 tablespoons water
½ cup seasoned bread crumbs

Pinch of cayenne pepper
4 cups mixed salad greens
Optional: bell peppers, tomatoes, edible flowers
Vinaigrette salad dressing

Heat oven to 400 degrees. Spray cookie sheet with vegetable spray. Cut cheese into 8 equal discs. Wisk together egg and water. Mix crumbs and cayenne. Dip cheese into egg mixture and then into bread crumbs. Place on cookie sheet and bake for about 5 to 10 minutes, flipping half way through, or until soft and brown. Divide salad greens, chunks of bell peppers and thin slices of tomato onto 4 plates and top with warm cheese. Garnish with edible flowers. Serve with a light vinaigrette salad dressing and serve with fresh artisan bread.

Braised Greens with Feta

2 pounds of washed chopped greens (chard, spinach or a
   braising mix)
½ cup onion, chopped
2 cloves garlic, chopped fine
Olive oil
½ cup feta, cut into ¼ inch cubes
Balsamic vinegar

Heat olive oil in large, deep fry pan or wok. Sauté onion and garlic on medium heat until soft. Increase temperature to medium-high, throw in wet greens and toss as they cook. Add a little more water if necessary but keep the greens moving so they don't burn. When greens are wilted, add feta cubes and stir another few minutes till cheese is warm. Drizzle with balsamic vinegar and serve.

Dessert: Chocolate Chevre Truffles

12 ounces high quality semi sweet chocolate chips
8 ounces well drained plain chevre
Cocoa powder

Microwave or use double boiler to melt the chocolate chips. Stir in chevre. Mix well. Chill several hours until firm. Shape into 1-inch balls and place on a cookie sheet. Chill another few hours then roll in cocoa powder and serve. These will keep several weeks in the refrigerator.

grandfather had worked in Helsinki for the State Department, there was a bit of history for me there. For fundraising, I invented this cheese called Midnight Sun, a black ash cheese. Once you get an understanding of how the milk behaves, and what the different cultures do, and the different bacteria, and what you can expect over time, you can design how you want a cheese to be. I designed this cheese — a lactic, bloomy type — and took it to market, and made enough money for my trip. With that cheese, as well as some others, over time I've made some money. There's a constant flow of comments about how lucky I am, how great it is to be learning seasonality from the inside out. I have to admit, it's a great way to live.

Spinning Spider Cheeses are now kind of a local delicacy. Lots of the restaurants in Asheville serve them. We have a large variety that's growing all the time:

Fresh **chevre,** hand-ladled into rounds, logs, pyramids and buttons. It has a delicate texture, the flavor is fresh and tangy.

Bloomy rind **stackhouse,** loaf-shaped with a white rind, a thin layer of applewood ash down the center and a dusting of ash under the rind. It has a mushroomy flavor with a hint of fresh milk. This one was the named number one goat cheese in the south by Southern Foodways Alliance.

Camille, which is the farm's version of a traditional goat milk camembert.

Gabriel's Gold gouda, a raw goat milk cheese that's aged for four to six months. It has a smooth texture, tiny eyes and a nutty, buttery flavor.

Black Mountain Blue, a raw goat milk blue cheese aged for two to six months. Well veined with a rustic look and sharp finish.

And finally a **feta,** made with raw goat milk and aged for sixty days for a distinctive sharp flavor.

Although other restaurants and markets in the area want our farm's cheeses, we're at our capacity without jeopardizing the quality of our products. Recently we made a deal with a neighboring farm that will be designing their herd structure to meet our standards. We'll get more milk from them, and that will give us the necessary growth without sacrifice.

I know for sure that eventually I want to be a cheese maker. When I finish my associate's degree, I want to go to Europe for a three-month internship, to learn cheese-making from the masters. I have a contact with a fourth-generation Swiss cheesemonger. Our intern this year has a huge number of contacts in France, and she's going to help me get placed there. I want to spend time on at least two farms, maybe three, learn how to make the aged French-style cheeses, the traditional camemberts and bries. Provence is just this wonderful Mecca of goat cheese. But in the Alps, I'll also focus on the harder cheeses. I'll come home, go to UNCA [*University of North Carolina at Asheville*] and then I'll be ready for the full-on reality.

I admit that most of my time is spent with the goats. My social life revolves around the farm market, the 4-H program, the homeschooling program and some acting. I'm part of a student-run and -directed theater group in Asheville. Outside of the goats, my real love is contra dancing. At least once a week, I bargain with my brothers to take over my duties, so I can go off for an evening of dancing with the local contra dance group. A couple of weeks ago, I actually took a whole weekend off, and went to a music/art/contra festival.

During mating season (September to December), the does come into heat every twenty-one days. During that time, the ten male goats (or bucks) run ragged along the fence line, butting their heads together and kicking up the dirt. The does are restless, constantly bleating and wagging their tails. We pen breed the goats anywhere from when they are seven to eight months old and weighing in at least eighty to one hundred pounds. We'll select a doe and place it in a smaller pen with a chosen buck. After the connection has been made, pregnancy lasts about 150 days.

Then, during kidding season, all of us, even my younger brothers, Sylas and Morgan, get involved. This last year there were forty does due within five days. Somebody always has to sleep in the barn. Either my mom or myself are there for 90 percent of the deliveries, hands on, and so are my brothers. Sometimes the whole family is sleeping in the barn. It's an exciting time. A really emotional time, too, with all the babies sucking on our ears or licking us. It's exhausting. The sleep deprivation is stunning. It gets pretty hairy when more than one is coming out at the same time.

Down the road, I think we will probably join hands with my uncle who has a much bigger farm, more pasture. There's nothing on it right now, it's just an old mountain farm that we're fencing. I'll probably move over there with the milking herd, transport the milk back to this farm so I can continue to help my mom with the cheese making.

Cullen flashes his Cheshire cat smile.

I pretty much know where my future lies. It's just a matter of time.

Amy and Jamie Ager
Hickory Nut Gap Farm ■ Fairview, Buncombe County, North Carolina ■
www.hickorynutgapfarm.com

Not far from the Spinning Spider Creamery, you'll come to Hickory Nut Gap Farm, six hundred acres of farmland that historically has produced apples, tobacco, corn and raspberries. Jamie Ager is the fourth generation to farm his share of the family's land along with his wife, Amy.

They feel a deep gratitude to be able to raise their two children, Cyrus and Nolin (a third's on the way), on family land. They're raising pastured cows, sheep, pigs and chickens on ninety acres of reclaimed pasture, striving to mimic nature in a "perennial polyculture" that includes open fields and woodlands.

Amy Ager: We met at Warren Wilson College.

Warren Wilson is committed to "experiential opportunities for international and cross-cultural understanding in a setting that provides wisdom, spiritual growth, and contribution to the common good."

I grew up in Louisville, Kentucky, and ended up at Warren Wilson. We met in chemistry class.

Jamie Ager: And there was some chemistry there! *(They both laugh.)*

Amy: We were both doing an environmental studies major with a sustainable agriculture concentration. It was something totally new and exciting and different from anything I'd grown up with. My

great-grandparents were potato farmers in Louisville, and my grandfather and his brothers worked the farm. They sold it about ten years before I was born.

I grew up in the suburbs, totally separated from all that. At Warren Wilson, because they have a farm, I was drawn to it. Who knows why? I like being outside working, and the learning is in a totally different way there.

We graduated in 2000. This family farm land was available for new management ideas. So we came back here and began working for Jamie's mother, who manages the farm, in trade for ownership in animals. We're gaining ownership in the sheep and the cows, so we have something to work with. There are six members who own the land, which we actually lease. We have our own business and a four-way partnership with Jamie's mother and

father. Jamie and I focus on raising the livestock, direct marketing and agritourism.

Jamie: When you're a freshman in college, nobody knows what the heck they want to do, right? You're just kind of flailing. You go to college because that's what everybody expects you to do. That first summer I came back here to the farm and worked, I thought, Man, this is fun! I like this stuff. The advice I was getting from everyone was, Don't farm, you can't make any money at it. I was never encouraged. And then, in the middle of my sophomore year, I had a good friend who was an intern up on Joel Salatin's farm in Virginia. She said, "I'm going up there for the weekend, would you like to come?" So I went up there, spent the whole weekend and came back absolutely inspired. It changed my life, honestly.

Amy: We did an independent study together and wrote the business plan for our farm. We didn't know what a business plan was supposed to be like, didn't really know what pasture poultry meant, or where to start. We looked at three years of records to see which enterprises were profitable, which would be smart to do.

Jamie and I leave Amy at the farmhouse to feed the baby. He takes me on a tour of the acreage. Down into the fields, straight into the middle of the cows, together we move them from one field to another. Jamie continues sharing all he's learned from Joel Salatin on pasturing cows and other sustainable practices: stewardship of the land, polyculture, pigs in the woods, cows on pasture eating grass and clover, drinking clean spring water.

Jamie shows me the chicken tents where chickens can easily be moved from pasture to pasture. He remarks how much sense it all makes, how easy it is, once you know what you're doing.

Jamie: We came back to this farm, which until 1989 had been a forty-cow dairy farm, typical Appalachian, not very profitable. In fact it fell apart in the '80s. My dad and my uncle had run it since the '50s. They'd sold the dairy farm, but my mom had kept the rest going. She loved it. They had ten

acres of apples, but she could see that it wasn't going anywhere. It was a great opportunity for us to come home, to have a chance to get involved. I realize more and more that young farmers don't have this opportunity very often, to have a whole farm that they can use without having Dad or Grandpa looking over their shoulder. When you're fifty or so, you seem to get more conservative, you don't want to do crazy new things with a farm. Which is what we're doing now, with all of what we've learned from Salatin and in school. Raising animals that have good fats like omega-3 fatty acids and conjugated linoleic acids, no hormones, no antibiotics, farming with the season.

So we refenced the whole thing. Put a lot of infrastructure in over the first couple of years, marketing. My three brothers aren't as interested in the place, or our vision. We've tried to figure out how to keep people involved. We're working on that.

We walk back to the farm stand where there's a *freezer with piles of frozen meat, and a few hanging items like caps, T-shirts and cups. James says that families have birthday parties and other celebrations at the stand. There are apples, free-range eggs and maple syrup.*

Amy: At this point in the life of our business, we don't have enough supply to meet the demand in Asheville. We're in the middle of developing protocols. Two other families are raising animals to help supply our business in accordance with our standards and procedures. They bring us two cows each week. We have about sixty steers that we'll do ourselves this year on top of that. We get a few others from another family. These cows grow up to our standards. One farmer has this amazing forage chain that he's planted. He's producing some beautiful marbled grass-fed beef. We use that for our wholesale market. Then for our retail we sell to two tailgate markets every Saturday.

Jamie: With the pigs, we'll raise about 350 or so

this year. That's all from just weaned piglets that we purchase and then finish out. With the sheep, we're pretty much raising those from ewes that we traded for this year's lambs. I'm not sure how we'll move forward with the pigs. With the price of grain being so high, it doesn't make sense to be feeding them all this grain when it costs twice as much as last year. People are starving and we're feeding it to the pigs. Grass-fed beef and grass-fed lamb make a lot more sense.

We just started leasing two hundred more acres, so we're actually working with about 290 acres. That's allowing us to have a lot more room to graze. That's helped with the bottleneck. This is really a pretty small farm, ninety acres, that's what we lease from the family. When compared to farms out West, that's pretty small. This road runs through the middle of the property. We've got houses going up all over. We're not really rural anymore.

We're doing more things oriented toward tour-ism. We plant a corn maze in the fall. We have a u-pick pumpkin patch right across the street. We have apples. Ever since my great-grandfather purchased the farm there's been an apple orchard. We have about ten acres of apples, probably fifteen to twenty different varieties. Yellow Delicious, Red Delicious, Rome, Hunter, Banana, Empire and Arkansas Black. We also purchase apples because we've had a couple of bad years in a row. My mom and aunt started this roadside stand up at the family home about fifteen years ago. We used to sell just to the juicing plant, but it went out of business. We started direct marketing off of the roadside out near Chimney Rock. We do school tours in the morning.

At one point we had a barn fire, and we built this building in its place. It's become our sales area.

For the most part, all the meat we eat comes from what we raise. The freezer-burned packages!

Amy: We have a garden. We buy rice, bread and dairy from other farmers. Our neighbor has some goats she's milking; we trade for things. Our grocery bill declines during the summer. During the winter we put things up. It's tough to prioritize that with the kids. But I do what I can. I always make apple butter and I freeze beans, tomatoes, peas, shredded zucchini for zucchini bread, strawberries.

I think my parents really respect that we're making a living at this. My dad's all about the entrepreneurial spirit. They enjoy coming to visit. Though it isn't a lifestyle they'd choose for themselves.

Jamie: I definitely see us here in the next five years.

Amy: The big hinge is whether or not this land will get funded for a conservation easement, which the family has applied for. At that point we would be eligible for a long-term lease with the family. Right now, it's year to year.

Jamie: It's pretty tentative. My grandfather died in 1999. My grandmother died in 2001. Our inheritance is this land. It's valuable, probably $30-35,000 an acre. My mom has five brothers and sisters. It's stressful for us, but incredible. Essentially, we started this business knowing it was a year-to-year lease. We built this farm store on land that we don't own. We spent $30,000 on it. We've done some things, businesswise, that aren't necessarily too smart. We felt we had to, in order to show that we could do it. So far, it's worked out.

The store is open two days a week right now, Thursdays and Saturdays. We're open seven days a week in September and October.

Amy: Jamie's cousin, Annie Louise Perkinson, raises ten acres of vegetables and flowers right down the road on Flying Cloud Farm. She's starting to use some of the bottomland.

Jamie has twenty-two cousins in his generation. Not everybody lives locally or even wants to be involved in farming or land-based occupations.

Jamie: The most important thing is that we keep the family together. That's more important than anything.

Amy is designing a website to incorporate everything. We're pretty into branding right now. We just developed a new logo for the farm and our meat business. These are exciting times no matter how you look at it.

Annie Louise Perkinson and Isaiah Perkinson
Flying Cloud Farm ■ Fairview, Buncombe County, North Carolina ■ www.flyingcloudfarm.com

A spitting distance from the Hickory Nut Gap Farm is the eleven-acre Flying Cloud Farm. Annie Louise Perkinson and Jamie Ager are first cousins. Annie Louise and her husband, Isaiah, have managed Flying Cloud for ten years now.

Annie Louise grew up in Fairview, North Carolina, weeding, gathering eggs, canning, jamming and freezing produce for home use. She also cared for her many brothers, sisters, and twenty-one cousins. Annie did her undergraduate work at UNC Chapel Hill for two years. She graduated from Warren Wilson College in 1996.

Isaiah Perkinson was born in Philadelphia and moved to Chapel Hill when he was in high school. He attended UNCG for a year before he figured he could learn more on his own. Isaiah takes care of all the mechanical aspects of the farm. The family depends on him for everything from tractor work to irrigation to refrigeration. Isaiah can fix anything.

I drive over a rickety bridge that sounds like a garage band: cymbals, drums and bells. A group of huge dogs waits on the other side, so I decide to leave Luna in the car.

Annie is dressed in a summer skirt, T-shirt, and a string of pearls which she tells me she wears all the time.

Annie Louise Perkinson: I got the pearls one Christmas. The first day I went on a horseback ride, I lost them. I went back the next day and found them. Since then they haven't come off. My father will tell you that I started the whole farm with a hand fork, eight years ago. Now I've got these pearls!

My mom is third generation here. My dad is English and he's a doctor. They bought the house in the late '70s. I was born in London and lived there until I was three. Then we moved here. My mother is an artist and takes care of children. She has a summer camp and teaches art classes in the fall and winter. I'm one of five siblings, the oldest in fact. My brother William, who is next in line, has a portable sawmill. He milled all the wood we used to build our house and barn.

Our farming practices rely on cover cropping, amending the soil with OMRI *[Organic Materials Review Institute]* approved minerals and fertilizers, annual soil testing, crop rotation, beneficial insect habitat, and careful planning for insect and weed issues. At this point our land is not organic, although we do follow the rules of OMRI at all times. In the past we have been certified organic. When the certification switched from a North Carolina agency to the USDA, the cost was really prohibitive for us. Since we do primarily direct marketing — one hundred CSA shares this year, and three or four tailgates a week, we have immediate contact with all the people who eat our foods.

This gives everyone a chance to ask us questions or visit our farm. Since we do no wholesale distribution of our produce, we don't need to be certified. Our CSA is now at $500 a share for twenty-one weeks — but if you need to, you can split it with someone.

We rent land from my parents and several neighbors. We have about fourteen acres. We do a cover crop on many of those acres, and then we have our gardens.

Growing up, my mom spoiled us rotten with homemade bread. Our grandparents had a dairy, so we had milk and butter and yogurt. We had a hayfield and a home garden. Actually I'm not a very good cook, I prefer eating. I like the idea of having a lot of preserved food, but I don't love canning. I got a grant to use a local production kitchen to help with the canning. I'm going to make strawberry jam and hot pepper jellies, a few other things to sell. Our goal is to figure out how to make money all year. We do markets all the way through Christmas. We do vegetables and wreaths in the fall. January is our down month, then in February the greenhouse is full on again.

Isaiah and I met in Chapel Hill. We were working at Pepper's Pizza. It was pretty much love at first sight, but we didn't see each other for a few years in between. We have two girls, eleven and seven years old. They go to the same public school I went to.

RECIPES ■ Annie Louise and Isaiah Perkinson

Breakfast: Make a smoothie with berries you have frozen throughout the season.

Blend 1 cup frozen strawberries, 1 cup frozen blueberries, 1 cup frozen blackberries with some grape juice (from the farm next door) and a few ice cubes until it is smooth and drinkable My daughter Ivy, who is only 7, makes these by herself for snacks.

Lunch: Simple Tomato-mozzarella Salad

1 sweet onion, thinly sliced
4 tomatoes, sliced
1 pound fresh mozzarella, sliced
1 cup fresh basil
3 cloves garlic, minced
2 teaspoons red wine vinegar
2 tablespoons olive oil
Salt and pepper, to taste

Place layer of onion on serving dish. Add layer of tomatoes and layer of mozzarella. Sprinkle with basil, garlic, salt and pepper. Drizzle with oil and vinegar.

Repeat layers until all ingredients are used. Serve at room temperature. One of my favorite ways to eat tomatoes! Serves 2.

Dinner: Baba ghanoush

Bake eggplant on a baking sheet until skin is soft and flesh feels soft. Scoop the flesh into a colander, and press to extract excess liquid. Transfer to a food processor and add:

2 tablespoons tahini
1 to 2 cloves garlic
1 tablespoon lemon juice
2 teaspoons salt

Pulse until smooth. Taste and adjust the lemon juice and salt. Transfer to a shallow bowl and garnish with:

1 tablespoon olive oil
1 tablespoon parsley, finely chopped

Serve with warm pita bread. Serves 2.

Isaiah: I grew up in Philly, in the city, going to public schools. I went to high school in Chapel Hill and have been down here for about twenty years. I love farming. I get to be close to my family — my wife and my kids. My father died a while back, but my mother is on her way down. We convinced her to move here.

We make our way to the back of the property. Annie points out the lay of the land.

Annie: We have a bamboo forest.

Isaiah: Our older child bites the bamboo shoots in the spring when they first come out of the ground. She loves strawberries, eats them right out of the patch.

We walk down toward the main road where there are vegetables and flowers. Annie points out four rows of dahlias that will bloom in September and October.

Annie: We have some poppies, radishes and turnips. We irrigate out of this creek. It's our life-line, Ashley Creek. It joins Brush Creek and Cane Creek, goes on to the Swannanoa River, then the French Broad River.

This is our blueberry patch. Last year we had a late freeze and lost all our blueberries. This year we should have plenty! We have about five hundred plants, four different varieties.

And at the end of all these rows we have our peppers, eggplants, squash and tomatoes. We grow these on black plastic and landscaping fabric and use drip irrigation.

This is a pile of manure from our dairy farm neighbor across the way. He grows corn over there, and rye. He has a dairy farm so we're getting manure from him. He feeds the corn to the cows. He makes silage, so it's fermented. They basically cut up the whole stalk and then animals eat it. It's very good for them, good bacteria.

Those are beets, carrots, turnips, white turnips, greens and lettuce. I can remember when I planted

all of this because Isaiah's sister had just had a baby. I was at the birth all night and came back and planted all this.

If you come to market this afternoon, we'll have all the produce out.

One of our dogs, Mona, got run over yesterday. We're all very sad. She was chasing a rabbit. I didn't cry until this morning when I got up and was waking the kids.

My parents own this side of the driveway. The other side belongs to the Lynches. We rent their field for hay because we also have cows and horses. We also rent a few sections over there. This is our strawberry patch. Try them, they're the real deal, sweet and tart.

We grow flowers on either side of the strawberries for beneficial insects. Larkspur and poppies. The ladybugs are hatching right now. We have a CSA member who keeps twelve beehives out here. She read *The Secret Life of Bees* and got inspired.

She grew up on a farm and she wanted to do something, but didn't have the land. She won the State Fair for the best honey.

This is all larkspur, nigella. It's all about to bloom. We plant the flowers in mid-September so they'll bloom in the spring. There are others that are biannuals that we start in the summer. We have sweet williams, here. The blooming stops when we get frost. Then we dry the flowers and make wreaths.

We're doing cows on a very small scale, and ten piglets that we got from Warren Wilson College.

Look at these poppies. They're from my great-grandmother's seeds. They're not blooming yet, but they will. She was actually an artist in the south of France when she was eighteen. She lived in the area where Monet lived. Monet was eighty at the time. My great-grandmother and her husband were the first people in our family to come to Fairview in 1916. This is seed she planted, and it keeps coming back. The pods I use for the wreaths — the flowers, the petals all fall off. They're still full of beneficial insects.

My great-grandmother bought this house. It was a stagecoach inn, built in the 1830s. The landscaping around here is all hers. When she put her paintbrush away she started on the garden.

I feel rooted here. Buying land is really hard for young farmers, so we're very happy that we can rent. When my parents first came here, land was about $2,000 an acre. Now it's about $50,000 an acre.

Before Isaiah and I were married we registered at Biltmore Hardware. The people there thought it

was a joke. I went in afterward to buy a rope and they gave it to me. They were so thankful for all our business!

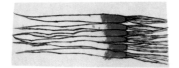

I'm driving between the rolling hills and sheared granite outcroppings of North Carolina. Suddenly shiny wet greenstones of Virginia are all around. I've been holding on to the steering wheel like the reigns of a bucking bronco. I pull off the windy road and stop to fully gaze upon the glory of the Shenandoah Valley. At one time this was tobacco farms, and Civil War battlefields.

The Polyface Farm is owned by the Salatin Family. Daniel belongs to the third generation in his family to farm the land. His parents, Joel and Teresa Salatin, lead the movement toward "management intensive grazing" or pasture-fed farming.

Even before Polyface Farm became the centerfold of Michael Pollan's book The Omnivore's Dilemma, *everyone in the farming community knew about the Salatins. Joel has written half a dozen books and is on the lecture circuit.*

Daniel and his wife, Sheri, run the Polyface Farm on a day-to-day basis just the way his dad taught him: "Grass is everything."

Sheri and Daniel Salatin
The Polyface Farm ▪ Swoope, Virginia ▪ www.polyfacefarms.com

APRIL ▪ *Back on a small winding road, I pass tobacco sheds, huge weathered silos and pillared homes. I make a quick stop in a cemetery, so Luna can run. At the back of the cemetery, I spot a pyramid tombstone:* COLORED FOLK BURIED HERE.

I arrive a little before expected. Daniel is still out in the fields doing chores. His wife, Sheri, a petite, fresh-faced blonde, invites me in. She totes three-month-old Lauryn on her hip, and is trailed by Travis, who is four, and Andrew, who is two. "I have a farm job," Travis tells me. He helps his dad move the cows from pasture to pasture. He also gathers eggs and helps butcher the chickens.

Sheri Salatin: Daniel and I met after my mother and father read Joel's book *Pastured Poultry Profits*. We came up from Austin, Texas, for a couple of days to learn how to butcher chickens. I was sixteen. My family had a little fifteen-acre farm adjacent to my grandparent's thirty acres, so we had forty-five acres in all. After our visit, we stayed in touch. A few years later, Daniel and I started corresponding. Our parents all went to the same college.

Daniel arrives, out of breath. He scoops up Andrew, then Travis, then Lauryn. He leans over to kiss Sheri.

Daniel Salatin: I started butchering chickens when I was three or four, like Travis. I'd watched my dad do it one-hundred and fifty times, and then it was my turn. Before that, he'd explained it five hundred times. My sister was in charge of starting the chicks and the flower gardens. When I was about seven I started raising rabbits. I wanted something that was my own. My dad didn't know anything about rabbits. I wrote a little anecdote about them and put it in the farm's spring newsletter. Suddenly orders came in for 150 rabbits. At seven, I could pretty much do 90 percent of the work. I really got into looking at feed rations and ratios, looking at how things were done before soybean meal and pellet feed. I learned how to keep records on everything from the genetics to the finances. I purchased the feed by just keeping a cash account, learning that if I only had enough money for one bag of feed, then that's all I got.

I remember one time I went into the feed store and had exactly enough money for two bags. The store manager was kind of ribbing me, saying I should just get ten bags since I'd be back in a week or two anyway. I told him I only had money for two. [*Laughs*] He told me I knew more about finances than most of the adults he worked with. I should always remember, above all else, budget. Starting my business from scratch, building it, doing the

marketing, gathering customers, getting positive rewards from them — "This is the best rabbit we've ever eaten," they'd say.

I have New Zealand White–California crosses. I've been line breeding for twelve years now, running a closed herd. I selected a rabbit that would do exactly what I wanted it to do, from handling grass to forage. Those two breeds, New Zealand and California, are each kind of an industry standard, just like a Cornish crossed chicken, or a Holstein cow for dairy. Standard fare. They can't handle anything out of the ordinary. They're used to being grain fed and kept in a pen. They grow fast. They can't handle being pastured or having chickens underneath them in cages. A little bit of dust, a little bit of wind, can't handle any of it.

The rabbits live in wire cages hanging along the wall of the barn. The chickens run free underneath them. The chickens keep the ground stirred up, which keeps everything composting. Then the chickens lay eggs. We have two levels of production, two usages in the same building. If we were to fully utilize the building, we'd have worm beds underneath the rabbits and plants on top. There are only so many hours in a day.

Like all kids, I toyed with the idea of being a policeman, a fireman, a soldier or a knight. I always wanted to be a farmer. I really wasn't into book studies. I spent a few summers doing some carpentry, but I wasn't really into building houses for someone else.

I liked building our house, but 365 days a year— nope. I want something where I can see improvements year in and year out. I want to see my accomplishments, walk by them every day. All our fields are named for events, or people in our lives, or things that have happened in those fields. This here is "Hail Field." Grandpa was baling hay in it one time and a storm came up. Hailed on them. They ran into the barn.

I'm rooted in this land. It's important to have a sense of purpose in life. We can leave the earth and the soil in better shape than when we took it on.

I'm a realist. I'm a day-in, day-out person. I like systems, patterns, grind-it-out dailiness. When my father and I don't butt heads, about him dreaming and me working, we're a great team. You can't have one without the other. Living with my father has given me an appreciation for pop stars. People come here to take photos, wanting autographs. I want to shout, "Dad, there are chores to be done! Let's get going!"

Management-intensive grazing, the ideas my dad has explored on our farm, have been a wild success. As we attempt to carry on and stay viable in this growing explosion, we have to stay focused. I'm old enough to remember the days when the organic and alternative food movement was still considered a whack job. When I was a kid, we'd go to a farmers market, just talk to people about clean food. It was all about trying to convince people that paying an extra 10 to 25 percent to have local food was worth it. If you look at global trade and the industrial market, we're still whacko. More and more we're working with consumers who accept our ideas and love our food. Our buying club has grown from thirty shares to 1400 shares.

For a long time we were perceived by big farmers as cute with our one hundred acres. They had five hundred cows, huge spreads. They said our land-management ideas wouldn't work for farms their size. Now we have one thousand acres and five hundred cows and we can tell them, "This is still working for us. It still makes a lot of sense." We've expanded our arena by renting additional property for pastures. Folks drive by, see me rolling up cross fence, giving the cows a new paddock. They're still hauling hay. They now give some thought to what we're doing. When I buy calves, they ask if I make corn silage. I tell them no, my cows are pasture-fed.

This movement is huge. It includes folks from all over the United States and the world. But we don't have any friends locally who are involved in the movement. There's a young farmers' organization in our county; they're all conventional. We're at the

point where we're starting to bring folks into the area. Some of our interns are staying on.

Sheri: My sister and a former apprentice of ours recently married and are coming back to the area to farm.

Daniel: I'm taking over the full-time, day-to-day operation of the farm, teaching the apprentices, having my hands in the dirt 100 percent of the time. My father is still working 50 percent on the farm. The other 50 percent he's on the lecture circuit and writing books pushing the movement into the mainstream. Those of us who use our parents as stepping stones still know what it feels like to find our own way. We want to add to what's already in place.

For instance, looking at where the exports, or the waste, is going. Just because your dad is growing corn and beans, you don't have to go next door and buy a farm and grow corn and beans. If your parents are conventional it doesn't mean you have to be conventional.

We are in discussions about the continued multi-generational nature of this farm. We're all trying to work this out amicably. My parents don't believe in an equal inheritance for each child. Sheri and I have a house here, rent free, if you will. I didn't purchase the land that the house is on, but I work every day on that land, 24/7. My sister is making her own path somewhere else. There's the possibility that Sheri and I will receive the land. My sister will receive all other assets that can be moved. My grandfather was an accountant by trade. He didn't believe it was fair for those of his children who stayed on the farm to have to buy out their siblings. I think some of the land is still in my grandmother's name. As it transfers to my dad, it's not going to be equal either. That's the second generation not to have an equal inheritance to pass on.

For now, renting land rather than paying a mortgage just makes much more sense. For about a month's worth of mortgage payments, we're

renting land for an entire year. I see us returning to more of an aristocratic farming society, like England, where you have multiple land owners and a land-management society. After working on other people's land for the last ten years, where they're so hands off, I like it. They want to see their land improved but they don't want to deal with it themselves. They just want to see that it is there for future generations to enjoy. Virginia recognizes agricultural and conservation easements. Polyface has been able to operate strictly as an entrepreneurial enterprise.

We have a list of core values that we hold to. One of them is not going into debt for more than a five-year loan. That limits you from getting into an overhead situation that locks the next generation into paying for it.

Both Sheri and I really enjoy farming, and neither of us feels the need to get away from it. There are times we take breaks, when I go somewhere to

lecture, but we love being here. I do some hunting and we're very involved with our church. I have to say, Sunday is my favorite day.

Sheri: Mine, too. It's our only day of real rest. We take naps. We're so busy these days we finally had to get a secretary. We get close to forty to fifty phone calls a day. Sunday is my favorite day, too. No one comes to the door, no phone calls.

Daniel: We love people. That's one of the reasons for our success. We embrace people both as customers, and by sharing our ideas and getting input on what we do.

Daniel takes his cowboy hat off and scratches his head.

Yesterday we butchered 680 broiler chickens in our processing facility, which is just over there.

He points behind where we are standing.

Sheri: Great-Grandma watched the kids for us.

Daniel: We were all there, my dad, my mom, a couple of interns and a couple of neighbors who

come in as short-term help. Earlier in the day we'd come by a group of locals, two college girls and a family passing through from California. We call them OD'ers. They've read *The Omnivore's Dilemma* and want to see if we're for real. We open our doors wide to visitors.

We're pushing our limits right now, though, and would never do anything to affect the integrity of our product.

Sheri: We won't cut corners.

Daniel: For example, we've been asked by chefs to provide chickens year round. The only way to do that from October to March is to ship them in from Florida. You can't have our fresh local chickens when there's no grass. Another option during the winter months is to put the chickens in a heated building. But they won't have pasture. They're closed in. No sunshine, no fresh air. You'd have to go to a completely heated, climate-controlled facility with sanitizers and chemicals to keep everything clean.

We need to help the chefs understand that it's not in their best interest to get this product in December.

Sheri: We collaborate with other farms with transportation. Every Tuesday we do deliveries for our high-end restaurants. There's a group of vegetable growers, Chef's Garden, they put their produce on our truck. It pays our driver more to deliver everything, since he gets paid by the pound. The chefs are happier because they get more coming off the truck at one time.

Daniel: We are growing like crazy and people ask us what keeps us from becoming another Walmart. That's one of our biggest fears. Dad wrote this in our spring 2008 newsletter:

Core Distinctives: Because some of you have expressed concern that we are turning into an empire – and frankly all of this scares us too – we have articulated some core distinctives to keep us from Wall

Streetifying. We aren't finished yet, but these are a start at least:

1. No Shipping. No delivery beyond 4 hours (close enough that a patron can drive to the farm and inspect us and return home in a day).

2. No sales or marketing targets and objectives. Growth completely organic.

3. No manure hauling offsite — only as much manure generation in an area as that land base can metabolize. No trafficking in manure. Ecology dictates concentration. (This immediately cancels out CAFO, Concentrated Feedlot Operation, where you take the manure and haul it someplace else.)

4. Never go public with stocks or the business (eliminates tempting and prostitutionary infusion of cash). Not to be confused with interested, knowledgeable investors.

5. No trademarks or copyrights. No secrets. We've helped start hundreds of folks, and if we fear competition, then we don't have confidence in our own creativity to stay viable.

6. No regular public advertising. Expansion only by word of mouth through satisfied patrons. Specialty ads in targeted spots for singular events is okay.

7. Every worker should have a commission-based opportunity. Jobs must be free of repetitive motion syndrome. As few employees as possible — use subcontractors and commissions.

8. Expansion can never compromise quality. Beyond that, quality must increase. If it's not healing, it's not Polyface.

Number nine would be avoiding multi-year debt, or having a benchmark payback for capital investment — like a five-year payback. If we have to invest in something that takes more than five years to pay off the capital outlay, then it's too much. We need to figure out a cheaper way to do it.

Marriage was a big adjustment for me. Living here on the farm with my parents close by and finding my own identity was tough. I went from being single, being able to work sunup to sundown, coming in, snagging a bite off of Mom's table, then going back out, continuing to work all day long . . . to having a family and responsibilities at home. My own trash to take out. My own phone messages to return. We had to keep communicating about all of it.

Sheri: We'd love to travel, but we decided to have a family young, so we'll be out of that earlier and then we can travel.

Daniel: The difference between my generation and my dad's is, I think his is more into philosophical ideas. The younger generation wants to know how to get a market going, how to build a chicken pen and process birds.

Sheri: A typical day for me begins at breakfast. There's nothing that says a farmer's wife has to get up early. *[Laughs]* Daniel gets up at the crack of dawn with the roosters, but not me. I get up at 7 to 7:30, when the kids come and drag me up. For the most part breakfast is eggs, sausage, bacon, muffins or occasionally my granola. We pretty much eat every meal together. The only one we might skip is lunch. Daniel does chores first thing and then comes in for breakfast. On Tuesdays I call restaurants in order to put their orders together. If it's a buying club week, I'll do emails.

Daniel and Sheri offer to walk me around the farm. Everyone starts down the road, including the kids, all talking at once.

Sheri: This is the Raken House, a combination of rabbits and chickens.

Open at both ends, sunlight streams through, but it never gets too hot. The hum is like a buzz saw.

Sheri: These chickens are young pullets. The only reason that they're in here is for the rabbits. They stir the bedding and keep down the ammonia

[rabbit urine is very high in ammonia]. Otherwise you'd pass out from the smell! We just keep adding bedding. Then at the end of the year, in the wintertime, we put the pigs in here. They turn it up. Then we spread it out in the fields.

Sheri glances at her watch, then reminds Daniel about a birthday dinner with Daniel's mother at a local hamburger joint. The kids say, Yeah!

My mother-in-law and I take turns feeding the guys dinner. I have everybody on Monday and two other nights a week. Nobody cooks on Sundays. It's fend for yourself night!

At the processing facility, Daniel describes the process of butchering chickens.

Daniel: You place the chickens upside down in the cone. Their head comes out the bottom. You're able to just slice the throat and they bleed out. They go flatline in about five to ten seconds. There's no pain. You don't cut the windpipe, because that would shock them and cause suffocation and stress. If you cut the jugular, there's a bleed out and very little stress. Just lightheaded passing out as opposed to a panicked death. There's always the reflex, kicking of death, the muscle spasm, but there's no fighting it. There is a way of lulling the bird, then slicing their jugular and the bird feels nothing.

We run up to two hundred birds an hour in this facility. We'll do five hundred tomorrow. We do evisceration by hand. Sheri and Dad are the A-team. From bird death to the chill tank is about ten minutes.

Sheri: I honestly think that children are not naturally afraid of this process. It's part of life on a farm. Even little girls do not say euwww or yuck.

Daniel: When the death of an animal is dealt with in a respectful way, and the animals have been respected during their lives, there is no feeling about having "used them." They live out a full and fulfilled life. This is a continuation of that life. It leads them to benefit us in their end. And when

RECIPES ■ Sheri and Daniel Salatin

Breakfast Tacos

3 to 4 potatoes
1 pound breakfast sausage bulk
6 eggs
Tortillas

Cut the potatoes into small, bite-sized cubes and fry in either olive oil or lard until almost tender. Add the sausage to the pan and fry until browned. Mix eggs in a bowl and then pour over sausage and potatoes. Stir around until eggs are cooked. Serve on warm tortillas with salsa, sour cream, cheese, tomatoes or anything else you would like.

You can adjust the amount of eggs, potatoes and sausage as desired. There really is no set number of any.

Chef's Chicken Salad

2½ cups cooked chicken, chopped (not pureed)
Add to taste:
About ½ cup pecans, chopped
About ½ cup green pepper, chopped
¼ cup green onion, chopped
¼ cup dried apricots, chopped
¼ cup red pepper, chopped
1 cup mayonnaise
2 tablespoons dijon mustard
2 tablespoons honey
1 teaspoon dried tarragon

Mix all together and serve on crackers or sandwich bread. Keep chilled.

Oven Fried Chicken

1 broiler, cut up
1 cup flour, divided
1 teaspoon salt
1 teaspoon paprika
1 teaspoon pepper
¼ cup butter
¼ cup lard
1 egg, beaten
3 tablespoons milk

Preheat oven to 415 degrees.

Melt butter and lard in bottom of 9×13-inch pan in hot oven. Mix milk and egg together in a bowl. Place ½ cup flour in a bag. Then mix remaining dry ingredients separate in another bag. Shake each piece of chicken in the flour, then dip it into the milk mix. Shake it into the flour mix and lay skin side down in the butter/lard mix. Bake for 30 minutes. Then using tongs, flip chicken over and back for an additional 30 minutes until crispy fried. Remove to chicken to a platter and keep warm.

If desired, use the drippings to make gravy and serve with mashed potatoes.

---

the end does come for the chickens, it's done out in the open air without chemicals or bleach or nasty smells. It's dignified. It's not Disneyland, this is reality. If you eat meat, you're going to have to deal with this. Last week, Travis got to kill one. There was no fear, and no yucky *euwws*. Right, Travis?

Travis nods.

We mosey over to where they house the broilers. Four pens, or "tractors," are moved each morning. Nearby, a small group of cows grazes. Daniel says his father can talk about grass for hours.

Daniel: The chickens are about ready to go out in the field. It takes about eight weeks to raise a broiler, from start to finish. We move the pens once

a day. We'll get about eighteen thousand broilers in a summer. Broilers are easy; the overhead is low. The pens are $250 each. That's $1.00 a bird.

Now that the weather is better, the boys will come with me to fill the feed buckets. They'll play in the water mainly, but that's okay. I'm right here, not going very far very fast. I move from pen to pen and they walk along with me.

We have two Anatolian shepherd dogs that are at the upper fields with the majority of the broilers. One's in training and the other's working.

We run about five hundred to six hundred head of cattle every year. We do seasonal mob stocking — eighteenth-century hammering. The bison

come in twice a year, once on the way, following the grass. And once on the way back. They just *whomp*! They'll come in and, in one day, change the grass from this high stuff to completely flat lands. Four hundred animals will completely level two acres. Then they move on. We load them into trailers, take them from rental farm to rental farm, run them as one big group. It's totally different, the whole idea of loading cattle up in trailers, trucking then ten miles down the road just so you can graze them. Trucking is cheap. We have subcontractors who come in and do their thing, these big cowboys running big diesel trucks. It's very, very exciting. It's my favorite part of it, really, the cows!

A small four-wheeler roars up with Joel Salatin. He has on his famous eye-catching straw hat. He carries a black rubber bucket. After quick introductions, he asks Daniel how he's done with moving the pigs.

Daniel: Picture perfect. We left at three, went up,

moved the TSI *[Timber Stand Improvement]* pigs, grabbed the other pigs and were home by 4:15. What about you and the cows?

Joel Salatin: We got along okay. Those 440 head filled that alley from the turnoff going into the wedge, all the way to the gate at the white barn. They came out of John's yard, so they filled it from there all the way to the gate. They made that turn, it was very cool.

Daniel: They came out of the gate nice, I bet, with that new, bigger gate.

Joel: Well, that didn't actually help us or hurt us today, just because they didn't have a lot of momentum going through it. They had to go up and around. It was fine.

I'm going to give the one up there some of this new mixture.

He passes me the bucket.

Joel: Ascophyllum Nodosum, from Iceland. Try it. It's the best kelp in the world. We don't give our animals anything that we wouldn't eat. It's geo-thermally dried at a very low temperature. They grow it in farms up there and harvest it. They have real high tides. It's mixed with food-grade soft rock phosphate called Nutrabalancer. The salt is from out in Utah, Redmond salt. Totally unprocessed, high in minerals. That's why it's got the red color, because of all the minerals in it, as opposed to the white salt, which is processed and iodized.

I take a pinch and put it in my mouth. It tastes like kelp and salt.

Joel takes off his hat and nods at me. See you at dinner, *he tells Daniel and Sheri.*

Daniel: Neat thing about the whole system — we can go to a piece of ground that's been worn down. It's got thistles, it's weedy, it's messy. We put up our fencing, our water system and start rotationally grazing. Soon we can double the carrying capacity per acre. We can get rid of the weeds. At the same time we create just awesome mob effect. The fertility cycle picks up. It's exciting to see what cows can do to heal the landscape. We joke about putting up signs, "Another land conversion project by Polyface Farms."

We work long hours, sunup to sundown, all the time, but it's more than a great life for all of us. We support it, and it supports us. My father's right. It's all about the grass.

Back in New York City, I begin to transcribe and organize the recent interviews. The weather is warming up. Now the cherry blossoms are in bloom. So are the apple blossoms. I have plenty of work to do. Still, I plan to leave for points west and Durango by the first of May.

It has been about eight months since Lora Krogman passed away. I have been waiting to decide how to approach her profile. Parker Forsell, who took over for Lora after she died, tells me that a note went out to the CSA list asking that, in lieu of flowers, people send seeds that could be planted around the farm in Lora's memory.

MAY ■ *Back at Angelic Organics.*

Parker: Things are still changing around here, nothing is really set. Lora was the hostess for the farm. When people come here to stay, like beekeeper Gunther Hauk just did, it now falls on Bob *[Lora's boyfriend]* or me to try and host. It just isn't in either of our characters to be a host-type person. Plus, Lora was a chef. After she passed away, we couldn't figure out who was going to cook.

Bob Bower approaches. He has on the same baseball cap I remember from the year before. I tell him how sorry I am about Lora, and remind him that I want to incorporate Lora's poetry and recipes into the profile I'd begun writing about her.

Bob: I will make a point, then, to figure out in the next week or two what poems she might have wanted me to give you.

One of the most difficult things is that Lora had gotten into probably the best space in her life. The last time I saw her, right over there *[he points to a spot not far from where we stand]* — she'd had kind of a tough day, but she was feeling so happy about how much better some of the workers were doing. She was excited.

Bob disappears into his apartment and brings out a box Lora had given him. Inside are photos of the two of them, drawings and some poems.

Bob: Here's one of her haikus:

> Full Moon
> On the way to Japan
> She changes her wardrobe

He turns away from me looking toward the fields.

We're harvesting some great carrots out there now.

Later, Parker shows me the biodynamic "stirrer." He explains the manure compost mixture and the quartz mix; how and when they are applied to the fields. We discuss a recent piece in The New York Times *in which Angelic Organics was highlighted. We talk about how consumers are getting more and more educated, beginning to ask questions about their food and produce.*

I stand close to Lora's one remaining beehive. Only one survived the rough winter. It's about 80 degrees and I'm perspiring. I listen to the katydids, the drone of the bees and farm flies. All around, pink and purple clover rises knee-high. Behind me extend row after row of neat crop fields. It feels like it will storm any minute.

Excerpts from *Bee Poem Beginnings*
an unfinished poem by Lora Krogman

in the morning mist, my car cloaked
in anticipation and early sun, I drove 50 miles north
on 51 to the mustard colored barn with brown trim
to pick up metal cages two hives, two pounds of bees in
metal cages trimmed with wood

I remember that they are sentient sensitive workers who suppress their sex,
little monks, messengers with wings who build bridges

(I rest my hand) on the wood of their cage to feel their vibration

THIRD SUMMER ■ *This time when I arrive in Durango, although the air smells clean and fresh, it's still cool. A late spring. The back garden is filled with daffodils and the tulips are about to burst open. Summer follows quickly, with its hiking and swimming and the delightful work of pulling my book together, testing all of the recipes.*

I have two last interviews to do, one in Durango and one in Chimayo, New Mexico.

"The Acequias of the upper Mora Valley are the highest and most famous traditional irrigation system in New Mexico. Almost in defiance of gravity, they elevate water from three west-flowing forks of the Rio Pueblo in the Sangre de Cristo Mountains."

This is the prologue to a folktale recently translated by Enrique R. Lamadrid and Juan Estevan Arellano. To learn more about this water system, I search out Estevan Arellano, an award-winning journalist, farmer and native of northern New Mexico. He tells me an acequia is a manmade ditch that brings water from a river or stream to a piece of land through earthen and sometimes concrete culverts. Acequias recharge ground water aquifers, saving energy and avoiding wasteful piped irrigation.

Arellano says to imagine the way blood flows through the body, from arteries to capillaries. In the same way, the water from a river is diverted into channels that run into the Acequia Madre (the mother ditch). Individuals tap into the water supply to irrigate their fields. The Mayordomo makes sure everyone along the Acequia gets an equal share.

El Agua Es La Vida Congreso De Las Acequias
Statement of Principles

1. We recognize, honor and respect that water is sacred
2. We reaffirm the connection between land, water and our communities as the material and spiritual basis for our existence
3. We practice the principle that water is life in our customs and traditions of water sharing
4. Because it is scarce and precious, the utmost care must be taken in using our water

5. We honor the indigenous knowledge of our elders, which guides the day-to-day operation of Acequias

6. We recognize that our ancestors viewed water as a communal resource attached to the land

7. We honor water as part of our heritage and believe that treating water as a commodity for generating profit is a fundamental disrespect of our way of life

8. We seek to sustain our ancestral connections to water

9. We believe that decisions about reallocations or transfers of water rights should be made through a cultural and spiritual attachment to place, through a feeling of *querencia*

10. We believe that our Acequias are fundamental to our culture and our identity as land-based people

11. We maintain that water we use for growing food supports our self-determination as a people

Adán Trujillo, Omar Trujillo, and Pilar Trujillo
Chimayó, New Mexico ■ www.lasacequias.org/programs/sembrando-semillas/

JULY ■ *I visit the Trujillo family in Chimayó. Their Acequia de la Cañada Ancha is five and half miles long and irrigates two hundred acres, twenty of which belong to the Trujillos. Three Trujillo siblings, Adán, Omar and Pilar work to keep the tradition of the Acequias alive. Their homestead is El Rincon Farm.*

Pilar Trujillo: Our mom is from south Texas, Mexican-American. Our dad is a native New Mexican. They farmed this land in the '70s, when they were first married. They had Adán, then Omar. In 1979 or 1980 they all moved to El Rito, another little river town where I was born. After that we moved to Española so they could get better jobs. They kept the land and this house. We always came back to Chimayó during the summer. My grandfather built this house. There was an apple orchard, plum trees and apricot trees. In the summers we would return to harvest the fruit.

My grandpa tended sheep when he was growing up. He worked the fields. It was difficult work, subsistence farming. He did it to survive. As soon as he was able to get out of Chimayó, he took the opportunity. He became a teacher and kept a small garden.

My parents split up in 1995. They agree that the happiest years of their marriage were when they lived here in this little home with not much money. Growing their own food, having their two little sons running around with animals — chickens, goats, ducks, pigs.

In 2007, Adán was already living here; so was Omar. I was living in Santa Fe. None of us had gotten very far from Chimayó. The previous winter, one of Omar's friends came down from Vermont. That changed everything. The spring of 2007, we decided to start farming again.

Adán: I was having a conversation with my dad. We work together every day in our law practice. I think in the course of the conversation I told him, "You know, the land is just a liability. All you do

is pay property taxes on it. You're never going to develop it, you're never going to put houses on it. It's irrigated agricultural land connected to old land-based traditions. It should be available for agricultural use."

Omar's friend called him up and said, "Hey, I'm going to take a bike ride through Mexico. I'm going to pass through New Mexico and I'd love to see you and hang out." They hadn't seen each other since they'd met in Costa Rica, three or four years before.

His name is Daniel James Harding. Typical Vermont kid, long red curly hair. A really good guy — twenty-two or twenty-three years old. He was on a train, and somewhere in the Midwest the train ended up hitting a soybean truck. They all had to get off and move all their stuff to some lot where everything was supposed to be protected. The big canister where Daniel had stored his bike, his tent, and all his gear for this six-month trip through Mexico was stolen. So he shows up in Santa Fe

with nothing. Prior to that he'd been working on an organic farm.

Pilar: He saw our land and just freaked at how amazing it was!

Adán: Daniel had never irrigated. In Vermont they just plant, then wait for the rain. The weeds grow pretty slowly because they don't have to compete much. It's different out here in the desert. Once you have weeds, and you add water to that, and you add sun, they just keep coming.

The timing was perfect. We had just begun having these conversations about wanting to start this farm and then poof! Out of nowhere this young, motivated, organic farmer from Vermont shows up. Daniel agreed to stay on, at least through the first season. That's how we got started. He encouraged us to do more crop variety. At first we'd wanted to focus on the native Chimayó chili pepper. He said, "No, you need to grow more, you need to grow a variety of crops."

So we developed a crop list. Some of them we didn't enjoy. We're not big turnip fans. It was extremely important for us to have that variety because we could see the benefit of eating that food. We started to think about food processing and food preservation and food storage throughout the winter months. If we'd just had chiles and a little bit of squash, we definitely wouldn't have had the experience we did. We wanted to get back to the lifestyle our parents had in the '70s, with chickens wandering all around, and pigs and goats. My dad's friends used to come over and they'd slaughter a pig. They'd have meat all winter long. He even built shelves in the family room for Mason jars, so they could can everything and eat throughout the winter.

I acquired a piece of property right next door so we could expand the farm. We hired Mario. He brought his entire family along. Now they live right across the way from here, helping us to cultivate the land.

Omar: Daniel stayed with us for ten or eleven months. We bought a new tractor and began to figure out how to get the property ready. Daniel hadn't worked with furrows, he hadn't worked with channels, he hadn't worked in the desert. So it's been a learning process. Each year we learn more. We stick to the traditional ways. We irrigate by flood irrigation. Most of the farms around here do drip irrigation. We pulled out all the weeds by hand (we learned that's a big mistake). We'd like to be able to grow everything that we need right here. We'd also like to encourage other people in the valley, in Chimayó especially, to do the same.

Adán: When I was eighteen, I went to Colorado College, in Colorado Springs. I didn't move back here until I finished University of New Mexico Law School in 2004.

Pilar: The furthest I got was Albuquerque. I went to a community college for about eight months. Then moved back to Santa Fe and spent the last nine years there finishing my degree, environmental studies, through a long-distance program at Prescott College. I moved back to Chimayó a year and a half ago.

Omar: I left Española after I graduated from high school. I did my first year of undergraduate study in Las Vegas, New Mexico. I ended up at UNM in 2003 studying media arts. After I graduated, there wasn't much going on in New Mexico as far as the film industry, so I worked as a waiter and bartender. I took off to Costa Rica for nine months. In 2002 I came back to work with my dad in his law office. For the last seven years I've been back and forth between Chimayó and Albuquerque doing any film work I can get.

I can see myself having a family on this land. The history of this place is very important. El Rincon de los Trujillo is named after us. Our family has been here for hundreds of years.

Adan: In Spanish, *rincon* means where the natural hills create an inside corner. Our Trujillo ancestors settled this little corner of land: "Trujillo Hollow."

Omar: Our parents reacquired much of the land that had been in the family. We've now got twenty acres, one of the biggest farms in Chimayó.

Adán: In the Spanish era, this land was all part of a land grant. The federal government ended up taking these lands from the people. What they did was to isolate the people. You can't go beyond those hills a mile that way. You can't go beyond those hills 1200 yards this way. It's a very small strip of land that Chimayó has.

When you have such a tiny land base, and you have a population that's been there for hundreds of years, what they own gets smaller and smaller. If I have an acre and I have four kids, when I pass away I give each of them a quarter of an acre. If they have four kids, then they have to split it up into smaller and smaller pieces. My dad said it used to be a requirement that the smallest pieces of land had to be just wide enough for you to turn an oxcart around and plow. There were many Trujillo landowners who had all gotten their tiny parcels over the years. When they started to pass away, my dad began to purchase them, consolidate them, like

El Rincon Recipes:

Most of these ingredients are things we grow on the farm . . . except for olive oil, salt, pepper and the dessert ingredients. It's always best to use the freshest ingredients possible, and a real treat when we can make almost our entire meal with ingredients from the garden.

Breakfast: Calabacitas with Eggs

4 to 6 small/medium squash (zucchini, crookneck), sliced into smaller pieces

4 ears of fresh corn, husked and with the corn taken off the cob

5 green Chimayo chili peppers – roasted, peeled and chopped

4 to 6 tablespoons olive oil

1 small onion

Few garlic cloves

Salt and pepper to taste

4 eggs

Shredded cheese (can use goat chevre if you prefer for a tangier flavor)

Saute the onions and garlic in olive oil for a few moments. Add the squash and sauté for 3 to 4 minutes. Add the fresh corn and chopped green chili. Cook over medium heat for about 5 minutes, making sure squash does not get overcooked.

When finished cooking, top with shredded cheese and cover with lid to melt the cheese (or put under broiler). Fry 2 to 4 eggs in olive oil. Spoon calabacitas onto dish and top with a fried egg or two, depending on how hungry you are! Serves 2 to 4 people.

Lunch: Veggie Tacos with Green Chili

Fresh corn tortillas, if possible

1 onion

Few cloves of garlic

2 to 4 tablespoons olive oil

2 to 3 carrots, cut into small pieces

1 bunch fresh chard, rinsed and chopped

1 bunch fresh spinach, rinsed and chopped

Goat cheese (chevre or other soft cheese)

Few sprigs of fresh basil, sliced into strips

Salt and pepper to taste

Chimayo green chili, roasted, peeled and chopped with garlic and salt added into it

Sauté onions, garlic and carrots in olive oil for a few minutes. Add the chopped chard and spinach and cook over medium heat until the greens are wilted and the carrots have softened to your liking. Warm up the corn tortillas on a skillet with a few drops of olive oil. Spoon the veggie mixture into warm tortillas, top with goat cheese, slivers of fresh basil, and a little bit of chopped green chili. Enjoy! Serves 2 to 4.

Dinner: Red Chili Enchiladas

This is a heavy meal best reserved for a Sunday afternoon when you have time to make a fresh pot of beans and, of course, the red Chili – it's all about the quality of the ingredients and the red Chili in this recipe!

Red Chili recipe (courtesy of my mama!)

1 pound lean pork (or beef, turkey, chicken), cubed or ground

1 cup water

1 tablespoon olive oil

2 teaspoons salt

8 cups whole red Chimayó chili pods

6 cloves garlic

3 cups chicken or vegetable broth *plus* 3 cups water, or 6 cups water

6 tablespoons flour

Pinch of oregano

Heat the oven to 300 degrees. Brown the meat in 1 tablespoon olive oil. Add 1 cup water and simmer while preparing the other ingredients. De-seed and de-vein the chili pods if necessary.

Toast the chili pods for 3 to 5 minutes in the oven, turning once. Quickly rinse the chili pods after toasting. Place approximately half of the chili pods, half of the broth/water, half of the flour, and half of the garlic in a blender. Puree until smooth, then add to the cooked meat. Place remainder of ingredients in blender and repeat. Add pinch of oregano. Stir gently, adjust salt to taste. Simmer for 45 minutes, stirring occasionally to prevent sticking. Makes 8 cups (A LOT!)

You can adjust the spice level by either using less/more chili pods, or by mixing with milder/spicier chili.

Ingredients for enchiladas

 Large pot of fresh pinto beans with the juice (look up
  how to make them on the internet)

 Fresh corn tortillas, 1 dozen

 Large pot of red chili (recipe above)

 Shredded cheese

 4 to 6 eggs (optional)

 Chopped onion, lettuce, tomato, avocado for garnish

Take one corn tortilla and dip it into the hot pot of
chili (or into the pot of beans for a less spicy version).
Lay the tortilla on a plate and repeat with additional
tortilla – up to 3 or 4 tortillas per serving, depending on
how hungry you are! Smother the tortillas on the plate
with more beans and chili. Top with cheese and put
under the broiler for a few moments. Top with a fried
egg, if desired. Garnish with lettuce, tomato, onions
and avocado. You can lightly fry the corn tortillas before
dipping them for a firmer texture.

Desert: Biscochitos

Biscochitos are actually the state cookie now! My mom
and I make these every year for Christmas – they are a
holiday staple, along with tamales and posole. It is pretty
important to use lard – not vegetable shortening – for
true biscocho flavor.

 2 cups lard

 1 cup sugar

 2 eggs

 2 teaspoons anise seed or anise extract

 ½ teaspoon salt

 ½ cup brandy, wine, or water

 6 cups sifted flour

 3 teaspoons baking powder

 Cinnamon sugar

Cream lard and sugar. Add anise and eggs. Sift flour,
baking powder and salt together. Add alternately to first
mixture flour and liquid. Roll out ⅛ inch thick and cut
with cookie cutter or fancy shapes. Sprinkle with cinnamon sugar. Bake in 375 degree oven 8 to 10 minutes
until golden brown.

pieces of a puzzle. Owning twenty acres in Chimayó
is a huge piece of land.

Omar: We want to maintain the integrity of this
place. We want to use it not only for ourselves, but
to show others the beauty of farming, of sustainable living, of doing something with the family. We
stuck out at the farmers market right away because
of the quality of our products. Our soil was rich
with nutrients and everything we grew was delicious. We were looking at our ancestral land in a
way that we hadn't before. If we can make that
change, then I think there's a lot of hope for other
people. We can move back to an era where we don't
need to be dependent on other countries, on other
parts of our country to live prosperous lives.

Adán: Much of what we have is agricultural land
– and we are talking about a conservation easement
to make sure that the land will continue to be used
this way in perpetuity.

Most people have to leave Española or northern
New Mexico in order to make a living. If you're
not happy driving up to the labs *(Los Alamos)* and
suffering severe health effects thirty years later, then
you have to go somewhere else, Santa Fe or Albuquerque. Most of my friends from high school don't
live here anymore. If they wanted to be an engineer,
they had to go. I'm starting to notice though that
for the people who are from northern New Mexico,
getting back here is always on their mind.

Omar: Although northern New Mexico is incredibly beautiful, it also has hideous problems that
affect people all over the nation, but even more here
in percentages, per capita— drug abuse and domestic violence, teen dropouts, teen pregnancy. They're
all really high in Chimayó. We grew up amidst that.
The trick now is how to manage these problems,
where to start. First step is to give kids something
to do. Pilar does that in her work.

Pilar: I'm the Youth Coordinator for a program
called Sembrando Semillas. I oversee five different
sites in northern NM and southern Colorado with
the New Mexico Acequia Association. Sembrando
Semillas is an inter-generational agriculture program.

Youths work with mentors in their community doing seasonal, agriculture activities related to the Acequia; growing traditional crops, traditional food processing and storage, traditional cattle ranching. The mentors train their own children. Then the friends of their children get involved, so it grows organically. It's very much word of mouth.

We're trying to reaffirm what these kids already know. They've grown up in small, mostly farming communities. They've seen their neighbors growing food all their lives. We're trying to reaffirm their identity as land-based people. We're trying to show them that it is economically valuable. We're trying to get them to have their own relationship with the land instead of just seeing their neighbors or their grandparents. One of the ways we encourage them is to give them cameras and tell them, "Shoot as many pictures as you want. Take short videos on your camera. Let's make a movie about it, let's enter into a local film festival. Let's go to some of the schools and show it to other kids."

The kids are anywhere from eight to eighteen years old. It really is family, we aren't focusing on any one particular age. If one of the families has a little five-year-old boy and he's out there helping, he's part of the program. We want to get them to see how incredibly important and special what we have is. The kids travel to Albuquerque for youth conferences and are some of the only rural kids. The kids from the city are completely blown away. They ask questions like, "What do you do? How do you do it? What's an Acequia?"

I'm blessed that my work deals with all the things I'm passionate about. When I was in Santa Fe finishing my degree, I created a course of study around traditional farming methods. I did it with the help of Miguel Santisteven, who is very passionate about native crops, seeds and water. He got me excited about the possibility of planting and farming. At that time he worked with the New Mexico Acequia Association and was instrumental in starting the Sembrando Semillas. Miguel decided to go back to school to get his Ph.D. in biology at the exact time that I finished my undergraduate degree. Since Miguel knew me, he recommended me for the job of youth coordinator. Synchronistic.

Adán: There are farmers out there who are generous with their knowledge. They recognize that if you get people excited and passionate about this, it's going to pay dividends, not only from a market standpoint in terms of increasing the production, but just with that connection to the land-based culture. There's another local farmer, Don Bustos, who has taken the time to come out here and look at our land and give us pointers and lend us equipment. Matt Romero allowed us to go out to his farm and look at his drip system, his sand filter and the type of irrigation he's set up. All the vendors at the Santa Fe Farmers Market are always there for us. They've told us about the rhythms of the land, the changing seasons, or when it's the best time to plant. They're mostly older and native to northern New Mexico. Farming is second nature to them.

Of course, there's some resentment because it's gentrification. Although some of the new people have small gardens, they don't farm much. They raise the property values. Too many locals who don't have any resources are too willing to sell out their water rights, sell out the land that has been in their family for centuries because they need that money. Or they want that money. Once the land is gone, it's difficult to get it back. The fact is you place a multi-million dollar home, or even just a nice small home on the land, you raise the property value so much that no local person is going to be able to afford it. We know we've got a big responsibility and we need to make sure we capitalize on it. Our goal is to make this the best piece of property we can.

Pilar: It has to be economically viable.

Omar: The last two years, we've put in so much money and work as a family. Very little has been returned monetarily.

Pilar: But eating the food has really been a reward.

Omar: There's nothing better on a late summer evening than going out and picking everything you need for dinner.

Last year we planted a couple of varieties of squash, a couple of varieties of corn, and our Chimayó chilis. We had carrots, radishes, beets, potatoes, onions, garlic, tomatoes, a variety of lettuces and herbs as well as peas and beans and fruit trees.

We all go on a tour of the property. We hike up and down the hills, in and out of arroyos, back and around all of the structures on the property. There's a strong scent of scrub oak and Russian sage.

Pilar: Our Acequia is over five miles long and serves a large community.

Adán: I don't know how many *parciantes*, but you can imagine how many landowners — we are at the halfway point. In fact, every spring we have a crew that starts at the beginning of the ditch, another crew at the end and we meet somewhere in the Rincon. You can choose either to work it, or

you send someone on your behalf. You can pay a "peon," which is what they call it. That's around $40. In 2005 I did it, and we had a relatively small crew, probably twenty people. Each year there have been more and more people working. This past year there must have been around sixty people. If you clean your own property you don't have to pay anything.

We're lucky to have a perennial ditch. It diverts off the Rio Ouemado that runs year round. They keep the head gate open, which means that we have water in this ditch year round. Many ditches dry out in March and have to partition the water. They have very strict rules about who gets water when. They have less water and more users. There aren't that many farmers farming along our ditch. If there's water in it, for the most part we can take it.

Pilar: This is a system that has worked for

PHOTO COURTESY PILAR TRUJILLO

hundreds of years so everybody can grow their crops. Of course, water levels are different now, and we've been in a never-ending drought. The climate's changing. It's still a system that's successful, that allows for every person on the Acequia to get water.

If the land comes with water rights you can use the water in any way you want. On a lawn, to drink, whatever. My grandmother would go to visit family in southern New Mexico. When she'd return she'd begin drinking water out of the ditch again and she'd get sick. Then she'd acclimate. Think about how much worse the water must be today.

Omar: Even the well water is bad.

Adán: Within five years I'd like to establish an intern program. I would like to have a much cleaner infrastructure, where everything has been organized. We need garages for our tractors. We need our trees pruned. Fencing — interior fencing to

introduce livestock. There are some buildable areas just down the road where we can make our own adobe. Maybe look into building houses in the next three to four years that would house either family members, interns or renters. Have a viable, sustainable farm that provides food for our family, but also brings in supplemental income to offset whatever we spend on labor, whatever we spend on travel to the farmers market.

I'd also like to start thinking about incorporating some kind of CSA, where we approach some of these neighbors and say, "Look, if you're interested in the CSA you could come by once a week. We'll have a box of whatever fruits and vegetables are ready that week." We want to start feeding our own community instead of taking our food up to Santa Fe.

Omar: I can see the Rincon becoming not only a place where we're able to grow for ourselves and others, but bring people in as a kind of agritourism. My mom's a massage therapist. I'd love to have a place we could rent out, where people could come and stay with us, visit. Have some horses to ride, stock the pond with fish so we could fish for our dinner.

Pilar: We all basically have the same vision for the place. I will go along with the agritourism, but really, I just want to keep planting. I want to make sure we continue to put seeds in the ground and to grow native crops.

I'd like to get into more food processing, keeping animals. We plan on keeping chickens. We already have a few. I want to make a chicken tractor when they're bigger, move them down the field. This is home for me!

In my job, we have big plans for the youth program and for the food system in northern New Mexico. We have big plans for creating networks, for getting the youth involved on every level. For everything we dream of, we will be deliberate, conscious.

Katrina Blair
Turtle Lake Refuge ■ Durango, Colorado ■ www.turtlelakerefuge.org

AUGUST ■ *My last interview before starting back to New York City is with Katrina Blair, who has mentored Samantha Johnson (one of my first interviews) as well as many other young people who pass through the Durango area.*

The Local Wild Life Café is open every "Turtle Tuesday" and "Frog Friday" from 11:11 A.M. until 2:22 P.M. A plate of flaxseed crackers is set before me by one of Katrina's interns, a full-headed beauty, with dreadlocks to her waist and a clean white apron. I've been to the café many times. I've become addicted to the crackers, addicted to the fresh raw foods that show up on the white lunch plate twice a week.

Today for lunch they serve a minted wheatgrass drink, followed by a zingy cold carrot soup with sprouted beans and ginger. The main course is alfalfa sprouts with chopped nuts topped with a light green goddess dressing. Next comes zucchini and yellow squash lasagna. And finally, for dessert, apricot cobbler. All the ingredients come from Katrina's backyard garden.

Katrina's house is located in Hidden Valley, an overgrown valley less than five miles from town, close to the beginning of the Colorado Trail. It has a cold cellar to store vegetables and several outside decks.

On one of the decks two young interns harvest a pile of recently picked kale. There are two more interns in the kitchen trying to figure out how to use the cheese wheels from the malo plants. The one from Guatemala decides that they will pickle them. "They are a delicacy."

Across the road from the main house there's more

RECURRING ■ Katrina Blair

Breakfast: The Breakfast Apple Cobbler

Crust:

1 cup sunflower seeds (soaked and drained)
1 cup almond (soaked and drained)
2 cups dates

Grind them in cuisinart until they become dough consistency. Form this dough into a pie pan for the crust.

Filling:

4 apples
1 lemon
1 teaspoon cinnamon
1 teaspoon vanilla

Grind the apples in the food processor until it become apple saucy. Fill your pie pan with the filling, decorate the top and serve for a breakfast of champions! Serves a group.

Lunch: Veggie Nori Wraps

The Cheese:

1 tablespoon fresh ginger
1 clove garlic
2 tablespoons soy sauce
1½ cups walnuts

The fillings:

1 avocado
1 carrot
1 cucumber
½ cup bean sprouts
Diced cabbage (approximately ½ cup)
Buckwheat lettuce (approximately ½ cup

Create your walnut cheese by adding the walnuts, ginger, garlic and soy sauce in the food processor until smooth. Use a nori seaweed to make a wrap for lunch. Spread on the "cheese" and layer in avocado, buckwheat lettuce, sliced carrots, cucumber, cabbage and sprouts. Roll it up, slice into pieces and serve with soy sauce if desired, or just eat in one whole delicious bite. Serves 3 to 5.

Dinner: Zucchini Linguini with Dandelion Pesto

4 large zucchini
2 cups of dandelions
2 cups of basil
1 cup cashew
1 lemon
1 teaspoon good salt
½ cup good oil
½ cup good water
2 to 3 cloves of garlic

To make your pesto sauce blend all ingredients in the blender until smooth. Take your zucchini and spiralize (with a Salad Co hand crank Spiralizer) or shred it into noodles with a cheese grater. Mix the two together and serve a fine feast for dinner, made of local goodness right from the earth. Serves 4 to 6.

Dessert: Green Revolution Ice Dream

3 lemons
2 avocados
3 cups of good water
1 cup local honey
1 teaspoon of local dried weed powder if possible (made with dandelions, mallow, plantain, lambsquarter, amaranth and osha greens)

Blend all ingredients into a very creamy green pudding. Place into a metal bowl in the freezer. Mix every hour to keep smooth and serve when it becomes ice cream consistency. Be part of the Green Revolution! Serves a group.

So on January 11, 2000, we opened Local Wild Life Café amidst the growing wheatgrass, buckwheat and sunflower greens we'd planted on trays in the backyard of the Rocky Mountain Retreat. The RMR was founded by my mom and my aunt. They'd set up the building as a healing retreat center where guests could come to learn about living foods and biofeedback. It was no longer active. We renovated the space, tiling the floors, adding glass windows, creating a new dining area. It was ready for a new kind of health inspiration — Turtle Lake Refuge. We chose our lunch hours, 11:11 to 2:22, to coincide with the moment we first opened. This honors the ageless myth — when we catch time at double, triple or quadruple digits, the divine is with us. We're at the right place at the right time.

We call ourselves Local Wild Life for three reasons:

Local: We believe in the value of locally grown foods. Foods nurtured into life in the same environment we exist in are more easily assimilated into our systems than food imported from far reaches of the planet.

Wild: Wild foods have chosen for themselves to thrive in this region. They are deeply connected to the land. When we eat wild harvested food we deepen our connection to this region of the earth. "Weeds" often hold the greatest value for our bodies.

Life: Life gives life. Eating foods in their fresh living form provides the full enzymatic benefit the food has to offer. By eating living foods we conserve energy, decrease stress on our bodies, and gain maximum benefit with minimal effort.

Nature is our best teacher and finest example of sustainable living. When we look outside and observe all the other species living on the planet, we see them eating exclusively local, wild and living foods. By imitating nature's design, everyone benefits.

We originally asked for a donation instead of setting a price, to raise money and awareness for the preservation of the sixty acres of land adjacent to Turtle Lake. Although our lunches were not quite enough to raise the money to buy the land, we were blessed with the good fortune of a neighbor. They bought the land and ultimately placed forty-seven acres of it into a conservation easement, which included the lake and the majority of the wetlands.

The Café serves as many as sixty guests a day now, a celebration of people coming together around health. We still serve lunch only twice a week. The other days of the week, we create fabulous wild, living treats that we bike over to Durango's stores and restaurants.

We grow organic microgreens and sprouts year round for all ten public schools in Durango. The students take field trips to our place and learn how to plant the greens themselves. They learn to make wild fruit smoothies on the bicycle blender, and how to make apple juice on our hand crank juicer. We've been involved with the local Farm-to-School group since its inception in 2005. We provide educational programs focusing on sustainable practices in the schools.

We've had a booth at the Farmer's Market for over ten years. We bike all our wares there on two three-wheel bikes. Then we set up our bike blender for smoothies, our wheatgrass bicycle for green juices. Recently, I started playing music at the farmers market with my band, ABunDance. We're a smorgasbord of musical talents from drums to didgeridoos. We sing about picking fruit and eating weeds.

One of our current focuses is the Turtle Lake Refuge Organic Farm School, a school for sustainable living. We have honeybees, fruit trees, greenhouses, cold frames and a cold cellar *[in progress]*. We have dwellings for interns/residents. One of our projects is called Grassroots, an organic lawncare business. We use compost tea as grass food. By eliminating the use of herbicides, pesticides and chemical fertilizers, we support the immune systems of honeybees and all the wild pollinators.

I just finished a book I've been working on for years called *Local Wild Life: Turtle Lake Refuge's Recipes for Living Deep*. It's a compilation of our favorite recipes and wild foods, how to use them, and our stories and philosophies. It's filled with tons of pictures of our last eleven years of adventures.

Every year I take a walkabout, where I hike into the woods with little or no food. It's a delicious time of centering with the wild spaces around me and within me. I feel this solo time is essential to recharge my spirit. I simply walk, sleep outside, eat wild food, drink wild water and sing. The whole journey is a prayer.

Makenna Leiner Goodman
Farmer/Writer/Editor ■ Washington, Vermont ■ www.chelseagreen.com

THIRD FALL, THANKSGIVING ■ *Luna and I drive up to Vermont for Thanksgiving. My daughter, Makenna, has left New York City, packed up all her belongings, moved herself up to Vermont where she has some good friends, and is now living on a ninety-acre farm that she is co-operating with her boyfriend, Sam. The ninety-acre spread of forest and pasture land is covered in fall color. In the last year Sam and Makenna have raised a large vegetable garden, four cows, two pigs, two lambs, and 156 chickens. Everything on our Thanksgiving Day plate is either grown on their land or traded for something grown on their land. My daughter takes me around the farm, showing me where the pigs have lived and died, introducing me to the two sheep, the two cows, the hens; showing me the henhouse they have built as per Joel Salatin's books*

and personal advice. In her own right, my daughter has become one of the people my book is about. I ask her if I might interview her for the book. With some hesitation, she agrees. We settle out by the pond, sitting across from each other at the picnic table. I turn my tape recorder on.

Makenna: Growing up, you and Dad were these artsy parents who served "thoughtful" food. At lunchtime I got my avocado and cheese whole-wheat sandwiches out of wax bags, while my friends were getting fun foods like Lunchables. That's what I wanted. I wanted to be like them.

When I went to the Mountain School in my junior year of high school everything changed for me. That year — when I was sixteen — was really my first experience of being on a farm, being around

RECIPES ■ Makenna Leiner Goodman

Chard Pie

We always have piles and piles of chard in the garden. This is an incarnation that was passed from Sam's sister to him, which he morphed, and passed onto me . . . sometimes it's exact, other times it's a leftovers pie. Either way, it's a staple in our house!

Crust:
    2 cups flour
    ½ cup olive oil
    ½ cup water

Mix everything in a bowl until it balls up. So easy! Then, plop it in an ungreased glass pie dish, morph it into a crust, and keep it on hold for a second while you make the filling.

Pie:
    3 eggs (we use the ones from our hens)
    A healthy splash of milk or cream
    Handful of parmesan cheese
    A bunch of kale or chard or beet greens
    1 onion or leek
    Raisins
    Salt and pepper to taste

Preheat oven to 400 degrees. Sauté the onions or leeks in a cast iron pan with olive oil (or any kind of pan). Add the chopped greens, and salt and pepper to taste. Then throw in the raisins, sauté some more, and let cool a little bit. In a mixing bowl, mix eggs, milk, cheese. Add the greens, etc., and stir. Then dump into your crust and bake for 45 minutes or until the pie has set and browned a bit. We eat it with hot sauce, and it's better cold the next day, as far as I'm concerned.

Cabbage Salad

    1 head of purple or green cabbage (or a little of both)
    1 sweet onion, thinly sliced
    A bunch of cilantro

Dressing:
    3 tablespoons or so of yogurt
    Splash lemon juice
    2 splashes olive oil
    2 splashes rice vinegar
    ½ splash soy sauce
    Squirt of agave nectar
    Squirt of dijon mustard

Slice the cabbage as thin as you can, same with the onion, and toss in a bowl. Dice the cilantro and add. Shake dressing in a mason jar until creamy and tangy. Add more of something if you think it needs it – more yogurt makes it thicker, more lemon juice makes it more sour. This salad keeps in the fridge for days, and is amazing in burritos. I take it to work with a side of rice and some salsa. Yum.

"Red Sauce" Easy Pasta – But One For The Books!

This recipe is the best on a night you're not really in the mood to use a lot of ingredients, but you want a delicious meal that's also fast.

    1 can of peeled whole tomatoes (sadly we got tomato blight, so these are store bought)
    2 onions
    Splash of lemon juice
    2 squirts agave nectar
    Olive oil
    Salt, pepper, garlic powder, oregano, basil
    One can of cheap beer! Or nice beer. Whatever.

animals, living and studying outside, and weeding. I hadn't been doing very well in science back in New York City — but at the Mountain School science was taught within the context of the outside world. I could make a connection between the facts and life, it was fun and I did well. I felt connected and alive, and it reminded me of my childhood in Colorado, before we moved to New York City. I took care of Murray, the ram. I fed him, watered him, let him in and out of the pen. I loved the way he smelled. I also took care of the chickens — they were weirdos! I liked seeing the social mechanisms of the animals living in their own environment.

I went back to the Mountain School the summer after my junior year of college to be a part of the farm crew.

1 package spaghetti
Parmesan cheese

In a big pan, sauté onions in olive oil until translucent. Add the can of tomatoes and lower heat. Mash up the tomatoes a bit so they're not all large. Add lemon juice, agave nectar, and spices. Cover and let simmer over medium-ish heat for a while – until it's bubbling and looking like sauce. Then, my secret recipe which came out of desperation one night when we had no wine – pour in a can or bottle of beer. This makes the sauce so buttery and amazing. It really changes everything, and I will never ever go back. Boil water with salt (the water should taste like seawater but not too too salty, salt is what makes pasta not taste glunky and is crucial when making any kind of pasta). Drain the noodles and then put them back in the big pot, adding the sauce. Stir with a pasta spoon until every noodle is covered. Top with parmesan and hot pepper flakes, if you want.

Poor Farm Farm Breakfast

My personal favorite and not for the faint-hearted. Keeps you satisfied for long hours though.

1 piece bread (recipe to follow)
Fresh fruit jam (or honey)
Salted butter
1 egg
1 small piece of cheddar cheese

Toast the bread, and while it's toasting fry up an egg in a pan with a little piece of cheese on top (cover the pan for the last portion of it). The key to a well cooked fried egg is to turn the stove off before you think it's done, because it keeps cooking in the pan. Then butter the toast and spread jam or honey on it, and put your egg on top! So salty, so sweet, just perfect.

Homemade Country Bread

4 cups white unbleached flour (I use King Arthur)
1 ½ cups warm water
1 teaspoon baking yeast
2 teaspoons salt

In a mixing bowl, add flour, yeast and salt. Use a fork to stir. Add the warm water, and keep stirring. it's going to be weird feeling, like there's not enough water, but there is. At a certain point you'll have to use your hands to gather up the wet dough and the dry dough. Keep the faith! It will become a messy looking ball at some point. Once it does, leave it covered and out on the counter for 4 hours or overnight, which makes the bread sweeter (4 hours is fine if you're in a rush). Preheat the oven to like 500 degrees. Take that dough ball and work it in your hands a little bit, but not too much. If you hold both of your palms facing slightly up, you'll notice the dough begins to fall over the sides of your hands. This is GOOD! Take one of the falling sides and tuck it under the other side, pinching the seam shut. You want a boule, which is basically a ball that's been sealed well, tucking one side in. Roll this ball in a small amount of flour. Then put it on a baking stone or pan, and make 3 slashes from side to side on the top with a serrated knife. This lets air out and also looks pretty. Bake for 45 minutes or so, with a dish of water in the oven. This makes the crust crisp. So either 45 minutes or until the bread is yellow-brown. You'll get the hang of your oven and you'll be able to time it according to your own rhythm, but to test it, if you flip over the loaf and tap on the bottom, it should sound hollow. Let cool before you cut! If you think you've overcooked it, don't let it cool. Cut it right away to let some of the heat out, because bread keeps cooking even when it's out of the oven.

I applied for the summer position at the beginning of the school year. Gerry Coleman was the manager of the farm, and I knew she thought I was a little spacey (at least she said so back in high school). She became my mentor during that summer—I loved her.

After the first week I was exhausted and my body was 100 percent sore. I was working from early morning until late at night. I don't know what I expected, but it was the hardest work I'd ever done. In the beginning I was doing electric fencing. I didn't really like electricity. I was nervous around the roping. I ended up switching with one of my friends and began working with the chickens—I wanted to work with the animals.

That summer was life changing for me. Not only

did I learn how to farm but I had all this incredible produce to cook with. My community was so amazing there. The other crew members were musicians, artists, landscape architects and teachers.

At the end of that summer I met and fell in love with Sam. He was actually already a farmer, had been farming for five years. I looked up to him. I hated to go back to college. That last year, my senior year, I worked in the prison system part-time, teaching poetry to women at a maximum security facility.

When I graduated from college, I went back to New York City and got a job in the publishing world. I found that I hated working in a cubicle, in a high rise; I hated midtown Manhattan and those soggy salads. It was a confusing time in a way, an alienated time. The work became all about earning enough money to be able to afford a life I wasn't

sure I wanted. I do know how lucky I was to work for those two years in top publishing jobs, to learn some of the business of art. It was most definitely *not* for me, though. I decided to move to Vermont.

I moved into a huge, unheated house with two male friends. Pretty soon I started looking for a job. Then by February I moved in with my boyfriend, Sam, and we started farming together. February is down time in the world of farming, the month to order seeds. For the first time ever, I sat down with a seed catalog. I was really excited about artichokes and lettuce. I wanted to be responsible for the garden. Once the seeds arrived, we started them inside. When those little sprouts started to show, it was like a miracle! At first I thought it was because of me that they'd come up. Then I realized it had almost nothing to do with me. I had merely coordinated things for them. I had created a healthy environment, but they had done everything else all on their own. It was meditative. I had to be gentle and careful. I had to be steady and consistent. I couldn't miss a day. I had to be part of the circle all the time. I was amazed at how fast they grew. Sometimes I'd come back from work and suddenly there would be a whole head of broccoli.

In the beginning of my chicken rearing, I put the chicks out when they were too young. Ravens swooped down and got many of them. They were extremely free-range and unprotected. When they were bigger, I lost about five of them. One to our dog, Frida, one to a neighbor's dog and two to coyotes. One morning at dawn I heard serious squawking coming from the henhouse. I climbed out the bedroom window onto the roof to check it out. There was a coyote trotting off with a hen in its jaws. I yelled out, "Hey!" It turned back to look at me, then just kept on going. I felt sorry for the hen, but it was pretty wild to see this ferocity first thing in the morning. I respected the coyote. We built the henhouse and fenced them in a bit more.

Harvest time was amazing. Picking food that I was going to eat was just the most incredible thing I'd ever done. And picking it from my own garden was the best. I hardly ever went to the store all summer. Everything was from the garden. And at the end of harvest we didn't turn the garden over, we didn't put it to bed. We just left it. Then we will roto-till it in the spring, using cow and horse manure.

This fall, we killed 130 chickens. We did it in one day. Chicken killing is gruesome, but I pulled through. Then two local men came and killed the cows. I know that they were very gentle and quick. Soon after that it was time for the pigs to go. Several weeks later, Sam killed the lambs. We butchered them together. That was a lot harder, for both of us. Lambs are so gentle to each other and so sweet — they don't have a mean bone in their body, unlike piggies and chickens, who can be mean. Sam got a deer, too. I helped butcher it. Butchering is such a quiet and respectful activity, gruesome as it sounds.

PHOTO COURTESY MAKENNA GOODMAN

We'll be keeping the last forty chickens through the winter. By spring they will be a year old, but they will continue to lay until next winter, when we'll kill them for stew.

I feel really lucky because I got to move onto this farm. Sam is more experienced than I am, so I get to learn from him. I've found other mentors, too. We all need mentors. It's too hard to do it from scratch by yourself. I would suggest anyone who thinks they want to do this, find someone to apprentice with. Decide where and what you want to do. Let's say you want to live in California, want to be able to farm most of the year. Then Google organic farms in California. If you want four seasons, then you want a northeast growing season — then google Vermont, New Hampshire or Maine.

There's a big difference between growing tomatoes on your balcony and farming acreage. An apprenticeship, will give you so much information and no matter what you ultimately choose to do with that information, it will change your life. If

you want to spend all your time fencing, building sheds, working with animals, growing food, harvesting it, you've got to love it.

Sam recently built a sugarhouse out of the tractor shed. One of his loves is sugaring. Maple sugaring is still popular in Vermont. We're always gawking at other people's sugarbushes. It's also a potential moneymaker. You can invest money in equipment and make it back in the first year. Come early spring, March, when Sam and I are rested, have ordered our seeds, and are ready for socializing, we'll get together with friends and neighbors and sugar the maples. We'll do bucket sugaring.

The one thing I know for sure is this: If you're going to be a farmer, you can't be afraid to fail. The best advice I ever got was from Joel Salatin, who said exactly that. He said do what you like. If you don't like to weed, then mulch. Do permaculture. Start an edible forest garden instead of a traditional French bed garden. If you love chickens, raise chickens. Don't take on too much.

Am I talking too much? *[Makenna smiles.]* I guess I love my life.

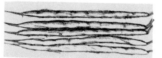

For now, my journey across this wide nation, talking to the new generation of farmers and food lovers comes to an end. Researching and writing this book allowed me to reconnect with the spirit of my mother's pantry and to celebrate as my daughter makes her own way in this world.

Finding our "life work," as the poet Donald Hall calls work that both sustains and impassions us through a lifetime, is not easy. It means being able to hear one's own heart, to feel the swell of it, and to recognize its beat of joy, and finally, to have the courage to follow wherever it leads. This is a divine process that must be revisited again and again.

Bibliography

Acevedo, Karen Keb. *Urban Farm* (premier issue). Los Angeles: Fancy Publications/ BowTie, 2009.

Acheson, James M. *The Lobster Gangs of Maine.* Hanover, NH: University Press of New England, 1988.

Ash, John, with Sid Goldstein. *From the Earth to the Table.* New York: Dutton/ Penguin, 1995.

Baum, Dan. *Nine Lives: Death and Life in New Orleans.* New York: Spiegel and Grau/ Random House, 2009.

Berley, Peter. *The Modern Vegetarian Kitchen.* New York: Regan Books/ HarperCollins, 2004.(Anna Lappe — around p. 350, cast-iron jalepeno cornbread)

Berry, Wendell. *The Mad Farmer Poems.* Carrollton, OH: Counterpoint Press, 2008.

———. *Remembering.* San Francisco: North Point Press, 1988.

Blair, Katrina. *Local Wildlife: Turtle Lake Refuge's Recipes for Living Deep.* Durango, CO: Turtle Publications, 2009.

Brotman, Juliano, with Erika Lenkert. *RAW: The UNcook Book.* New York: HarperCollins, 1999.

Cadwallader, Sharon. *The Living Kitchen.* San Francisco: Yolla Bolly Press/ Sierra Club Books, 1983.

Carpenter, Novella. *Farm City: The Education of an Urban Farmer.* New York: The Penguin Press, 2009.

Cheney, Ian, and Curt Ellis, dir. *The Greening of Southie.* Wicked Delicate, 2008. DVD.

———, writers. *King Corn.* Dir. Aaron Woolf. Mosaic Films, Inc., 2007. DVD.

Child, Julia, with Alex Prud'homme. *My Life in France.* New York: Anchor/ Random House, 2006.

Christopher, Tom. "Can Weeds Help Solve the Climate Crisis?" *The New York Times Magazine* 29. June 2008: 42-47.

Clancy, Kate. *Greener Pastures.* Cambridge: Union of Concerned Scientists, 2006.

Cox, Jeff. *The Organic Food Shopper's Guide.* Hoboken: John Wiley & Sons, 2008.

Crawford, Stanley. *Mayordomo: Chronicle of an Acequia in Northern New Mexico.* Albuquerque: University of New Mexico Press, 1988.

Dailey, Anne. "The New Crop." *The Valley Table* June/July 2008: 59-61.

Denevan, Jim, with Mara Stets. *Outstanding in the Field: A Farm to Table Cookbook.* New York: Clarkson Potter/ Random House, 2008.

Dunea, Melanie. *My Last Supper.* New York: Bloomsbury USA, 2007.

Edible Communities-Local Food Magazines. Edible Communities, Inc. Web. 8 October 2009.

Fallon, Sally, with Mary G. Enig, Ph.D. *Nourishing Traditions.* Washington, D.C.: New Trends, 2001.

Farley, Tom, and Deborah A. Cohen. *Prescription for a Healthy Nation.* Boston: Beacon Press, 2005.

Fisher, MFK. *How to Cook a Wolf.* New York: North Point Press, 1988.

Food, Inc. Dir. Robert Kenner. Perf. Michael Pollan, Eric Schlosser. Magnolia, 2008. DVD.

Frasier, Clark, et al. *The Arrows Cookbook.* New York: Scribner, 2003.

Fresh, the Movie. Dir. Ana Sofia Joanes. Perf. Will Allen, Michael Pollan, Joel Salatin. Ana Sofia Joanes, 2009.

Frye, Keith. *Roadside Geology of Virginia.* Missoula: Mountain Press Publishing, 1986.

Goldman, Amy, and Victor Schrager. *The Compleat Squash.* New York: Workman Publishing, 2004.

Graves, W.H. *Medicinal Value of Natural Foods.* Columbia: Dr. W.H. Graves, 1955.

Green, Aliza. *Field Guide to Produce.* Philadelphia: Quirk Books, 2004.

Greenlaw, Linda. *The Lobster Chronicles.* New York: Hyperion, 2002.

Growing Roots: A Documentary about Turtle Lake Refuge. Dir. Brian Barnes. Fort Lewis College Student Project, 2008. DVD.

Gussow Dye, Joan. *This Organic Life Confessions of a Suburban Homesteader.* White River Junction, VT: Chelsea Green, 2001.

Hall, Donald. *Life Work.* Boston: Beacon Press, 2007.

Harris, Richard, with Lisa Fox. *Artisan Farming: Lessons, Lore, and Recipes.* Layton, UT: Gibbs Smith, 2008.

Hayes, Joanne Lamb, et al. *Recipes from America's Small Farms.* New York: Villard, 2003.

Hayes, Shannon. *The Farmer and the Grill: A Guide to Grilling, Barbecuing, and Spit-Roasting Grassfed Meat.* Richmondville, NY: Left to Write Press, 2007.

———. *The Grassfed Gourmet Cookbook.* Bala Cynwyd, PA: Eating Fresh Publications, 2004.

Heart and Soil. Dir. Mara LeGrande. Skydance Productions, 2007. DVD.

Heekin, Deirdre, and Caleb Barber. *In Late Winter We Ate Pears: A Year of Hunger and Love.* White River Junction, VT: Chelsea Green, 2009.

Heron, Katrina, ed. *Slow Food Nation's Come to the Table.* New York: Rodale, 2008.

Herrera, Gabriel Alonso de, and Juan Estevan Arellano, comp. *Ancient Agriculture.* Layton, UT: Ancient City/ Gibbs Smith, 2006.

Hesser, Amanda, ed. *Eat, Memory: Great Writers at the Table.* New York: W.W. Norton & Company, 2009.

Howard, Manny. "My Empire of Dirt." *New York Magazine* 17 September 2007: 22+.

Jackman, Ian. *Eat This!* New York: HarperCollins, 2007.

Jaudas, Ulrich, and Seyedmehdi Mobini. *The Goat Handbook.* New York: Barron's Educational Series, 2006.

Jones, Judith. *The Tenth Muse: My Life in Food.* New York: Anchor Books/Random House, 2007.

Kafka, Barbara, with Christopher Styler. *Vegetable Love.* New York: Artisan, 2005.

Kagel, Katherine. *Cooking with Café Pasqual's: Recipes from Santa Fe's Renowned Corner Cafe.* Berkeley: Ten Speed Press, 2006.

Kamp, David. *The United States of Arugula.* New York: Broadway Books, 2006.

Katz, Sandor Ellix. *The Revolution Will Not Be Microwaved.* White River Junction, VT: Chelsea Green, 2006.

Kelly, Melissa, with Eve Adamson. *Mediterranean Women Stay Slim Too.* New York: Collins/ HarperCollins, 2006.

Kennedy, Diana. *Nothing Fancy: Recipes and Recollections of Soul-Satisfying Food.* Garden City, NY: The Dial Press / Doubleday, 1984.

Kessler, Brad. *Goat Song: A Seasonal Life, A Short History of Herding, and the Art of Making Cheese.* New York: Scribner/ Simon & Schuster, 2009.

Kingsolver, Barbara, et al. *Animal, Vegetable, Miracle: A Year of Food Life.* New York: HarperCollins, 2007.

Kramer, Jane. "The Hungry Travellers." *The New Yorker* 24 November 2008: 100-107.

Kurlansky, Mark. *Cod: A Biography of the Fish that Changed the World.* New York: Penguin, 1998.

———. *The Big Oyster: History on the Half Shell.* New York: Ballantine/Random House, 2006.

———. *The Food of a Younger Land.* New York: Riverhead/ Penguin, 2009.

LaDuke, Winona. *All Our Relations.* Cambridge: South End Press, 1999.

———, with Sarah Alexander. *Food Is Medicine.* Ponsford, MN: White Earth Land Recovery Project, 2008.

———, with Brian Carlson. *Our Manoomin, Our Life: The Anishinaabeg Struggle to Protect Wild Rice.* Ponsford, MN: White Earth Land Recovery Project, 2003.

———. *The Winona LaDuke Reader: A Collection of Essential Writings.* Stillwater, MN: Voyageur, 2002.

Lamadrid, Enrique R., and Juan Estevan Arellano. *Juan the Bear and the Water of Life.* Albequerque: University of New Mexico Press, 2008.

Landrigan, Phillip J., et al. *Raising Healthy Children in a Toxic World.* Emmaus, PA: Rodale, 2001.

Langholtz, Gabrielle, ed. *Edible Manhattan.* Santa Fe: Edible Communities, Inc., March/April 2009.

Lappé, Anna, and Bryant Terry. *Grub: Ideas for an Urban Organic Kitchen.* New York: Penguin, 2006.

Lappé, Frances Moore. *Getting a Grip.* Cambridge: Small Planet Media, 2007.

Lappé, Frances Moore. *Diet for a Small Planet.* New York: Ballantine/Random House, 1991. (Anna Lappé — p. 312 feijoda — tangy black bean)

———, and Anna Lappé. *Hope's Edge: The Next Diet for a Small Planet.* New York: Tarcher/Putnam, 2003.

Levenstein, Harvey. *Paradox of Plenty.* Berkeley/ Los Angeles: University of California Press, 2003.

Lipman, Frank, with Mollie Doyle. *Spent: End Exhaustion and Feel Great Again.* New York: Fireside/ Simon and Schuster, 2009.

Locavore: Local Diet, Healthy Planet. Dir. Jay Canode. The Living Farm/Lynn Gillespie, 2009. DVD.

Lovenheim, Peter. *Portrait of a Burger as a Young Calf.* New York: Harmony/Random House, 2002.

Madison, Deborah. *Local Flavors.* New York: Broadway Books, 2002.

Madison, Deborah, and Patrick McFarlin. *What We Eat When We Eat Alone.* Layton, UT: Gibbs Smith, 2009.

Mascarino, Monica, ed. *Almanac of the International Slow Food Movement.* Italy: Slow Food Editore, 2008.

Masumoto, David Mas. *Wisdom of the Last Farmer.* New York: Free Press/Simon & Schuster, 2009.

McDonough, William, and Michael Braungart. *Cradle to Cradle.* New York: North Point Press, 2002.

McNamee, Thomas. *Alice Waters and Chez Panisse.* New York: The Penguin Press, 2007.

Mendelson, Anne. *Milk: The Surprising Story of Milk Through the Ages.* New York: Alfred A. Knopf, 2008.

Moosewood Collective, The. *Moosewood Restaurant: Simple Suppers.* New York: Clarkson Potter, 2005.

Moskowitz, Isa Chandra, and Terry Hope Romero. *Veganomicon.* New York: Marlowe & Company, 2007.

Nabhan, Gary Paul. *Coming Home to Eat.* New York: W.W. Norton & Company, 2009.

Native Harvest. *Jiibaakweda Gimiijiminaan: Let's Cook Our Food.* Kearney, NE: Morris Press Cookbooks, 2003.

Nestle, Marion. *Food Politics.* Berkeley/Los Angeles: University of California Press, 2002.

Outwater, Alice. *Water: A Natural History.* New York: Basic Books/ Perseus, 1996.

Palmer, Charlie. *Charlie Palmer's Practical Guide to the New American Kitchen.* New York: Melcher Media, 2006.

Paniz, Neela, and Helen Newton Hartung. *The Bombay Cafe.* Berkeley: Ten Speed Press, 1998.

Pollan, Michael. "An Animal's Place." *The New York Times Magazine* 10 November 2002: 58+.

———. *In Defense of Food.* New York: The Penguin Press, 2008.

———. *The Omnivore's Dilemma.* New York: The Penguin Press, 2006.

———. "Why Bother?" *The New York Times Magazine* 20 April 2008: 19+.

Pouillon, Nora. *Cooking with Nora*. New York: Park Lane Press/Random House, 1996.

Prentice, Jessica. *Full Moon Feast*. White River Junction, VT: Chelsea Green, 2006.

Reichl, Ruth. *Garlic and Sapphires*. New York: The Penguin Press, 2005.

———, cd. *The Gourmet Cookbook*. New York: Houghton Mifflin, 2004.

Remnick, David, ed. *Secret Ingredients: The New Yorker Book of Food and Drink*. New York: Random House, 2007.

Richard, Michael. *Happy in the Kitchen*. New York: Artisan, 2006.

Roahen, Sara. *Gumbo Tales*. New York: W.W. Norton & Company, 2008.

Roberts, Jeffery P. *The Atlas of American Artisan Cheese*. White River Junction, VT: Chelsea Green, 2007.

Roberts, Paul. *The End of Food*. New York: Houghton Mifflin, 2008.

Rose, Chris. *1 Dead in Attic*. New Orleans: Chris Rose Books, 2005.

Roulac, John W. *Backyard Composting: Your Complete Guide to Recycling Yard Clippings*. Ojai, CA: Harmonious Technologies, 1992

Ruhlman, Michael. *The Elements of Cooking: Translating the Chef's Craft for Every Kitchen*. New York: Scribner/ Simon & Schuster, 2007.

Sass, Lorna. *Recipes from an Ecological Kitchen, Volume One*. New York: HarperCollins, 1992. (Anna Lappé — split pea soup with coriander seeds)

Schloss, Andrew, and David Joachim. *Mastering the Grill: The Owner's Manual for Outdoor Cooking*. San Francisco: Chronicle Books, 2007.

Schlosser, Eric. *Fast Food Nation*. New York: HarperCollins, 2002.

Schwab, Alexander. *Mushrooming Without Fear*. New York: Skyhorse, 2006.

Shadle, Mark. *It's Only Natural Restaurant: Vegan Recipes*. Middletown, CT: It's Only Natural Restaurant, LLC, 2005.

Shapiro, Harry, and Peyton Young. *Harry's Roadhouse Cookbook*. Layton, UT: Gibbs Smith, 2006.

Silverton, Nancy, with Carolynn Carreño. *A Twist of the Wrist*. New York: Alfred A. Knopf, 2007.

Smith, Alisa, and J.B. Mackinnon. *Plenty: Eating Locally on the 100-Mile Diet*. New York: Three Rivers Press/ Random House, 2007.

Smith, Kathryn. *Frank Lloyd Wright's Taliesin and Taliesin West*. New York: Harry N. Abrams, 1997.

Spalding, Blake, Jennifer Castle, and Lavinia Spalding. *With a Measure of Grace: The Story and Recipes of a Small Town Restaurant*. Santa Fe: Provecho Press, 2004.

Stewart, Keith. *It's a Long Road to a Tomato: Tales of an Organic Farmer who Quit the Big City for the (Not So) Simple Life*. New York: Marlowe & Company, 2006.

Stewart, Kimberly Lord. *Eating Between the Lines*. New York: St. Martin's Griffin, 2007.

Tasch, Woody. *Inquiries Into the Nature of Slow Money*. White River Junction, VT: Chelsea Green, 2008.

Terry, Bryant. *Vegan Soul Kitchen*. Cambridge: Da Capo Press/Perseus, 2009.

Thoreau, Henry D. *Wild Apples and Other Natural History Essays*. Athens, GA: University of Georgia Press, 2002.

Tooker, Poppy. *Crescent City Farmers Market Cookbook*. New Orleans: market umbrella.org, 2009.

Wann, David. *Simple Prosperity*. New York: St. Martin's Griffin, 2007.

Waters, Alice. *Chez Panisse Fruit*. New York: HarperCollins, 2002.

———. *Chez Panisse Vegetables*. New York: HarperCollins, 1996.

Weinstein, Norman. *Mastering Knife Skills*. New York: Stewart, Tabori & Chang, 2008.

White, Courtney. *Revolution on the Range*. Washington D.C.: Island Press, 2008.

White Earth Tribal & Community College Student Services. *White Earth Reservation Cookbook*. Waverly, IA: G and R Publishing Company, 2005.

Williams, Merrill, ed. *Maine Food & Lifestyle*. Rockland: Mainely Living LLC, 2008.

Winston, Steve. *The Spanish Table Cookbook*. Seattle: Steve Winston, 2005.

Witherspoon, Kimberly, and Peter Meehan. *How I Learned to Cook*. New York, Bloomsbury USA, 2006.

Zimmer, Gary F. *The Biological Farmer: A Complete Guide to the Sustainable & Profitable Biological System of Farming*. Austin: Acres USA, 2000. A

Index